D1766902

Please return / renew by date shown.
You can renew at: **norlink.norfolk.gov.uk**
or by telephone: **0344 800 8006**
Please have your library card & PIN ready.

12/8/16		

NORFOLK LIBRARY
AND INFORMATION SERVICE

NORFOLK ITEM

30129 077 665 892

Zeppelin

THE STORY OF LIGHTER-THAN-AIR CRAFT

Ernst A. Lehmann

Zeppelin

THE STORY OF LIGHTER-THAN-AIR CRAFT

ERNST A. LEHMANN
Commander of the *Hindenburg*

Edited with Notes and Illustrations by Alan Sutton

with a New Introduction by Ian Castle

FONTHILL

Cyclist (taking initiative on being caught without a light). 'Douse your glim, mate; we'll be having them Zeppelins all over us.' *Punch*, 7 October 1914.

629.13324

Fonthill Media Limited
Fonthill Media LLC
www.fonthillmedia.com
office@fonthillmedia.com

First published 1937. This revised and illustrated edition published in the
United Kingdom and the United States of America 2015.

British Library Cataloguing in Publication Data:
A catalogue record for this book is available from the British Library

The original text in German was primarily the work of Captain Ernst A. Lehmann,
Commander of the *Hindenburg*, and who was fatally burned when the ship caught fire
at Lakehurst on 6 May 1937 and died the following day. The text was edited and
completed by Leonhard Adelt, and translated by Jay Dratler.

Edited with notes and illustrations by Alan Sutton

ISBN 978-1-78155-012-0

Typeset in 10pt on 13pt Sabon
Printed and bound in Great Britain by CPI Group (UK) Ltd, Croydon, CR0 4YY

CONTENTS

PUBLISHER'S PREFACE
TO THE 2015 EDITION

*Z*EPPELIN! THE WORD conjures images to the mind and there is little doubt that during the First World War it created fear and genuine concern among city dwellers as some of the *Punch* cartoons in this edition aptly demonstrate. The author of this book, Ernst A. Lehmann, was close to the Zeppelin story from its early days and had great faith in the ever increasing success of the Zeppelin on international routes. It is sadly ironic that this talented man and strong advocate of the Zeppelin should die in a Zeppelin disaster shortly after he had produced the draft for this book. He died following the fire that destroyed the *Hindenburg* on 6 May 1937; he survived the fire itself but was badly burnt. Ernst Lehmann was visited the following morning by Charles E. Rosendahl:

> The morning following the accident I went to see my friend Ernst Lehmann as he lay in the hospital not suffering particularly though badly burned. We had a rather extended conversation and then to permit him to conserve his strength, I departed intending to return in the afternoon as the medical pronouncements were that his chances for surviving were at least even and that the crisis would not be reached for at least three days. But his injuries were worse than had been diagnosed. In what therefore turned out to be practically his last conversation on the subject, I discussed with him the future of airships. Although completely baffled over the possibility of any natural phenomena having caused the loss of the *Hindenburg*, Lehmann told me of his still firm conviction that the airship will go on. No words were wasted in agreeing, however, that the salvation of the type lies in the employment of helium.

It is surprising that Rosendahl was allowed to visit at all! Contrary to Lehmann's conviction the airship did not live on. The *Hindenburg* fire was a sharp stab that destroyed confidence, but the final death blow was the onset of war. In April 1940, Hermann Göring issued the order to scrap both *Graf Zeppelins* (LZ 127 *Graf Zeppelin* and LZ 130 *Graf Zeppelin II*—sister-ship to the *Hindenburg*) and the unfinished framework of LZ 131, since the metal was needed for other aircraft. By 27 April, work crews had finished cutting up the airships. On 6 May 1940, the enormous airship hangars in Frankfurt were levelled by explosives, three years to the day after the destruction of the *Hindenburg*.

The text prepared by Lehmann is well-written and has an immediacy which makes for compelling reading. The reader, however, should realise that this was written down in early 1937 with no knowledge of the all-consuming apocalypse which would consume German cities and the flower of German youth over the coming eight years.

In this edition the original text, plus the final chapter written by Charles E. Rosendahl has been left exactly as first published in 1937. Editorial changes for this edition have been relatively minor but there were considerable errors with place names and proper names, many of which were misspelt and one senses that the publisher was rushing to get the book to press. Lehmann's text was prepared for press by Leonhard Adelt, (1881–1945), a German translator and writer. The translation was further tidied by Jay Dratler and the book was published less than fourths months after the *Hindenburg* disaster.

In preparing this edition for publication I have been struck by a two interesting facts; and the first relates to the Allies' blockade of Germany:

> The German people hoped for and expected extraordinary accomplishments from the airships. Their animosity was directed principally against England, who had laid a hunger-blockade while she herself remained impregnable from land and sea. Consequently, the cry of German public opinion for an attack from the air was doubly vociferous.

The First World War came to an end through hunger and revolution and not on the battlefield—even if that would later have become an inevitability, therefore Lehmann's comments about hunger amplify know facts for the period. In November 1916 one German seaman wrote home:

> There was much complaining about the food this week. Each day we got a soup mixture which was so thin and weak and so poorly prepared that I always felt hungrier after the meal than before it. As an additional treat, the soup was almost always burned. I pilfered potatoes whenever I could and cooked them over steam at night.

The sailors, however, were better off than the dockworkers, for the latter were reduced to begging for food scraps from the sailors. Even though Navy ratings may have been better off than the general populace, it was the Kiel mutiny by sailors of the German High Seas Fleet on 3 November 1918 that triggered the revolution which was to sweep aside the monarchy within a few days.

A German Holiday. *Punch*, 9 February 1916.
Child: 'Please Sir, what is this holiday for?'
Official: 'Because our Zeppelins have conquered England.'
Child: 'Have they brought us back any bread?'
Official: 'Don't ask silly questions. Wave our flag.'

A second interesting point about this book is the striking contradiction regarding bombing policy, for Lehmann initially makes great play about the Zeppelin bombing being limited to 'strategic targets' only:

> There were many who considered this circumscribed aerial warfare an insufficient reprisal for the unbroken hunger-blockade, and suggested that the attacks should be confined not to single air-raids but should be extended to combined assaults of whole air-fleets over Britain. Twenty great airships with three hundred incendiary bombs each could fly over London. Six thousand bombs, it was maintained, would start so many fires in the metropolis that it would be impossible to extinguish this gigantic conflagration. And even if every third Zeppelin were to be shot down, the crews could still drop their bombs while falling.
>
> When I was asked my technical opinion, I admitted that the plan, as such, was feasible. But the thought of subjecting a defenceless civilian population, outside the actual war zone, to all the horrors of aerial warfare, and destroying priceless cultural treasures, was reason enough for all of us to reject the plan. The Kaiser had at first opposed any air attack upon England at all and

only later, under the pressure of his Admirals and Generals, consented to the bombardment of points of real military significance. But certain places in the capital, such as Buckingham Palace, Westminster Abbey, St Paul's Cathedral and the government buildings were under no circumstances to be affected, not even by accident! As I was piloting one of the army airships that were to fly over England, I was quick to realize what the Imperial command signified and what the consequences for me would be if I disobeyed it.

Later in the narrative, this pretence at the angelic intensions of precision strategic bombing somewhat fall away:

Frightened out of their sleep, millions of people fled to the cellars, stumbling through the darkness and cowering together at every detonation. No one knew where the next bomb would strike, and this uncertainty was nerve-racking. Women broke out in hysterical crying jags, children wept, and men, no longer able to endure it down below, rushed out into the streets with balled fists, as if wanting to strangle an enemy hovering invisible in the clouds above. This enemy was, God knows, only concerned with the military objectives which made the capital of the British Empire the storehouse of the World War; but it was inevitable that many bombs missed their mark and demolished dwellings around the docks. Those poor people saw their little goods and possessions go up in flames, and when they fled from their burning houses, they ran into a murderous rain of splinters, shrapnel and debris; it is immaterial whether the German attack or the English defence caused more victims.

This is a fascinating insight into the German mind-set at the time, and which propaganda was the more correct? Were the British populace cowering? Were German spies reporting correctly? Is it true that anti-aircraft fire created substantial casualties? Logic would dictate that what gets fired upwards must fall somewhere, but how much damage did this do?

This book is, without doubt, a great contribution to the Zeppelin saga by one who was closely involved. Lehmann tactfully does not touch upon his differences with Hugo Eckener regarding the use of the airships for Nazi electioneering—for Eckener was strongly against it. Nor does he touch upon Göring's manoeuvring which broke up the Zeppelin company, thereby leaving Eckener as an outsider. Instead, although he may not have become a party member, Lehmann makes his Nazi sympathies quite clear. He believes in the superiority of German engineering and beyond that the superiority of everything German. It remains a forever unanswered question about how he might have felt in 1945 had he survived the *Hindenburg* disaster and the subsequent demise of the Third Reich?

Although the text remains as Lehmann wrote it and Adelt/Dratler edited and translated it, I have added some notes which expand upon a few themes.

Count Zepp takes the Surrender. *Punch*, 27 June 1917.

Furthermore, although the 1937 edition was illustrated we have expanded upon the illustrations to provide a more comprehensive contribution to the Zeppelin story.

It is worth a final comment to point out to the reader that the structure of the book is most odd. It starts with a trip to Brazil in 1935, then moves on to the First World War, following which Lehmann reverts to a short history of Count Zeppelin. Also later in the text, Lehmann oddly introduces himself, providing a short biography. I conclude that this was an early draft for a book which he would have presented in a more logical sequence had he lived to do so. In their desire to get the book on the market, the publisher and translator took the materials to hand, tidied it quickly and presented it to the public. Notwithstanding this sequential oddity, Lehmann's work remains a superb contribution to what we know about the Zeppelin era.

Alan Sutton
Publisher

THE FLIGHT THAT FAILED.

THE EMPEROR. "WHAT! NO BABES, SIRRAH?"
THE MURDERER. "ALAS! SIRE, NONE."
THE EMPEROR. "WELL, THEN, NO BABES, NO IRON CROSSES."

[*Exit murderer, discouraged.*

A Bernard Partridge cartoon for *Punch*, 27 January 1915.

NEW INTRODUCTION
BY IAN CASTLE

O N 6 MAY 1937, a devastating fire engulfed Zeppelin LZ 129—better known throughout the world as the *Hindenburg*—as it came in to land at Lakehurst, New Jersey. The sensational dying moments of this colossal airship, the pride of a re-emerging German nation, were captured for posterity by a dramatic radio broadcast. Later, this impassioned commentary, when dubbed to the harrowing newsreel footage of the death throes of the *Hinadenburg,* created the haunting memory of the disaster that remains sharp to this day.

Of the 97 people aboard, 35 died, as did one of the ground crew. Most of those died immediately, but a few lingered on for a while before succumbing. Amongst the latter was Ernst Lehmann. He staggered alive from the blazing wreck with terrible burns to his back but died in hospital the following day.

Lehmann was no ordinary passenger. He had previously commanded the *Hindenburg* on ten trans-Atlantic crossings to the US, but this time he was aboard as a director of the *Deutsche-Zeppelin-Reederai* (German Zeppelin Transport Company). This flight, from Frankfurt to Lakehurst was the first of 18 trans-Atlantic flights scheduled for 1937. It proved to be the last.

Ernst Lehmann's life was one inextricably entwined with the development of airships, and in particular, those that bore the Zeppelin name. Lehmann trained as a naval engineer but quickly became dissatisfied with his chosen career. Aware that Count von Zeppelin's company, *Deutsche Luftschiffahrts-Aktiengesellschaft (DELAG)*, was looking for applicants to train as airship commanders, Lehmann applied and was accepted. He joined *DELAG* in spring 1913, training on the *Viktoria Luise* and *Hansa*, under the direction of Hugo Eckener. By the autumn of that year Lehmann had command of the latest Zeppelin, *Sachsen*, in which he made 550 flights, both in peacetime and in war.

Reading through the pages of this book, Lehmann's passion for lighter-than-air flight is clear. Even when returning from a destructive bombing raid over Antwerp in 1914 he still finds time to appreciate the natural beauty of the sky.

A thick layer of fog and dense clouds melted together in the valley and removed our view of the earth as if a magic cloth had been stretched beneath us. In the west the stars were still shining, while in the east the sun rose, a golden wheel of fire with spokes of violet, purple, orange, rose and green.

The sheer delight he found in flight is further emphasised when he writes:

If I were not an airshipman, I'd like to be a passenger and devote myself entirely to the observation of the thousand-fold play of colours and forms which Nature contrives out of nothing more than air and water.

When war finally came, it shook him from his reverie:

War! We had never seriously considered war. We were much too preoccupied with our airships.

But war had come and, with the army immediately requisitioning *DELAG's* three civil Zeppelins, *Viktoria Luise*, *Hansa* and *Sachsen*, Lehmann became involved in training Zeppelin crews for the new airship fleet under construction, as well as undertaking the occasional foray over enemy lines.

At the beginning of 1915, the Army gave Lehmann command of the latest Zeppelin, Z XII. At the same time he recalls the clamour of the German people as they demanded an air offensive against Britain.

[They] hoped for and expected extraordinary accomplishments from the airships. Their animosity was directed principally against England, who had laid a hunger-blockade while she herself remained impregnable from land and sea. Consequently, the cry of German public opinion for an attack from the air was doubly vociferous.

Lehmann attempted a raid on Britain on 17 March 1915 in Z XII, but, thwarted by the weather, he diverted his attack to Calais. At times like these he recognised how the shared experience served to draw the crew together in an ever-tighter bond. He writes:

It is self-evident that in the narrow community of the airship, where all our fates were bound together, I was intimately acquainted with my men even beyond the line of duty. The commander on board is not solely a superior officer, he is also comrade, friend, father, doctor and spiritual adviser all in one.

And while serving on Z XII he voiced the feelings of many who take to the air when he wrote, 'An airshipman must have luck.'

Luck certainly seems to have followed Lehmann and his crew through the war. They survived a very active spell on the Eastern Front in the second half of 1915, yet Lehmann still found time to conduct a personal war against Grand Duke Nicolas of Russia! Enraged by Russian devastation in Poland, he attempted to track down the Grand Duke's private train and bomb it, demonstrating in the process 'the grim hatred of the hunter trailing a wolf.'

On his return from the East, in October 1915, Lehmann took command of the new LZ 90, in which he reached England for the first time. He now experienced the difficulties shared by most Zeppelin commanders in accurately locating targets in a blacked-out landscape.

On the night of 31 March 1916, Lehmann was over Suffolk when two of his four engines stopped. While the crew worked feverishly to repair them, Lehmann tried to establish his position.

> We sought in vain for some landmark or light, for the enemy had done a good job of darkening the land.... There remained nothing for me to do but turn homeward. Just then a battery opened fire upon us, and we thereby ascertained our position, which was over Norwich.

The British authorities, however, pinpointed LZ 90 coming no further inland than Ipswich that night—some 40 miles away to the south.

Two days later Lehmann was back over Britain. On approaching London he describes how the 'smoke and vapours of the metropolis' hid LZ 90 from the defences below but also how they prevented him from seeing his target. In these difficult conditions, Lehmann approached:

> ... a battery of searchlights and an anti-aircraft nest which was firing at us with unusual fury. I had saved my entire load of bombs, 5,000 pounds of them, and now judged it to be the right time to make use of them.

Briefly shielded by cloud, LZ.90 then emerged and Lehmann:

> ... once more sighted the Thames, foggy and vague, but still visible enough to recognize by its course.... we navigated in the direction of the river flow and dropped our bombs one after another on a spot where, according to our map, the eastern docks and factories lay.

Lehmann then adds a heart-rending tale of destruction and terror played out on the ground below. This is, however, fabrication. Detailed reports of all raids were carefully compiled by the British authorities. On this occasion they record the anti-aircraft guns at Waltham Abbey, on the River Lea, engaging LZ 90, and some 90 bombs falling on the town where they damaged a few

houses but caused no injuries. Waltham Abbey lay at least 13 miles north of
any of the London docks. If, as seems possible, Lehmann mistook the Lea for
the Thames, then he would not be the first Zeppelin commander to make that
mistake during the war.

Towards the end of April 1916, Lehmann assumed command of another new
zeppelin, LZ.98. Perhaps the most interesting aspect of Lehmann's wartime
experiences comes in his account of his part in the great Zeppelin raid of 2–3
September 1916, the largest of the war. As Lehmann, in LZ 98, neared Woolwich,
anti-aircraft guns opened fire. Lehmann turned away from the guns then, when
the time was right, commenced a textbook attack.

> Three times my ship had been caught by the searchlights, and three times I
> succeeded in withdrawing into a cloud before the 'Archies' found our range.
> Finally, some clouds passing at a 10,000-foot altitude, came to my aid. I
> zigzagged toward them, sailing from one to the other until we stood directly
> over the Thames. We dropped our bombs on the docks and then, protected
> by the nearest clouds, climbed to 14,000 feet.

Lehmann's bombs fell on Gravesend. But, as he set a course for home, his second
in command let out a scream. Looking back, Lehmann saw 'a bright ball of
fire'; he instantly understood its meaning. 'We knew that the blazing meteor
on the further rim of the city could only be one of our airships.'

That 'blazing meteor', was *Schütte-Lanz SL 11*, another of the Army's airships.
Lehmann looked on as:

> The flaming mass hung in the sky for more than a minute; then single parts
> detached themselves from it and preceded it to the earth.... We remained
> silent until it was all over, and then realized how easily the same fate could
> have overtaken us if we had not been fortunate enough to find clouds when
> we needed them.... As we subsequently learned, Lieutenant William Robinson
> shot down the *SL* after he had been in the air for almost two hours vainly
> attacking one of the other airships.

Lehmann's summary is correct, but he misses one important point; the other
airship that the British airman had been 'vainly attacking' was actually his own.
Robinson's report details his unsuccessful pursuit of Lehmann.

> I saw nothing till 1.10 a.m., when two searchlights picked up a Zeppelin
> about S.E. of Woolwich. The clouds had collected in this quarter, and the
> searchlights had some difficulty in keeping on the aircraft.

Robinson gained slowly on LZ 98 for ten minutes, then:

It went behind some clouds avoiding the searchlights and I lost sight of it. After 15 minutes fruitless search I returned to my patrol.

Lehmann and the crew of LZ 98 never noticed the tiny hunter slowly stalking them in the dark sky. That night they were fortunate to experience what Lehmann considered ideal conditions.

We needed visibility and scattered banks of clouds in which we could hide from the searchlights, anti-aircraft batteries and pursuit fliers.

In the early hours of 3 September 1916, those very conditions had probably saved the lives of Ernst Lehmann and the crew of LZ 98. For, frustrated by his failure to engage Lehmann's airship, Robinson turned away to pounce instead on *SL 11*. Moments later *SL 11* became the 'blazing meteor' that so chilled Lehmann and his crew.

By 1917 Lehmann reports that the offensive role of the army airships was over and now, commanding the new LZ 120, he moved to the Baltic in an observation and reconnaissance role. Here life was much more relaxed and a sense of joy emerges again in his writing as he talks of endless peaceful patrols, with home comforts on board and the joy of impromptu music nights complete with guitar, harmonicas and music boxes. He even recalls enjoying the previously unthinkable luxuries of showers and sunbathing. All this was part of what he describes as 'the nirvana of our world-record flight', for in July 1917 the LZ 120 broke the airship endurance record by staying aloft for 101 hours.

And it was endurance or long-distance flying that dominated the rest of Lehmann's life. In the last year of the war, now based at Friedrichshafen—the home of Zeppelin airships—he took on a new development role while also commanding delivery flights of new Zeppelins to the naval authorities, who, unlike the army, retained their belief in the offensive value of airships.

By the end of the war Lehmann was already considering the prospects of a first trans-Atlantic crossing to the US—a prize ultimately claimed by the British airship R 34 in 1919. Then, in 1923, he lost his endurance record when the French airship *Dixmude* (former Zeppelin L 72) recorded a flight of almost 119 hours over the Mediterranean. Twelve years later, in 1935, Lehmann proudly—although unintentionally—reclaimed the record in *Graf Zeppelin* when it landed in Brazil after a flight of 120 hours.

Lehmann's personal dream of a trans-Atlantic crossing finally became reality in 1924 when he flew from Germany on the delivery flight of LZ 126 to the US Navy. As First Officer under Hugo Eckener, and as a proud German, he felt the enormity of the mission. Remembering the moment that LZ 126 left the European mainland, he writes, 'Our hearts beat faster. It was a solemn moment.' But as the flight neared its end and, with America in sight, he recalls the enormous sense of achievement when he writes, 'now we know how Christopher Columbus and his crew felt when … the lookout on the *Pinta* sighted land.' In America, Lehmann and Eckener embarked on a dizzying whirl of social engagements that leave the reader exhausted, but which paved the way towards securing a regular trans-Atlantic Zeppelin service. This, Lehmann believed, marked an important step 'in the peaceful development of world aviation.'

Back in Germany again, a new Zeppelin was under construction, LZ 127, the *Graf Zeppelin*. In describing this new airship, Lehmann explains that:

> Although the airship was equipped for transporting mail, passengers and cargo, it had been designed and built merely for a series of demonstration flights over great distances…. It was neither a genuine passenger airship, for there were accommodations for only twenty travellers, nor a mail airship, since it was not fast enough for that purpose but it had just enough of the qualities of both to carry out all the necessary demonstrations.

And carry them out it did. In October 1928, as the *Graf Zeppelin* prepared to make its first trans-Atlantic flight, enthusiasm and excitement grew. Eager travellers snapped up the 20 passenger tickets for $3,000 each, a staggering $42,000 in current terms. And in America the welcome this time was even more ecstatic then for the arrival of LZ 126 four years earlier; this time Zeppelin fever gripped all America. On that first occasion Lehmann believed America

> … regarded the conquering of the Atlantic as a technical demonstration and a sporting proposition. This time, however, they stretched out a friendly hand, honouring, in the enemy of yesterday, the friend of today.

After the *Graf Zeppelin's* successful completion of the American journey, German president Paul von Hindenburg expressed the feelings of many when he informed the crew that, 'The heart of all Germany beat proudly for the airship.'

The following year, Lehmann flew as Eckener's First Officer, on the *Graf Zeppelin's* historic round the world flight. A flight that he considered signified an important moment in Germany's rehabilitation in the eyes of the world.

> So many good wishes and prayers accompanied us! For it was not only our little dockyard affairs we were furthering this time, it was all Germany's affair.

Before this trans-global flight of 31,000 miles was safely completed, Lehmann had the honour to command the *Graf Zeppelin* on the final leg of its momentous journey. In all, between 1928 and 1935, he commanded the *Graf Zeppelin* 272 times. After *Graf Zeppelin* came Lehmann's final airship—LZ 129, the *Hindenburg*.

From his first encounter with the *Sachsen*, to the technology of the *Hindenburg*, Lehmann had witnessed dramatic progress; the old *Sachsen*, with its gas capacity of 19,500 m³, dwarfed by *Hindenburg*, which held 200,000 m³ of hydrogen. Then, in comparing the first Zeppelin to this latest model, Lehmann remarked:

> No one—not even the inventor in his wildest dreams—could foresee that, three and a half decades later, a dirigible of the same type.... would contain in a single one of its sixteen gas-cells more hydrogen than the entire capacity of the first Zeppelin.

Yet Lehmann's belief in the future of the airship remained boundless.

> The Hindenburg is the result of thirty-six years of airshipping, and its crew is too... And already they are dreaming of an entirely new airship beside which the LZ 129 will be a mere experiment.

But it was not to be, the 'experiment' marked the end of the line. With the *Hindenburg* disaster so visible to the world, that same world, which had once stood electrified by the achievement of the trans-Atlantic flights, now recoiled in horror and airship travel never recovered. Ernst Lehmann, a man who had devoted his life to airships, never had to come to terms with that reality. He died in his hospital bed still believing that airships had a future, still believing 'world traffic via airships has begun.' That dream died, alongside Ernst Lehmann, at Lakehurst on 6 May 1937.

Ian Castle
February 2015

PREFACE TO THE 1937 EDITION
BY COMMANDER CHARLES E. ROSENDAHL

IT IS AN unhappy task that is given me to write this preface and the last chapter to this book of Captain Ernst A. Lehmann. Even so, I am now more than grateful for the opportunity of expressing, if only briefly, the eminence and meaning of the life and achievement of my friend and fellow-airman; and that the final chapter allows me to present a report of the loss of the *Hindenburg* as I observed it.

Those who read the pages of this book will find abundant evidence of the mixture of genius and common sense which form the keynote of this great airship commander's career. Knowing that his natural modesty would conceal his attributes, I cannot but comment on those features which give full measure to his stature and define his human qualities.

During the fourteen years I knew this man, I never found anything that could affect his natural simplicity. While never seeking the plaudits of an admiring crowd, he was always gracious enough to answer 'just one more question' for the press, to stand for 'just one more shot' for the photographers, to gratify just one more autograph-seeker. Dapper, polished, suave, conversant with world affairs, a talented linguist, he was the one assigned to meet and talk with interested captains of industry and distinguished visitors. On board ship, while his orders were given in a manner unmistakably determined, no one ever knew him to raise his voice above the conversational tone.

Pride in worldly success and in his own remarkable rise to prominence played little part in a life some of the happiest moments of which were spent on duty in an airship control-room or off duty dragging out folk-tunes from an old accordion in the officers' mess. I recall riding with him only last summer in his small German car, discussing his garden as we drove along winding country roads to his home, and there inspecting his boat-shed and landing on the banks of the beautiful Bodensee where he found relief and rest from the demands of the ever-broadening airship world in which he was a directing figure. As he sat on occasion after dinner aboard the *Hindenburg* rendering classical music from the ship's grand piano, it seemed to me that these were not only moments of relaxation but moments when his progressive vision was wandering far ahead, reflecting on the part which his beloved airships were to play in man's romantic conquest of atmospheric oceans. His whole existence was bound up in a great ideal—the perfection of the Zeppelin principle of airships for the commercial transportation of the peoples of the world. To this ideal, he gave of his courage, ability, integrity, and finally, his life.

It is all the more tragic that his end should have come at a time when the final achievement of Zeppelin's dream seemed to be near at hand. As he left the scene of the blazing *Hindenburg*, practically dragged away for medical assistance, fatally burned and sick at heart, his entirely clear mind running rapidly over his profound and basic airship knowledge that dated back to the most perilous airship duties of the World War, Lehmann could only repeat, 'I don't understand it; I don't understand it.'

So many years of trial and effort, research and improvement, so much of his own genius and travail, and now he was not privileged to live to see the full goal attained. It seems the pioneering path of progress must ever be punctuated by the loss of such men as Ernst Lehmann to shock the rest of us into realization of how much the world can owe to some individuals and to make us appreciate the price of advancing civilization.

The name and memory of Lehmann are now inseparably linked with those of Zeppelin and his fellow-pioneers who have given and are giving their lives unselfishly to the furtherance of the airship ideal. To all of us his book is a fitting monument to what he gave and did for civilization. The world is indebted to Ernst Lehmann; it owes and concedes him a place of honour.

One of the final photographs of Ernst Lehmann, taken in the dining room on board the *Hindenburg*. Lehmann is at the head of the table with spectacles studying the menu. To the left is steward Fritz Deeg. He survived the disaster and on 7 May 1937 he, along with two other crew members, had the unenviable task of identifying the bodies.

A Bruce Bairnsfather cartoon from 1918.

1

GRAF ZEPPELIN TO BRAZIL WITH MAIL

ON A CLEAR bright Sunday we flew out of the autumn and into the spring. We had no passengers aboard, only mail, and we defrauded Nature both by escaping winter and by gaining three good hours' time in our westward flight. We were carrying mail between Africa and America.

In a way, this was a new mission strengthening the bond between aviation and airship transport. Until then, the *Graf Zeppelin* had carried passengers and mail from Friedrichshafen to Rio de Janeiro and back again—a distance of over 6,250 miles each way. Now she was substituting, so to speak. The mother ships *Schwabenland* and *Westfalen*, which served the German Lufthansa mail-pilots as floating bases in the Atlantic, were withdrawn for a month, to be overhauled. During this time, the *Graf Zeppelin*, taking the place of the Dornier-Wals, maintained the shuttle-service between Bathurst, Africa, and Pernambuco, Brazil.

The *Graf Zeppelin* took off from Friedrichshafen under my command for her fiftieth American crossing at 7 a.m. on 7 November 1935. As on each of her other trips during her seven years of operation, the ship was booked to capacity. She returned to Recife de Pernambuco from Rio de Janeiro, obtained gas and gasoline at the mooring-mast and, on 15 November, began the first of three scheduled shuttle-trips without passengers to Bathurst.

The Atlantic Ocean is 1,900 miles wide between Recife and Bathurst, which is the capital of the British colony of Gambia and lies on the river of that name. The German Lufthansa Airline, carrying the mail via Stuttgart and Seville, enters upon its actual transoceanic stretch at that point and the company therefore maintains a station and airfield at Bathurst.

Since Bathurst has no mooring-mast, we exchange mails without landing, and deliver the South American load at Pernambuco, from which point the Condor Syndicate mail planes forward it along the coast and in ray-formation over the entire continent. On Sunday, 24 November, the *Graf Zeppelin* again appeared at Bathurst and, from an altitude of 650 feet, dropped the tiny parachute containing the European mail, hoisted the American mail on board with a grapple, and began the return voyage over the Atlantic.

It was a clear bright Sunday, and the air simmered over the hot white sand. The barracks of the air station receded, the slim mail plane became a miniature, and our comrades and their black assistants became small white dots. The tiny city, residence of the Royal British Governor, lay like driftwood in the estuary, and from the far bank of the Gambia the cannon of Fort Sullen demanded respect. The droning of the motors drowned out the rolling of the surf, which laid a white ruff along the coast. From the steep headland of Saint Mary, the flag on the Baku Recreation Home waved Africa's farewell.

There is, admittedly, no great difference between autumn in Africa which we were leaving, and spring in South America toward which we had set our course. One perspires here and one perspires there. But over the blue Atlantic, the heavens curved off into infinity, the headwinds of our own speed cooled us, and there was eternal difference and change in the seeming monotony. If I were not an airshipman, I'd like to be a passenger and devote myself entirely to the observation of the thousand-fold play of colours and forms which Nature contrives out of nothing more than air and water.

But I was the responsible officer and I was on duty, and during the rest periods, when my comrades von Schiller and Wittemann replaced me, I ate and slept and took my ease. Then, a telegram jolted me out of my smug calm. The wireless operator, his face a mask of consternation, brought it to me himself. It was from the Condor Syndicate in Rio de Janeiro and it was addressed to 'Denne.' Denne is the *Graf Zeppelin*'s code-name; the Brazilian stations sometimes over-politely wired 'Comte Denne.'

Rio, 24, November, 20.05 (8.05 p.m.)
Recife telegraphs in translation stop minor revolutionary movement in city stop according official communication consider this landing Zeppelin inadvisable stop request immediate transmission to Zeppelin suggest return Spain if possible stop Signed Aeronauts stop further from us stop political disturbances in Natal all intercourse interrupted mail-delivery impossible stop disturbances in Recife also government in control except in Olinda and an armoury in city stop federal troops prepared to occupy Giquia with militia stop

Syncondor

Well, that was a fine state of affairs. But after all, it was not the first time that the *Graf Zeppelin* had become involved in the domestic politics of the great South American republic. But the central government in Rio de Janeiro had always been able to suppress the opposition, and if our landing-field at Giquia, near Recife, was protected by militia, we could drop the European mail in Recife, instead of Natal, and land there to replenish our fuel.

Therefore, I sent our wireless message No. 16 to the Condor Syndicate in

Rio de Janeiro (to which I must add that by international usage '9 gmt' signifies nine o'clock Greenwich Meridian Time).

Condor Rio
For Recife must land Recife for fuel arrange military guard and ground crew tomorrow morning 9 gmt confirm
Command Grafzeppelin

No sooner done than Recife reported urgently twice in succession:

Recife, 23.50
Command Grafzeppelin No. 199
Your number 16 landing preparations for 9 gmt impossible since all streets unsafe and telephone communication interrupted tonight request postpone landing until I re-establish communication and notify you
Station Recife

Recife, 23.55
From Recife number 197 2.24 urgent for Grafzeppelin after further communication with officials advise Zeppelin landing here be delayed as long as possible if return impossible stop the situation is serious
Aeronauta Recife

What was to be done? Giquia, with gas and gasoline supplies awaiting us at the mooring-mast, lay in the zone of battle, and the airfields of Recife and Natal, which could at least have supplied us with gasoline, were likewise military objectives. We could set our course for Rio de Janeiro, but the gasworks, which was to provide hydrogen at the new landing-field, was not yet in operation. Should we turn back and land in Seville to supplement our supply of gas? Against the northeast trade-winds the distance was too great for the quantity of fuel still at our command. Furthermore, we did not wish to leave a mission unfulfilled while the possibility of carrying it out still remained. At the first alarm, I ordered the motors throttled to save fuel. Using only two out of five motors, we flew slowly over the ocean, and I radioed back:

Aeronauta Recife
Cruising slowly direction Recife will await your report stop can postpone landing until Tuesday if necessary but urgently request utmost acceleration all necessary measures including production of gas since must replenish before European return which only possible Recife
Lehmann

The wireless messages flew thick and fast throughout Sunday night and Monday; the messages came from our landing-field at Recife, from our representative, Hans Sievert, business manager of Herm. Stoltz & Co., exporting corporation, and the Condor Syndicate.

For Aeronauta Recife
No. 19 Is gas supply certain question-mark who is causing the disturbances
                                                                    Grafzeppelin

Recife 25, November, 1.25 a.m., Monday
Command Grafzeppelin
To your No. 19 Unable communicate gas-works disturbances apparently caused by reds
                                                                    Station Recife

Recife, 02.25
No. 202 143 q Your 16 18 and 19
In constant communication with headquarters government troops since midday period movement started in Socorro barracks last night where troops revolted simultaneously with communist disturbances in various parts of city period Rebel portions of army have advanced toward city as far as Largas da Paz consequently occupying zep-field and all streets en route period shooting continues in city commander of troops has received War Minister's order to safe-guard zeppelin-field which at moment impossible because of above situation period arrival of relief troops from Maceio and Parahyba doubtful before tomorrow morning when mop-up of landing-field planned period consequently landing tomorrow morning out of question postpone same temporarily until Monday afternoon but expect possible additional postponement until Tuesday morning if necessary period last communication with zep-field 17 o'clock at which hour everything quiet production of gas running normal period at present conferring with commander of troops will inform you significant developments continuously
                                                                    Sievert

Rio, 03.10
This War Ministry reports colon local government officials urgently advise postponement landing as long as possible so that assume such out of question before tomorrow night stop area of conflict moving toward Giquia stop government troops advancing hope to have suppressed everything by tomorrow forenoon
                                                                    Syncondor

Condor Recife and Rio

No. 20 We have apportioned fuel to last until Wednesday even until Thursday if favourable weather continues will wait out of sight of Recife for opportunity to land stop have not and shall not consider return flight Europe will ourselves transmit no information there without previous arrangement with you stop suggest you give news report of situation for Friedrichshafen and press through us stop inform whether desirable drop mail Maceio late this afternoon

Grafzeppelin

Recife D 9.20

Denne No. 208

Your official reporting of situation agreeable troop commander colon Monday 7 o'clock gmt part of federal troops barracked outside city limits Pernambuco revolted Sunday morning in their quarters while political disturbances apparently of leftist origin broke out simultaneously various portions of city period police together with troops stationed in inner city were able to control situation in city as well as prevent entrance of revolutionaries period relief troops just arrived from neighbouring state Parahyba comma more expected period it is thought order will be restored entirely during course of day full stop for you confidential colon mop-up has begun stop will probably be able to give another report this afternoon situation already brighter since arrival above-mentioned strong relief troops but meanwhile landing before Tuesday morning still out of question

Sievert

Aeronauta Recife

No. 8 messages all received stop postponement until Tuesday afternoon entirely agreeable if necessary even Wednesday stop Hamburg notified according our no. 6.

Grafzeppelin

As an international postman, the *Graf Zeppelin* was expected to deliver the European mails punctually. But since this was possible, at the time, neither in Natal, the capital of the federal state of Rio Grande do Norte lying north of Pernambuco, nor in Recife, the capital of Pernambuco, I decided to make for Maceio, the capital of the state of Alagoas in whose harbour the Condor Syndicate's Dornier-Wall had an emergency landing station on the route between Natal and Rio. I wirelessed this information to Rio who wired back their confirmation.

The *Graf Zeppelin*, therefore, set a direct course for Maceio. From a distance, the small city revealed itself by its tall cathedrals. Beneath the subdued rhythm of our motors, we heard the sound of hammers in the dock-yard; ships were loading and unloading in the harbour. There was no sign of a revolution here. Leaving behind us the lagoon and the headland on which Maceio lies, we descended to

850 feet and floated over the French company's flying field. Employees of the Condor Syndicate accepted the mail by means of a parachute we dropped; a short greeting passed from man to man; and then we were on our way again toward the sea. An auto brought the American mail to the harbour, where it was reloaded on a plane which, like our own ship, came from Friedrichshafen.

Shortly after five Monday afternoon, the Condor Syndicate in Rio received our report:

Have delivered mail Maceio cruising slowly northward remaining out of sight vicinity Recife

Command Grafzeppelin

and then Sievert came through again:

Recife 17.18
Denne no. 2 16-1 7
Am at station request contact in 15 minutes

Sievert

Recife 17.40 Denne No. 224
For you confidential stop latest developments normal but considerable opposition Largo da Paz brisk firing artillery brought up stop troop commander hopes as stated mop-up field district completed tonight field itself apparently already occupied government troops through flank movement but situation presumably not yet finally determined even by tomorrow morning therefore and in consideration impossibility make landing preparations until tomorrow morning postpone landing temporarily until Tuesday afternoon period remaining here at station until 15 o'clock tomorrow awaiting your possible advice period no further news of situation before tomorrow morning excepting unusual circumstances

Sievert

Denne 54-55 18.00
Condor Recife and Rio
Since Friedrichshafen apparently worried request your or government permission immediately to release following report colon landing Recife instead today Monday night as scheduled probably not before Tuesday morning because army revolt in Pernambuco since Sunday night which by very energetic intervention of government instantly suppressed stop for safety's sake at present awaiting advice landing preparations Pernambuco have beautiful weather and fuel and food until Thursday

Command Grafzeppelin

Zep-yards Friedrichshafen and Berlin
Took off Recife Friday night because southern mail late therefore landing actually scheduled today Monday night but have postponed same until
tomorrow stop army revolt quickly suppressed nevertheless delaying landing
as precautionary measure celebrating 500 flight

Command Grafzeppelin

During all these news-flashes, Monday night had come and the revolution
went to sleep. Through the night, we heard nothing but repetitious or contra-
dictory reports; of the conditions at our landing field we heard not a word.
Even Olinda, on the picturesque heights above Recife, wired us twice.

Olinda, 25, November, 17.10
Service from post and telegraph of Brazil Pernambuco no down now

Olindaradio

Olinda, 26, November 8.10
Here is revolution please give me information if expect landing field or if
destiny rio pse to inform our chief

Olindaradio

'Here is revolution'—yes, we seemed to have noticed that a day or so ago;
and as to whether we could land, we hoped to find that out from the very ones
who so naively asked us about it.

2

Revolution in Brazil

TUESDAY MORNING CAME and the sun rose as the *Graf Zeppelin* cruised high over Recife. We made our normal rounds and waited. Actually, we were not in a great hurry. We had been under way four days having only transferred mail at Bathurst and, if we found it necessary, could remain aloft for another four days. Since we were economical, we still had gasoline and oil. We were rather short of food because we had not anticipated such a prolongation of the voyage; but we could manage. However, since the SS *España* of the Hamburg-South American Steamship Company was on our course, I seized the opportunity to experiment with provisioning an airship from a steamer and wired as follows:

Captain España dhgt
Set course for delivering following provisions if possible
65 pounds bread as available
leg of veal
piece beef
10 pounds bologna
55 pounds potatoes
Tinned sardines for 50 portions
25 bottles beer cold
5 pounds flour
5 pounds spaghetti
50 packages zwieback

Grafzeppelin

Grafzeppelin
You can have everything but bottled beer keg instead potatoes fresh only in sacks stop how will you receive and when question-mark if necessary can send out boat stop position 12 o'clock gmt 6.42 south 33.04 west course 2424 rw greetings

Schneekloth

España

Thanks for cooperation request provisions without beer be prepared stop to manoeuvre set course against wind full speed ahead stop deliver with cord net stop will accept on second run

Grz

The plan was carried out as promptly and smoothly as if steamer and airship had practised it a hundred times. The *España* steamed full speed ahead and the *Graf Zeppelin* moved over her from the rear, described a circle and descended. Headed into the wind, with its engines retarded so that it barely held its own, the airship glided over the fruit-boat. The *Graf Zeppelin*, in military parlance, marked time.

The airship was so close to the steamer that we were able to exchange greetings and news with the crew while Schiller's men lowered the net through the trap-door in the gondola. This net was considerably larger than the shopping-bags used for marketing by our women at home but it served the same purpose.

No sooner was the cable with its 240 pound load hauled up again, than our engines resumed full speed. The *España* fell behind us, small as a ship in a toy-shop window, her crew like tiny dots on the deck. From our radio cabin we wired our thanks to the captain:

Graf Zeppelin picks up provisions from the *España*.

Captain Schneekloth dght
Sincere thanks now we can await the end of the Pernambuco revolution
Greetings

                                                            Lehmann

We cruised on between the coast and the Fernando Noroñha Islands whose rock monoliths are the outposts of America. The surf thundered house-high on the cliffs, and the white spray seemed to condense into odd shapes, like flying animals; seagulls, albatrosses and herons swooped around the craggy rocks, and in the glassy blue sea the airship's violet shadow glided over torpedo-shaped sharks and brown giant rays. The main island, one and a half miles wide and seven and a half miles long, reminded me of Heligoland. Over the wide strand, the red rocks rose to 100-yard heights. On them, between corn and bean fields, manioc and castor-oil plants, clung a few flat stone houses, towered over by the steel skeleton of the wireless station. I saw only a single person; motionless, he stood on the shore, staring after the airship.

We wondered whether the man on the beach was one of the 160 wardens; whether he was one of the political prisoners exiled to the white-hot island, three degrees from the equator and 475 miles from the nearest point of the coast. Only once a month does a steamer put in from Recife de Pernambuco, bringing mail and provisions for the prisoners and their wardens.

Besides the hundreds of reports of weather and positions, our receiver in the wireless room greedily picked up all the political announcements regarding the present disturbance from Rio de Janeiro. The President summoned the cabinet for a special session. Garrisons, navy and police were warned. Banks, railway stations, and factories were placed under military guard. Parliament declared martial law throughout Brazil for the next thirty days. And all Communist leaders in the country were arrested. The severity and scope of the adopted measures proved that, although everything still seemed quiet in Rio, this was not a coup of purely local character.

On Saturday night, 23 November, the revolt had broken out simultaneously in the three neighbouring federal states of Rio Grande do Norte, Parahyba, and Pernambuco, indicating that it was the result of a carefully organized plan. In Grao Para, situated near the equator between the mouths of the Para and Amazon Rivers, the preparations for the revolt were discovered and frustrated in the nick of time.

In Natal, the capital of Rio Grande do Norte, the mutinous 21st Chasseurs occupied the government buildings and radio station, thereby winning the support of other troops. The state President, Rafael Gernandez, took refuge in the police barracks. The radio station prematurely reported the triumph of the revolution, which was to be climaxed by a general strike of 200,000 workers. In Rio de Janeiro, the federal government denied the report.

In Parahyba, capital of the state of that name, the revolutionists had entrenched themselves and were being attacked by police and government troops. Our route brought us via Parahyba to Pernambuco. In Recife itself, capital of Pernambuco, rebel soldiers— non-coms, cadets and Chasseurs—had occupied the barracks and were advancing against the government buildings and the harbour. Bloody street-battles were being fought between government militia and rebel troops.

A hundred times, we of the *Graf Zeppelin* had had a bird's-eye view of Recife, and we were familiar with its topography. We knew the long narrow line of the coral reef for which Recife is named and which protects the incoming ships from the vicious surf. Between Riff and the peninsula, Bairro do Recife, we saw in our mind's eye the entranceway guarded by forts, and freighters at the quay were taking on snow-white cane sugar, bales of cotton and the great sticks of Brazilian wood which gave Pernambuco its name. We saw swarms of yellow, brown and black natives, heard the imperative horns of the automobiles, and watched the street-cars crossing the bridges leading to Bairro do Antonio Vaz and entering the suburb of Boa Vista. Were they fighting at the station, the Arsenal, the Customs House? Was the Vrijborg of Sao Antonio, built by Moritz von Nassau, German General in the service of the Dutch, still in the hands of the government? Mentally, we wandered again through the main thoroughfare, so many of whose sign-plates bear German names. There the German trade flag flies from the roof of the Herm. Stoltz & Co. counting-house, and there the Aeronauta, representative of the German Zeppelin Works, has its offices. If, and we had no doubt of it, the rebels were repulsed by the government, they would have to retreat over the Rio Capiberibe bridges to Boa Vista, where our German compatriots live with their wives and children.

We had often been guests of the German Club, bowling and drinking ice-cold beer and even visiting the school-rooms in the top storey of the club-house, which is a building dating from the time of the Brazilian empire. The coco-palms peered with giraffe-like necks over the roof-top. A yellow banana plantation, thick as a corn-field, displayed great branches loaded with fruit. The breadfruit trees offered their unbaked loaves to the children in the playground. Along the black slimy pools, tyrant or king birds pecked hungrily for insects. Iguanas sunned themselves on the hot wall surrounding the club-grounds. The throats of the long-tailed lizards pulsed with excitement when a child approached, but they remained gripped by curiosity until a hand reached out and they turned and fled.

Four miles from Recife, and connected to it by a trolley line, the city of Olinda lies on a hill overlooking the plain. German Benedictine nuns run the teachers' seminary there, and in a nearby cloister German Franciscans carry on their missionary work. This city of baroque churches was occupied by the 29th Chasseurs who had joined the revolt and were protecting the rear of the rebels in the port city. Such speculations and scenes occupied our minds as we cruised around awaiting an opportunity to land.

Our landing-field, Giquia, lay outside Recife on the edge of a mangrove swamp which offered cover for mutineers and mobs alike. It was reported that the rebels, who had lost a hundred dead, seventy wounded, and ninety captured in the street-fighting, were being forced back toward the swamps by Captain Reis. But the crux of the situation seemed to be in Natal, where the central government had concentrated all available troops and the two cruisers *Bahia* and *Rio Grande do Sul*.

Our middleman on land, Mr Sievert, was in a difficult position during all this confusion. Part of his written report covering Sunday and Monday, which I read later, follows:

Since I received the news of the revolt on Sunday morning, I haven't slept a wink. At that time, I was still able to get a taxi to take me to the Secretaria. The answer to my question of what to do about the Zeppelin was 'E inconveniente o Zeppelin vir!' I immediately sent a telegram to Rio and urgently advised the return of the airship to Spain.

Whether that was possible I naturally did not know, but it seemed to me the only safe solution, since the outcome of the revolution could not be foretold. At headquarters they were gravely concerned by the ramifications of the movement. I tried to get to the Pina radio station, but it was impossible to get a taxi, even for gold.

By good luck, I was able to get to Derby, where I hoped to arrange for the protection of the field and the ground crew. As is understandable, they had no time for such questions at the moment, since they first had to send out troops to the various posts in the city. Without having accomplished very much, I returned to the German Club, to start out from there with my own car. But just as I was entering the garage furious shooting began around me. The communists had slipped from behind through the fields and into the water-shed to keep a fiery rendezvous with the police troops attacking from the other side of the bridge. For a good half-hour we were forced to take cover.

But that passed, too, and at about 4 p.m. I was able to get my car out of the garage, although I could still hear rifle shots. The telephones were no longer working, but fortunately, after a thousand difficulties, I was able to get through to the Pina radio station. There were no messages from the Zep. Apparently she had not yet received our warning. I again wired that if the return voyage was impracticable, the landing here should be delayed as long as possible.

It was useless to try to get to the Zep-field. You could get only as far as the Afogados Bridge where the firing began. So I went to the Quartel General, where they characterized the situation as 'extremely delicate', and could offer no advice as to the Zeppelin's arrival. They had already received a telegram from the War Ministry ordering them to occupy the Zep-field and protect the airship during its stay. But they had no troops available at the moment, and the field was in the hands of the rebels. Natal, which at present seems to resemble a soviet republic, was a proof of the danger of the movement.

At the time, I could do nothing though I still hoped the Zep was in no danger. I was still unable to obtain reports from her. At about eight o'clock in the evening, however, I learned in a roundabout way that a telegram from the Zep had arrived for me with the information that she would arrive on Monday morning at six and had to land immediately.

This information worried me no little, and I once more drove back to the city to the Quartel General. And they were no less dismayed than I, for the troops from Parahyba were not due before morning.

But the contents of the telegram seemed so unintelligible that I hurried to Pina to read it myself. Attempts to get through by car were unsuccessful. A special pass assured my safe conduct, but I was forbidden to use my headlights. Nevertheless, I came through the up torn roads of the Rua Imperial without mishap, only to learn, when I was about to turn off to Pina, that the Pina Bridge was under fire and impassable.

So I once more returned and attempted to phone. That was finally arranged, and I learned through another telegram, from Lehmann himself, that the landing could be postponed until Tuesday. I then spent the entire night in the counting-house, from which, with some difficulty, we could communicate with Pina. Acting upon my advice, Captain Lehmann so apportioned his gas as to be able to remain aloft until Wednesday or even Thursday.

Meanwhile I continued to communicate with the Quartel General, for I had to keep informed on conditions until I had made certain that a later landing was possible. Nevertheless, we prepared everything for Wednesday afternoon, though fearing sabotage. I determined to use as many Germans as I could for the ground-crew.

Largo da Paz was in a bad state. The entire electrical supply was cut off, and the field was completely dark, which was why it seemed best to land on Thursday morning, refuel during the day and leave again at nightfall. Today the city is quieter, since the Socorro is supposed to have surrendered. At any rate, I am in constant contact with the Zeppelin, and am keeping them informed.

3

The End of the Revolution and the Return to Friedrichshafen

Tuesday morning, the radio messages continued to arrive from land in a steady stream. Pina relayed Sievert's confidential report:

Recife, 26 November 11.35 a.m.
Command, Grafzeppelin
For you strictly confidential stop just received information from general staff apparently indicating battle vicinity zep-field period general staff still hopes advance areas by tonight and consolidate positions during course of tomorrow morning period inner city quiet but isolated by patrols and entirely without transportation facilities period consider necessary delay landing until Wednesday afternoon better still Thursday morning refuel during day and take off Thursday evening to avoid overnight stay period consider consequent technical problems stop according Herrmanns report 22,000 cubic meters hydrogen ready attempting get through to field with Herrmann period you were seen yesterday about 14 o'clock please remain out of sight period in case of urgent message please communicate immediately hope to be back Pina station by 10.30.

Sievert

Aeronauta Recife
No. 10 for Sievert considering imminent change in weather conditions landing and refuelling should not be postponed longer than absolutely necessary therefore please inquire general staff whether sufficient degree safety not obtainable by Wednesday afternoon.

Lehmann

By half past three Sievert had replied in confidence that the main body of the rebel troops were retreating toward Socorro and that the landing field and environs were undamaged, the only problem being whether power and electricity could be restored by Wednesday afternoon. We obtained a complete resume of the situation from the official and press reports. According to them, the revolution in the northern states was practically over. The government troops, aided by National Militia and volunteers from the interior, were now strong enough to complete the mopping-up of the federal capitals. Artillery was brought up against the mutinous barracks which were about to be stormed. Army and Navy air squadrons dropped bombs on the barricades and machine-gunned the fugitives. A couple of ring-leaders attempting to escape from Natal on the steamer *Santos* found the sea blockaded by battleships and turned back hopelessly. The barracks in Olinda and Socorro were evacuated, and aerial bombardments broke the last resistance at Jobotao. The rebels everywhere were surrendering their arms or fleeing into the interior.

Meanwhile, we kept requesting weather reports, for though we could stay aloft until Thursday morning if the weather remained fair, we wished to be prepared for an emergency landing on Wednesday. Message followed message as we exchanged words with various points on land. One report from the Secretary of Public Safety was so encouraging that we began to make plans for landing early Wednesday morning. But Sievert recommended that we give the government time to clean up any remaining rebel nests and that we allow him time to organize a landing crew. This we agreed to do and set 5 p.m. Rio Time Wednesday as the time of landing.

Wednesday morning, Sievert reported progress on preparations for landing. I wired Rio to request the punctual arrival of the south post, for I planned to take off for Bathurst early Friday morning with the European mail. At 3.10 p.m., the following message was picked up:

Berlin 15.10
Command Grafzeppelin via Hamburg
With permission air ministry request code report of position latest developments and particulars wireless reply requested
DNB Berlin
(Deutsches Nachrichtenbüro—
German News Agency)

We replied:

Took off Friday night last week post exchanged Bathurst Sunday morning stop first report of Recife revolution arrived on board Sunday night stop since Rio gas-works unfinished and trip Seville against northeast trade winds too far decided immediately economize fuel by reducing engine speed whereby another weeks flight possible stop furthermore refuelling from land or steamship was considered stop for practise and because of food shortage accepted about 110 kilograms food from steamer *España* yesterday morning stop cruised near Recife in constant communication with Recife reports indicated disturbances and fighting over by end of week and we could wait that long especially while exceptionally good weather continued stop last night rebels surrendered to government troops from Maceio Bahia Parahyba stop will land today at sunset flight until then nearly 120 hours

Lehmann

At the prearranged time, the *Graf Zeppelin* sailed over the thickly populated city and landed. On the wide sandy field the landing-cross was laid out, the friends and helpers waved, and the ground-crew in khaki smiled happily at us as they grasped the handling guys. A few moments later the ship's nose was fastened to the mooring mast, and the rear engine car rolled on the rails whenever a puff of wind tried to push the ship out of position.

According to Central European time, which is four hours ahead of Brazilian time, it was 9.25 p.m. when we landed. Effortlessly and unintentionally we had exceeded by an hour the longest flight yet made by an airship, that of the French naval cruiser *Dixmuide*. Incidentally, the *Dixmuide* was also a German Zeppelin and, before the peace treaty required its surrender to France, was known as the L 72.

Without delay, the empty gasoline tanks were refilled, the mess was freshly provisioned and gas was replenished. In the tropics, the difference in temperature between night and day is greater than in our climate, and the airship had lost a great deal of hydrogen which was now being replaced by the gas-works on the landing-field.

According to the schedule, the *Graf Zeppelin* had to complete still a third mail-flight between Bathurst and Recife and follow that by proceeding to Rio for her last passenger flight of the year. But there was bad news from the capital. In reply to President Vargas' radio appeal to the rebels to surrender and avoid further bloodshed, political and military opportunists, adopting the slogan 'Down with foreigners and their lackeys!' began a revolt in the capital itself. The 3rd Infantry Regiment mutinied in its own barracks and was besieged by government troops who battered breaches in the walls with field cannon. Non-coms and air cadets attacked their officers, and artillery cadets brought up heavy guns against the airport. Hangars and planes went up in flames. Fliers circled over Urca and dropped their bombs on friends and foes alike. And eight hours later the smoking ruins of barracks, flying-schools and the Exhibition Hall, holes in the houses, wrecked automobiles and pools of blood in the streets bore mute testimony to the scenes of horror in the metropolis.

These events took place 1,250 miles to the south of us, while 225 miles to the north the government troops were still ridding Natal of the insurgents. Naturally, it was vitally important for me to know what condition Brazil might be expected to be in when the *Graf Zeppelin* returned from Africa. I could learn nothing, however, without going into the city.

On the way into Recife from the field, our auto drove by swampy black pools, where flocks of vultures hovered and swooped, horrid scavengers of death, the natural sanitation officers of the tropics. Naked pickaninnies wrestled in the dusty streets, making a deafening noise with gasoline cans which, after discharging their original functions, served as milk-cans, water basins and other household makeshifts. The earthen houses on the outskirts were simply constructed of mud and bamboo poles. On wooden verandas, negro women operated sewing machine treadles while listening to gramophone music coming from rusty horns. The trucks and high-bodied model T's with dilapidated tops presently increased in number, the houses became higher and seemed to draw closer together, and suddenly there was a cosmopolitan bustle and to-do. With elegant gestures of their staffs traffic policemen wearing white tropical helmets directed the confusion of buses, donkey carts and pedestrians; only the cars of doctors and officials sped by, irritably sounding their horns.

The loyal government troops quartered in Recife were commanded by General Rabello. At the outbreak of the revolt he was on an inspection tour, and his Chief of Staff, together with the eminently dependable Chief of Police, held the city for the government. The latter considered the revolution over; but the Chief of Staff declined to give us the necessary assurance until three or four days had passed.

I could not wait that long, but took on the American mails and started for Bathurst on Friday, according to schedule. The mail pilots had no more permitted the revolution to interfere with their duties than had the airshipmen. Punctually, the Condor Syndicate planes flew from Chile, Argentine and Uruguay to Rio de Janeiro, picked up the mail sacks and, with bombs exploding under them in the civil war, continued on their way to Pernambuco. Our crossing to Bathurst was uneventful. I was determined to return directly to Friedrichshafen from Bathurst if the necessary guarantee for the safety of the ship was not forthcoming. The European mail, which the fast plane of the German Lufthansa was carrying toward us from Seville, would then have had to remain in Bathurst until 6 December when the mother-ship *Schwabenland* resumed service. Furthermore, that would have eliminated the last passenger flight to Rio where we were to pick up twelve passengers on 4 December. But both of these considerations were insignificant beside the danger that the *Graf Zeppelin* might again become involved in hostilities or be subjected to sabotage. Before going any further, therefore, I decided to radio and the following exchange took place:

Denne 30 November 14.50
Syncondor Rio
Request complete weather forecast Europe North Atlantic sometime Saturday stop notify Zeppelin-works Friedrichshafen and Berlin that we are equipped for return trip but will decide on Saturday night at Bathurst whether to do so

if on basis of arrangement with Rio and Recife opinion of political conditions there and their probable development does not fully guarantee the safety of the airship in Brazil and the abandoning of the remainder of the schedule therefore seems advisable

Lehmann

From Rio to Denne, 16.46
Present conditions give no grounds for anxiety

Syncondor

Denne to Rio 18.10
Our question did not concern present conditions but development of situation which according responsible authorities is to be expected up to sixteenth of December especially in Recife and Natal stop urgently request reply before 20 rio time since we otherwise proceed to Friedrichshafen

Lehmann

The official and press reports which our radio picked up sounded comforting, and so, after exchanging mails at Bathurst, on the morning of 1 December, I wired:

Denne 3.20
Dr Eckener and Zeppelinreeder Friedrichshafen
Setting course Recife will complete remainder program on schedule

Lehmann

On the night of 2 December, at 10.15, we dropped the American mail by parachute over the brightly lit harbour of Natal, and on the next morning, at about eight o'clock, we landed in Recife to replenish gas and gasoline.

And so our substitution for the German Lufthansa Dornier-Wals in the postal service between Africa and America was completed as per schedule. The airship continued her voyage to Rio de Janeiro and returned to Friedrichshafen with mail and passengers.

On 10 December, at 6.41 in the morning, the *Graf Zeppelin* landed on the snow-covered dockyard and came to her well-earned winter rest. She was to be thoroughly overhauled in her berth near the factory, where her sister-ship, the LZ 129, was built, and the keel—to use a nautical but not quite correct expression—of the LZ 130 was being laid. In 1935, her seventh year of operation, the LZ 127, which is the *Graf Zeppelin*'s dock-number, covered 222,000 miles on 82 trips, and carried 30,715 pounds of mail and freight, and 5,227 persons of whom 1,437 were passengers. At the end of 1935, the total distance traversed by the LZ 127 since her first workshop flight amounted to more than thirty

Graf Zeppelin flies over Rio de Janeiro.

times the circumference of the earth, namely 850,000 miles; the net weight of mail and freight was 143,000 pounds; and the number of passengers carried was 12,000. Never, since commercial Zeppelins first came into existence—more than twenty-five years before—had an accident befallen a passenger! Of what other means of transportation could the same be said?

Meanwhile, peace and order had been restored in Brazil. No one in Berlin or Buenos Aires, Santiago or Warsaw had to wait even a single day longer for his mail; cooperation in international commerce had triumphed over the mischief-makers and fomenters of rebellion.

Still, it gave me a queer feeling. We had been hostages of the revolution, so to speak. In the peaceful performance of our duty, we had inadvertently become involved in a civil war. It seemed to me that I had lived through all this once before. I remembered the years when Germany fought for her existence against a world of enemies. The Zeppelins which I commanded at that time did not stop at the edge of the zone of fire; they fought, too; and it was during the war that I first made a hundred-hour flight in an airship.

In the following chapters I shall tell about those eventful times.

4

THE FIRST DAYS OF THE WAR

OR WEEKS I had flown the commercial dirigible *Sachsen* on passenger flights from Leipzig and this time we landed in the capital of Saxony. On Sunday we were hosts to a number of inventors endeavouring to make airship travel safer. One of them brought with him an involved object resembling a monstrous folded umbrella. He said it was the latest type of parachute.

'Would you like to try it?' he asked me. We were hovering some 4,000 feet over the earth and down below us a crowd waited for something to happen.

'No, thanks,' I replied. 'Surely you must have enough confidence in your own invention to try it yourself.'

But he declined my repeated invitations to bail out in his 'chute, much to the amusement of the other inventors who proceeded to display their creations like proud mothers at a baby parade.

'I'll tell you what,' I said. 'We can test it this way.' I tied a dummy to the thing and tossed it overboard. It struck the earth like a stone and the dummy burst apart spraying its sand filling in all directions.

The others laughed heartily at the discomfiture of their rival—all but one. He had held himself apart from the trials which were a pleasant diversion in the monotonous flight schedules. The man was a professional parachute jumper and always drew large crowds when he leaped from balloons at fairs and similar places. Today, he had come with an entirely new apparatus, and he intended to test it from our ship.

'Next!'

He did not hesitate, but with a small package clutched under his arm, stepped coolly through the cabin door into space.

'I have sent a lunatic to his death,' I thought, as I saw him falling. He turned over and over in his descent, shooting directly toward the spectators massed like little black dots below us. Horrified by his foolhardiness, I stared down, firmly convinced that the impact would smash him. I saw the package fall away from him as if he had abandoned it as useless. But to my astonishment it billowed out, opening with the sound of a pistol shot. When I again spied the jumper under the opened 'chute, he was swinging to and fro like a pendulum and sinking slowly and safely to earth. We had witnessed the first demonstration of the folded parachute that is in use everywhere today.

We ourselves often jumped from airships, but our leaps were made without parachutes and consequently were confined to negligible heights. Naturally, we were sometimes obliged to land with a 'heavy' ship; for instance, in rain or snowstorms, when the reserve ballast was exhausted. For such occasions, every superfluous member of the crew had been trained to climb outside shortly before the landing and cling there, clutching the hand-rails. As soon as the ship came within seven feet of the ground, I gave the signal and the men dropped off. In that way the ship was lightened by a few hundredweights, and its descent slackened. Moreover, the men were then in a position to grip the handrails and prevent the ship from striking the earth. This landing trick, which appears almost like desertion to the uninitiated spectator, was always effective. Men went overboard as ballast. But with the aid of dependable parachutes, our method was improved, and we were able to bail out, if necessary, from any desirable height.

Until then—this was the summer of 1914—such emergencies had never arisen. The Deutsche Luftschiffahrts-Aktiengesellschaft, better known as 'Delag,' was making passenger flights between cities in Germany, and had become affiliated with the Zeppelin Company. Thus, we had at our disposal, besides the Friedrichshafen shipyards, the airship hangars at Baden-Baden, Potsdam, Frankfurt am Main, Düsseldorf, Johannisthal, Gotha, Hamburg, Leipzig and Dresden. Certainly, in these pre-war times, every German saw a Zeppelin in flight, either the *Deutschland* or the *Schwaben* or, later on, the *Hansa, Viktoria Luise* or *Sachsen*. Altogether, 37,250 passengers were carried on 1,600 flights, and the ships spent 3,200 hours in the air, covering 100,000 miles—all without accident. Tickets were obtainable at all branches of the Hamburg America Line. The Delag was founded as the basis of an airship system that was some day to link all German cities and perhaps the more important ones throughout Europe. Furthermore, we were even then considering a flight to the North Pole. Count Zeppelin and Prince Henry of Prussia, the Kaiser's brother, had undertaken an expedition on the Lloyd steamer *Mainz* to seek a likely base for the contemplated dash to the Pole. Then the great catastrophe overtook the world.

On the evening of 31 July 1914, as I was leaving the control stand, I received a telegram from the War Ministry forbidding me to fly the *Sachsen* more than thirty miles from her home base.

War! We had never seriously considered war. We were much too preoccupied with our airships. I had served as a naval engineer at the Imperial docks in Kiel, but, finding a naval career far too unexciting, had resigned as a reserve officer sixteen months earlier and joined the Delag. Since then I had commanded commercial airships on hundreds of flights; and as smooth and calm as these

LZ 11 *Viktoria Luise* cabin. Notice the release of water ballast at the right-hand side.

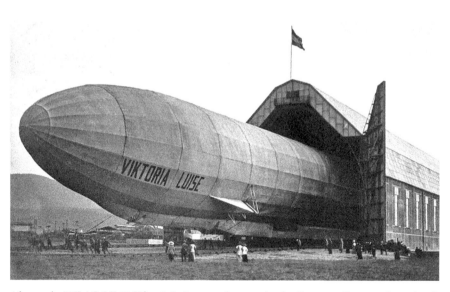

After use by DELAG, LZ 11 *Viktoria Luise* was taken over by the German military on the outbreak of the First World War. It broke apart while being put into its hangar on 1 October 1915.

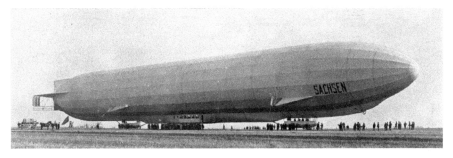

LZ 13 *Sachsen* made its first flight on 3 May 1913. Before the First World War it transported 9,837 passengers in 419 flights, travelling 39,919 km.

trips may have been for the passengers, they were eventful enough for the responsible commander of the ship.

At that time, Dr Hugo Eckener, in the operation of those as yet imperfect Zeppelins, had already had the opportunity of demonstrating that intuitive gift for weather-forecasting which, in the navy, had earned him his nick-name of 'Pontiff.' He was selected for the job of training young naval officers in operating the commanding airships, and I was permitted to help him. Even the F. d. L. (Führer der Luft-Schiffe—Commander of Airships) of the World War, Peter Strasser, was trained in airship operation on the *Sachsen*. King Friedrich August of Saxony, who inspected us during our service with the Saxon Aviation Corps, wondered about the layman, Dr Eckener, and asked him in what field he had earned his doctorate. Eckener replied that he was a Doctor of Philosophy, whereupon the King, in his blunt manner, said, 'Well, then, you don't know much about airships!'

But I like to remember a real test of the great airship master's abilities, when Eckener brought the *Sachsen* through a snowstorm to Hamburg and couldn't see the Fuhlsbüttel landing-field in the thick fog. Finally, he made a bold decision, and brought the clumsy ship over a high-tension wire and down into a pasture. There he got his bearings and, on the next day, with the aid of a hurriedly assembled ground crew, manoeuvred the *Sachsen* neatly into the Fuhlsbüttel hangar. Nothing else happened; only the electric lights went out in the neighbouring villages because the crew had carefully cut the wires after the landing.

Well, I dug my naval lieutenant's uniform from the trunk in the attic and wondered what the war had in store for us airshipmen. We had no idea what would be done with us, for there was no provision for Zeppelins in the General Staff's plans. Although Zeppelins had already been used in manoeuvres, their military value was considered trivial.

Besides our three commercial Zeppelins, the *Viktoria Luise*, the *Hansa* and the *Sachsen*, there were at that time nine other rigid airships in Germany. Seven of

Viktoria Luise at the Kiel Regatta in 1912.

these were in the possession of the army: four new Zeppelins of 22,000-cubic-me-
tre capacity, on the western frontier; two older ones of 19,000-cubic-metre
volume; and one ship of the Schütte-Lanz design, the 25,000-cubic-metre SL 2,
on the eastern frontier. Of the two naval airships, one was stationed in Hamburg
and the other was still under construction. Not one of these ships was equipped
for warfare. In July, when the situation became critical, the commander of the
army airship Z VIII, which lay deflated in Metz, a few miles from the French
border, sought permission to inflate her for service against the French cavalry,
which was being mobilized on the other side of the frontier. For if war was
declared, there was danger that the enemy would advance upon Metz and
destroy the helpless ship. But the War Ministry summarily rejected the petition.

    That was significant. It revealed how unprepared we were for war, and it
indicated, furthermore, that the authorities in Berlin had no idea of what to
do with such a ship in the event of war. Yet, to tell the truth, we were no better
off. We had had some training and experience in aeronautics and we were
enthusiastic young officers in the new merchant marine of the air. Even Count
Zeppelin himself, old in years, but more enthusiastic than many a youngster, at
that time occupied himself not with the military potentialities of his invention,
but with its peacetime development. The army and navy airships were built
for purely experimental purposes, in order to collect various data, and the
government endeavoured to support the new science with contracts. But if
anyone had prophesied then, that, during the war, we would build eighty-eight
Zeppelins, each one larger and more efficient than its predecessor, I should
have considered him a visionary. And yet, more important than the military

results, were the tremendous technical and practical advances made in this hard, prodigal school.

But before it was decided how we were to be employed, I received a surprising kind of baptism under fire. While the mobilization was proceeding with clockwork precision, the wildest rumours circulated through the country. It was said that France was sending automobile loads of gold to its Russian allies through—of all places—Germany. To the guards on bridges, railways and country roads, therefore, every automobile looked suspicious, and if it did not stop when challenged, they fired at it.

Upon my application, we had received a new motorcar, and as we were riding out to the Leipzig airship base one night, we noticed, some distance ahead of us, a red light, swinging to and fro. We thought it was a railway signal, and paid no more attention to it. The next thing we knew, we were in a hot cross-fire from infantry. The lead hummed by our ears like a swarm of bees, ripping holes in the car; and they would have bored holes in us, too, if the driver, with keen presence of mind, had not turned out the lights and stepped on the gas. We reached the airship base on a roundabout route and in a veritable wreck of a car. I was never so furious in my life. It was a ridiculous way to receive one's baptism under fire, and when I found the officer who commanded those loyal sharp-shooters, he was obliged to listen to a great many complimentary remarks. Thereafter, we were not bothered and came and went as we pleased.

A week later I received orders to transfer the *Sachsen* to Potsdam, where she was docked, so to speak, and transformed into a military craft.

Like everything else, civil aircraft, now, were commandeered by the War Office. The *Sachsen*, built in 1913 as the seventeenth ship of the Zeppelin Company, was 470 feet long, had a maximum diameter of 47 feet, and contained 19,550 cubic metres of hydrogen, which enabled her to lift 18,040 pounds of useful load. Like her two predecessors, she was enlarged to 495 feet and thus, with a volume of 20,870 cubic metres, could lift 20,680 pounds exclusive of her own weight. But this increase in volume did not alter the fact that the Zeppelin airship of that time did not yet possess the qualities which, under the demands of military use, it developed during the war. Its external form was still not adapted to the streamlines of the displaced air, but instead was spread out evenly and cylindrically. The ship's frame was not yet made of the duralumin alloy, but of aluminium, and the gas cells were not of light goldbeaters' skin, but of rubberized cotton. My *Sachsen* had only two gondolas, of which the foremost served as both control car and engine-room. The walkway, which connected the control car and the stern engine car, had not yet been placed in the body of the ship, but hung under it like a keel. The propellers, coupled directly to the motors in the later types, were fastened high on the body of the ship by means of outriggers. The three Maybach motors, totalling 540 horsepower, gave the good ship a top speed of 45 miles per hour. With her passenger cabin, built into the walkway, the *Sachsen* was decidedly a commercial airship for mail and pleasure flights of modest proportions, and it was not rendered especially war-like simply because a little radio booth and a device for dropping bombs were installed, or because the control car as well as the platform on the ship's back was armed with machine-guns.

In Potsdam we learned that the airships were not to be assigned to particular troops, but were to operate independently. With my three officers and fifteen men, it was my duty to remain at the disposal of the High Command for special missions, but, beyond that, I was my own master. The first order from above was to take off at night, cruise far behind the enemy lines during the following day and return on the next night. Each of the accompanying airships was to drop bombs on the railway bridges and other military objectives along the route. A General Staff Officer, who was assigned to the commander of each airship, was to determine the course and the objectives. Now, this would have been quite all right if, at the time, we had had the airships which we were to have two years later. But the Zeppelins which were at our disposal at the beginning of the war could fly neither high, nor fast, nor far enough, nor carry sufficient bombs, to accomplish the feats which the General Staff demanded of them. But they tried; with the result that three of them were lost.

At the beginning of August, the Z VI took off from Cologne to support the attack on Lutetia. The ship dropped its bombs over the fort, according to orders, but the thick clouds and its heavy load forced it to fly low. Thus it was struck repeatedly by shrapnel, and even provided a convenient target for the enemy infantry behind the fort. On the return trip, the crew was obliged to ground the ship near Bonn, and there it remained, a total wreck.

The Z VII was ordered to seek out the French army which had withdrawn so rapidly from Alsace that the Germans were no longer in contact with it. The airship took off from Baden-Oos toward the Vosges, constantly in danger of running against a mountain-peak in the clouds because it could not climb above 5,000 feet. In the early morning, the Z VII discovered a French camp, which it bombed; and after another flight through the clouds saw, more than 2,700 feet below, the main force of the enemy army. Instantly, the air was filled with bursting shrapnel, and many thousands of soldiers competed in the attempt to hit a bull's-eye in the 520-foot-long airship. The ship limped off with its gas-cells punctured, and was wrecked near St Quirin, in Lorraine.

On the same day, the Z VIII had taken off from Trèves. As it flew over our troops, our over-zealous countrymen greeted it with heavy rifle-fire, thereby giving the crew a foretaste of the reception that was in store for them at the hands of the French a few hours later. When the enemy force suddenly appeared under it, the ship was only a few hundred feet high. There were rifles and bombs on board, of course, and use was made of them, but the enemy had the advantage. The controls were shot off the craft, and thousands of bullets and shell splinters punctured the gas-cells. The Z VIII hovered defencelessly over

No Man's Land, which at that time was an indefinite strip of territory many miles in width, and stuck in the trees in the forest of Badonvillers. The crew swung themselves overboard and the commander destroyed his ship's papers and ordered the wreck burned. But so little hydrogen remained in the cells that it would not take fire. At that moment, a squadron of French Cavalry dashed into the woods and attacked the airship with drawn sabres. The airmen defended themselves with rifles and pistols, determined not to surrender. But the enemy preponderance was too great to be resisted for any length of time, and the handful of Germans suddenly stopped firing and fled into the woods, where the pursuing horsemen soon lost their trails.

For eleven hours, the airmen marched eastward, until at a lonely farm they came upon the German advance guard. When they stepped into the farmhouse, they saw a captain lazily polishing his boots.

'Where have *you* come from?' he asked in surprise.

'From the French lines,' they answered. 'Twelve hours from here.'

This was the first report indicating with what speed the French had withdrawn. The Germans had hesitated to follow too closely, fearing a trap, and the French Army had consequently won enough time to retreat unhindered to fortified positions. The Captain telephoned the news to Headquarters, and soon the whole German Army began a forced march westward. Within twenty-four hours, the gap was closed and No Man's Land was in German hands.

Unfortunately as this scouting flight turned out for the Z VIII, it belatedly justified the petition of her commander, who had asked permission to take off immediately after the declaration of war. Perhaps the Germans might not have lost contact with the enemy and might have forced them into open battle before they could entrench themselves in the fortified lines at the rear.

LZ 23 (Z VIII). On 21 August 1914, Z VIII engaged the French army while at an altitude of a few hundred feet. According to Lehmann Z VIII received 'thousands of bullets and shell splinters', forcing it to drift and make a forced landing in no man's land near Bandonvillers. The crew destroyed all documents and tried to burn the wreck but so little gas remained it would not burn: the airship crew were captured by the French Army.

5

THE EARLY MILITARY USE OF *SACHSEN*

$\mathbf{P}$OTSDAM ALWAYS SEEMED to me to be peaceful and quiet, and I found it scarcely changed when we landed there with the *Sachsen*. While I had breakfast on the terrace of the Hotel Königsberg, two officers approached my table. The taller of the two was Lieutenant-Colonel Baron Max von Gemmingen,[1] nephew and colleague of Count Zeppelin and now assigned to the *Sachsen* as General Staff Officer. Gemmingen was over the age of military service, but had volunteered and expressly asked to be assigned to the *Sachsen*. For my part, I was particularly happy to get him, and not some other General Staffer who understood nothing of airships. Gemmingen was an expert and at the same time a nobleman in the finest sense of the term: upright, able, fearless and free. Everyone on board liked him, and we two became fast friends, although the division of authority did not make service any easier. Together we faced the changing fortunes of war, until the Baron, in the spring of 1917, after the death of Count Zeppelin, became chairman of the Board of Directors of the Zeppelin Company. He died in the spring of 1924 in the midst of great plans for a transatlantic mail-service.

The other officer, who was with Gemmingen, was a Lieutenant Ackermann.[2] A rich young sportsman, he had a few months earlier become a Zeppelin pilot out of sheer enthusiasm for the thing, and had been assigned to me as Bombing Officer. Shortly after, he was transferred from my ship to the LZ 37, Commander von der Hagen, with which he was shot down. I learned the details of his death from his Chief Helmsman, who, through a curious freak of chance, was the only one to live through the catastrophe.

Besides the officers,' the helmsman relates, 'we had ten men on board. Our ship took off late at night from Brussels, flew over the North Sea in an arc toward Calais and bombed a junction of the English lines. The enemy anti-aircraft fire didn't even come near us in the dark, and when it became light, we doubled back to avoid the zone of fire. This manoeuvre delayed us considerably; and later we had to fight strong head-winds, so that we did not reach the Gontrode airship base, near Ghent, until daylight. We breathed with relief because we thought we were out of danger.

I was at my elevator rudder, when the observer on the upper platform reported through the speaking-tube: 'Airplane two thousand feet aft, above the ship!' We all knew what that meant; the enemy flier was already in the most suitable position for an attack, for we could not repulse him from the control-car. Without waiting for the command to do so, the observer on the back of the airship sent a burst of machine-gun fire at the attacking flier. But already I felt a hit. The ship quivered, and my helm turned loosely in the air. It found no more resistance—a sign that our steering mechanism had become useless. The control car swayed back and forth as if drunk, and I fell. While I was still trying to get to my feet, the entire crew either jumped or were thrown overboard; at any rate, I never saw them again. The whole immense hull above me was ablaze, instantly becoming a roaring, hissing inferno. Instinctively, I threw myself flat on the floor of the car and clawed the rails, desperately trying to avoid the merciless fire roasting down upon me. I wondered how long it took to fall 5,000 feet. I knew this was the end, but I actually welcomed it as preferable to the slow torture of incineration. At last the gondola struck, and everything went black. I regained consciousness in the hospital.

I can supply the missing portions of the story: the control car broke loose from the burning ship and fell to the roof of a convent. Like a shell, it crashed right through to the attic. The impact threw the helmsman out of the car, and he landed flat in a bed which had been vacated by a nun only a few moments before. That saved his life.

The *Sachsen*, meanwhile, had been transferred to Cologne to replace the ill fated Z VI. But the fact that three airships had been lost simultaneously had evidently shaken the High Command's confidence in Zeppelins, for they were now ignored entirely. For weeks we waited for orders that never arrived. Then Gemmingen and I got a motorcar and sped to headquarters at Koblenz. Curtly and clearly, he told the gentlemen that they had been ill-advised to send pre-war types of such limited climbing capacity over the enemy lines in broad daylight. The General Staff was reasonable enough to perceive this, and granted my comrade and me full power in future to arrange for all the necessary measures of precaution. That was exactly what we wanted.

At that time, General von Beseler was preparing to besiege the fortified city of Antwerp to which the Belgians had withdrawn. The Germans had already cut all avenues of retreat with the exception of a railway line running along the Dutch frontier to the west of the fortified city. We suggested the destruction of a junction of this railway line some miles outside the fortifications, proposing to use as many explosives as the *Sachsen* could possibly carry. This would delay the enemy long enough to enable the attackers to close the circle around Antwerp.

LZ 17 *Sachsen*. This photograph was probably taken during its first flight on 3 May 1913. It was taken over by the German Army and had bomb racks and a bomb drop station fitted, together with an improved radio room, machine guns in the cars below and a gunners' nest in the tail. In its first attack on Antwerp it carried 820 kg of bombs and spent 12 hours in the air. It was decommissioned in the autumn of 1916.

Unfortunately, General von Beseler had greater confidence in his cavalry than in our airship. He had already ordered his mounted forces to destroy the railway, and informed us that he did not want us to interfere with his men. The result was that the despatched cavalry met with Allied troops at the junction and was neither swift nor strong enough to stop them. Part of the Belgian troops were withdrawn from Antwerp on this railway and later played an important and perhaps decisive role in the Battle of the Marne. But we were yet to take part in the siege of Antwerp.

At the beginning of September 1914, the General Staff thought it time to send a Zeppelin on a night flight over the fortress. While waiting in Cologne for this order, we had not been idle. We went aloft day after day to familiarize the officers and men with their particular duties. The officer who was to drop the bombs acquainted himself with his instruments and learned to judge the drift of the bomb in the wind. The helmsman practised the most precise cooperation with the Bombing Officer. Our day began at three in the morning. We went up at four and cruised for four hours over the field where we had laid out a variety of targets. When our supply of practise bombs was exhausted, we were obliged to land and collect them again.

At first we had only artillery shells, and very few of those. To make the shells strike head-on, we tied bits of horse-blankets to their ends. Of course, we knew that somewhere in Berlin new bullet-shaped bombs were being made, but since it was not definitely known whether we would get them before the attack on

Antwerp, or at all, for that matter, we obtained the permission of the High Command and ordered a large munitions factory near Cologne to produce bombs according to our own design. We tested these bombs over an artillery range and were so pleased with the results that we preferred them even later, when the 'official' aerial bombs had been issued. The bombs supplied by Ärar had much thicker walls than ours and were consequently heavier, although they were no more effective, and so we continued to use our own, much to the annoyance of a high official. At this time, too, we were already testing various types of incendiary bombs which a number of firms had produced according to our demands. Furthermore, to protect our airship hangars and other important buildings from air-raids, we experimented with a great steel net which was supposed to catch the bombs and cause them to explode. The bombs which we dropped from a 2,000 or 2,500-foot altitude did not miss their mark but proved the net itself to be a complete failure, for they slipped neatly through the mesh and, no matter how the fuses were timed, exploded on the ground.

In the midst of these experiments, we received the order for the attack on Antwerp. On a warm moonlit night at 11 o'clock, we climbed over Cologne and followed the railway line to Aachen, which was brightly illuminated. There I took the ship up higher.

We had 2,000 pounds of bombs on board, a heavy load for the ship which was supposed to rise to 6,700 feet above sea-level. We had left the machine-guns behind, but the crew was armed with automatic rifles and pistols.

Behind Lutetia we struck a cloud-bank and rose above it. Vibrating with the thunderous rhythm of the motors and the humming of the propellers, our ship hovered over a silvery sea of clouds. It required an effort to tear myself from the magical sight. Off Antwerp, the clouds thinned out and at last disappeared altogether. In order not to make a too convenient target for the artillery in the fort, we had to wait until the moon set. That would be shortly before the break of dawn, and so only a few moments would remain for the attack.

When we had cruised for an hour between Antwerp and the Dutch frontier, the moment arrived. It was unusually warm, and only with difficulty were we able to maintain our altitude of 5,700 feet. The inclined position into which we were thus forced was so severe that the men in the control car were slipping backwards. To reach the fortress, we flew full speed ahead, and the accelerated motors warned the defenders. Instantly, the white fingers of searchlights searched the pitch-black night, sliding over us time and again without fixing us permanently. The anti-aircraft guns fired blindly, and the first shells exploded several hundred yards behind us. Directly beneath us, innumerable little points of fire sparked like glow-worms; this was the infantry lying between the first and second belt of fortifications. We let go a few ten-pound bombs.

Meanwhile, however, the artillery fire increased and came uncomfortably close. One searchlight, much stronger than the rest, discovered us and held us tightly in its circle of light. A few shells sped by so close that we felt the wind-pressure.

Mutely and in complete darkness—for all lights on board were extinguished during an attack—my crew remained at their posts. Gemmingen spotted the objectives through his binoculars and I gave the orders to fire. In the two engine cars men stood ready to throw small hand-bombs.

First we flew over the hateful searchlight. A dose of hand-grenades and rifle-bullets and, in an instant, it was extinguished. My Chief Helmsman Laux grabbed a twenty pound hand-bomb, swung it high over his head and grimly heaved it overboard as if thereby giving it an additional one per cent in speed of impact. Then it was the turn of the outer forts. The firing apparatus released the large incendiary bombs, which squirted fountains of fire when they exploded. On the way to the interior, where we intended to pay our respects to the central railway station, we bombarded the two inner forts and two high-blazing fires signalled our success. I looked at the clock; already we had been within the city limits for twenty minutes, and it was high time to leave Antwerp, for a bright light was dawning in the east.

Relieved of the released bombs, the *Sachsen* began the return flight. A thick layer of fog and dense clouds melted together in the valley and removed our view of the earth as if a magic cloth had been stretched beneath us. In the west the stars were still shining, while in the east the sun rose, a golden wheel of fire with spokes of violet, purple, orange, rose and green. We reached Cologne at eleven in the forenoon, after having been under way exactly twelve hours.

The Dutch newspapers which we received contained news items from Antwerp, reporting that our airship arrived over the city on a north-westerly wind to bombard the Arsenal near Beschen, the military slaughterhouse at Schietschotel, the barracks near the Borsbeekschen Gate and the railway yards.

Awakened by the first warning shot, the inhabitants saw a feeble light to the east. Immediately thereafter, a terrific detonation near the Borsbeekschen Gate shook the nearby houses, shattering the windows and causing them to tremble as if in an earthquake. The frightened people ran out into the streets in their nightshirts, stumbling over torn telegraph wires, and were greeted by a hail of debris. Holes were torn in ten houses on the Steenbrough Street as if by pickaxes. The first bomb missed the factory at which it was aimed and tore a hole three feet deep and ten feet wide in a nearby field. But the next bomb struck a diamond cutting establishment and reduced it to ruins. The third bomb crashed through the home of a factory owner, van Geel, and penetrated to the second floor. The seven members of the Defray family, who lived on the top floor, drew on their clothes in all haste and fled down the stairs into the cellar just as the upper story disappeared as if it had been shaved off. Glass splinters and stones wounded the fugitives, who were immediately attended to by doctors in the vicinity. The inhabitants of the next house were likewise alarmed by the crash and flash of the bomb that landed in the field. They fled to the cellar just as a second bomb destroyed their house also. A direct hit sliced the Gewichtenkuis Inn neatly in two. The whole series of bombs fell within a half-mile of the wireless station which, according to the reporter, was the objective of the raid.

Shortly after our attack on Antwerp, the Zeppelin Company completed a new army airship, which was stationed at Düsseldorf and was assigned to Captain Horn, one of the ablest airship commanders of the World War. Horn's Z IX and my *Sachsen* together undertook a few scouting flights to Antwerp and Ostend. We must have dropped about 11,000 pounds of bombs on the two forts, and if we didn't cause any appreciable damage, we at least managed to restore the High Command's confidence in airships. But the General Staff was apparently still not aware of our limitations, for they would not otherwise have issued such orders as this to the Z IX: *Carry out bombing attack on Antwerp, Zeebrugge, Dunkirk and Calais. Return via Lille, which also to be bombed.* That was asking a little too much, for even under the most favourable conditions, the airship could not carry more than ten bombs for all five cities. Furthermore, the enemy had meanwhile so far perfected their air units that their pursuit planes and heavy bombers were beginning to make life very uncomfortable for us. From then on we had to reckon with them whether we were in the air or at home in the hangars.

The English were the first to attack a Zeppelin in its hangar. On 27 September, 1914, an aviator named Marix appeared over Düsseldorf to bomb the Z IX and destroy it in its hangar.[3] The surprise was complete, for no plane of that day was capable of flying from the English front to Düsseldorf without an intermediate landing, unless he took the route over neutral Holland. And, as we later learned, this was the route the English pilot chose. This violation of neutrality was in vain, however, for the first raid was a failure and served us as a warning. We armed the hangar-roofs with machine-guns and installed as many anti-aircraft batteries as we could possibly obtain in those first months of the war.

But the English flier was stubborn and returned again on 8 October. From a great altitude, he descended in a power dive over the hangar, and released a bomb which killed a mechanic standing on the roof, crashed through, and set fire to the Z IX. Though the machine-gun posts on the corner towers remained unharmed, the beautiful new airship went up in flames. I immediately came over from Cologne and found the hangar almost undamaged; but the airship was a twisted heap of ruins, and only the motors could be salvaged. The bombs, hanging under the hull of the ship, were without fuses, and when the metal supports melted in the burning hydrogen, they had fallen harmlessly to the ground.

The Englishman's success encouraged his comrades, and twice the allied planes violated the neutrality of Switzerland to raid the Friedrichshafen Zeppelin works from Bodensee. But they accomplished nothing by it. They had more luck a few months later, however, with two air raids undertaken on the same day: the LZ 37 was destroyed in the air near Ghent, and the LZ 38 was demolished by an aerial bomb in its hangar at Brussels.

When Maubeuge fell, von Gemmingen and I inspected the French airship hangar. The enemy had attempted to blow it up, but had done such a poor job that we were able to repair it in short order and lodge a Zeppelin in it. At Maubeuge we even found snapshots of the French airship which had last been stationed there. It was of the pressure balloon type, like all the other French dirigible balloons built at the Aéronautique Militaire, Nieuport-Astra, and Zodiac factories. Their limited radius of action and insignificant lifting-capacity made them unsuitable for major operations.

The same applied to the 162 little pressure balloons of the Pony Blimp, Coastal, and North Sea type, which England used in the World War and which covered some 2,000,000 miles in coastal defence service. One of these was shot down by a German naval flier who, during the course of the war, rose from bos'n's mate in the reserve to the rank of Lieutenant-Commander and received the Pour le mérite for bringing down nineteen enemy planes and sinking many submarines. Fifteen years later, this man, our most successful naval flier, brought to America the Do X, the first of the flying boats constructed by the Dornier Works of the Zeppelin Company. He is Friedrich Christiansen, today a major-general and Commander of the Flying School in the German Air Force.[4]

LZ 37 was brought down by Sub-Lt Reginald Warneford, 1 Sqdn RNAS, flying a Morane-Saulnier Type L, during its first raid on Calais on 7 June 1915. LZ 37 crashed at Sint-Amandsberg, near Ghent. Warneford was awarded a VC for his actions. This sketch was drawn by Reg Warneford himself.

LZ 38 was one of a new 'P' Class of Naval Zeppelins and it carried out the first bombing raid on London on 31 May 1915 killing seven and injuring 35 people. This was followed by raids on Ipswich, Ramsgate, Southend (twice) and London, dropping a total of 8,360 kg of bombs. On 7 June 1915 this Navy Zeppelin, along with LZ 37 was returning to Evére to the east of Brussels and they ran into a counter-raid by RNAS aircraft flying from Furnes, Belgium. LZ 38 was destroyed on the ground. As a consequence of the RNAS raid both the German Army and Navy withdrew from their bases in Belgium.

Italy used non-rigid dirigible balloons of from 4,700 to 12,000-cubic-metre capacity. One of these, the *Citta di Jesi*, was shot down over Pola on the night of 5 August 1915, and its crew of six were captured. Another dropped eighteen bombs on the Royal and Imperial Headquarters in Portogruaro during the battle of the Piave.

In the fourth year of the war, a young Frenchman distinguished himself. On patrol in the English Channel, the motor balloon VA 5, stationed at Le Havre and commanded by naval ensign Albessard, sighted a German submarine that was just capturing a merchant ship. Albessard attacked the submarine with bombs. The Germans returned fire with their ship's guns and sent nine shots through the bloated body of this Lilliputian of the air. The gas escaped and the balloon envelope became slack and sank to the sea with its gondola. Nevertheless, the spirited Ensign continued to throw bombs at the submarine, which was in danger of losing its submerging capacity by a direct hit, and consequently would have been unable to slip through the blockade. So the German commander abandoned his prize, gave orders to submerge, and thus escaped the approaching enemy destroyers. These arrived just in time to rescue the airman and take the VA 5 back to Cherbourg. Fourteen days later, Ensign Albessard was again under way in his patched airship.

The Allies maintain that their little coastal airships time and again discovered submarines through oil-spots on the surface of the water and that in at least one instance they caused the destruction of a German U-boat by summoning destroyers by wireless. For our part, we can neither confirm nor deny this assertion; but, at any rate, the net profit of the German airships was much greater, thanks to their superior efficiency. Fifty times, our naval airships discovered and attacked enemy submarines, and six times the battle ended in disaster for the attacked. Each of the airships, L 9, L 10, SL 3, L 54, and L 63 destroyed an enemy submarine. L 31, under Lieutenant-Commander Heinrich Mathy, once even took up the fight against a whole fleet of English submarines.[5] Her commander relates the story:

> I was flying half a mile from the Dogger Bank on a northerly course, when I sighted a submarine at a great distance. Instantly, I steered my ship into a cloud in order to approach unobserved and make certain whether it was an enemy or a friend below. When I was still about five miles away, I carefully left my hiding-place and saw not one, but four English submarines, which were apparently lying in wait for a German ship. Whereupon I withdrew into the clouds again, and when I emerged, I was over the subs. Only then did they sight the airship. Their guns began to bark, shells and shrapnel burst over us, and one hit struck against the floor of the control car. I wasn't going to stand for that, and I released a bomb. It was only meant to be a practise shot, and it fell about 400 feet short of its comparatively small target. The second bomb burst only 200 feet from the submarine, the third was within 100 feet, and the fourth struck right in front of the conning tower. The percussion could be felt 2,500 feet up. And when the black cloud of smoke dispersed, we saw the stern of the submarine sticking upright into the air and its crew struggling in the water. A few seconds later there was only a large oil-spot on the surface.
>
> Then I drew back into the clouds again to get over the next submarine. But when the L 31 emerged, the entire flotilla had submerged and fled. Nor was I sorry, for I had other and more important worries at the moment: the L 31 was sinking at the stern. Two gas cells were leaking badly. All the aft water ballast was released immediately, and my men brought gasoline tanks, machine guns, bombs, and even their clothes forward to lighten the stern. Slowly, the ship regained an even keel. At the examination, three direct hits were found. Two shells tore neatly through one cell, and splinters punctured another. One shell passed through the tail. A few feet higher and it might very well have damaged the rudder. But as it happened we got off easily.

Nor did the performance of the enemy pressure airships in the army service compare with that of the German army ships. The war activities of the French airship fleet confined themselves to bombs dropped on the unprotected cities of the Rhineland by the *Adjutant Vincenot*, a dirigible balloon of the Clément-Bayard type. Her sister-ship, the *Alsace*, was shot down by German guns in an attempt to break through the front over Rethel, and fell behind our lines almost

LZ 36 (L9) made 74 successful reconnaissance missions in the North Sea and took part in four raids on England dropping a total of 5,683 kg of bombs. It also made several attacks on British submarines, at least one of which was successful. It burnt out in its hangar at Fuhlsbüttel in the north of Hamburg on 16 September 1916 after the Navy Zeppelin LZ 31 (L 6) it was alongside caught fire during inflation.

LZ 40 (L 10) undertook five raids on England dropping a total of 9,900 kg of bombs and also destroyed a British submarine. It was destroyed in a thunderstorm on 3 September 1915 near Cuxhaven killing 19 crew members.

LZ 72 (L 31) was commanded by Kapitän Leutnant Heinrich Mathy, one of the most famous of Zeppelin commanders. The L 31 once took up a fight against a whole fleet of British submarines. It was intercepted and destroyed by British fighter pilot 2nd Lt W. J. Tempest on 2 October 1916 near Potters Bar, north of London. Mathy with his entire crew died after jumping from the flaming Zeppelin.

undamaged, a striking proof of the impracticability of the pressure balloon, which depends entirely upon its envelope.

The dirigible balloon, whose photograph we found at Maubeuge, met a still more deplorable fate. All soldiers, without exception, apparently have a passion for shooting at airships, and they are sometimes careless about what national insignia such an enticingly large target bears. Even German air-cruisers occasionally heard German bullets whistling through their cells. But since our airships are divided into a row of gas cells which correspond to the bulkheads of a sea vessel, the tiny bullet-holes mean nothing more serious than a slight loss of gas. The French dirigible likewise flew into the cross-fire of its own troops as it was leaving Maubeuge and either the French had better aim or they used larger calibres, for they shot their own airship to shreds.

6

The Invention of the Observation Car

AFTER THE FIRST six months of the war, Zeppelin construction at Friedrichshafen took a tremendous upswing. Another dockyard was erected at Potsdam, and plans provided for no fewer than twenty-six army and navy airships by 1915. At last the construction time had been accelerated to such an extent that, for a while, the two factories together completed a new airship every fourteen days.

At the beginning of the year, von Gemmingen and I were transferred from the *Sachsen* to a new airship, the Z XII. Although even this newly constructed craft, with a gas volume of only 25,000 cubic metres, a twelve-ton useful load, and a scant speed of 60 miles per hour did not meet the demands of aerial warfare, it was nevertheless a noticeable improvement over the pre-war types. The hitherto open cars were enclosed, and the walkway was already at least partially removed to the body of the ship. Some improvements had been suggested by Von Gemmingen and me; others, such as the transition to streamlining, were impossible of realization because of technical limitations. The primary consideration at the moment was the building of as many airships as possible, as quickly as possible; hence, the rings, of which the rigid frame was composed, had to be as nearly identical in diameter as possible, in order that they could be easily replaced or interchanged.

The German people hoped for and expected extraordinary accomplishments from the airships. Their animosity was directed principally against England, who had laid a hunger-blockade while she herself remained impregnable from land and sea. Consequently, the cry of German public opinion for an attack from the air was doubly vociferous. The Military High Command did not ignore this pressure, but their motives were not of such an emotional nature. For them, it was more important to counteract the disruption of our sea trade and the throttling of our sources of supply. The airships and fliers were ordered to drop explosive and incendiary bombs exclusively on points of strategic importance in Britain, such as docks, arsenals, munitions factories, storehouses and railway stations, and thereby cause the retention of considerable military forces at home. The army command counted on the air-raids to boost civilian morale while weakening the resistance of the enemy.

There were many who considered this circumscribed aerial warfare an insufficient reprisal for the unbroken hunger-blockade, and suggested that the attacks should be confined not to single air-raids but should be extended to combined assaults of whole air-fleets over Britain. Twenty great airships with three hundred incendiary bombs each could fly over London. Six thousand bombs, it was maintained, would start so many fires in the metropolis that it would be impossible to extinguish this gigantic conflagration. And even if every third Zeppelin were to be shot down, the crews could still drop their bombs while falling.

When I was asked my technical opinion, I admitted that the plan, as such, was feasible. But the thought of subjecting a defenceless civilian population, outside the actual war zone, to all the horrors of aerial warfare, and destroying priceless cultural treasures, was reason enough for all of us to reject the plan. The Kaiser had at first opposed any air attack upon England at all and only later, under the pressure of his Admirals and Generals, consented to the bombardment of points of real military significance. But certain places in the capital, such as Buckingham Palace, Westminster Abbey, St Paul's Cathedral and the government buildings were under no circumstances to be affected, not even by accident! As I was piloting one of the army airships that were to fly over England, I was quick to realize what the Imperial command signified and what the consequences for me would be if I disobeyed it. So I spread out my map of London and drew around those buildings red circles resembling the so-called danger circles which a sea-captain uses to mark dangerous reefs and sand-banks. 'See how careful we have to be?' I said to Gemmingen. 'They will scarcely allow us enough time to drop all our bombs over the city of London at one time. We'll have to describe an arc and we'll undoubtedly enter one of those danger zones. And if we don't want to be discovered too soon, we'll need clouds to hide us, and under the clouds we'll need clear air, so that we can see the objectives. Unfortunately, such conditions will force us to forego many chances at the Bank of England, and we'll have to satisfy ourselves with the docks and military objectives on the outskirts of the city.'

At that time, Captain Masius, commander of the LZ 35, received a code telegram just as he was about to make a flight over various towns behind the English lines—Cassel, St Omer and Hazebrouck. But by express command of the Kaiser, he was forbidden to bomb St Omer, and instead was ordered to attack Poperinghe. The reason soon became known: Headquarters had learned that the commanders of the Entente had arranged a meeting in St Omer, at which the Kings of England and Belgium were also to be present. When Masius told me about it, he added with a shrug of his shoulders, 'The Allied commanders are meeting in the city hall at St Omer. The city hall stands alone in the centre of a wide open square. Nothing would be easier than to polish it off with a single direct hit.' We all understood that the places at which either King George or King Albert were staying were to be avoided by our bombing squadrons. On the other hand, the Entente was not so considerate, for Charleville and Stenay were at various times subjected to aerial attacks when, or perhaps because, the enemy fliers knew that the Kaiser and the Crown Prince sometimes stopped there.

The respect for non-military conventions of a purely humane or even dynastic nature became more difficult the more the enemy interfered with our military operations. Their planes constantly improved in speed, dependability and climbing power, their searchlights became stronger, and their anti-aircraft defences more efficient. The enemy fliers now climbed to our altitude, the night sky was illuminated as brightly as daylight at the first alarm and the anti-aircraft batteries occasionally showed better aim than their targets. Every time we crossed our own frontier we had to count on getting into a hornet's nest. Gemmingen and I racked our brains for some means of meeting this dangerous defence.

We finally struck upon the plan of lowering from the airship a small observation car, from which the observer could set the course and direct the bombing while the airship followed its course in a cloud bank thousands of feet overhead, unseen by the enemy. As an engineer, it fell to me to work out this idea technically. Other people had had the same idea, and the civil engineer Hagen, in Cologne, who had approached us with it, supplied us with a hand windlass and a 3.8 millimetre steel cable one thousand feet long. We found an old butter-tub and equipped it with a tail-piece which was intended to function as a sort of weather-cock, to prevent swerving. Amidships, in the bombing compartment, we mounted the windlass, from which the steel cable was paid out. To counteract jolts, the tub was fastened to the cable by a couple of strong steel springs. An ordinary field-telephone connected it with the control car.

After I had blindfolded the helmsman at the control stand, I crawled into the butter-tub and gave the order to lower away. At first, this was done smoothly, and as the steel cable began to roll out, creaking and groaning, I sank like a bucket into a well. But when I was hanging about 500 feet below the ship, I began to be tossed around rather painfully, and I had some difficulty retaining control of my butter-tub. I squinted mistrustfully at the cable, which was not over-strong, and expected to see the windlass fall overboard at any moment. This uncomfortable feeling accelerated the calculations which I was making. With a pocket-compass I determined the direction to be taken by the ship and telephoned my orders to the blind-folded helmsman in the control car. The orders were carried out promptly, and the ship moved where and how I wanted it to. Satisfied with the result, I had myself hoisted aboard again.

As soon as the Z XII had landed, I ordered an efficient windlass. It was no longer to be operated by hand, but by means of one of the large gasoline motors of the airships.

Furthermore, we had a 3,000-foot length of cable of high-grade steel man-ufactured for us. A copper wire, insulated with rubber, was introduced into the centre of the cable to serve as a telephone circuit. The observation car was made of willow withies and resembled the stern of a tiny airship, complete with tail and rudder. This was to enable the observer to parry the side-swings when the ship was in bumpy air. In practice, however, this precaution proved to be unnecessary. The basket contained a comfortable chair, a card-table, compass, telephone, electric light and a lightning rod. So equipped, we were eager to be the first ones to seek out the British on their own island. But we had difficulties, and the two naval Zeppelins L 3 and L 4, under naval officers Fritz and Count Platen, stole a march on us by visiting the English coast on 19 January 1915. We still hoped to be the first ones over London.

The difficulties that confronted us in the two first and coldest months of the second year of the war were attributable to the fact that the oil-tanks and pipe-lines of the engines on the new Z XII were not sufficiently protected against the cold. During a raid over Nancy on an exceptionally cold day in February, our ship climbed to 11,000 feet without much difficulty, a remarkable height for those days. The thermometer sank to 50 degrees below zero; actually it was much colder, but our instruments were not gauged for lower temperatures. We were unable to heat the control car.

The crew, working outside, were bitterly cold, and I feared that the mechanics' fingers would be frozen. The situation became grave when one of the three motors stopped. While we were attempting to start it again, another one went dead. The oil in the tanks had formed into hard lumps. To carry out the attack with only one motor would have been suicidal—we would be lucky enough to

LZ 24 (L 3) participated in the first raid on England on 19 January 1915.

LZ 24 (L 3). On 17 February 1915 L 3 was abandoned by its crew after a forced landing in Denmark, caused by engine failure compounded by strong headwinds and insufficient fuel. The wind was so strong it blew the airship, now unmanned but with engines still running, out to the sea.

get home at all. We had to tear open the tanks, extract the thick clumps of oil, cut them into small pieces and feed them in chips directly through the purifier and into the motor. In this manner we kept one motor going and even brought another into operation again, but we crept home at a veritable snail's pace.

Because of this bad experience, the gasoline and oil arrangements were altered. Then, on 8 March 1915, we moved to our new hangar at Maubeuge, in the occupied French zone. Only three days after our arrival we received the long-awaited orders: *Until further notice you are to bomb military objectives wherever possible in England, especially London.*

The order was couched in general terms, and that pleased me no little. For this permitted me to decide when and where we would go. But the decision depended upon weather conditions, and we were badly supplied with weather forecasts during the war. The German weather bureau was set up in Belgium, and its information originated along the front, which was no more than 100 miles away. For us airshipmen that was almost useless, because a storm-centre travelling at a speed of 30 to 40 miles per hour would have passed over or changed its direction before we could be warned of it. Consequently, we were often forced blindly to undertake flights which might last twenty hours. Under these circumstances there was nothing for us to do but draw our conclusions on board from the change in cloud formation, the velocity of the wind at various altitudes, and the temperature and barometer readings. According to my estimate, at least thirty per cent of the air-raids launched against England and France were interrupted by unforeseen changes in weather; and even that is an extraordinarily favourable result when one remembers that the airships went up in every half-way tolerable sort of weather. Moderate headwinds alone placed our success in doubt because they held the heavily laden ship within reach of the enemy longer than was prudent; and severe rains could weight it down so heavily that it could no longer rise high enough to elude the counter-attack.

To these weather obstacles was added the difficulty of getting our bearings. In times of peace, cities are brightly illuminated, lighthouses blink on every coast, and the airship can fly as low as is desirable. During the war, on the other hand, not even the usual topographical aids were of any use. In order not to betray our position to the enemy, we used the wireless only on a lengthy trip or in the event of unforeseen emergencies arising during the homeward stretch. Astronomical observations were impossible when the stars were not visible. At that time we did not yet have our searchlights, by means of whose circle of light on the ground, the velocity of the wind may be gauged. Our sole landmarks were the lighthouses of Ostend and Steenbrugge. An imaginary line drawn horizontally between their two vertical beams of light pointed directly to the mouth of the Thames.

Hungarian born Paul Jaray, (1889–1974) in a gondola. From 1915 Jaray worked at Luftschiffbau Zeppelin, and it is unclear if this is a separate development from what Lehmann describes, or if it is all the same thing.

7

THE FIRST ATTEMPT AT LONDON

N 17 MARCH 1915, the weather improved, and the radio repeated, 'Attack on London.' When I arrived at the hangar to give the order to 'Ready ship,' I found my men at work. My officers reported; the chief engineer tested the engines; the helmsmen checked the rudder controls and elevators; the gas valves and water ballast bags were in order; and the sailmaker used a paintbrush to retouch the camouflaging of the cover. Hydrogen hissed through the inflation tubes, the gasoline tanks were filled, and the cap less bombs were hung in the release mechanism.

As soon as the airship was reported clear, I took my place in the control car while the Watch Officer remained outside to direct the launching. The sandbags, which weight down the ship, were removed, and it rose from the wooden blocks on which the bumper bags rested. The ground crew grasped the handling lines, and at the command 'Airship march' they drew it out of the hangar. The Watch Officer was the last to swing aboard, and the man who substituted for him, or rather for his weight, jumped out. The ship was set against the wind and after releasing water ballast was 'weighed off.' Then with thundering motors it climbed up in wide curves to gain altitude and took course over Ostend to the North Sea.

The air was clear and calm and we searched in vain for a cloud behind which we could slip through the English coastal defence. Under us, on the shimmering sea, cruised enemy patrol boats; I prudently ordered the lights out. The airship became a ghostly apparition. In the control car, the only light was on the dial of the machine telegraph. The two helmsmen stood like phantoms beside the wheel. In his narrow cubicle the radio operator sat with his headset over his ears, listening to the confusion of signals and voices whispering in the infinity of space. Under our keel the end-weight of the antenna followed the airship like the spawn of a mother fish. The cold penetrated the control car through the floor and open windows. Despite two pairs of underwear, and leather jackets and helmets, we were cold. The thermos bottle was passed around, and the hot coffee stimulated us.

To pass the time while waiting, von Gemmingen and I made an inspection tour. The Watch Officer and Navigation Officer remained in the control car with the helmsmen. We climbed the smooth aluminium ladder leading to the walkway inside the ship. The head-winds blew icily between the car and the body of the ship, pressing me to the ladder, and my gloved hands involuntarily clutched tighter around the rungs. It sometimes happened that a man was overcome by vertigo and slid off, falling 8,500 feet into the North Sea.

Even the walkway which extended through the entire ship was no promenade. In the darkness we made our way not so much with the aid of the self-illumined plaques marking the route as by habit and instinct. On the narrow catwalk between the rigging and the tanks, we balanced ourselves as skilfully as if we were walking in broad daylight down a wide street. Like the rest, I was wearing fur-lined shoes; and this thick footwear was not solely a protection from the cold. The hobnailed army boot might have damaged the ship's metal frame, and shoes with rubber or straw soles were therefore regulation.

Near the gas-cells, which threw shadows along the walkway like giant mushrooms in a prehistoric landscape, I heard a noise. In the light of my pocket-torch I saw the sailmaker climbing about with monkey-like dexterity. In his button less overalls (so that he couldn't get caught on anything) he braced himself between two gas-cells like a mountain-climber in a rock chimney. He was searching for a leak in the cover. Brush and cellon pot (fabric glue) were below him, close at hand if a bullet hole in the fabric had to be temporarily repaired. The sailmaker's duties involved great responsibility and were in themselves not without danger. Under certain circumstances he could be rendered unconscious by escaping gas almost before he knew it. Consequently, he always had an assistant or a comrade to attend him during his work.

On bombing raids I had no superfluous men aboard, and there was no such thing as relief after short watches, as in peace-time service. Thus the hammocks in the crew's quarters, which were eked out between the girders, were empty now. There was only a man relieving himself of his inner feelings on the throne-seat in the background. He jumped up in fright when he recognized me; but I smilingly motioned him back. The non-com who was the cook on board, reported in the darkness; I ordered him to give all hands a plate of soup from the aluminium pot on the fireless cooker—they could use something hot as long as the enemy was not making it hot for us. We didn't carry much in the way of provisions for they would have been superfluous—either we returned in twenty hours or we did not return at all. Our food was limited to bread, butter, ham, bacon, a few eggs, some preserves, a few bars of chocolate, and tea and coffee; we permitted ourselves a swallow of cognac only when we were back on land after a fulfilled mission.

Amidships, the narrow defile of the walkway widened out. Perpendicularly below me, the sea looked like lead. In the pale glimmer coming through the hatchway, I saw the bombs hanging in the release mechanism like rows of pears; besides explosive bombs weighing from 125 to 650 pounds, there were phosphorus bombs for igniting fires in the bombarded objectives. The safety catches were not yet off, but my Bombing Officer was already lying on his stomach, staring impatiently through the open trap-door. He was a fine fellow and in peace-time wouldn't have hurt a fly, but now he was eager to spill his murderous load overboard. We were at war, and war knows only severity toward the enemy, who repays in the same coin.

While Gemmingen discussed with the Bombing Officer the cooperation between him and the control car, I continued the inspection and descended to the aft engine car, which swayed under the airship like a celestial satellite. The car was enclosed and so crowded by the two 210-horsepower Maybach motors that the two mechanics could scarcely turn around. The noise of the motors drowned out every word, and the Chief Machinist simply raised his hand, which meant that everything was OK. The air in this nutshell was saturated with gasoline fumes and exhaust gases. I almost choked, until I opened the outlet and let the icy air stream in. To exist for hours in this roaring devil's cauldron, where glowing heat and biting cold alternated, required a stone constitution and iron nerves. Yet it was as nothing compared to the demands made upon the mechanics when, during a battle with the enemy or the elements, the lives of the entire crew depended upon the repairing in mid-air of damages to the motor or propeller.

It is self-evident that in the narrow community of the airship, where all our fates were bound together, I was intimately acquainted with my men even beyond the line of duty. The commander on board is not solely a superior officer, he is also comrade, friend, father, doctor and spiritual adviser all in one. Thus, I was familiar with the personal lives of my crew, and knew that one had a wife and child at home, another had married young, and a third was the only son and sole support of aged parents. Emotional ties bound each one of them to life. No one wanted to die all wanted to return after the war. Yet this longing for home did not make them cowardly or fearful in time of danger, but strengthened them ten-fold in their determination to repel the overwhelming enemy forces.

Proud of being permitted to lead such gallant men into the enemy's territory, I strolled through the marvellous structure that was our weapon and our home. In the darkness behind me, the stern, with its control and rudder fins, merged with the delicate filigree of girders. I passed the shaft way which led between two gas-cells to the back of the airship, fifty feet up. There, on the platform beside his machine-gun, hunched up in the winds created by the speed of the ship, the gunner acted as look-out and reported through the speaking-tube the instant he sighted an enemy flier. He was forbidden to shoot until he had received the order to do so. For when the ship climbed, gas escaped upward, and there was danger that a volley of gun-fire might ignite the mixture of gas and air. Consequently, there could be shooting on the platform only when the ship was not releasing gas.

It was eleven o'clock when I returned to the control car. The Z XII had been cruising long enough, and now I set a direct course for England. The sharp coastline, with surf foaming against it, rose out of the dip of the horizon. And suddenly we had a queer feeling, as if our nerves were tightening in an almost joyous anticipation. Would we succeed in breaking through the chain of coastal batteries and remaining unobserved or at least undamaged? Strange that we could see so little of the mainland; it couldn't possibly have been that dark. The mystery was solved when we came closer, for suddenly we were in a thick fog. The island was protecting itself from the flying invaders as it had protected itself from the invasions of enemy seamen centuries ago.

I brought the heavily laden ship as high as she would go. But at 10,000 feet the fog was just as thick. We cruised in all directions, constantly hoping to find the Thames, since the clouds are generally thinner over rivers. Finally I brought the ship down almost to the earth—in vain; the great metropolis was simply not to be found. We did arouse the furious fire of an anti-aircraft battery, which we were unable to find either. We had to owe it our reply.

In order not to waste the entire night in fruitless searching, we turned and steered for Calais. Much to our surprise, the weather conditions there were actually ideal for the testing of our observation basket under fire. The clouds were 4,000 feet high, and the air beneath them was clear as crystal. We could see the lights of Calais from miles away, and we prepared to attack. Gemmingen and I had a friendly quarrel because both of us wanted to get into the observation basket. Then Gemmingen pointed out that he was assigned to the airship as General Staff Officer and Observer, whereas I, the commander, was obliged to remain in the control car. I had to admit that he was right.

Before we reached Calais, we throttled the motors so that they made the least possible noise while still permitting us to manoeuvre. The ship dove into the clouds, and Gemmingen was lowered 2,500 feet in the observation car. In the infinity of space he was suspended like a disembodied ghost. But as events were to prove, he was a dangerous ghost. When we arrived over the city, the observer hung 2,500 feet above it and had a clear view, whereas his tiny gondola was invisible from below. The garrison of the fort heard the sound of our motors, and all the light artillery began firing in the direction from which the noise seemed to come. But only once did a salvo come close enough for us to hear the crash of the exploding shells. When we leaned out of the car, we saw nothing but darkness and fog, but Gemmingen directed us by telephone and set the course by compass. Following his instructions, we circled over the fort for forty-five minutes, dropping small bombs here and larger ones there on the railway station, the warehouses, the munitions dumps and other buildings. From time to time we noticed large oval spots on the clouds; they were the searchlights gleaming as through an outspread tablecloth.

Later we learned that a panic broke out in Calais not only as a result of the air attack, but because the airship remained invisible. There was a great deal of theorizing as to how we had succeeded in concealing ourselves. They suspected a system of mirrors and colours, although science had already proven that to be impossible. At any rate, the authorities arrested a few innocent inhabitants who had been outside the city limits with their bicycles on that night. They were accused of having signalled us with their bicycle lamps.

Back from our raid, I had brought the Z XII down to 400 feet and was weighing off; that is, I had stopped the motors in order to leave the ship to its own buoyancy. Our forward motion had ceased, the elevator helmsman reported that we were descending slowly, and I was just about to start the motors again when I suddenly saw a great black smokestack looming against the sky. The weather had changed, the barometer had fallen more than ten millimetres in less than twelve hours, and the altitude gauge had indicated 325 feet too many. Before we could drop ballast, the ship touched ground. It fell on a railway track between two factories in the vicinity of our landing-field. The forward gondola came down on a foot-bridge and the rear portion of the ship squatted on the rails. Part of the steering apparatus was torn off by a telegraph pole. I jumped out, inspected the damage and sent out a man to stop all trains. After we had moored the Z XII to a number of telegraph poles, we waited for daylight and then dragged the limping giant back into its hangar, where it was hospitalized for the next fourteen days.

Apparently, we were due for a streak of bad luck during this time, for no sooner was my ship in order again than it suffered a second accident. Once more we had started for a raid on London when we struck heavy rains at night over the North Sea. The rain streamed from the hull and encumbered the ship to such an extent that the execution of our plan was out of the question. In order not to bring our bombs back home again, I took course for Dunkirk and emptied one and a half tons of explosives over the fort, which in turn plastered the air with shrapnel. Suddenly, the ship quivered, there was a crash, and immediately thereafter the crew in the aft motor gondola telephoned that the starboard propeller had disappeared. A large tear in the outer cover and a smaller one in the underside of a gas-cell betrayed the course of the propeller which had evidently been struck by a splinter. We made for home, somewhat downcast, because we had once again failed to reach our real goal.

But some of my comrades had more luck with their raid on Paris than we had with ours against London. On 20 March 1915, the commanders of the army airships Z X, LZ 35, and SL 2 received orders to attack the French capital on the following night. By blinking their code names, German searchlights at Douai, Cambrai, Noyon and other places served as directional beacons. The wooden SL 2, built by Professor Schütte at the Lanz works, was struck on the outward journey over the trenches and therefore dropped its bombs over the French Headquarters at Compiegne and returned to its hangar. The other two airships continued their raid on the metropolis.

Paris had been warned. Its searchlights played in all directions, and a battery to the south fired furiously at a cloud which, in the gleam of the searchlight, they mistook for an airship. For reasons best known to themselves, the French left their capital brightly illuminated, in sharp contrast to London, which always lay in darkness. My comrades could clearly see the fire from the muzzles of the heavy guns in the forts. Most of their shells fell back into the city again, and some of them struck the government quarter, where they caused considerable damage. Even the 'Archie' was a failure, its shells bursting far beneath the German airships. As Commander Horn of the Z X told me, he reached the French capital fighting strong head-winds and, at an altitude of only 8,000 feet, cruised around for half an hour in order to drop his bombs carefully and accurately. Even the Reuter newspaper agency was obliged to acknowledge the German success, and reported that a large munitions factory had been hit. 'Half of the factory operating at the time was blown to bits. The rest of it looked as if it had been struck by a cyclone. An enormous hole in the earth was filled with beams, girders and stone debris.' A large power house was destroyed in the same manner.

The LZ 35 likewise reached Paris, bombarded it and, upon leaving the city, was followed by motorized units of anti-aircraft guns and searchlights. Commander Masius shook off the pursuers by altering his course over the forests north of Paris. When the airship crossed the frontier it was again fired upon, but despite hundreds of holes in its outer cover, returned home safely.

The Z X was less fortunate on its homeward journey. 'Dawn broke just as we were passing the front near Noyon,' Captain Horn relates. 'The French were waiting for us. Although we flew as high as we could, nevertheless, at an altitude of 10,000 feet, the Z X was struck by two full salvos from a battery. Shells and shrapnel burst around us, and their splinters tore through two or three cells simultaneously. A whole shell went through the ship, and two shrapnel shells missed the control car by inches.

> We escaped behind our own lines by speeding away. German planes convoyed us in case enemy fliers appeared, but the latter didn't even take off, not wanting to risk getting into the hail of shells. The Chief Engineer, who made the rounds with two mechanics, reported that no less than five cells were rapidly losing gas, and the elevator helmsman supplemented this news with the information that the Z X was losing more than five feet per second. I brought the ship down to 4,000 feet in order that the buoyant gas would be forced upward, where the cells were not so full of holes. We lightened the ship by throwing machine-guns, gasoline tanks, oil reserve tins, tools and equipment overboard. Our coats and shoes followed. And when nothing else seemed to help, we resigned ourselves to the inevitable and brought the leaking ship to an emergency landing in a field near St Quentin, without injury to the crew.

Despite his misfortune, I envied Captain Horn, for he had been able to carry out his mission. On my third foray against England I got only as far as Harwich, where I emptied my load of explosives. Two days later the LZ 38 was over London, thus being the first airship to bombard the capital of the British Empire.

8

TRANSFERRED TO THE EASTERN FRONT

EPRESSED BY THE short-comings of the Z VII, I was having her thoroughly overhauled, when I received orders to transfer her to Hindenburg, on the eastern front. The Marshal had a very high opinion of airships, and this despite the fact that he at first had to get along with pre-war types which, at best, could only be called experimental. Of the three airships stationed on the German eastern frontier at the beginning of the war, one was the SL 2, which supported the Austro-Hungarian army at Cholm and Lublin and once stayed aloft for sixty hours, with a stop-over at the Przemysl fortress. She was afterwards transferred to the western front, where we have already met her. The second airship, the Z IV, was a veteran of the German air fleet and served on the eastern front under Captain Quast's command from August to October, 1914. Meagrely equipped with machine-guns and small bombs she got into a stiff fight with the Russians at an altitude of a few hundred feet and finally returned with no fewer than 300 holes in her gas-cells. She bombarded the forts of Warsaw and repeatedly attacked railway junctions in the neighbourhood of the Polish capital. Later, the Z IV was withdrawn from service at the front, but still found valuable use as a training ship for the development of additional crews.

The third airship in the east, the Z V, under Captain Grüner, betrayed the mobilization of Russian troops near Novo Georgievsk, and three days later bombarded a whole regiment of Cossacks, returning with vital information concerning the Russian main force which was advancing against Hindenburg. When on 28 August 1914 she attacked the railway yards of Mlava, the Z V was no more than 3,500 feet high. The Russian artillery sent its shrapnel into the body of the ship, which fell behind the enemy lines, badly damaged. As the shipwrecked airmen were attempting to burn the wreck, they were overpowered and captured by the Russians. In 1917, one of them succeeded in escaping into Germany from a Siberian prison camp. Through him we learned that most of his comrades had died of starvation. Captain Grüner and a companion had likewise escaped and, dressed as peasants, had wandered across Siberia to China, where they were shot down by Russian patrols as they were crossing the border.

During the first winter of the war, then, Hindenburg was without airships. After the victory at Tannenberg, he would have been unable to do anything with them anyway, since he was involved mainly in strategic warfare. But now, after breaking through the lines with a slashing attack near Gorlice, he was prepared, with the aid of our Austro-Hungarian allies, to roll back the broken Russian front, and he therefore required airships of the latest and most efficient type for scouting purposes. Whereupon he received my old *Sachsen*, the Z XI and the LZ 34. Commanded by George, Gaissert and Jacobi, respectively, all three made raids on Warsaw, Grodno, Kovno and other strongholds, but the LZ 34 was destroyed after a successful raid on Kovno in a forced landing in May, and on the same day the Z XI was dashed to pieces by a squall as it was being launched from the hangar. As replacements, my Z XII and the LZ 39 under Horn were assigned to the Field Marshal with our airship base at Allenstein.

On the day after our arrival in Allenstein, von Gemmingen and I proceeded to Lötzen to report to eastern Headquarters. Lieutenant-Colonel Max Hoffmann, Chief of the Operations Division and later Ludendorff's successor on the eastern front, received us, explaining the military situation as we strolled through the city. We were pleased with the exemplary order which characterized Hindenburg's headquarters and to which even the posters on the streets and in the public places bore witness. Beside an old-fashioned Hamburg-America-Line placard inviting the reader on a pleasure cruise to Corfu, hung an Agricultural Department appeal to smoke meat and make sausages—an appeal which, unfortunately, was answered only too willingly and hastened Germany's meat-shortage during the war. The prices of all foodstuffs were established by proclamation of the commanding officers at Fort Boyen. The Royal Prussian Railway Board of Königsberg requested public support in the prevention of sabotage. There was an army order against looting, and another poster detailing the scale of rewards for the delivery of valuables:

1 kilogram Infantry munitions, 25 pfennig
1 kilogram Artillery shells, 3 pfennig
1 kilogram iron, 1 pfennig
1 kilogram clothing, 15 pfennig
Gold, 5%
Field glasses, machine guns, cameras, etc., 5-9%
Empty preserve tins, 50 pfennig

Hoffmann left us at the Hotel Kaiserhof, where we had breakfast with officers of the German and Austro-Hungarian General Staff. At the prearranged hour we returned to headquarters which were in a private house. The ground floor was the telephone and telegraph centre, the wires running through broken windows to the trees in the street and along these to the front. In the depths of the house, electric bells rang, telephones jangled, and ordinance officers and adjutants hurried in and out. On the next floor, it was much quieter. It was Hindenburg's custom to keep his staff small in order to move the army commanders as close as possible to the front, and he followed this practice in the east, too. His intimate staff consisted of only sixteen officers. Non-coms of the Staff unit, wearing real Mayor's chains and breast-plates decorated with an eagle, announced us to their Chief of Staff, Lieutenant-General Erich Ludendorff. Gemmingen, who had been on the General Staff with him, entered first. After a few moments, I was asked inside, too. Dressed in smart field-grey, his glance directed at me clearly and penetratingly, the General held out his hand. 'Gemmingen has told me about you,' he said. 'I bid you welcome as the first naval officer under my command. Let's look at the maps.'

In a large adjoining room, the tables were covered with papers and maps; still larger maps, hanging on the walls, were marked by coloured lines and pins. Hoffmann and a young General Staff Captain were at work there. Ludendorff marked the points of attack on the map and then left us in order to occupy himself with other problems without losing any time. Hindenburg and he were excellent examples for everyone at headquarters. They rose at six in the morning and sat at their desks until eight. After breakfast, they took a short walk, and from nine o'clock on they read the incoming dispatches. Their simple midday meal took no more than a half hour, and from one to seven, and after dinner

General Paul von Hindenburg, Kaiser Wilhelm II, General Erich Ludendorff at Headquarters, 1917.

until midnight, they worked on without stopping.

On the night after our arrival, we were invited to Hindenburg's quarters. As a mere naval lieutenant I felt somewhat out of place amid all the gold and silver decorations for all the others were of far higher rank. I had never before seen such magnificent uniforms as those worn by the Austrian and Hungarian cavalry officers.

Shortly before we were called to the table, the Field Marshal entered the room, shook hands and exchanged a few words with everyone. Before his Adjutant, Captain Kemmerer, could introduce me, Hindenburg turned to me and said in a slow deep voice, 'Why, hello, have we a sailor here now? Are we perhaps getting a couple of submarines?'

'No, Your Excellency,' I replied, 'but a few airships.'

The Field Marshal then greeted Baron von Gemmingen and asked about Count Zeppelin's health. Meanwhile, he led us into one of the two dining-rooms reserved for guests. Although, according to my rank, I should have been at a nearby table, I found myself at my host's table with Gemmingen, Ludendorff and other German and Austro-Hungarian Generals.

The meal was over in fifteen minutes, and the Field Marshal took Ludendorff aside for a conference. Half an hour later he returned, spoke to a few of the other guests and then sat down with Hoffmann, von Gemmingen and me. The conversation turned on the present situation. Hindenburg was convinced that there could be no decisive result on the western front until the Russian army was entirely destroyed. He believed that he could achieve this by summer if the necessary forces were placed at his disposal. The outcome of the world war proved how accurate was his judgment. When I met Hoffmann again that autumn, he assured me that Hindenburg would unquestionably have destroyed the entire Russian army, and consequently Russia's power, if the two additional divisions had been granted him.

9

ZX II on the Eastern Front

A T THE END of June 1915, we began our activities with General von Gallwitz' army. The front lines ran close to the old political boundary which Russia had fortified with well-equipped strongholds from Warsaw to Kovno. For miles, the River Narev was the line hindering our troops from attacking Warsaw from the rear. North-east of Warsaw lay the strong fortress of Pultusk. It was our job to bomb the defence lines and outer forts of Pultusk on the night before the attack, thus confusing the enemy and giving Gallwitz' army the opportunity for a surprise attack.

When we upped ship shortly after nightfall, we found the entire locality covered by a thick fog. For hours we remained aloft, but the fog did not disperse, and we returned with our task uncompleted. But under the protection of this very fog, our infantry advanced anyway and succeeded in breaking through the Russian front.

While the Germans pushed farther forward on the north flank, and the royal and imperial troops, reinforced by Germans, pushed back the Russians in the south, our three airships harassed the retreating enemy, destroying railways and preventing them from escaping the German pursuit.

The main route between Warsaw and Petersburg, and especially that from Warsaw to Dünaburg, was still in Russian hands and was carefully guarded. The only way to approach them was by means of our airships. While the *Sachsen* under Captain George, and later under First Lieutenant Scherzer, attacked Lomza with conspicuous success, and the LZ 39 under Captain Horn raided Tluscz and Novo Georgievsk, my Z XII concentrated on the railways lines to Dünaburg and especially the Malkin and Bialystok railway stations. In these northern parts the July nights were comparatively short and on cloudless nights the moon was too bright to permit raids; but despite this we only once let the weather interfere with us. In August we were active uninterruptedly, and the Z XII dropped about ten tons of bombs on the railway stations.

Once we took off from Allenstein on a beautiful summer night, carrying gasoline for eight hours, and almost three tons of bombs destined for Bialystok.

At an altitude of 5,500 feet the Z XII crossed the front without being discovered; only infantry fire crackled below us. We were within five miles of the city when suddenly every light in it went out and two batteries on the railway line began firing at us. But the shells exploded so high above us that I determined to remain at only 5,500 feet, for to rise above the danger-zone would have meant passing through their point of fire. I deduced from this that the enemy had only simple field guns set at a definite angle. Apparently they had expected us to travel at least 2,500 feet higher, and this error kept us from being bracketed for they had no time to dig-in their gun-carriages.

The railway yards were in feverish commotion. Heavy trains were being shunted to safety before our bombardment began. But already our small bombs were exploding on the rails. Instantly the station resembled a disturbed ant-heap. Everyone ran about panic-stricken, seeking any sort of shelter. On the main line, I noticed a suspiciously long train which was placed off on a siding between two other trains. Something told me that this train was important, so I brought the ship down to 2,500 feet, until we were directly above it. Then I ordered the release of half of our supply of heavy bombs. The result was terrific. The cars were loaded with munitions, and with every hit, one load after another flew into the air until the station was a seething hell of flames. The deafening explosions drowned out the roar of our motors. The percussions struck at our gondola like hammer-strokes, and the flying shells and bits of wreckage were like a cyclone behind us.

Immediately after the searchlight went out and the batteries ceased firing, we rose over the danger zone and, from a height of 8,400 feet, were better able to view our work of destruction. The great Bialystok railway centre was no more. Satisfied with this result, I made my entry in the ship's log and, on the homeward trip, dropped the rest of our bombs on two way-stations, demolishing another small junction and a bridge. Luck was with us. We had not received a single hit. I rejoiced inwardly, but I rejoiced too soon.

The return journey led over the Russian stronghold of Ossoviec, and I had to pass over it because our gasoline supply would suffice only for the shortest route to Allenstein. A thick layer of fog and low clouds concealed the swamps and forests, and I depended upon being invisible from the fort. Aroused by the sound of our motors, the garrison trained searchlights toward the sky. The beams pushed against the underside of the clouds and painted lovely circles and ellipses on the black cloth outspread a thousand or more yards below us. Like a sinister shadow our ship glided through the night with its motors droning. But then the guns began to boom, and their barrels were aimed, as we knew, in the direction from which our motor noise was coming. We paid scant attention to the thundering until suddenly, without warning, the clouds beneath us drew away and we were in the clear air, at the mercy of the enemy fire. A searchlight caught us in its circle, lost us for an instant, caught us again and then held us fast. The guns in the fort and the trenches peppered one salvo after another directly into our path. They were shooting short, and when we again were able to slip into a cloud, we were no longer in such great danger. But they continued to fire blindly into the sky, and a last salvo accidentally exploded right under our stern. That meant that our aft gas-cells were punctured by splinters, and we began to lose gas and buoyancy. But our own lines were just on the other side of Ossoviec, and we were only two and a half hours from home. Everything seemed to be going all right.

Day broke when we arrived at the point where, according to my calculations, Allenstein should have been. But we saw nothing. Thick grey fog had swallowed the land. We could not communicate with our station for we had dismantled the wireless set in order to carry more bombs. If the Allenstein base had had a pilot balloon, they could have sent it up and we would have known where to land. The next air-base was at Königsberg, but it was scarcely likely that the weather conditions were any better there.

I had hoped that by daybreak the sun would warm our lifting-gas and thus enable us to regain altitude, but at five o'clock in the morning it was still concealed by high clouds. The situation became grave. We could not rise any further. Neither could we cruise at will, for the gasoline tanks were almost empty. Yet we were obliged to keep the propellers turning fast enough to retain control of the airship. We lifted the nose of the ship upward to avoid sinking any further. Already our ballast and everything portable, such as the windlass and paraphernalia of the observation basket, had been thrown overboard. After cruising around for two hours without any sign of improvement in the weather, we had fuel enough for only forty-five more minutes. Under those circumstances, I had to land.

The following ten minutes are among the most uncomfortable of my life. No commander wants to lose his ship. We pushed through the fog with the bow lowered, and I still hoped it would not be as thick on the ground and that we would find one of the many small lakes where I could set the ship down safely.

But the fog reached all the way down to the earth. Our altitude gauge already showed such a low height as was scarcely to be found in this locality, and still we could not see the ground. We were falling at the rate of 20 feet a minute, for the enormous cotton hull absorbed the moisture like a sponge, and the gas-cells were shrinking almost visibly because of the colder air down below. Finally, I ordered the motors speeded up to keep the ship under control, although normally, when we were so close to the ground, I retarded the speed. I do not know how my men reacted to this order, but they were a cold-blooded band, and every man took his orders and carried them out as if we were on a harmless practise flight.

I looked out of the control car window just as a wooded knoll appeared no more than two ships-lengths ahead of us. It was too late to get over it, because one of the motors coughed and stuttered just at that moment, so we jerked the rudder around and slid past it at a speed of 45 miles per hour, no more than 35 feet from the ground. If only a lake had come into sight.

No sooner said, than one of them appeared. It was a very small lake, really no more than a duck-pond, and before we could stop we had reached the further bank. The surface of the water disappeared behind us, and the wild ducks, who had flown up in alarm, settled down again. I gave the order to come about, and when the lake came into sight again, we were prepared. All the motors were stopped, then set full speed astern, bringing the ship to a standstill. The aft engine car splashed down into the water, and the forward car followed. The lake was shallow and the impact tore the two rear motors from the struts. Now I had only a single motor with which to bring the 500-foot-long ship out of a lake surrounded by forest. There it floated, a large duck on a small pond.

The surface of the lake was large enough to permit us to turn, but that was all. We were sitting as in a mousetrap, for, excepting the clearing through which we had slipped in, the trees cut off every avenue of escape. The propeller of the one undamaged engine was in the water, and I attempted to use our airship as a sea-vessel. But the propeller didn't turn slowly enough to prevent its being shattered by the resistance of the water, and I quickly abandoned the attempt. We had no anchor and the wind tossed us around until a few men waded to the bank, threw a cable around a tree and thus secured the stern of the ship. We did as much as we could toward lightening the ship so that it couldn't swing into the trees.

Meanwhile I had sent out a man to phone the airship base and obtain aid. Just after he reappeared with a few farmers, an old soldier approached with a troop of Russian prisoners who were working in the fields. They formed a splendid ground crew. As we soon learned, we were only ten miles from the Allenstein airbase, which sent gas and fuel on a truck and offered additional aid. But we were too proud, and declined. For in the meantime, the sun had come out, drying the ship and expanding the remainder of the gas, and although one rear cell was entirely empty and two others were half limp, I was certain that the Z XII still had sufficient buoyancy to get away if we limited the crew to three or four men.

I ordered only two helmsmen and a mechanic to remain aboard besides myself, and put the others ashore. They and the Russians grounded the ship until I gave the command to up ship. Slowly and ponderously the ship rose from the surface of the lake, and with the hum of our sole remaining motor sounding like sweet music to our ears we limped to Allenstein and landed. A half hour after the take-off from the lake, the Z XII was in its hangar.

A few moments later a storm broke out; the doors of the hangar creaked, the windows rattled. Hearing it, I wrapped myself tighter in my blanket, dead tired, and smiled sleepily to myself. An airshipman must have luck.

During the next few days, while the Z XII was being repaired, I had plenty of time to hear what had happened to my comrades. The LZ 79, an 840-horse-power army airship of 31,900-cubic-metre capacity, was stationed south-west of us, at the Posen airship base. This improved type of ship was built in streamline form, tapering toward the stern. It was consequently faster, and superior to its forerunners even in lifting capacity. On the same night we were over Bialystok, Captain Gaissert set out with the LZ 79 for the fortress of Brest-Litovsk, where the defeated Russians hoped to make a last stand against the Germans and Austro-Hungarians. As beacon-lights, he used the flames of the villages which the Russians had set afire in their retreat, and at midnight he threw a full dozen of his heaviest bombs down upon the overcrowded Brest-Litovsk railway station. He then veered to the south-east and, at 2.30 dropped the rest of his load at the junction at Kovel. Against stiff north-west winds, Gaissert again reached Posen on the next forenoon, without incident. In seventeen hours he had covered 1,000 miles and dropped about 3,000 pounds of bombs.

When Gaissert visited Brest-Litovsk again two weeks later, the Russians were just destroying the city and the forts. Seen from above, Brest-Litovsk resembled a single sea of flame over which hung black palls of smoke. Gaissert had no intention of flying the LZ 79 over this blazing furnace, and prudently made a circle around the city. When he reached the railway line at Luninecz, through which point the Russians were transporting their troops, he dropped bombs on every train he saw—and the trains stopped running. After the LZ 79 had once again left its visiting card in this manner, it was withdrawn from the eastern front and returned to service in the west.

The reparation of the Z XII had been delayed because the holy bureaucracy was obliged to consider whether it would permit me the necessary spare parts. Nevertheless, at the beginning of September, 1915, we were able to move into our new airship base at Königsberg and were already busily engaged in transforming the railway stations on the Vilna route into crater-holes.

As exciting and dangerous as this work may have been, we were not quite satisfied with it. Secretly, we had set ourselves another goal—and this was the Grand Duke Nicholas, uncle of the Tsar and Generalissimo of the Russian army. During his retreat through Poland, the Grand Duke left the country devastated behind him, dispersing the people and leaving the women and children to miserable deaths in the swamps. The constant sight of the gutted villages and trampled fields filled us with a dull fury, and though we were usually sorry for every victim of our bombardments, we felt toward Nicholas the grim hatred of the hunter trailing a wolf. Today, I can admit it; we were on a veritable man-hunt for the Generalissimo of the Russians. Of course, this was more in the nature of a private war which we were carrying on, and we took care not to reveal our intentions at the German headquarters. We knew that the Grand Duke had no permanent headquarters; he used his special train, which at night was halted at some station which had telegraph connections. But by shrewd questioning, we finally learned from one of the younger Staff Officers the whereabouts of that station presuming, of course, that the Supreme Command East itself knew that. When the hunt for Nicholas could be combined with our regular duties, we attacked those stations which we suspected of harbouring the Grand Duke. Once, on our second trip to Malkin, we made a side-trip of 60 miles to visit Syedlets, where, according to the latest reports, the Russian High Commander was supposed to be. Since I found no real opposition, I descended to a low altitude and found, in the darkness of a siding, a *de luxe* train that was certainly no troop transport. Six of our best bombs plunged downward, and the cosy cars flew into bits, their ruins whirling hundreds of yards high in the air.

Perhaps the Grand Duke was not on the train at the time; perhaps it was not his train at all; at any rate, I waited in vain to hear his death confirmed. On the contrary, he was more active than ever before, and with a strategic talent indisputably his own, retreated in far-sweeping closed formation.

His lines, however, did not reach to the Baltic, and if Hindenburg had at that time received the necessary reinforcements, the entire northern Russian army would have been surrounded and captured.

Before operations on the eastern front came to a close in the winter of 1915–16, we were reinforced by two additional airships. One, the new LZ 85, under Scherzer, dropped twelve tons of explosive and incendiary bombs on the railways and bridges near Dünaburg, Riga and Minsk. The other, the LZ 39, bombarded the fortress of Rovno. But in so doing, its rear gas-cells were punctured by shrapnel and a shell nicked a strut on the forward engine car. When the commander, Dr Lempertz, subsequently began his homeward journey, the stern of the ship sank and its inclined position became dangerous. Suddenly, the strut snapped, and the gondola, including the mechanics, dropped off. Since the same fate threatened the forward control station, Lempertz and his officers retreated to the inside of the ship. Thus, out of control, the LZ 39 began to drift back toward Russia. But the crew did not give up hope. All hands worked feverishly; all the ballast in the stern was thrown overboard, even the fuel tanks; the cargo was brought forward from the stern; and finally Lempertz was able to make use of the emergency controls in the rear part of the ship. In this way the small group came back over the lines and brought the ship down not far from Luck, which was in German hands. Unfortunately, there were no materials with which to complete the vital repairs on the spot, and the LZ 39 went to pieces and was later dismantled.

Much later, after the war, when Dr Lempertz was at the Friedrichshafen airship docks developing a gaseous fuel to be used in the Maybach motors of the *Graf Zeppelin*, we talked about the old days and about how carelessly the goddess of fortune distributes her favours, for the same thing that happened to Dr Lempertz in the LZ 39 could easily have befallen me in the Z XII.

Soon thereafter, the break of winter put a stop to our activities on the eastern front. Together with my orders to transfer the Z XII to Darmstadt, I received a telegram: 'On the occasion of their transfer from my command, I wish to express my gratitude to the commander, the officers and crew of the Z XII and wish them luck in their future activities. Von Hindenburg.'

10

THE *KING STEPHEN* INCIDENT

I HAD ORDERS TO transfer the Z XII to Darmstadt. But I could not obey them. This was due to the wind blowing crosswise to the single door of the Königsberg hangar. For two weeks we waited for a few minutes' lull in which to undock the ship. We did not even leave the hangar, but slept in our hammocks, in order not to miss the first favourable moment. On a rainy night in October, the wind finally died down and we could risk undocking.

Our journey took place at night between two layers of clouds from the upper one of which it rained in buckets; the other obstructed all vision of the earth below. We had no radio apparatus, and navigated by compass. At daybreak we pushed the ship's nose down through the clouds and saw Hanau below us. Near Darmstadt we found a stiff wind directly in our face. Wind resistance and motor power were equalized and by running the motors and sinking the ship's nose downward, we descended like an elevator.

In Darmstadt there were further orders awaiting Gemmingen and me. We were to deliver the Z XII to another crew and take over, at Potsdam, the new LZ 90, which was the equal of the LZ 79 in size and efficiency. Soon after receiving my new ship I resumed contact with my old outfit, the navy, which had its own airship squadron.

The association of Zeppelin airships with the Imperial German Navy had at first been under a tragic star. One year before the outbreak of the war, the first naval airship went down in a North Sea storm off Heligoland, and the second burned in the air a month later over the Johannisthal airfield. In the first disaster, the commander of the L 1, his engineers and a part of his crew were drowned; in the second, the entire crew, including the captain, met a frightful death.

In spite of this, Commander Peter Strasser, who was in command of the naval air force during the World War, believed faithfully in their future. While I was awaiting the completion of the Z XII in Frankfurt am Main, I was ordered to deliver a lecture to the army and navy experts on the use of our observation gondola. Though the War Ministry later consented to the introduction of our observation car, it first charged its specialists to complete technical

The Johannisthal Air Disaster, 17 October 1913. LZ 18 was destroyed by an explosion caused by escaped hydrogen being sucked into an engine compartment during a test flight; the entire crew was killed.

improvements; and the specialists fussed around with it for over a year. Strasser, on the other hand, in his swift, decisive manner, made no fuss at all, but tested the car which the Zeppelin Company had built according to my instructions. Each of his subordinate airshipmen was obliged to permit himself to be lowered in it at least once; but Strasser himself tried it first. I know the following story only at second hand, but his men must have done something wrong, for they say that when the Commander was suspended 350 feet below the airship, the tail of the car caught in the wireless antenna or some other trailing line, and the basket tipped. The cable, still being paid out from the windlass, then formed a considerable loop, so that the occupant had to cling tightly to the basket in order not to fall out. Suddenly, the antenna released the car, and Strasser dropped down into space until the cable snapped taut with a sharp jerk. Thus, our invention did not enjoy a very auspicious introduction into the navy.

Thanks to Strasser, the first two naval airships were soon replaced by two new constructions which, at the outbreak of the war, were used for reconnaissance flights over the North Sea. During the first months of the war, the L 3 undertook 141 flights, among them one of thirty-four hours' duration, and the L 4 undertook fifty. Another ship was completed in October, 1914 and, by the end of the year, had made fifty successful scouting flights over the Baltic. For the first Christmas of the war, the Highest Army Command provided the navy with three additional airships, the L 6, L 7, and L 8. From the second year of the war on, the naval air fleet was increased rapidly, but the growing losses prevented their number from ever exceeding fifteen units at one time.

Four naval airships were lost in battle with the enemy. In February 1915, the L 3 and L 4 were wrecked in a storm while returning from a scouting flight along the Norwegian Coast. The commanders of the two airships, Fritz and Count Platen, were exceptionally capable men. Lieutenant-Commander Fritz, commander of the L 3, later told me:

When we came about, shortly after mid-day, I knew we were due for trouble. An increasingly stiff wind had sprung up from the south; the horizon was dark and bulging with ugly cloud-banks. Our second engine had stuttered a few times and we knew it was not going to hold out. Over The Skagerrak, the headwinds stiffened and began to churn up the sea below us, and when the first drops of rain splashed down, I knew that we would no longer be able to reach our home base at Hamburg. For a moment I considered letting the tailwinds drive us over The Kattegat and Belt toward the Baltic, but that would have increased the route to Germany at least three-fold. And how did we know that the weather conditions were any better there?

Therefore I decided to hold a direct course along the Danish coast in order to land as soon as it was advisable. Shortly after two o'clock, our ailing motor stopped. I had long ago given up any hope of reaching our own hangar, but thought we might be able to reach Northern Silesia. There, I could have obtained aid from the Tondern air base, which was just being constructed.

At three o'clock, the wind strengthened to a gale and heavy snow flurries set in. When we looked down at the foaming sea, it sometimes seemed as if we were no longer moving at all. That the ship might weather the snow-storm through the night was out of the question; I had to come down before dark. When we neared the Danish mainland, I gathered all the ship's papers, including the code-signal book with its lead covering, and dropped them into the sea.

Over the level ground, we set the ship into the wind by running the two other motors full speed ahead, and followed this by a landing manoeuvre exactly like those we had practised during our training period at Hamburg. In every gondola, I ordered four men to cling to the hand-rails, and, no more than seven feet over the earth, I signalled through the control car window for the men to drop off. Before and during this operation, I released gas, to prevent the suddenly lightened ship from rising again. All eight men lighted on their feet and grasped the hand-rails. Quickly, I threw both anchor-lines from the nose of the ship, and my men caught them and held the vessel down to earth.

'Just then another snow flurry approached, and I ordered all the remaining crew into the forward gondola and opened the gas valves. At my command, some of my men jumped off, just as a puff of wind pushed the ship down.

Become heavy through the loss of gas, it struck heavily on both gondolas and then the rest of my crew jumped. I remained on board with the elevator helmsman, but then we, too, left the ship, which, being no more than an empty envelope with running motors, was sentenced to destruction.

It was plain that we couldn't hold the ship for any length of time, and even if we had been able to, it would have been confiscated by the Danish government. Still, I hesitated; that was my first ship, and it was bitterly hard to give it up.

Then the snow squall struck. It came upon us with terrific force, blinding our eyes and darkening the earth as if night had come. The ship was pressed hard against the ground, but it nevertheless began to toss my crew around violently. By raising my voice to its highest pitch, I made myself heard above the storm. Both sides close together! Clear the lines! Ready! Then came the command, Let go!

The L 3 reared up and leapt away from us like a phantom. In the next moment it had vanished into the snow and darkness, driven out to the North Sea. I left my men no time for moody contemplation. We waded haphazardly through the snow, making our way inland. The Danish peasants whom we met an hour later were at first dismayed, thinking that Germany had declared war on Denmark. We reassured them and they gave us coffee and lodging, until a Danish military escort arrived and transferred us to a concentration camp.

The sister-ship, the L 4, under Lieutenant-Commander Count von Platen, suffered an almost identical fate, except that her crew had less luck or were less skilful when the ship came down during the storm. Two of the men were injured and four others, apparently misjudging the instant for leaping, were carried away in the runaway airship. No trace of them was ever found.

The two other naval airships which were lost were the L 8 and the L 7. At the beginning of March 1915, the L 8, under Lieutenant-Commander Beelitz, was returning from a raid on the English coast and flew too low over the enemy lines near Nieuport. Artillery hits emptied four of its gas-cells, but in spite of this, it might still have reached its Rhenish home base at Düren if bad weather and heavy rainfalls had not forced it down near the Belgian village of Tirlemont. The crew saved themselves and anchored the damaged ship, but within a few hours the storm had damaged it to such an extent that it had to be dismantled.

The L 7 had been raiding England together with two other airships and struck murky weather on the return trip. At 4,000 feet, it unexpectedly passed over an enemy flotilla. The Commander, Naval-Lieutenant Hempel, changed his course and thus flew over a still stronger fleet whose shells ripped holes in the various gas-cells. Broken-winged, the L 7 got away, and its commander wirelessed that he would have to come down at sea. German destroyers and submarines rushed out but were unable to find the airship. The enemy had caught up with it again. An English submarine attacked the craft as it was lying helpless on the surface

LZ 24 (L 3) participated in the first raid on England on 19 January 1915. On 17 February 1915 it was abandoned by its crew after a forced landing in Denmark, caused by engine failure compounded by strong headwinds and insufficient fuel. The wind was so strong it blew the airship, now unmanned but with engines still running, out to the sea. It is pictured here before it left Germany.

of the water. Gunfire killed the Commander, the First Officer and nine men of the crew. Those remaining alive were fished out of the wreckage and taken prisoner. This happened near Horns Reef, on the Danish coast.

This series of misfortunes was followed by a second, of which I heard upon my return from the east. The L 10, under Lieutenant-Commander Hirsch, had taken off from the Nordholz airbase and, apparently disregarding the proper precautions—for the ship was inclined upward—pushed into a thundercloud. The escaping hydrogen mixed with the air to form explosive gas, which was ignited by a thunderbolt. An enormous blazing sack, the L 10 crashed down out of the clouds.[6]

On 9 August 1915, the L 12 was badly damaged during an attack on London. The Commander of the L 12, Naval-Lieutenant Peterson, held the leaking ship at an angle of 20° until he reached the open sea. To decrease the angle of inclination, all hands except the two mechanics in the aft gondola were ordered forward, and all furnishings, including gasoline tanks, oil containers, machine-guns and wireless apparatus were thrown overboard. In spite of these efforts, the ship struck the water and Machinist's Mate Frankhänel was thrown from the aft gondola. While the wreck floated with the tide, the mate relieved himself of his leather clothing and began to swim after the ship, which was disappearing in the darkness. Whenever he was about to grasp the floating gasbag, a mischievous wind would push it out of his reach again. But after three hours, Frankhänel succeeded in grasping the great stern fin and clambered aboard. From there he crept forward over the back of the ship, climbed through the hatchway and joined his comrades, who had given him up as lost and now greeted him as one returned from the dead. Later, a German destroyer towed the vessel back toward Ostend, but there it caught fire and the flames completed the destruction begun by the sea.

Three additional airships fell sacrifice to the flames at this time: the L 6 and L 9, which lay side by side in the Hamburg hangar, were destroyed through an accident during the process of inflation, and the L 18 at Tondern because of a leaky gas-pipe connection. The L 6 had given its commander, Naval-Lieutenant von Buttlar Brandenfels, his first opportunity to distinguish himself.[7] During the course of the war, this dashing officer, like Strasser and Bockholt, received the highest German war decoration, the Pour le Mérite.

On 25 December 1914, off Heligoland, Buttlar sighted three English mine-layers convoyed by two small cruisers and eight destroyers. Since the board sender was out of order, Buttlar attempted to report his observations by means of searchlight signals to a flying-boat from the naval air base at Heligoland, the flagship *Seydlitz* of the Chief of the Scouting Forces.

Not inclined to stand by while the minelayer continued its dangerous activities, the L 6 flew over the three steamers and, from an altitude of 4,000 feet, dropped the only three bombs available. For some reason or other, the bomb-sighting device was not on board; the bombs, each weighing 110 pounds, were aimed at random, and a hit could only have been a lucky accident.

The bombs did no damage, but instead the L 6 received the well-directed anti-aircraft fire of the English cruisers. The airship withdrew from the shell-bursts and retired into a cloud; then, concealed, it flew very low over the enemy flotilla and opened fire with machine guns from the two gondolas and the upper platform. The Englishmen returned fire with their rifles and, punctured by bullets, the L 6 began its homeward journey. Buttlar was obliged to throw overboard all the gasoline tanks in order to keep his ship from sinking, but despite this circumstance he reported to the Chief of the Scouting Forces by dropping a message to the *Seydlitz*. He arrived at Nordholz with his supply of ballast and gasoline entirely exhausted.

Such an exploit, to the success of which both audacity and luck must contribute, could only have happened in the early part of the war, when anti-aircraft defence was still in its swaddling clothes. I heard this story from the Bombing Officer of the L 6, who manned the machine guns on the back of the airship during the battle. His name is Hans von Schiller, and he is not unknown to the passengers to our commercial airships.[8]

In the same capacity, Schiller took part in the L 6's first night attack on the English coast, and again used his three bombs. They fell on the old Norman city of Maldon, on the Essex heights. His hands stiff with cold—it was winter and the airship gondolas of that time were still open—Schiller dropped a number of small incendiary bombs over the same place.

Like my friend Pruss, another Captain of the Deutsche Zeppelin Reederei, Hans von Schiller was considered one of the bulwarks of the air-cruiser commanded by Lieutenant-Commander Buttlar during the war. He had another exciting experience at Hartlepool on 18 August 1916 when, after a squadron attack by seven naval airships, the L 11, 13, 21, 22, 30, 31, and 32, an apparently harmless flotilla of fishing boats off the Dogger Bank suddenly uncovered 'Archies' and came within a hair of bringing down the L 30, which was flying at a height of only 1,000 feet.

Soon thereafter, Buttlar, with the nucleus of his crew, was transferred from the L 30 to the newer and stronger L 54, and there Hans von Schiller had further opportunities of proving his courage and wit in the face of desperate circumstances. Over the North Sea, the L 54 was homeward bound with three empty gas-cells, and threatened to break in two pieces. Reporting for duty, the First Officer smartly saluted the Commander and asked dryly, 'Will the Captain take command of the fore part of the ship or the after part?'

When the army gave up its airships, the LZ 88 was turned over to the navy. The Navy Board equipped it for experimental purposes, numbered it L 25, and placed von Schiller in command. After the armistice, Schiller joined the Zeppelin Airship Works as Navigation Officer and Pilot.

But let us return to the second year of the war. Eventually, the Zeppelin Works accelerated their construction time to such an extent that, as I have already indicated, a new airship was completed every fourteen days. So we did not lack ships. But the training of the necessary crews was a difficult task and required a great deal of time. Actually, at least a year of intensive schooling is required

LZ 45 (L 13) undertook 45 reconnaissance missions. In one flight on 31 January 1916 it pushed forward from the Midlands to the west coast and managed to transmit important messages regarding British ship movements. It took part in 15 raids on England dropping 20,667 kg of bombs. L 13 was decommissioned on 25 April 1917.

to weld together a crew that the commander of the airship can depend upon. He and his closer staff, First Officer, Navigation Officer, and Flight Engineer, should have twice as much time at their disposal in order to acquire a sufficiently thorough acquaintance with their duties under all conceivable circumstances. Naturally, that was impossible during the war, and I am sure I shall not be offending any of my brave comrades by saying that most of the accidents to our airships were attributable to inexperience.

Every airship base was garrisoned with a hundred men; but it was the commander's duty to see that his ship was in proper shape. He was the captain and he alone was responsible. At the air base his crew was supplemented by a landing-crew of the same strength, and these twenty or twenty-five men were permanently assigned to the airship, following it wherever it was transferred. Even when the ship was not on a flight, the crew had plenty of work to do. In their hours off duty, our airmen cultivated their gardens or played soccer. After twenty hours of duty against the enemy amid exploding shells, they were happy to devote a few short hours to peaceful work on the earth and to bloodless contests with the leather ball.

While our army airships sought their targets principally on the mainland, the naval airships carried the war to England and maintained an effective patrol service over the North Sea. Their alertness made it almost impossible for the English Fleet to carry out important movements without the knowledge of the German Admiralty. At the same time, the airships served as scouts, supported the German Fleet in its raids against the English coast and, on the other hand, protected the German coast from enemy attacks.

Consequently, the naval airships were often forced down at sea. When the sea was calm, the entire manoeuvre, including remaining stationary by means of a floating sea-anchor, was child's play. But the cool winds of the upper strata having been lost, the ship soon regained buoyancy and would ascend of its own accord, if the ballast-tanks were not instantly filled with additional water. With the aid of its motors and control surfaces, a floating airship can be manoeuvred almost as well as a sea-vessel—not only in calms but in winds also, since winds increase the efficacy of the control surfaces. Even before the war, we had often practised this during our training at the Naval Air School at Hamburg. Now, in the bitter warfare against our submarines, the English attempted to block every exit from the German waterways by means of mines, and ultimately were laying nearly 10,000 mines per month. They themselves estimate the number of mines placed in the North Sea during the war as 61,679. They were wise enough to do their work only on dark nights, during thick fogs or in stormy weather, when no airship could risk going aloft. Thus our airships were for the most part confined to discovering the mines which had already been planted and flying ahead of our minesweepers to give them timely warnings of the approach of the enemy.

From the bird's-eye view even smaller objects can be pretty clearly seen under water to considerable depths, depending upon the weather. If it was a single mine which we discovered, it was sunk from on board by machine gun fire. On the other hand if we were dealing with whole mine fields, which generally were laid out checker-board fashion, we would drop at the corners a buoy with a bright flag as a marker, and then notify the minesweeping fleet via wireless. On a single day, the L 5, under Naval-Lieutenant Hirsch, sighted and marked 368 mines. Sometimes the airship landed beside the minesweepers, took on one of its officers and sailed over the minefields at a low altitude. The officer was then returned to his boat and the mines were destroyed according to his instructions.

The patrol service of the naval airships over the North Sea extended, in addition, to the observation of merchant ships which often carried contraband for the enemy although they flew neutral flags. Once, one of the naval airships halted an English and a Swedish sailboat cruising about one sea-mile from the Danish light-ship. Before the two vessels could sail away, the airship came down to a hundred feet and the Swedish captain received the order, 'Heave to until further orders!' The English captain received the order, 'All men abandon ship and row to the light-ship!' Why did they obey, why didn't they shoot at the airship? Because they knew that they could not open fire without being instantly blown to bits by bombs from the airship.

Two minutes after the British sailors had abandoned the ship, the airship dropped two bombs. They crashed through the deck, tore open the hull and sent the ship keel-upwards into the depths. Then an airship officer leaned out of the window of the control car and gave the Swedes permission to weigh anchor.

One day the L 23 sighted the Norwegian bark *Royal* about fifty sea miles off the light-ship at Horns Reef. Lieutenant-Commander Bockholt brought the airship over the sailing vessel and, when the captain pretended to be deaf, dropped a bomb off its bow. Then, suddenly, the Norwegian understood, and with suspicious haste lowered his boats and ordered the crew to pile in. With all possible caution, the L 23 came down on the water, and its commander politely requested the neutral's papers. The bark proved to be carrying a cargo of wood for the English coal mines. Thereupon, Helmsman Gegert and two non-coms boarded the ship and, after a 43-hour trip, sailed her into Cuxhaven as a trophy of war.

The L 40, under Sommerfeld, even halted a steamer in this manner. But since, at the time, the enemy began to use small calibre incendiary shells in defence against our airships, Commander Strasser soon forbade this practise.

Our naval airships did not even hesitate to give battle to enemy warships and aviators. One night Lieutenant-Commander Löwe, commander of the L 19, who was under way with two sister-ships, wired: 'Sighted smoke clouds north of Terschelling.' This first message was followed a few minutes later by a more detailed report. Three English airplane carriers, recognizable by their plump outlines, were speeding toward the German coast. They were convoyed by various light cruisers and armoured ships which in turn were protected from German submarines by a number of destroyers. Evidently this armada planned to come as close as possible to the German coast, and from there send airplanes aloft.

The English thought themselves undetected, and they were about to lower the planes to the water when the three airships appeared. But before the airships could dispose of their bombs, a battleship came upon the scene and put them to flight. The strong headwinds retarded their speed and the battleship sent whole salvos of shells after them. As the muzzle fire indicated, they were using their largest calibre. The airships were making slow progress, and it seemed an interminably long time before the crews saw the coast of Holland appear upon the distant horizon. One of the Zeppelins lured the battleship after her, while two smaller British cruisers attempted to cut off her retreat. Six miles from the neutral coast, the cruisers ceased firing and went about in order to catch up with the convoy again. The airship, which meanwhile had gone higher, slowly trailed along behind.

While the English cruisers pursued their sister-ship, the two other airships again flew over the airplane carriers and dropped their bombs. The amphibians had already been lowered and were just about to start for the attack upon the German coast. The resultant excitement and confusion on the water can be easily imagined, for the wireless alarm sent out by the L 19 now brought a number of German battleships upon the scene. Quickly, the amphibians were hoisted aboard again, the airplane carriers, including their convoys, steamed away, and the three airships followed them at a higher altitude. The chase lasted the entire day, and it was nightfall before the airships returned home, with a few holes in their gas-cells, but otherwise undamaged.

By this timely and fortunate reconnaissance action the naval airship L 19, together with the others, prevented a large scale attack, an attack that without doubt was intended as revenge for the German air-raids on the island. This same airship played the major role in a tragedy soon thereafter, on 31 January 1916.

Nine airships had attacked Liverpool at night; eight of them returned, but the L 19 was missing. Its commander, Löwe, had trouble with the new type motors, which did not become dependable until months later. Destroyers searched all night for the missing airship, but they could find nothing.

According to Löwe's last wireless message, which reported engine trouble, the L 79 should have been somewhere along the coast of Holland. The weather was bad, it was bitter cold, and thick fog hung low over a large portion of the North Sea.

On the next morning, Headquarters received a report stating that an airship was seen in the fog over Holland. The ship was travelling at a low altitude and was fired upon by the Dutch garrison because it was violating neutrality. A few days later, Reuters reported: An English fishing steamer, the *King Stephen*, encountered a drifting airship in the North Sea, but was unable to rescue the crew. That was all, until months later a number of bottles were hauled up in fishing nets on the Norwegian coast. One of these bottles contained a message from Löwe and was addressed to Captain Strasser, Commander of Airships. It read:

With fifteen men on platform and back of the L 19, floating about 3 degrees east, I attempt a last report. Light headwinds and three motors out of commission delayed us on our homeward journey and brought us into fog, which followed us to Holland, where we received considerable gunfire. The ship became heavy; the three engines stopped simultaneously. On 2 February 1916, about 1 o'clock in the afternoon; this seems to be the end. Löwe.

Chief Engineer Baumann, in civil life a foreman of a south German electricity works, entrusted his last message to his wife and five small children to a thermos-bottle which, after some months, was picked up by a Swedish ship.

Dear Grete and children,

I find myself in great danger at the moment, having fallen into the sea with our ship. Dearest Grete, I still hope to be rescued; if it is to be otherwise, then it is God's will. Love and kisses for you and the children.

Your faithful George.

Baumann's note was dated 1 February at four in the afternoon. The drifting wreck stayed afloat overnight, and on 2 February, Naval-Lieutenant Erwin Braunhof, Watch Officer of the L 19 and son of a Hanover minister, placed his farewell in the hands of the sea.

Two days and two nights afloat. No help. Bless you. An English fishing steamer wouldn't rescue us.

Erwin.

The truth of this report was confirmed by a third message in a bottle.

My dear Ada and Mother,

It is II in the morning, February 2. This morning a fishing steamer, an English one, passed by but refused to rescue us. It was the *King Stephen* out of Grimsby. Courage failing; storm coming up. Still thinking of you.

Hans.
At eleven thirty we prayed and said farewell to each other.

Your Hans.

The *King Stephen* had come alongside but had refused to take the ship-wrecked men aboard, thereby delivering them, contrary to all seamen's honour and humanity, to a slow and miserable death. A few months later one of our submarines captured the fishing steamer *King Stephen* and brought it to a German harbour. The Captain at first denied ever having seen an airship, but all the other members of his crew admitted it in individual interviews. They said the crew of the airship could easily have been rescued, but that nothing was done. Whereupon the Captain of the fishing steamer likewise admitted the facts of the case and excused himself by maintaining that he feared he would be overpowered by the Germans and thus lose his ship. The crew of the *King Stephen* were interned as prisoners and sent back home at the end of the war.[9]

The case of the L 15 is very similar. I learned the details from the commander, Breithaupt, who is a lieutenant-colonel today and has charge of the Airship Division of the Air Ministry. Obeying orders to raid important points in central England—for he had already commanded the L 15 for half a year on bombing flights over England—Breithaupt, in March 1916, became embroiled in a battle over the suburbs of London. English planes swarmed around the L 15 like hornets, flying above it and dropping bombs which, however, were not well aimed. The machine guns of the airship were finally successful in repulsing the enemy fliers. But the anti-aircraft batteries on the ground shot at the tremendous target with rare accuracy and sent one shell after another crashing through the body of the ship. Four aft gas-cells were slashed to pieces. All bombs had to be dropped immediately.

Breithaupt steered for Ostend. He temporarily lost control of the leaking ship, which from an altitude of approximately 10,000 feet fell in great curves until he regained control at about 3,000 feet over the English coast. But then, at one in the morning, fifteen miles from the coast, the ship collapsed in the air and sank down near the mouth of the Thames.

Breithaupt had sent his men inside the ship, where the impact would not endanger them; he himself remained in the control car with the helmsmen. Great masses of water flooded the gondola and threw the men around like chips of wood. The elevator helmsman was drowned, and not a single man inside the ship escaped without injury.

Broken in two, the L 15 lay in the water, sinking rapidly. The crew climbed to the upper side of the hull, and Breithaupt and the rudder helmsman followed them. Two hours later a fishing steamer arrived but left again without replying to the plea for a boat. The bow and stern of the broken ship made a sharp angle out of the water, and the wreck was visible at a great distance. Attracted by this, four fishing boats approached from the other side and came within 100 yards. The first words to reach the ears of the shipwrecked men were 'Go to hell!' The airshipmen called back '*King Stephen*!' A volley of rifle fire was the answer. The shots whistled through the wreck. Breithaupt and a number of his comrades lost their footing on the slippery hull and fell fifty feet into the icy water.

The shooting had lasted scarcely two minutes when it was ended by the appearance of the English destroyer *Vulture*. A boat was sent out, but the commanding officer insisted that the shipwrecked men relieve themselves of all their clothes before being taken aboard. All except Breithaupt, who declined to take off his uniform, received woollen shirts on the destroyer, and with this clothing they began the journey to the English military prison at Chatham. Incidents of this sort were extremely rare.

The L 15 sinking near the mouth of the Thames.

11

Commander Schütze and the L 11

T HE ANXIETY OF the English refuted their official claims that our airship raids were ineffectual. I myself piloted army airships over England and I shall tell about that later, but since I am now concerned with our naval dirigibles, I shall confine myself here to a report by Commander Victor Schütze, showing what a single ship, boldly and skilfully handled, was able to accomplish.

It was a stormy winter's night at the beginning of March 1916, when a look-out on an English patrol boat heard the drone of motors approaching over the North Sea. Other ships likewise heard the sound, and soon a number of searchlights flared up. Their beams of light struck against the cloud-banks which were being driven along by an icy north-west wind at an altitude of 8,000 feet. The thinnest portions of the clouds were pierced by a few rays. Up there, over a dark-black sea, three airships fought their way against a storm which was attempting to push them back to Germany. All the patrol ships opened fire, their shells howling through the clouds and exploding close by their targets. But the airships flew on to England.

Near the Flamborough Head lighthouse, the L 11 turned northward along the coast whose steep shore rose sharply against the black surf. It was an ugly night. The sudden snow-storm was interspersed with hail and rain squalls; the highways were transformed into swamps; the telegraph wires were down. No one expected German airships on such a night. As a matter of fact, they might not have taken off if they had known the weather conditions awaiting them.

The frost soon enveloped the L 11 in an icy mantle, pulling it downward. The weight of the ice and the heavy load of bombs made it almost impossible to keep the ship at a safe altitude over the enemy territory. Our entire supply of water ballast had already been exhausted. In view of the strong headwinds, I abandoned my proposed raid on the Rosyth navy yards, in Scotland, and instead decided upon the Middlesbrough munitions works. Then the wind began to blow at a speed of 55 miles per hour, conveniently giving the ship additional lift. The snow fell in thick flurries, blowing into the motor gondola and covering the observation nest on the upper platform of the hull. With teeth grimly bitten together, my crew laboured to keep the ship high in spite of snow and ice.

At one in the morning the clouds withdrew and the air became clear. Taking my bearings, I found that for hours we had made little progress. Again I changed my plans. The Humber lay to the south, a small black ribbon winding along the earth. The great city of Hull could be only a few miles away. Though the city was darkened and completely invisible, I determined to find it.

Just then a few flames flashed up like fireworks in the direction toward which we were flying. They were exploding bombs. Another airship of our trio, the L 14, was attacking Hull. From the window of my gondola I saw the city intermittently illuminated by the flash of hits. That sufficed. But before I could get to Hull, I had to fight the storm. Great mountain ranges of snow-clouds crowded under the ship, so that I was obliged to cruise about, waiting for a lull in the storm.

Since I had plenty of time, I remained in the same position for an hour or two until the weather cleared. Shortly after two in the morning, I began the attack. My Bombing Officer first threw a few bombs in the vicinity of the city to arouse the activity of the searchlights and anti-aircraft guns. Thus, they revealed to us their exact positions. I knew that because of the strength of the north wind I could not return a second time if I missed my objectives; but just then the clouds parted completely and, in the bright starlight, the city and its suburbs lay quiet under the thick snow. Directly below me I could distinguish streets, docks, shipyards and warehouses as clearly as if they were on a map. But now a few lights appeared in the streets. I flew the L 11 full speed ahead and arrived over the city with the wind behind me. For a time we dropped our bombs without being bothered. The first hit a dock and partially destroyed it. The second struck a canal-lock, and a few surrounding buildings collapsed like houses built of cards.

Every explosion sent masonry high into the air, until that portion of the city looked like a crater-field in the midst of a snow-covered landscape. I noticed another section similarly demolished, evidently by the bombs from the L 14. One of our bombs struck a munitions dump and caused a whole series of violent explosions. Through my glasses, I could see people running here and there in the garish flash of the bombs. The sluice-locks destroyed, the ships in the harbour began to drift. A few weak searchlights played up at the sky, but they were as ineffectual as the scattered gunfire.

Relieved of its death-dealing load, the L 11 rose to 8,500 feet, and I saved the last five bombs for the nearby city of Immingham, whose forts, as I had observed, were making it hot for the L 14. Two uncomfortably strong search-lights greeted us from the forts, but were unable to hold us and were small help to the heavy guns which were booming furiously upward. The beams of the searchlights repeatedly illuminated a thin layer of clouds which we happened to be right behind. Finally, however, about fifty incendiary shells whistled around our ship. Then, fortunately, our first large bomb blew up the nearest searchlight and the others were quickly extinguished.

A few moments after we had dropped our last five bombs, we left the coast of England and ran into another heavy snow-storm. This soon became a hurricane. It gripped the L 11 and tossed it a hundred yards high; and when the ship had recovered, a rudder-wire had become fouled. Before we could free it again, the ship was once more thrown hundreds of yards high, and I could bring it to an even keel only by ordering my crew back and forth like a human sliding-weight. And so we continued until the damage was repaired.

But then one of the motors stopped, its gasoline and water pipes frozen. Although we were unable to repair it, we arrived home in excellent condition after a flight lasting twenty-six hours.

Shortly thereafter, the L 11 again set out for England, and my destination this time was London. But over the North Sea I found myself delayed by strong headwinds, and I therefore headed instead for the shipyards on the Tyne. To do that I was obliged to fly over a fishing fleet which naturally wirelessed the warning to England; so I was prepared for a warm welcome. I made every effort, therefore, to attain a higher altitude, but even after dropping two full fuel-tanks overboard, the L 11 would not rise above 6,300 feet.

When we approached the Tyne, the batteries of big guns lining both sides of the river opened fire. I did not dare to try to get through this formidable defence, for my ship was flying low against a headwind of 30 miles per hour. But still I was determined to trick the Englishmen. At Sunderland were situated the great foundries and smelting furnaces which, in uninterrupted day and night shifts, were supplying the Allies with war-materials. The L 11 sped off in that direction. One, two, three high-powered explosive bombs struck the largest factory-building. The smelting furnaces and everything around them crumbled to ruins. The detonation roared like thunder, and the whole locality was illuminated by the flames that here and there pierced through the clouds of thick black smoke. Yet even this illumination was unnecessary, for a whole row of factories invited disaster by their brightly lit windows. The L 11 laid its eggs as quickly as possible, the buildings collapsed, and the streets were torn by craters and sowed with wreckage.

One of the bombs caused a veritable display of fireworks in the midst of a huge cloud of smoke. Instantly I released another bomb, and this had the same result. We must have been over a railway yard; locomotives, car sheds and roundhouses and, I hoped, a good many tons of war materials, flew into the air.

The anti-aircraft batteries made scarcely any effort to repulse us. Consequently the L 11 was not struck by a single bullet over Sunderland, although a large shell exploded so close to the envelope that the percussion felt like a direct hit.

Zigzagging over the searchlights, I made a detour to Middlesbrough, where the rest of my bombs made two additional smelting furnaces cease operations. On the next morning, the L 11 returned to its base at Nordholz, where after working for another hour and a half helping the landing crew dock and service the ship, my weary men fell into their beds, only to take off again on the following day for another westward flight.

This time I took forty-five bombs with me, but for reasons of weight economy, I restricted the engine crew, left spare parts and machine guns behind, and calculated my supply of fuel to a bare sufficiency. It was 2 p.m. when the L 11 took off from Germany, and it was thus scheduled to arrive over the English coast not later than 10.30; but fog and unfavourable winds delayed us until about three in the morning. I could no longer make London, and attempted to find Norwich instead; but the city was so carefully darkened that I could not discover it even when I knew I was flying over it. Perhaps I could succeed in finding Yarmouth or Lowestoft. The seaport of Yarmouth had been the objective of the first airship raid in January 1915, and it seemed to me about time to bombard the garrison and inhabitants again. But this city, too, we were unable to find. When the air-cruiser was already over the sea, the English tried to bring it down by shooting furiously into the mist. But although they could not see the airship, their muzzle fire betrayed their position. The L 11 instantly went about and, in the grey of dawn, flew over the batteries. Three full salvos crashed down upon the 'Archies' causing considerable destruction.

Again the L 11 returned to Nordholz undamaged. Three days later it was over England once more. In exceptionally clear air north of Hull it was caught by the beams of four searchlights and presented an excellent target to the batteries. Shells burst above, below and all around it. Then a bomb extinguished the nearest searchlight. The L 11 turned away and then remained undisturbed until the moon came up. A crank-shaft bearing melted in one of the rear motors, and the L 11 again changed its course to fly with the wind. At Hartlepool, the forward motor balked, and I therefore avoided the city and steered for Whitby where we had seen a smelting furnace operating at full blast. This was the famous Skinningrove Iron Works, whose numerous factory buildings and smelteries covered a wide territory. My Bombing Officer aimed carefully; and I did not proceed until I was convinced that the works had been destroyed. As is understandable, the English later announced that there had been no serious damage.

On the homeward journey, the L 11 got into heavy fog and I headed inland to make navigation easier. We were able to ascertain our position and, at an altitude of only 160 feet, held our course and landed at Nordholz at 3 p.m., when the fog lifted.

So much for the report of Commander Schütze. The layman can hardly understand the significance of that curt, dry closing remark. Returning from raids in the early hours of the morning, airships often got into fog. This meant, at that time, hours of careful navigation as close as possible to the earth, with the fuel reserve almost at the zero point and the ship sometimes unmanageable because of damages to motors and gas-cells. In such cases, the airshipmen were obliged to feel their way through the fog, so to speak, playing blind man's buff with fate. Now, all this uncertainty and danger is eliminated by radio direction finders and landing-beams.

I remember an uncomfortable night when, together with me, half a dozen naval airships left England in the face of a threatening storm. The whole fleet returned safely, except the L 20, which was furthest north. The storm carried the ship over North Scotland and forced the commander, Lieutenant-Commander Stabbert, to detour over the North Sea to Norway. There the supply of gasoline was exhausted. The L 20 landed near Stavanger and was destroyed by its crew. Stabbert and his men were interned in Norway.[11]

The command post on a Naval Zeppelin.

12

LZ 90 AND ATTACKS ON LONDON

URING THE FIRST months of 1916, while my naval comrades were giving the English plenty to think about, I piloted the new LZ 90, one of the seven airships directly under the Highest Army Command. It was a beautiful ship of 32,000-cubic-metre gas volume, constructed in streamline form, with a tapered stern and more efficient control organs. Its armament consisted of eight machine guns, two in each engine car, one on the upper platform and one on the stern; and its wireless apparatus was of the latest model.

But it was two months before the new motors were operating efficiently. We had trouble with the lubrication system and the crankshafts. Because of the emergency, the motors, which together developed 960 horsepower, had been hastily constructed. Once during a test flight to the Spich airship base at Cologne, all four of them stopped simultaneously and for a half-hour we were obliged to manoeuvre our ship as if it were a free balloon. But by the end of February, we finally had things running smoothly, and we undertook an especially long test-flight to experiment with our radio compass, still a novelty at that time.

A few days earlier, after an attack on the railway junction at Revigny, near Brabant-le-Roy, the LZ 77 had been shot down in flames. This was astonishing, for generally the shells went straight through the envelope, and even during shrapnel fire the damage was confined to a few gas-cells so that the ship could still remain aloft. Thus, when on the last day of February 1916 we started towards Verdun to replace the LZ 77, we did not realize what a decisive turning-point in aerial warfare her destruction signified.

After an hour's flight, the crankshaft broke in one of the motors, and we returned to Trèves, where we replaced two motors. A couple of days later we were on our way again. It poured in buckets, and between times it hailed and snowed. For eight hours we fought the storm, and finally we were more than content to be able to get back to our old hangar again. It was three days later before we succeeded in making an attack.

Our goal was the railway yards at Bar-le-Duc, which supplied France's key-position at Verdun. The LZ 90 carried almost 7,000 pounds of bombs. By throttling our motors and concealing ourselves in the clouds, we crossed the front at an altitude of 10,000 feet. I do not know whether we were detected or not, but, at any rate, Bar-le-Duc was not warned and at first greeted us only with a few ordinary shells.

Though the railway station was an important one, it was small, and since it was well darkened, we had difficulty in finding it. No sooner had the first load of bombs been released, than we were obliged to stop because the LZ 90 had overflown its mark. We circled around and were just making a second attack on the station, which by now was marked by fire and smoke, when we saw a number of thick yellow rockets coming toward us. They moved fairly slowly, but rose steadily, climbing past our ship, which was then at an altitude of 10,600 feet, and then continuing on still higher!

Incendiary rockets! The latest and surest method of igniting an airship filled with hydrogen. A single hit infallibly sufficed to destroy any airship. I ordered full speed ahead, brought the ship to its greatest possible altitude and fled in haste. The incendiary shells had come from a point near the station, and I hoped quickly to get beyond their range. But they continued to follow us, and a few came uncomfortably close to our stern. We discovered that the guns were mounted on motor-cars which were following us along a highway running parallel to our course. Instantly, we changed our course and escaped them. Passing over the lines we slipped into a cloud and remained there until we were again in friendly territory.

Now we knew why the LZ 77 had gone down in flames. Nevertheless, the indirect cause of its destruction was a new order compelling us to go aloft even on moonlit nights. Until then we had limited our raiding and scouting flights

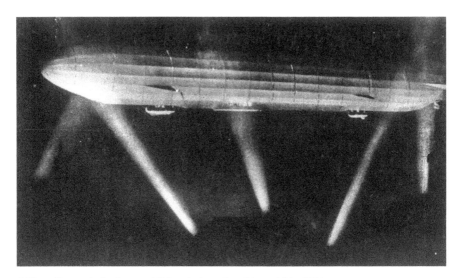

A Zeppelin caught in the searchlights during a bombing raid in 1916.

to dark nights, because test-flights undertaken especially for this purpose had proved that on a bright night, an airship was visible from a great distance, either as a black silhouette against the moon in the bright part of the heavens or as a shimmering silver mass against the other portion of the sky. I myself had taken part in earlier experiments of this type; but, since then, the climbing ability of our ships had increased considerably. The General Staff therefore ordered additional test-flights in the neighbourhood of Cologne, and these had indicated that at sufficiently high altitudes night-flights by moonlight were not dangerous. This conclusion was false; for during the last test-flights of the LZ 77, the observers were stationed too close to the thickly populated industrial centres. The pall of soot and smoke that always hangs over such localities dimmed the visibility, and the noises of the industrial plants overtoned the motor noises received in the observers' listening apparatus; circumstances which they had not taken into account.

Subsequently, various airships were sent over the lines by moonlight. Two of them had some luck even in misfortune. The LZ 74 struck snow storms and stiff head-winds which forced it to turn back. The LZ 95, under Captain George, flew into French artillery fire over the front at moonlight. The ship had more than four tons of bombs on board and with such a load could not even reach an altitude of 10,000 feet. A few gas-cells were shredded by direct hits, and George veered to the side, getting beyond the range of the guns. But the LZ 95 was finished, for this night and for ever. It was wrecked near the Namur airship base.

LZ 65 (LZ 95) was destroyed by French anti-aircraft fire on 21 February 1916 during an attempted attack on Vitry-le-François.

The unlucky LZ 77, under Captain Horn, had pushed through the French defence lines and, as we later learned, was sighted and slightly damaged by gun-fire. By direct observation and through wireless communication—which was also intercepted from another airship—the French had been kept well posted on his movements and had finally brought him down with incendiary rockets.

Instantly, the Zeppelin Airship Works took steps to meet this new danger. First of all, the climbing capacity of the airships was increased. This was especially important for attacks on London, whose anti-aircraft defence had gradually reached a high degree of efficiency. The English strengthened their searchlights, improved their defensive weapons, and built a series of new planes a few of which could climb higher than the airships of that time.

During air-raids on England, army and navy airships often worked together; in a different manner from sea-vessels, however, which remained close together and held their formation during all manoeuvres. The individual airships of a squadron proceeded in different directions and at different times, for the appearance of a mass would have made it easier for the defence to strike a hit, and would not have caused such uncertainty and confusion. Therefore, airship commanders informed each other of the time, direction and altitude of their flights over London, and the objectives which they had chosen.

On 31 March 1916, I started on a squadron flight to England with my new ship, the LZ 90. The weather held great promise. Nevertheless, we had to avoid a number of storms between Trèves, our point of departure, and Ostend, as well as over the North Sea. In the darkness, I recognised the headland south of Harwich by its lagoon-like contour. Shortly after nine o'clock I learned that two of our motors had stopped. With only two running motors, I couldn't risk the flight over London, and we therefore cruised between Colchester and Ipswich while the mechanics got to work. In the distance, we could see the London searchlights sweeping the heavens. I knew that according to orders there must be five airships over the metropolis, and I was therefore prepared for defence fire. But since we remained at an altitude of 8,300 feet, and our two running motors were throttled, the English listening-posts must not have heard us; at any rate, we remained unmolested. Meanwhile, we sought in vain for some landmark or light, for the enemy had done a good job of darkening the land. After two hours, the Chief Engineer reported that he lacked a few spare parts and could not repair the motors without them. There remained nothing for me to do but turn homeward. Just then a battery opened fire upon us, and we thereby ascertained our position, which was over Norwich. And this city then received our load of bombs as a parting gift.

Two days later we were again under way to England; the LZ 88 and the LZ 93 (Commanders Gerstenberg and Schramm) accompanied us, and various naval dirigibles had taken off to attack Scotland. I wanted to fly over London. At Ghent we waited almost an hour before going out in darkness over Ostend towards the sea. It was my plan to slip unnoticed into the island kingdom near the mouth of the Blackwater River. I hoped thus to be able to remain at a height of only 3,300 feet to economize on ballast, gas and fuel, and to avoid the head-winds in the upper strata.

But over the mouth of the Thames we were discovered, and a group of sea-vessels opened fire at us just as the searchlights began their restless playing in the sky. Without replying, we swung away at a right angle and climbed to 10,000 feet. There we resumed our course. The moon shone brightly through the windows of the control car, but it was due to set soon. A peculiar feeling overcame me as we hovered so high over the enemy's territory. Before going to sleep, every human being down there on the thickly populated island probably prayed to God that bad weather or moonlight might keep the German airships away, or that, if they came, they would be shot down.

The moon went down and there was nothing but black space around us. From the window of the control car I could see nothing but a few clouds; before us and down below the fog had become thicker, protecting us from detection by the searchlights as we crossed the outskirts of the city.

The powerful beams of light were stopped at an altitude of 6,700 feet by a thin layer of clouds while, only 1,300 feet above that, we crossed the defence zone in a direct course for the Albert docks.

There 'Archies' opened fire at us, awakened by the clamour of our motors. The searchlights transformed the fog into an opalescent, milky fluid. The air was filled with bursting shells which were aimed at random and fell back down upon the sea of houses. The English anti-aircraft guns in this way anticipated us, for a great deal of the damage subsequently attributed to us was actually caused by them.

The smoke and vapours of the metropolis were at once welcome and disadvantageous. They could not see us from below, but neither could we see anything from above. Then we approached a battery of searchlights and an anti-aircraft nest which was firing at us with unusual fury. I had saved my entire load of bombs, 5,000 pounds of them, and now judged it to be the right time to make use of them. First I dropped the smaller bombs to get my aim and extinguish the searchlights. And at that moment, my alert friend von Gemmingen noticed the first sample of a new kind of incendiary shell just as the rays of a gigantic searchlight broke through the clouds and fixed upon the grey hull of the LZ 90.

This sort of phosphorus shell was quite different from the French type. They looked like little blue sparks hissing toward us with extraordinary speed. More and more of them filled the air, and a few of them came so close that we could have caught them through the window of the control car. When an especially bright incendiary shell flew close by us, one of my men involuntarily cried out, 'Look out!' That in itself was fairly funny, but another man, who was just getting into the control car, stiffened up at this warning and stood at attention as if he were on parade ground. Our ringing laughter revealed the joke to him.

But that was not quite the time for jesting. At any moment we expected one of the incendiary shells to strike its brightly illuminated target and bring it down in flames. But fortunately there was a cloud on our path, and when our ship came over it the searchlight lost us. Reappearing, we once more sighted the Thames, foggy and vague, but still visible enough to recognize by its course. Using a searchlight as a landmark, we navigated in the direction of the river flow and dropped our bombs one after another on a spot where, according to our map, the eastern docks and factories lay. We ourselves were unable to judge the result of our raid, but according to eye-witness accounts it must have been terrible. The crash of the hits mingled with the thunder of the defence batteries, the rattle of machine guns, the noise of the fire-engines racing to the fires, and the shrill piping of the ambulances speeding to the scene. Frightened out of their sleep, millions of people fled to the cellars, stumbling through the darkness and cowering together at every detonation. No one knew where the next bomb would strike, and this uncertainty was nerve-racking. Women broke out in hysterical crying jags, children wept, and men, no longer able to endure it down below, rushed out into the streets with balled fists, as if wanting to strangle an enemy hovering invisible in the clouds above. This enemy was, God knows, only concerned with the military objectives which made the capital of the British Empire the storehouse of the World War; but it was inevitable that many bombs missed their mark and demolished dwellings around the docks. Those poor people saw their little goods and possessions go up in flames, and when they fled from their burning houses, they ran into a murderous rain of splinters, shrapnel and debris; it is immaterial whether the German attack or the English defence caused more victims.

I was relieved when the lightened ship carried us up to 12,000 feet where we saw no more of the city. Three or four times the searchlights caught us again, but the defence batteries under-estimated our altitude and we were out of range before their fire came closer. We were over London for only thirty minutes, but it seemed like an eternity to us. As we departed in the direction of the mouth of the Thames, I had the ship thoroughly checked. It had suffered not the slightest scratch.

Westerly winds, which we found higher up, favoured our return. Over the mouth of the river, we escaped the concentrated fire of forts and battleships. We set our course for Holland, sailed along the coast and up the Rhine and Moselle, and landed in Trèves exactly nineteen hours after our take-off. My returns from England were not always so uneventful.

13

THE BATTLE OF JUTLAND

I N MAY 1916, Vice Admiral Reinhold Scheer, Commander of the German North Sea Fleet, planned an attack upon Sunderland, on the eastern coast of England. He hoped thereby to lure the main British fleet to sea and force it into open battle. The entire German High Seas Fleet lay in wait south of the Dogger Bank and submarines were stationed everywhere along the English coast. Scheer's plan depended upon the cooperation of our airships, but fog over the whole of Northern Europe, as well as strong winds, prevented the ships from leaving their hangars.

The weather was still uncertain when on 30 May, Admiral Scheer decided to attack. That necessitated a change of plan. He himself wrote:

> For the thrust to the northwest against Sunderland, thoroughgoing aerial reconnaissance was indispensable because the attack led into a part of the sea in which we could not permit ourselves to give battle against our wishes.

Therefore, Scheer chose The Skagerrak as the direction of attack because the neighbouring Danish coast protected him on one side and the greater distance of the enemy fleet from its bases rendered the aerial reconnaissance of lesser importance.

In order that the enemy might have adequate knowledge of the appearance of our ships near and in The Skagerrak, the German warships were ordered to show themselves in sight of the Norwegian coast. Some German submarines were stationed off Scapa Flow, Moray Firth, Firth of Forth, and the Humber, and the remainder were north of the Terschelling Bank, in case the enemy forces approached from the south-west.

For scouting service before and during the battle, the following ten airships were called upon: L 11 (Commander Viktor Schütze), L 17 (Lieutenant-Commander Ehrlich), L 14 (Lieutenant-Commander d. R. Becker), L 21 (Lieutenant-Commander d. R. Max Dietrich), L 23 (Lieutenant-Commander von Schubert), L 16 (Lieutenant-Commander Sommerfeld), L 13 (Lieutenant-Commander d. R.

Prölss), L 9 (Commander z. D. Stelling), L 22 (Lieutenant-Commander Martin Dietrich) and L 24 (Lieutenant-Commander Robert Koch).

On 31 May, at four in the morning, the First and Second Scouting Divisions of our Battle Fleet, under Vice Admiral Hipper, left the Jade and advanced to the Skagerrak in accordance with orders. They showed themselves off the Norwegian coast and were to cruise in the Skagerrak overnight and join the main fleet again on the next day. The body of the fleet steamed out at 4.30 in the afternoon, in the following order: Third, First, Second Battleship Squadrons, convoyed by flotillas of torpedo-boats. A light breeze from the north-west ruffled the clear mirror of the North Sea. The heavily armoured colossuses and their small fleet convoys picked their way through the enemy minefields, which the mine-sweepers had searched and rendered safe.

At two o'clock in the afternoon, the naval airships L 16 and L 21 left their hangars. An hour later, the L 9, L 14, and L 23 started for their assigned sectors north and west of Heligoland, where they were to patrol. This trio did not come in contact at all with the two great fleets which met at 4.30. They heard and saw nothing of the battle, but their presence gave the German Admiralty the comforting assurance that its left flank was clear of enemy forces.

The first report of the sailing of the English battleships came via wireless from the submarines lurking off the eastern coast. The groups sighted were of varying strengths and steamed ahead without apparent cooperation. It could not be determined whether they had been lured out to sea by the German movements. But at any rate, their emergence was in accord with the intentions of the Chief of the German Fleet.

At 4.28, the leader of the torpedo boat flotilla protecting the German west flank saw smoke on the horizon. This vanguard of the enemy, eight small cruisers, became the object of a counter-thrust by Rear Admiral Bödicker, and was obliged to summon the support of six battleships and numerous light forces. In the ensuing engagement, the English armoured cruiser, the first victim, was blown into the air with a tremendous explosion. The German cruisers were being hard-pressed by the British Fifth Battle Squadron, and to relieve them, our torpedo boats closed in. The armoured cruiser *Queen Mary* exploded and sank. Clouds of smoke in the east heralded the approach of the German Fleet. The Second Squadron, which was leading, was just about to take the enemy in a cross-fire, when they were reinforced by a group of five battleships. But now the Third and First Squadrons were within ten miles of the scene, and when they opened fire, the enemy steamed off.

Toward evening the weather became misty, making pursuit difficult. Apart from the main force, Bödicker's reconnaissance group was again drawn into battle with overwhelming enemy forces. The bitter fighting around the badly damaged *Wiesbaden*, which was attacked from both sides by strong enemy forces, led to the real battle, which cost England a quarter of a million tons of ship's bottom and 10,000 men, and which is the greatest naval battle in the history of the world.

The situation was complicated for the German Command by the fact that during the battle around the *Wiesbaden* an enemy squadron of at least twenty battleships had come from the north and pushed between our fleet and the Danish coast. 'The whole arc from north to east,' said Admiral Scheer, 'was a sea of fire. The muzzle-fire of the big guns flashed clearly through the thick smoke and mist in which the ships themselves soon became unrecognizable.'

But the German Fleet Commander had not even for a moment thought of withdrawing from the enemy's embracing manoeuvre by putting about and not accepting battle. He was fully aware that the relative strength of both fleets made it impossible to destroy the enemy. But he trusted to the skill of our navy to outweigh our inferiority in number. The opportunity eagerly sought by every German sailor, to measure himself against the Englishmen, had arrived, and it was not to pass by without being grasped. Aware of the tremendous responsibility, Admiral Scheer, on the flagship *Friedrich der Grosse*, signalled the battleship squadron to close in upon the enemy.

The Fifth Division, which held the head of the line, struck the middle of the out-spread enemy battle line and, at a distance of eight miles, received fire from three sides. The reply of the German battleships and cruisers was more effective, as a group of English armoured cruisers soon learned: three of its units, *Defence*,

In action with the German Fleet during the Battle of Jutland.

Black Prince, and *Warrior* received direct hits and exploded. The steel giants continued to steam closer to each other, and the cruisers and torpedo-boats crowded in between them. To make room for them, Admiral Scheer swung about; a difficult manoeuvre that was carried out with peace-time precision. By neglecting to duplicate this manoeuvre, Admiral Jellicoe could not retain contact with Scheer. Perhaps he did not immediately interpret the about-face; at any rate, the open-mouthed English cannon thereupon became mute. The torpedo-boats had purposely laid a smoke-screen over the scene, and when this cleared away, the English battleship *Invincible* and an even dozen cruisers and destroyers were seen to be sinking. Of the German forces, the battleship *Lützow* was so badly damaged that the commander of the reconnaissance forces, Vice Admiral Hipper, was obliged to board the *Moltke*.

Admiral Scheer did not for a moment think of steaming away from the enemy. He proceeded to force action upon them by again reversing course and striking with all his power at the head of their line. Thereupon, Jellicoe was left no other choice but to veer around again for a running battle. This time the Englishmen's aim was better; our armoured cruisers suffered heavily, and our torpedo-boats were unable to approach the *Wiesbaden* to rescue their comrades, who were covered by larger calibres. But, grimly determined, the flotilla ran against the floating fortress itself and thus drew upon themselves the fire directed at the hard-pressed cruiser. Then, concealed in a smoke-screen, the torpedo boats disappeared and brought their Admiral the confirmation of the fact that he was now giving battle to the entire English Fleet.

Admiral Scheer had to face the following fact. It apparently was Jellicoe's intention to force the main German Fleet so far to the west during the course of the night that he could complete the embracing movement on the next morning and crush the German navy from all sides at once. But at night-fall, Scheer anticipated him by taking course, in closed formation, for Horns Reef, where, protected in the rear, he awaited attack.

On this night voyage to Horns Reef, the enemy dispersed and made numerous attacks from the east, but although they disturbed the movement, they could not prevent it, and they suffered heavier losses than we did. Scheer reports that at two o'clock a large English armoured cruiser, in complete recognition of the situation, closed in on the battleships of his First Squadron at about a mile's distance. It was no more than a few seconds before it was shot ablaze. In the glaring beams of the German searchlights, the crew could be seen running around helplessly as the heavy shells struck home blow after blow, throwing up showers of steel and dismembered human bodies. Four minutes after the firing began, there was a terrific explosion, and when the smoke parted, the North Sea had swallowed the ship and its crew.

During this time, five of our airships were over the sea. The muzzle-fire and flames of the death-locked fleets showed them the way; only rarely did the ghostly arm of a searchlight streak over the water or slant upwards when the droning motors became audible. For the beam inevitably revealed its point of origin and made it easier for the enemy artillery to get the range of the imprudent vessel. The German Fleet Command had therefore issued instructions restricting the use of searchlights during operations.

Even before midnight, the last ship of the departing fleet had lost sight of the badly damaged battleship *Lützow*. Airships searched for it, and four torpedo-boats took off the 1,250 man crew just as 700 tons of water poured through the gaping hole in the bow of the ship. At the end, the helmsman had navigated the ship backwards until the bow sank under water and the propellers turned in the empty air. A torpedo-boat gave the drifting wreck the *coup de grâce*.

The over-crowded torpedo boats battled their way through the double line of English cruisers and destroyers, and returned to German waters. Meanwhile, all the airships had reached their allotted sectors and searched them for enemy forces. At four o'clock in the morning, the first definite report came in from the L 24. Lieutenant-Commander Koch wirelessed that he had spied a flotilla of destroyers on the northwest coast of Jutland, fifty miles west of Bulbierg. The destroyers opened a furious fire at the airship and Koch replied with a few bombs. But the entire intermezzo did not seem to him to be important enough to bother about any longer, and he departed in a northerly direction. At five o'clock, between Jutland and the Norwegian coast, he reported observing an English Fleet of twelve warships steaming full-speed to the south.

This report, reaching Admiral Scheer just after he had arrived off Horns Reef with the body of his fleet, was the subject of a grave conference with his Chief of Staff Adolf von Trotha. Scheer was not disinclined to bar the way of this group and he was merely waiting more precise information from the L 24. But this was not forthcoming. At 4,000 feet, the L 24 struck cloud banks which obstructed its vision. Koch attempted to come down through the clouds and descended to 2,500 feet without being able to see anything. If the airship had possessed an observation gondola, it would have been a simple matter to lower the observer below the layer of clouds. In the same manner, it might have been possible for the three airships, L 13, L 17, and L 22, to make the requisite observations although they, too, were flying blindly in a fog. Admiral Scheer was in urgent need of swift, dependable information but he had only three of his fast little cruisers at his disposal. The airships, on which he had pinned his entire hopes, seemed to have left him in the lurch, when, surprisingly, at 5.10 a wireless message from the fifth scout of the air-squadron instantly altered the entire picture of the situation.

The L 11, sixty sea miles north of the coast of Holland, reported observing a strong English battle fleet steaming in closed formation to the north-east. Commander Schütze counted no less than twelve battleships besides a number of cruisers, destroyers, torpedo boats and sundry light forces. Half an hour later, Schütze sighted a second squadron of six battleships with convoys and, soon afterward, still a third group. The L 11 stuck to the enemy like a burr and was not even to be shaken off by the prodigal fire-works of the anti-aircraft guns until the clouds rolled under him and he could see nothing more. Schütze permitted me a glance at his log-book; I quote his entries word for word:

On 1 June at 1.30 in the morning the L 11 took off from Nordholz as the fourth ship covering the flank of the High Seas Forces, course NW by W off Heligoland. The complete crew was aboard. Freshening east wind, visibility diminished by ground fog and later by high, foggy mists which limited visibility to a maximum of two to four sea miles. Heligoland was not sighted in the fog. At five in the morning smoke clouds appeared in square 0 33 B, north of the ship; we set course in that direction. At 5.10 we were able to distinguish a strong enemy group of twelve great battleships with numerous light forces, steaming at full speed in a north-easterly direction. To maintain contact after sending the wireless report, the L 11 followed along behind, from time to time circling to the east. In so doing, the airship, at 5.40 in the morning, discovered east of the first group a second squadron of six English great battleships with light forces. This second group was proceeding on a northerly course, but upon being sighted swung to the west, apparently to seek union with the first group. Since this group was closer to our own main force than the first, the L 11 followed it; but at 5.50 we sighted a group of three English battle cruisers and about four light ships which came from the north-east, veered around south of the airship and pushed between the L 11 and the enemy's main force. Visibility was so poor that contact could be maintained only with great difficulty. Generally, only one of the groups was visible at one time; and apparently, the enemy saw the airship hovering against the rising sun at an altitude of from 4,000 to 6,000 feet.

At 5.15, shortly after meeting the first group of battleships, the enemy opened fire at us from all ships at once, using anti-aircraft batteries and big guns of all calibres. The heavy turrets fired broadsides. Laterally, the shots were well-placed; and the salvos were always close together. The muzzle-fire revealed the position of the line even when the group itself had disappeared in the smoke. All the vessels coming into sight instantly took up a vigorous fire, so that, for a time, the L 11 was in the concentrated fire of twenty-one large and many small ships. Though the fire was ineffectual, the heavy shells and shrapnel bursting nearby put such a strain on the ship's frame that it seemed advisable to draw off somewhat. The firing continued until 6.20. At about this time the battle cruisers advanced to close range from the SW and forced the L I 1 to fall back to the NE. Simultaneously, the visibility decreased considerably and the enemy was lost from sight.

The L II again took a northerly course and, at altitudes as low as 1,700 feet, attempted to find better conditions of visibility. But we were unable to see for more than two sea miles, so that, since the maintenance of contact was out of the question, we continued to strike curves to the North and South in order to remain between the enemy and our own main force. The enemy was not sighted again. At 8 a.m. the airships were dismissed by the Chief of the High Seas, and the L 11 flew home. On the return trip, the airship exchanged positions with a number of its own torpedo boats and accepted wireless reports for transmission. The airship remained close beside these boats as far as Sylt. The landing in Nordholz took place at two in the afternoon.

Thus, Admiral Scheer's information influenced his later decisions. The L 11 and L 24 had reported reinforcements which were obviously replacing Jellicoe's losses and would enable him to resume the conflict with overwhelming superiority. As little reason as the German Chief-of-Fleet had for avoiding another meeting with the Englishmen, it nevertheless seemed to him, in view of the poor visibility, inadvisable to advance with impaired strength against an enemy whose distribution and strength could not be more accurately determined. The outcome of such a battle in the fog would have been purely a matter of chance.

Apparently, the English Supreme Commander permitted himself to be influenced by similar considerations, for he knew that his reinforcements had been observed by the L 11 and he could safely assume that other airships had discovered the rest of his formations. Thus, the plan was revealed, and it was to be expected that the German submarines would do everything in their power to frustrate it. In view of this situation, Admiral Jellicoe preferred to withdraw his battle forces and forego his revenge. Apparently he issued the order to withdraw shortly after the L 11 lost sight of his fleet.

What weight the English attributed to the cooperation of the ten naval airships in the Battle of the Skagerrak[12] may be estimated from an English secret report which Admiral Moffat of the US Navy revealed to Congress during my stay in America. The report stated:

> From the results, it is plain that the confidence of the German Navy in their airships was more than justified. To the credit of the airships it may be said that they saved the German Fleet in the Battle of the Skagerrak, just as they saved the German cruisers during the attack on Yarmouth, and were instrumental in sinking the cruisers *Nottingham* and *Falmouth* off the English coast. If the situation at the Skagerrak had been reversed, if airships had enabled us to discover the whereabouts of the German High Seas Fleet and destroy it—who can deny the far-reaching effect this would have had upon the outcome of the war?

Two and a half months after the Battle of The Skagerrak, the German High Seas Fleet was again out on the North Sea, once more steaming for Sunderland, but this time in better weather and with eight airships. They were attempting to carry out the same plan that had once before been frustrated by inclement weather. Admiral Scheer had waited for the full moon when the airships were unable to carry out air-raids and were consequently available for other purposes. The German submarines likewise had been temporarily withdrawn from commercial warfare to support the thrust of the German High Seas Fleet against the eastern coast of England.

In the submarines and airships, Admiral Scheer saw a compensation for the overwhelming strength of the English Fleet. To force the enemy out to sea and into open combat, Sunderland was to be raided. The eight airships, among them three of the new 55,000-cubic-metre type, were given the task of patrolling the English coast from the Channel to North Scotland and from there straight across to the Norwegian coast. It was assumed that the airships would discover and report the presence of any enemy warships entering the sectors they were guarding. To get to the point, the plan failed. It was bound to fail, because too much was demanded of the airships. They were too few in number to patrol the entire North Sea. Each airship was supposed to patrol a section of over one hundred sea miles; and that was too much, unless visibility was exceptional. But, above all, there was no airship active within the tremendous space enclosed by the patrol lines. Thus, while the airships were flying over the North Sea to take up their posts, the English Fleet was already inside the patrolled area.

It was only by accident that four airships, keeping close to the English coast, saw parts of the English Fleet cruising on the North Sea. That afternoon, the vanguard of the German Fleet was within sixty sea miles of the English coast, north of the Humber, when the L 13, stationed farthest south, reported sighting about thirty units of the English Fleet. The English were steaming on a northerly course, about a hundred sea miles south of the Germans, and, expecting to meet them within two hours, Admiral Scheer turned southward. Meanwhile, the L 13 followed the enemy and kept the German Chief-of-Fleet posted. But a half hour later, Lieutenant-Commander Prölss lost sight of the British. A storm forced him off his course, and when he later returned to it, he could not find the enemy. Warned by the presence of the airship and by the increased wireless activity, the English Fleet had made a sudden right turn and, under cover of the storm clouds, headed westward toward the coast. Not even the patrol boats swiftly speeding ahead of Scheer's fleet were able to discover anything.

Meantime, two other naval airships, the L 11 and L 31, were on patrol before the Humber and the Tyne. They, too, observed part of the English Fleet, and at four o'clock in the afternoon, Scheer knew that the enemy was gathering much further north. Since the German Fleet had taken course to the south, the distance between the opponents had become so great that a meeting was impossible before nightfall. And since neither the Germans nor the English cared to give battle in the dark, both fleets returned to their home bases without incident.

14

THE EARLY DAYS OF THE ZEPPELIN

EANWHILE, I HAD surrendered the LZ 90 to another crew and was ordered to take over the new 35,800-cubic-metre LZ 98, at Friedrichshafen. At this point I am going to make a break in the narrative and tell something of the early days of the Zeppelin.

Old Count Zeppelin, who had often been our host during the war period, saw in the new LZ 98 only the forerunner of a much larger and more efficient airship constructed to serve world traffic in time of peace. At the outbreak of the war he had been working with Dürr on a design for a 70,000 cubic-metre airship intended for a flight to America. Although the Count was seventy-eight years old, he was still as active as the youngest of us, and constantly on the go. When he was not in one of the hangars, he was in a workshop; and if he was not there, he could perhaps be found in one of the laboratories. There was always something which he wanted to observe or personally supervise.

If a house reflects the character of its inhabitants, then Ferdinand von Zeppelin was easily recognizable by his.[13] He owned an estate near Constance, but he rarely visited it now. In Friedrichshafen, he had furnished a few rooms in a wing of the Kurgarten Hotel, which was owned by the Zeppelin Company. The furniture was modern and tasteful; the walls were covered with pictures of airships; and one large room contained the medals, cups, honorary diplomas and other decorations which the inventor of the rigid airship principle had received from governments, cities, universities and organizations. In view of these countless honours, it was difficult to believe that, at fifty-four years of age, this very man was ridiculed and humiliated when he first made public his design for a dirigible airship.

At the turn of the century, when he demonstrated his principle, Ferdinand von Zeppelin was sixty-two years old. It is characteristic of the spirit of this man and his work that today, after his death and the end of the World War, the descendants of his first workmen are still employed at the airship yards. Every one of them was the old gentleman's collaborator, in the best sense of the term. And that does not only apply to Ludwig Dürr, the director of the construction division and man of many honours. Marx, motor-boat captain during the 1900's, is a Chief Helmsman and trains the recruits. Dürr's brother-in-law, Losch, is superintendent of the foundry. Gassau, who was present, with tool-maker Peiss, at the crash of the second dirigible in Allgäu, is foreman of the manufacturing department; likewise, Schwarz, who escaped from the burning airship at Echterdingen. Rösch is Chief Mechanic. Kast works in the go-wheel factory. Grözinger, with more than 625,000 miles behind him, is a Chief Mechanic. Futscher was a machinist on the *Deutschland* and the *Viktoria Luise*. Schöb is a foreman. Kugler assembled the LZ 129 under Knud Eckener's direction. Of the engineers, Wilhelm Siegle fell into the hands of the French on the Z IV in 1913 and half a year later luckily escaped death in the crash of the naval dirigible L 2; and Karl Friedrich Beuerle was on hangar duty with the Delag before he circled the globe as a Chief Engineer.

To understand the magic which the personality of the inventor exerted upon us, one must hear those 'old-timers'—some of whom are not old at all—tell about it. The eyes of Helmsman Ludwig Marx, watery yet sharp, as if seeing beyond the dip of the horizon, gleam brightly when he rummages among his memories.

> The old gentleman was a man! A nobleman! Not because he was a Count, a General, a Chamberlain, 'His Excellency,' but because he was simply a fine person, strong of character, yet full of kindness, conscious of his worth, yet

Ferdinand Adolf Heinrich August Graf von Zeppelin, (1838–1917). He married, 1869, Isabella Constance Elisabeth Clementine née von Wolff, (1846-1922).

modest and religious. I think he said a silent prayer before every voyage, and after the voyage was over, he must have given thanks. When the first naval dirigible took off and everyone congratulated him, he removed his white cap as if at the command, 'Hats off for prayer,' and he said softly, to himself, 'How little I had to do with it.'

When one hears Helmsman Marx speaking, there is no need to ask about the Count's relations with his men.

Today, the Zeppelin Company is a great undertaking employing hundreds and thousands; but at the turn of the century, when everyone was laughing at the crazy count who wanted to build an airship, we were a woefully small group—you could count us off on your fingers. Even after the first triumphs, the entire personnel did not number more than sixty to ninety men. Every year there was one work-day free, and then Zeppelin hired a steamer and went on a picnic with the entire personnel. At the picnic grounds, one of us would make a speech. One time—it was at Immenstaad—our speaker got stuck. Count Zeppelin waited a while, and when nothing happened, he grinned. 'Mr Speaker, may I have the floor?' In dead earnest, our man answered, 'But it is I who am speaking to the Count!' But the old man, no whit abashed, spoke anyway. 'I shall try to finish the speech, even though not entirely as our comrade intended to deliver it. You workmen and officers do not owe me your thanks. On the contrary, I am indebted to you. For although this great work was my idea, it was you, my workers and employees, who completed it. Therefore, I thank you from the bottom of my heart, and drink to your health!'

The Count knew each of his men intimately, was informed of their domestic affairs and made a habit of remembering special occasions; he liked to give the children good books. Between him and the personnel there existed a genuinely patriarchal relationship. Although, as an old army man, he was a strict disciplinarian, when he was off duty he placed himself on a man-to-man footing with his personnel, and he never forgot to preface a request with 'please.' Even in his blackest hours, he thought of his employees; and when, after a severe reversal, he had no more money and was forced to discharge them, he made use of his connections to place them elsewhere, and consoled them with the promise to take them back as soon as it was possible.

The men would have gone through fire for their General Zeppelin. They repaid him, loyalty for loyalty—and he demanded it, too. For if once a man was disloyal, Zeppelin would never again have anything to do with him. Engineer Kübler, who had built the first dirigible, carried an insurance policy worth 50,000 marks. When he could not afford to pay the premiums any longer, he would not take part in the maiden flight, much to Zeppelin's annoyance. After the completion of the test flights, he resigned and migrated to the Argentine. Count Zeppelin never forgave him for that, and would not even consider any of the propositions Kübler later made to him by mail; as far as he was concerned, the man was through. The Count also broke with Eugen Wolf, who was on the maiden voyage of the first dirigible, when, after a few ships crashed, that famous African explorer publicly expressed the wish that the inventor might abandon his 'rigidity.'

The same constancy which Count Zeppelin displayed toward his 'old guard,' he showed toward his former war buddies. For as strictly as the mystery of Manzell was guarded from curious busybodies, the old soldiers obtained immediate access. Once, a lanky gruff blacksmith arrived, and his Excellency himself escorted him through the hangar to show him the ship, which at that time, 1899, was still under construction. The man was one of the Dragoons who, in July 1870, had taken part in General Staff Captain Zeppelin's bold patrol ride.

The King of Württemberg, when he came to Manzell for the first time, was not treated as courteously as was this smith. In fact, the Cerberus at the front gate curtly turned him back; he had orders to let no one in. When Count Zeppelin heard of this and apologized to his sovereign, the King turned aside the apology: 'What do you expect, my dear Zeppelin? The man was only doing his duty.'

The more the construction progressed, the more the public began to evince an irrepressible curiosity about it. Hundreds of travellers broke their journey at Friedrichshafen to get a good look at the mysterious 'flying ship,' as Count Zeppelin called it. Already, the real-estate operators scented the coming boom and were selling villa-sites 'with a view of the Alps and the Zeppelin balloon.'

At that time Ludwig Marx was the pilot of the motor-boat *Württemberg*, which daily transported the Count and his personnel from Friedrichshafen and aided in the launching and docking of the airship. Preiss, one of the 'old timers,' told me:

> Once, we played a mean trick on Ludwig Marx. Usually, when we were on the *Württemberg* crossing from Friedrichshafen to Manzell, the General would tell us to sing for him. One evening, on the return trip—we had been drinking the new wine and the six of us were garlanded with vine-leaves—we came by the Deutschen Haus and sang our favourite song under Zeppelin's window: *Wohlauf, die Luft geht frisch und rein*. Then, after we had had a couple of extra drinks, we exuberantly decided to steal the *Württemberg* for a night trip. No sooner said than done. Over there in Switzerland, we caroused some more, and Machinist Gross, the soberest of us, had difficulty in persuading us to break up at dawn. Motor trouble and a hunt for a rudder that had been tossed overboard caused us to be delayed considerably, and when we reached the Deutschen Haus, the rest of the personnel were waiting with Marx, who was furious, and with His Excellency, who was silent and imperturbable.

The next day there was a stiff investigation, and we were bawled out by Kübler. Every one of us was docked five marks; and when we objected to this severe penalty, the Chief Engineer crushed us by replying, 'You ought to be glad. You should have been locked up!' Well, he was right. But after that, we sang no more. Until Count Zeppelin one day, during a crossing, said, 'Well, don't you want to sing something?' We were obstinate, and grumbled that we wouldn't think of it. Whereupon the old Count casually suggested, 'Well, gentlemen, then sing the song you recently sang when you crossed over to Switzerland.' Then we knew that everything was all right again, and we all joined in with *Wohlauf , die Luft geht frisch und rein*! The Count grinned and looked pleased. He always appreciated a joke.

The Count's office was very modestly situated in three rooms above a former fish-market. The workshop was in Manzell, on crown property which the King of Württemberg had 'leased' to Zeppelin for 99 years—without ever again speaking about the payment of rent. Today, on this land, are scattered the buildings of the Dornier-Metallbauten-Gesellschaft, until recently a part of the Zeppelin Company. Since the Count did not wish prematurely to risk a landing of his airship on solid earth, he erected a floating wooden hangar, where the airship was to be assembled. This floating hangar was 450 feet long, 70 feet wide and 100 feet high, and rested on ninety-five pontoons.

One day a young technician named Ludwig Dürr came to Friedrichshafen.[14] He had been engaged in Stuttgart by Engineer Kober, since deceased, for the static calculation of the airship design and now, together with Engineers Burr and Endres, was assigned to Engineer Kübler. This Ludwig Dürr was an unimpressive and retiring young man; but when he opened his mouth he said the most essential and correct things, and when he himself took the hammer in his hand, he hit the nail on the head. Once when he was dissatisfied with a turnbuckle delivered by a factory, he went to work and forged a new one, which he submitted for the approval of the locksmith, Preiss. In point of fact, Preiss found that no skilled workman could have done a better job. But in order to uphold the superiority of the 'practical' workman as opposed to the 'university' man, he pointed out that a crack didn't fit together to a hair's breadth. Silently, Dürr took the turnbuckle and, after a few hours, returned with a completely new one in which the sharpest critical eyes could find no fault. The respect which Ludwig Dürr enjoyed not only before the world, but, more important as in this case, in the eyes of his workers, dated from this hour. For the plain workman quickly discovers whether an engineer knows only the theoretical side of his profession, and nothing strengthens the authority of a superior more than the acknowledgment of the men that he is a match for them from the practical standpoint as well.

Dürr, a beardless youngster, as shy as he was, nevertheless was bold enough to disagree with His Excellency regarding questions of construction. In his opinion, the pitching to which the floating hangar was subject, made it scarcely advisable to assemble the airplane there. In July, 1899, the hangar tore loose from its moorings and was driven away toward Constance. But it was towed back and, despite Dürr's warning, the airship was assembled in it.

The lattice girders and other parts of the airship frame were manufactured by the Carl Berg Aluminium Company at Eveking, near Lüdenscheid, and were shipped to Manzell by train. Early in November 1899, the rigid frame was assembled; but the installation of the gas-cells was so difficult that the maiden flight, originally planned for the same year, was delayed. Winter set in.

Helmsman Marx relates: On a January night, a storm came up while I was on night-watch at the airship hangar. The steel trusses, on which the pontoons were anchored, snapped like threads. In vain I threw out the emergency anchor. The enormous Noah's Ark drifted a mile before the storm tossed it up on land like a handball. The fact that the hull of the airship withstood this treatment was at once a miracle and an impressive proof of its elastic stability. The stranded hangar remained lying on the shore until the water rose again in the spring; only then were we able to tow it back to its old anchorage in Manzell Bay. It was later to cause us plenty of additional trouble.

In the middle of June the steel bottles of compressed hydrogen gas arrived from Bitterfeld, and at the same time Major Sperling, of the mechanized division, arrived from Berlin to supervise the inflation of the gas-cells. On 2 July 1900, the ship was ready to take off.

Although the entire undertaking was regarded as a curiosity—the whim of a retired General who had nothing better to do in his old age—the news spread like wild-fire, and many thousands of people were attracted to the lake. They lined the shore like a long black rope, and they swarmed aboard steamers and boats. The dockyard motorboat had difficulty in keeping the spectators far enough away not to endanger the ship which was filled with inflammable gas.

At about six o'clock in the afternoon, the float, on which the airship rested, was pushed from the hangar. It looked like a gigantic caterpillar slowly creeping forward. The crowd was astonished at its immensity and broke out into cries of surprise. As a matter of fact, the hull, 425 feet long, exceeded by far any dirigible balloon then in existence. No one—not even the inventor in his wildest dreams—could foresee that, three and a half decades later, a dirigible of the same type, 820 feet long and 135 feet in diameter, and bearing the dock-number 129 and the name *Hindenburg*, would contain in a single one of its sixteen gas-cells more hydrogen than the entire capacity of the first Zeppelin.

Outside on the lake, the little steamer *Buchhorn* took the strange monster in tow and pulled it against the wind. A screen protected the smoke-stack of the tug-boat so that no sparks could reach the floating airship. Beneath the

LZ 1 made its first flight on 2 July 1900. Here it is in *der schwimmenden halle*, the first floating hangar.

tremendous pencil could be seen the two gondolas, and in them the participators of this memorable voyage: Count Zeppelin, Baron Bassus, Eugen Wolf, the African explorer, Engineer Burr, and Machinist Gross—altogether, five people! The gondolas were at that time connected by an uncovered catwalk, and from this a lead weight of 550 pounds hung on a wire cable. When this sliding weight was shoved to the rear, the stern sank, and the airship climbed; when reversed, its nose sank, and the ship descended. On its first flight, the LZ 1 possessed neither elevator rudders nor stabilizing surfaces. A tiny rudder was situated on each side of the bow and stern.

Yet, despite everything, this first rigid airship was quite dirigible. When it had climbed high enough on the towrope and the motors had begun to turn, it veered into the wind and made a few fine turns. Its own speed was not great—the motorboat easily held pace with it—but what could be expected of two four-cylinder Daimler marine motors which at 800 revolutions together developed an average of 24 and a maximum of 32 horsepower! The *Graf Zeppelin* has five Maybach motors totalling 2,550 horsepower, and the four Daimler-Benz heavy oil motors of the *Hindenburg* develop a maximum of 4,200 horsepower.

Historians, when they evaluate the maiden flight of the LZ 1, should bear that in mind, and not only record that it lasted but eighteen minutes. For after eighteen minutes, the airship was obliged to land on the water near Immenstaad, because the sliding weight lever had broken, the ship's hull had buckled, and the rudder ropes had become tangled. Of all the places on the wide lake, this one particular spot had a marine signal on a stake; and on this stake, the airship impaled itself, causing a leak in the gas-cell. That night, the LZ 1 was towed away by the *Buchhorn*; and when the 'flying ship' lay safely in its hangar again, Zeppelin invited the entire personnel to the Seehof for a banquet, where Professor Hergesell and Baron Bassus congratulated the inventor and he, in turn, thanked his fellow-workers.

Not only the immediate participants and the spectators, but the entire world sensed that this first flight of a real airship was of historical significance, and that with the new century, a new era of transportation had begun. But soon there occurred an event which since then has frequently repeated itself in the history of the Zeppelin works; the inspiring triumph was soon followed by a reversal that threatened to destroy everything that hitherto had been achieved.

While they were still working to overcome the deficiencies revealed by the first flight—among other things, the sliding weight which served as an elevator rudder was removed to the inner catwalk—a sudden storm gripped the hangar and shook it violently from side to side, breaking a number of the ship's ring-girders and causing damage which required fourteen days of repair-work. Meanwhile, autumn had come, and it was 17 October 1900, before the LZ 1 could take off again. This second test-flight lasted eighty minutes, and it would have lasted much longer if the motors had not sputtered and stopped. The airship

A view of LZ 1 in flight.

fell fairly rapidly from an altitude of 1,000 feet. Marx was on the spot with the motor-boat and towed the winged bird back to the float, and then into the hangar. There were all sorts of rumours as to the cause of the motor-trouble; even sabotage was mentioned. The truth was that the man who was supposed to fill the gasoline tanks had inadvertently grasped a bottle of distilled water from among the gasoline-containers—and one really cannot blame motors for refusing to work under such conditions.

Three days later the LZ 1 took off again, to overcome the resistance of the wind (and of the experts). When the airship rode with the wind, Professor Hergesell calculated its speed as 9 m/secs, which corresponds to about the speed of a motor-car in city traffic. But against the wind, its weak motors did not do so well. After twenty-three minutes, however, the trip was over—and with it, the enterprise in general.

15

DISAPPOINTMENT WITH LZ 1 AND 2, SUCCESS WITH LZ 3 AND 4

THE COMPANY FOR the Advancement of Airship Travel, which had made the construction possible, was a stock company with an invested capital amounting to 800,000 marks. Count Zeppelin himself had contributed more than half of it, without gaining majority control. The grounds, workshop equipment, the floating hangar, salaries and materials consumed such huge amounts that a guarantee fund of an additional 150,000 marks had to be raised. To this, also, Count Zeppelin contributed the largest share.

When the first airship was finished, however, capital and guarantee fund were both exhausted. The three test-flights had not been spectacularly successful, and the army was cool. The government contract was not forthcoming, and the Order of the Red Eagle, First Class, with which Zeppelin returned from a lecture in Berlin, was not a sufficient substitute for it. The stock-holders declined to invest further funds for the continuance of the experimental flights, and instead decided upon the liquidation of the corporation. The Count, in his generous manner, thanked the gentlemen who had begun the great work, and promised to repay their investments if ever he was in a position to do so. 'Ah, Count,' one of the stock-holders good-naturedly replied, 'you don't have to promise that. When the corporation is liquidated, we stock-holders have no further claims.' Nevertheless, not one of the men who supported Zeppelin at the beginning of his work suffered losses because of their confidence; with the 120,000 marks realized from the sale of motors, aluminium, the wooden hangar and the equipment of the workshops, the subscribers to the guarantee fund were paid off, and even the members of the corporation later received their money.

After the liquidation of the Corporation for the Advancement of Airship Travel, the enterprise became the sole property of the inventor. At that time, the personnel consisted of only Dürr and two night watchmen. One million had been spent; no one would lend a second. Sixty thousand petitions which Zeppelin sent post-paid to all parts of the world, brought in all of 15,000 marks; a plea for the subsidizing of airship travel went unheeded; and the

Zeppelin-airship Construction Fund existed, for the time being, only on paper. But when Württemberg permitted a lottery which netted 124,000 marks, and Chancellor Count Bülow contributed 50,000 marks from the funds at his disposal, Zeppelin constructed a new floating hangar, an old wooden hangar on land, and a new airship, for all of which no more than 200,000 marks were spent. For three years, Ludwig Dürr, rejecting a tempting American proposition, had worked in all secrecy on improvements in construction. He replaced the latticed girders of the ship's frame with the triangular girders which have since been used on all Zeppelins; he based his improvements of the elevator rudder on researches which Professor Hergesell had made with Hargrave kites at the Meteorological Station in Friedrichshafen; and he increased the power plant to 170 horsepower.

If the first flight of the LZ 2 was a failure, then, according to the testimony of our old Chief Helmsman, Marx, the floating hangar was to blame for it. Of it, he says: 'At the end of November, the water in the Bodensee was so low that we could not launch the float with the airship. So we set the two engine cars on pontoons, and my motorboat, the *Württemberg*, towed the ship out of the hangar and into the wind. No sooner were we outside than a puff of wind from the stern lifted the airship over the motorboat, and the tow-rope fouled the elevator helm which at that time was still under the bow. I leaped to cut it, but it was already drawing the overloaded ship down to us while, at the same time, the wind continued to lift the stern. Just at this critical moment the propellers started turning and gave additional impetus to the downward motion. The ship hit the water headfirst. With great presence of mind, Count Zeppelin and Chief Engineer Dürr, who were on board with the mechanics, Karl Schwarz and Wilhelm Kast, pulled the aft release-valve in order to bring the ship to the water. That modified the gravity of the position, but the airship was so badly damaged that the continuance of the flight was out of the question.

> Professor Hergesell, who was standing beside me in the motorboat, began to swear at me in his initial excitement; and I, no less excited, swore back at him. What fault was it of mine that the wind was swifter than my motor-boat? Count Zeppelin, in the forward gondola, raised the megaphone to his lips and shouted down to us in good-natured Swabian, 'Of course, if Hergesell and Marx quarrel, that will make everything all right again.' Thus, we two gamecocks were shamed by the old gentleman, who had suffered most from the accident. Meanwhile, the tug-boat *Buchhorn* had hurried alongside and towed the airship back into the hangar on its engine cars. At least I had the satisfaction of proving that, from a practical standpoint, the float was superfluous.

Winter is not a good time for airship experiments; we know that today and we therefore schedule our test-flights for the spring or the summer. But at that time, there was no real knowledge of such things. Moreover, Count Zeppelin was dependent upon external circumstances which prompted him to make haste. So on 17 January 1906, after the damage was repaired, the second test flight began. When the two four-cylinder Mercedes motors began to hum, no one knew that this was the airship's swan-song. Locksmith Preiss, who was present, tells about it.

I had taken my place in the aft engine car with two other mechanics, Laburda and Gassau. In the forward gondola were Count Zeppelin, Captain von Krogh, a certified free-balloon pilot, and the mechanics, Kast and Brechenmacher. The order to launch the airship had come so unexpectedly that we had taken our posts on board in our work clothes; Hans Gassau even wore house-slippers.

The ship had too much buoyancy, and only attained its equilibrium at 1,500 feet over the Bodensee. Its weight distribution was out of balance. Down below, it made headway against the wind, but up above it, it could assert itself in the south-westerly air-streams only when it stood directly against the wind. Furthermore, the controls were stiff, and when the rudder jammed, we began to drift away. We were inclined at an angle of two degrees and were pitching up and down violently. Consequently the motors were alternately flooded with gasoline and then abruptly cut off without any supply at all. Thus, it was no wonder that first the forward and then the aft motor stalled; and when, in addition, the ventilator belt ripped, we stopped altogether. From then on we drifted rudderless as a free balloon. Beside me, Gassau sang softly and significantly to himself from Rigoletto, *Ah, why recall in misery.*

Almost imperceptibly, the wind had begun to carry us in the opposite direction, toward Allgäu. If we did not wish to crash in the mountains, it was time for us to think of landing. We didn't relish this; the earth, especially during winter, is harder than water, and we feared that our large airship would be broken by the impact, just as Schwarz's little aluminium balloon had been. But the time for deliberation was denied us; already we received a message slid along a wire from the control car: 'Lower the drag anchor!' In the control car, they pulled the valve, gas escaped, and the ship began to sink. The drag anchor rattled into the depths, bit into the frozen earth and the gondola struck hard, bounced up again and … crack! The chain broke and, at an altitude of 325 feet, the ship drifted straight toward two desolate farms. Before one of them, a girl was hanging out some washing. Seeing the huge monster approaching, she cried out angrily at us, 'Let me hang my washing!' Well, we were no gypsies, and we had other worries. The airship sank again, grazed two birches, denting a part of the hull, and then sat softly down in the swampy pasture. The first landing of a Zeppelin on solid earth had been effected without outside aid, thus refuting the predictions of the know-it-alls who said that an airship could land on water but never on solid ground.

Aided by the farmers, we moored the Zeppelin fore and aft with cables whose ends we weighted with boulders, earth and a variety of heavy objects. We considered ourselves very clever, not realizing that we were sealing the fate of our airship. For an airship moored fore and aft is defenceless before a cross-wind; whereas if anchored only by its bow, the ship automatically sets itself into the wind.

The two farms near our landing-place composed the hamlet of Fischersreut bei Sommersried in Allgäu. Colloquially, the locality was called 'Allwind.' That should have warned us; but there was not even a faint breeze at the time. Count Zeppelin returned to Friedrichshafen for the night, and Gassau begged to be permitted to return by train with him so that he could clothe himself decently. Kast and I took over the first watch on the ship until midnight, when we were relieved by Brechenmacher and Laburda. We retired to the quarters assigned us at Farmer Mohr's, and the first person we met there was the young girl who had been so incensed at our apparent attack upon her. We were dead tired and slept heavily until seven the next morning.

Unsuspecting, and in good spirits, we returned to the airship and at the anchorage found a Friedrichshafen crew busy demolishing our beautiful ship with axes and saws! We couldn't believe our eyes, and we didn't know whether we or they were crazy. But we soon learned the truth. During the night, a storm had come up and struck the ship from the side, tearing its covering and breaking the inner frame-work in a number of places.

At this late date, it is idle to discuss the question of whether or not it was necessary to take such drastic action. Certainly, individual parts, such as the gondolas, could have been spared and used in the new ship, instead of chopping the motors out with axes. Afterwards, it is true, they thought better of it and searched for the parts which could still be used. The wreckage of the LZ 2 was carted to Kisslegg on trucks; the metal was melted and sent back to the factory. The Count's employees, except for four or five, were again discharged and, for the time being, placed elsewhere.

For the second time in his decade-long fight, Ferdinand von Zeppelin was set back when he was just short of his goal. For although the three test-flights of the first ship had at least proved the practicability of the rigid principle, the failure of the second ship seemed to uphold its opponents, who had faith only in the non-rigid dirigible balloon. For an emergency landing, they argued, the crew ripped open the envelope, the gas escaped, and the envelope and gondola could be salvaged. On the other hand, the rigid form of the Zeppelin airship would always prove to be its undoing. In vain Count Zeppelin explained that this was precisely the advantage of his great airship, that it would not have to land, but would withstand storms in the air. The facts were against him.

Never before and never afterwards was the inventor as depressed as he was in those days, and it was small comfort to him that, at that time, the title of Cavalry General was bestowed upon him.

'An airshipman without an airship is like a Cavalry Officer without horses,' he said with a melancholy smile. 'And I am both.'

'The ship was too slow,' he sighed another time. 'Hergesell has proved that.' But, as before, the possibility that he had made a miscalculation wouldn't penetrate Ludwig Dürr's obstinate Swabian head; and he actually proved that Professor Hergesell's measurements applied only to the lower air strata, whereas the LZ 2 had held its own against stiffer winds at greater altitudes.

But Dürr! To him, a failure was only a means for learning something. First and foremost, he intended to overcome the vibration that had had such disastrous effect upon the motors and the controls. Not one whit disconcerted either by the unfavourable decision of the experts or His Excellency's diminished funds, Ludwig Dürr, with his own more than modest savings, built at Manzell a wind-tunnel by means of which he could study the effect of air-currents on a model of an airship. This experimental laboratory was constructed of the most primitive materials; the windows through which Dürr observed the occurrences inside the wind-tunnel were taken from the hangar itself, since no others could be afforded. The experiments proved that although the model without stabilizing surfaces was subject to severe pitchings in the artificially created wind, it floated calmly in the air-stream when, like a fish, it had stabilizing fins. Relying on this vital knowledge, Dürr designed the third airship, for whose construction not a single penny was yet on hand, but which nevertheless was eventually completed and brought Zeppelin's principle to fruition.

The LZ 3 was completed and was to begin its first test flight. At the start, Marx simply took up the tow-rope, attached it to the *Württemberg* and thus pulled the airship from the hangar. Dismayed, the Count shouted to him from on board. 'Say, don't you want to put the ship on the floats first?' 'It isn't necessary,' Marx called back. 'All right,' the old gentleman decided, 'have it your own way.' And it was accomplished without floats, as it later was accomplished without the floating hangar—although it was not until December 1907, when a storm damaged the airship as it hung suspended in the hangar, that this superfluous building was abandoned.

At that time there lived in Villa Monrepos, on the lake, a private scholar named Dr Hugo Eckener. He occupied himself with National Economy and, off and on, with Zeppelin's airship, much to the latter's annoyance, for he criticized it. So much greater was the general astonishment when the Count one day appeared on the landing stairs with this gentleman and invited him

LZ 3 (Z II) after conversion at the entrance to the floating hangar. Its first flight was on 9 October 1906. It was the first Zeppelin to be successful and made a number of flights of significant duration before being enlarged and purchased by the Army in 1908. It was used for training until being decommissioned in 1913.

to Manzell for a flight. Zeppelin, who was always honest and objective, had recognized the technical justification for Eckener's criticism, and thus won for himself a remarkable man who was to complete his life's work.

But the experts and military technicians proved to be less amenable to instruction than did Eckener, who as a sailor brought with him an intuitive feeling for atmospheric occurrences. When, after a 38-hour endurance flight on the fifth Zeppelin airship, Major a. D. von Parseval, designer of a dirigible free balloon, sceptically compared this hitherto unparalleled performance to the flight of a free balloon, the Count shook his head in despair.[15] 'What have I ever done to that man?' he asked. And when Parseval later doubted that the passenger airship *Schwabenland* was as fast as it was said to be, Zeppelin graciously invited him to take a trip to convince himself of the accuracy of the calculations.

But Major Gross, whom Zeppelin was obliged to tolerate as an expert for the Prussian War Ministry, but whose colleague, Chief Engineer Basenach, he forbade entrance to the dockyards, voiced his opposition in a sharper form. When this Commander of the Royal Prussian Airship Battalion and co-builder of the semi-rigid military dirigible balloon insinuated, during a lecture, that Count Zeppelin had adopted his rigid principle from that of the Agram lumberman, David , Schwarz, the Count's seconds called upon the Major. But the

Count Ferdinand von Zeppelin and Hugo Eckener, manager of the Luftschiffbau Zeppelin in the gondola of the Zeppelin LZ 10 *Schwaben*, Friedrichshafen, 26 September 1907.

Kaiser forbade the duel on the grounds that, in the battle to conquer the air, both gentlemen were 'Officers before the enemy' and as is well known, there can be no duels during war times.

The conflict between Zeppelin and Major Gross was finally settled personally by the Kaiser when Wilhelm II came to Manzell to inspect the LZ 3 which had flown to meet him at Donaueschingen with the Crown Prince aboard. He turned impulsively to Major Gross and said, 'You see? That dirigible is quite practical. And now it will be accepted.' So the LZ 3 became the first rigid airship in the Prussian army.

That was after the crash at Echterdingen, when the old ship had been rebuilt, enlarged and launched again to replace the LZ 4. At that time, too, Zeppelin's other military opponent, the Prussian War Minister von Einem, had made obeisance before the indubitable superiority of the rigid principle and given the permission, hitherto withheld, for a Zeppelin Lottery in Prussia. Only a few weeks before the crash at Echterdingen, General von Einem, returning from a vacation trip in Switzerland, had come to Friedrichshafen and asked permission to participate in the take-off of the fourth Zeppelin airship. The LZ 4 was not yet completely finished and the weather was stormy, but since it was important, perhaps imperative, to win the War Minister's support, Zeppelin asked Chief Engineer Dürr whether he would make the flight. Dürr considered the weather and made his decision quickly. 'Yes, I'll fly. But I will not accept the responsibility for the flight.' The Count turned angrily on his heel and departed to inform the War Minister. Von Einem appeared in a motor car, and a large crowd streamed after him.

LZ 4 before the first control change. LZ 4 first flew on 20 June 1908. It was intended for military use and completed a 12 hour flight on 1 July 1908 and attempted 24 hour endurance flight on 4 August 1908, but landed near Echterdingen after 12 hours to repair an engine. It was destroyed when strong winds broke its moorings. In this photograph the floating hangar can be seen in the background.

The Zeppelin landing in the presence of Count Zeppelin and the Crown Prince.

LZ 4, 1908. Although the photograph reads 'Z2', this is in fact LZ 4.

LZ 4, 4 July 1908.

The wind had stiffened, the floating hangar rocked and turned in a semi-circle, and the airship would have been dashed against the walls and wrecked at the start. Zeppelin, too, saw that; and, heavy of heart, he decided to refuse. 'Excellency,' he said to the War Minister, 'it is impossible to make the flight.' Von Einem made no bones about his displeasure, and brusquely turned away. 'I have nothing else to say,' he said; and stepping into his car, he drove off. The Count was very depressed. 'Why, he treated me like a recruit!' he complained.

The beclouded atmosphere was darkened still more when, a few days later, the Crown Prince attempted to comfort the inventor with a congratulatory telegram on his twelve-hour flight over Switzerland and wired: 'Keeping my fingers crossed for you. Wilhelm.' Zeppelin thought the signature 'Wilhelm' referred to the Kaiser, and he immediately wired his thanks. The Kaiser, who thus for the first time learned of the hoax, crossly wired the following message to his son: 'In future you will kindly keep your mouth shut and not your fingers crossed.' Count Zeppelin consequently never liked being reminded of the incident with the War Minister.[16]

It is well known that the great flight of the LZ 4 on 4 August 1908, brought about the decisive turn of events—not as a triumphal flight, which at first it seemed to be, but, miraculously enough, through the disaster which abruptly ended it at Echterdingen. Even now, those days seem like a fabulous fairy tale which one must have lived through in order to believe; no such spontaneous outburst of national enthusiasm was ever seen in Germany before. It deserves a separate chapter.

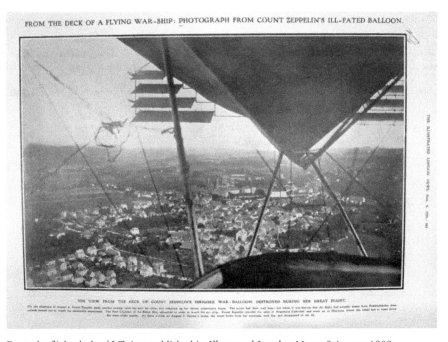

From the flight deck of LZ 4 as published in *Illustrated London News*, 8 August 1908.

16

THE DEATH OF COUNT
FERDINAND VON ZEPPELIN

I N THE DAYS when I took over the new army airship, the LZ 98, Friedrichshafen was more like a war-port than a country town on the Binnensee. At the Zeppelin Company's airship and airplane factories, the shifts worked night and day, and the personnel had increased to a total of 6,000 men. Besides those of the army, one saw many uniforms of the Imperial German Navy. Sailors, naval engineers and young officers familiarized themselves with the airships whose fates would be their own, but meanwhile, they enjoyed life. On the test-flights, Ensigns and Lieutenants would drop messages and packages to the innkeeper's daughter, who attended a very strict, convent-like pension; the hard-boiled eggs which the inn contributed to the trips would disappear mysteriously from the cellar; and on the training flight of the L 52, a stowaway suckling, painted half blue and half red, and wearing a coquettish bow on its curled tail, betrayed itself by its protesting grunts and was assigned to the ship's kitchen as Christmas fare.

At these exuberant escapades of youngsters who soon thereafter would risk their lives for the Fatherland, old General Zeppelin would smile with infinite understanding, concealing the disappointment he felt because he had not been called for active service. Nor was he pleased that his airships were being sent out singly against the enemy; if he had had his way, they would have waited until a whole fleet of air-cruisers was assembled for a big push.

He often told us of the battles he fought against the fury of the elements and the shortsightedness of the experts; and his old workers confirmed him. We had plenty of opportunity to convince ourselves of his unimpaired vigour. He thought nothing of jumping aboard a moving train. When he was starting for Manzell during low-tide one day, a stool was put into the motorboat to aid him in coming aboard. One of the young airship officers who accompanied him had already entered with the aid of the stool, and now offered his arm to the old gentleman. 'Why, that's nothing at all for us young folks,' Zeppelin replied, smiling, as he leaped from the quay directly into the boat.

When students of the technical school inspected the uninflated LZ 4, the inventor wished to give them the opportunity to enjoy the view of the dome-shaped

Fregattenkapitän Peter Strasser, (1876–1918) was Chief Commander of Germany's Zeppelin force during the First World War. He is pictured here, *c.* 1916, on the right, at Count Ferdinand Zeppelin's left side. To the left of the photograph is Hugo Eckener. Strasser died on 6 August 1918, on board LZ 112 (L 70) when it was intercepted and destroyed over North Sea by British de Havilland DH-4 flown by Major Egbert Cadbury with Captain Robert Leckie as gunner.

interior, and he led them over the side gallery of the hangar, where a thirteen-foot length of planking led into the bow of the ship. The foot-bridge was alarmingly narrow, and none of the young men dared to attempt the crossing at such a dizzying height. 'Well,' said the Count, grinning, 'not everybody can do this,' and he walked across with a feathery tread. Only one of them followed him; the others remained abashed and humiliated on the gallery.

When we were with Zeppelin, he usually had coffee passed around, and once, noticing that Captain Hacker was unaccustomed to this, he understandingly advised him to spill half a spoonful of coffee into his saucer, so that the cup wouldn't slip. He said, smiling:

I learned that trick from Duchess Robert. When I was at court with her one time, my cup slipped and I spilled the hot coffee over my dress-shirt. To console me, she gave me that piece of advice. It has stood me in good stead in all sorts of situations.

Once Count Zeppelin dropped a self-addressed post-card from the airship and enjoyed himself regally when it was delivered to him by a postman when he landed. 'I had never received any air-mail,' he said, 'and if I hadn't written to myself, no one else would have thought of it.' He, on the other hand, always thought of others, and he was infinitely considerate even when his head was filled with worries.

The LZ 4's first take-off on the acceptance flight of over 300 miles was unfortunate; the ship was badly damaged while it was being launched from the hangar. This meant not only further expense at a time when the inventor's funds were almost exhausted, but also cast a doubt on the purchase by the army board. Dejected, Zeppelin was returning to Friedrichshafen by motorboat, when he saw Captain Hacker's wife standing in the hangar. Turning to Hacker, he said, 'Your wife can't get home in the rain. Tell her that I should like to have her return with me on the *Württemberg*.' During the crossing, Zeppelin was silent, and it sounded like an apology when, taking his leave of the lady, he sighed and said, 'The gas content alone costs me 5,000 marks.'

Chief Mechanic Karl Schwarz, machinist on the third and fourth airships, and still at the Friedrichshafen dockyards today, was a witness to the take-off and a participant in the great flight which followed, and his eyes sparkle when he remembers how the miracle of Echterdingen happened:

The long-distance flight of the LZ 4, which was to last for twenty-four hours and was a condition of the purchase of the ship by the military department, was set for 15 July 1908. But when the new tug-boat *Weller*, was pulling

Count Ferdinand von Zeppelin in his element.

the LZ 4 out of the floating hangar, the tow-rope broke, and the south-west wind dashed the helpless airship against the walls of the hangar, damaging the propeller, the elevator rudder, and two gas-cells. The steamer *Königin Charlotte* helped rescue the injured giant, and the Imperial Commissioners departed.

The LZ 4 was repaired, and the Imperial Commission returned. The members of the Commission were Privy Councillors Hergesell and Mischke, Major Sperling of the Mechanized Division, and Captain von Jena, who later became the commander of the army airship Z 1 (LZ 3). Shortly after day-break on 4 August 1908, we took our posts on the LZ 4. Count Zeppelin piloted the ship, with Chief Engineer Dürr operating the elevator helm, and Lau and Captain Hacker at the rudder. Engineer Stahl and Baron von Bassus were with us in the aft gondola. Mechanics Laburda, Kast and myself tended the two 110-horsepower Daimler motors. When we took off, at about seven o'clock, there was no wind; but when we were underway it became sultry and close, and during the midday heat, over Strassburg, the ship ascended to a high altitude and thus lost gas. At six in the evening, over Nierstein, a cog-wheel slipped off the forward motor, and until it was replaced, the ship sank almost to the Rhine. We landed on a peaceful tributary, near Oppenheim, where a local wine-merchant gave us a bottle of fine Niersteiner which we shared with Count Zeppelin. While I repaired the damage to the forward motor, the LZ 4 was relieved of all superfluous weight, especially the gasoline tins; and Captain Hacker and Baron Bassus were sent ashore.

At 10.30 at night, the LZ 4, with the aid of a Rhine steamer and a company of Sappers, took off and continued the journey to Mainz, where we put about. Shortly afterwards the foremost of the two four-cylinder motors went dead; a connecting-rod bearing had burned out. But we flew on with one motor and finally reached an altitude of 6,000 feet. Near Echterdingen, we made a forced landing to repair the forward motor again, and to replenish gas and gasoline.

We had been on duty for twenty-four hours without any relief and we were dead tired. The clamour of the hundreds of thousands of people in cities and villages, the steamer sirens, the ringing church-bells—all were drowned out by the deafening roar of our motors. And when the first groups of people ran toward us and spoke to us, we couldn't hear a word they said. But they understood that we needed help, and they grabbed on with a will. The cable holding the bow of the ship like a bear's nose-ring was secured with a heap of earth; and not content with that, we buried a whole farm-wagon and fastened the cable to it. But even that later proved to be insufficient.

Soldiers arrived from Cannstadt and helped us arrange the ship so that it would be free to swing into the wind. From Untertürkheim, Daimler sent out a wrecking car with a portable workshop, and the damaged motor was taken out, repaired and reinstalled. Meanwhile, the news of our forced landing caused a veritable migration. By train, in carriages and automobiles, on bicycles and on foot, more than 50,000 people gathered on the field during the course of the forenoon. Count Zeppelin had gone to rest at the local hostelry at Echterdingen; the other members of the party were having their midday meal in the village. I remained in the aft gondola, the only one—as I thought—on the ship. I did not know that in the forward part of the ship, my comrade Laburda and one of the soldiers were still replenishing the water ballast.

At two in the afternoon, a storm came up, one of those savagely furious storms, like the one which caused the fire at Donaueschingen. The force of the wind overturned the airship and tossed it high in the air. The ground crew, fearing to be dragged along with it, released the tow-ropes. I saw somebody (it was a mechanic from the Daimler Works, who had been repairing the motor) leap from the forward gondola, and I ran along the catwalk as fast as I could to get to the forward gondola and pull the gas valves. My only thought was to bring the runaway airship back to earth. The individual valve-levers are placed beside each other on the control panel, and I took one in each finger and pulled with all my strength.

The gas escaped, but the ship continued to drift. The crowd faded away beneath me, and I found myself about half a mile away from the anchorage. I did not know whether the drifting ship had grazed a tree or the earth, but at any rate it seemed to me that I heard a cry of 'Fire!' The air ship was on an incline, with the bow sinking down; I leaned over the rail of the gondola. Within the airship envelope there was a suspiciously bright light which seemed to grow and come closer. And suddenly I knew. Fire. The airship was burning. I cannot say that I was either very frightened or prepared to die. Again, I had only one thought, and that was 'watch for your chance to jump!' I released the valve knobs which I had been holding tightly in my hands, and waited for my chance to jump. But the distance to the earth was still too great, and the burning ship was being driven along at a fast speed. Fifteen thousand cubic metres of hydrogen gas were burning, and the ballonettes were bursting with loud reports. The rings, supports and struts of the metal frame were glowing, bending and breaking; the envelope was being torn apart in blazing shreds; and soon the flames were eating through to the gasoline tanks. The heat was becoming unbearable; it was Hell itself in which I was burning alive.

If you ask me how long this lasted—I do not know. At such a moment, time has no meaning, and a second is longer than years or decades. There must have been a crash, the ship must have struck a tree; for suddenly I lay outside, flat on my face. Gas-cells, the envelope, and the whole net of girders crackled in livid red above me. As well as I could, I protected my head, breathing fire and trying to sit up and look around. Just then another mass caved in upon me. At such moments, one has terrific strength—I pushed the burden high, wound myself like an eel through the bent girders, slipped under the net of cloth covering me like a shroud, and I did not even feel the flames tonguing at me from all sides. I came free, stumbled to my feet and said grimly to myself, 'Now, run like hell!'

My lungs were filled with smoke and I gasped for breath. Falling as much as running, I nevertheless got about a hundred feet away from the ship. When I looked back, the proud giant airship was no more; the terrifying pyre had burned itself out, and only a few weak flames rose from the stern of the smoking ruin. A man in a singed uniform leaped toward me from the wreck, ran around blindly for a few seconds, and then stopped and stared. I got to my feet. He was a soldier. 'Where did you come from?' I asked. He fought for breath, and then said, 'I was in the airship; there's someone else back there.' I looked in the direction toward which he pointed, and saw another man lying near the edge of the ruins. It was my comrade Laburda. I stumbled toward him, and with the aid of the soldier dragged the unconscious form out of danger. Blood was running in two red streams from his nose. The impact had thrown him and the soldier out of the gondola, just as it had me. But Laburda was unfortunate and was knocked unconscious.

While I was still working over him, an excited crowd of people gathered to stare with dumb horror at the pitiful jumble of ruins which, only a few minutes before, had been a triumph of human endeavour and the symbol of German aspiration. Internes, taking the injured man from my care, wanted me to go along, but I refused and only then realized that my head and hands were badly burnt. In Echterdingen, the wife of the local doctor did an expert job of bandaging me.

How did I get to Echterdingen? I walked. There weren't as many autos then as there are now. Scarcely had I been bandaged, when I was again out at the scene of the disaster. There, the Stuttgart firemen were already extinguishing the remaining flames and cleaning up the wreckage. The Stuttgart Fire Commissioner, Jacobi, an efficient Berliner, had me re-bandaged by an interne, and then took me home with him in his auto. I dined with him and slept in his guest room. On the next morning, the clean new linen on the guest bed was in such a mess from my blisters that I was ashamed to face my hosts. But I couldn't help it. I looked frightful; the blisters had swelled so much that I couldn't recognize myself when I looked into a mirror.

Once more, the internes bandaged me, and at ten o'clock in the morning I took the train to Friedrichshafen, where I recuperated before flying again.

The brilliant progress of the LZ 4's flight was naturally followed with feverish excitement in our home town. Helmsman Marx and Zeppelin's daughter, Hella, decorated the *Württemberg* with flowers in the Count's colours, blue and white; there was a banquet awaiting the airshipmen; and a regimental band had agreed to play for us. Before the Deutsche Haus, an enthusiastic crowd sang national songs.

At midday, the songs and gaiety subsided; there were rumours that the airship had burned. Marx ran to the office, and found it closed. After a time, Dr Eckener came out of the Deutsche Haus, and it was plain that he had been crying. He went through the garden to the motorboat and told the boatman what had happened. Marx jumped on his motorcycle and sped away, far away, where he could be alone. He did not return to Friedrichshafen until nightfall.

On the next morning, Marx was on the way to the boat house when the balcony door opened in the upper storey of the Deutsche Haus and Zeppelin, smiling as if nothing had happened, called to him. 'Good morning, Marx! How are you?' The Helmsman was perplexed, and the Count continued, 'Why, Marx, you still seem to be hard hit by yesterday's occurrence. Come on up here a moment.' Marx went up, and Zeppelin opened the door. 'Well, Marx,' he said, 'what do you think of this accident?' The old salt growled, 'Can't say, Excellency.' Then the Count led him to a table on which lay a great heap of money. 'That was sent to me by the German people, and there's more coming! So, Marx, now we'll really begin to build airships. Please go to Dürr's home and tell him I want him to met me at Manzell at 8.30. With God's help, we start again!'

On the very day of the accident, and on that very scene, a man had swung himself on a table in full view of the smoking ruins and urged the crowd voluntarily to contribute toward a new airship. Newspapers had published the suggestion, and when the inventor returned, passing through a silent lane of people with their hats off, he found on his table a heap of telegrams pledging support to him. And that unanimous impulse was instantly transformed into action throughout the entire country. On the steamer *Königen Charlotte*, under way from Friedrichshafen to Constance, the passengers and crew collected 600 marks; and a Bädisch Bowling Club—the first of many organizations—sent 150 marks. The Aldermen of Stuttgart contributed 20,000 marks; Friedrichshafen 5,000 marks; and a host of other towns and cities followed suit. The newspapers continued to publish daily appeals, and printed lists of the contributors; the Mining Association at Essen gave 100,000 marks; Senator Possel of Lübeck a like amount; Dr Lanz, who later built airships with Professor Schütte of Danzig, contributed 50,000 marks. Rich and poor, old and young, even down to the children in school, cooperated in wiping out the consequences of an accident which everyone regarded as a national catastrophe.

Soon, the postman who came to the Deutsche Haus could no longer complete the sorting of the mail; he simply emptied whole sacks of letters, money-orders and packages on the floor. Count Zeppelin saw the heap growing and rising day by day. When the first few thousand marks were collected, he stammered, 'But I really can't accept that!' And when the public contributions totalling 6,096,555 marks were counted, he declined to use even a penny of it for himself. The Luftschiffbau Zeppelin (Zeppelin Airship Works) was incorporated with a capital of one million marks. Mr Uhland, the Count's business manager, took charge of the Zeppelin Foundation. The purpose of this organization, which Dr Eckener headed, was to use the fund of national contributions for the advancement of airship travel. The government reimbursed Count Zeppelin for his expenditures, and he in turn repaid the investments of the stock-holders in the liquidated Corporation for the Advancement of Airship Travel. His hints to these gentlemen that they decline this repayment and instead use it to create a Professorship at the Technical College in Stuttgart found small favour, especially with the wealthy stock-holders and only a scant 20,000 marks was realized. On the other hand, Zeppelin was inundated with begging letters from all the principal countries of the world. It was immaterial whether one had discovered the perpetuum mobile, or another wished to marry, or another was devotedly attached to the General as a former comrade-in-arms—all wanted his money. And all of them received an answer from the Count. Either he gave, and then did so from his own, and not from public funds, or he declined. Director Uhland complained to the Countess, who was more economical than her husband, that the postage alone for these letters of refusal amounted to 300 marks per month. It would have been so much simpler to throw the letters into the waste basket. But the Count good-naturedly replied, 'Well, then you answer them for a while.' When the flow of letters became a deluge, however, he took

In Skyland

AIRSHIP EXCURSIONS

by

ZEPPELIN AIRSHIPS

of the

GERMAN AIRSHIP NAVIGATION COMPANY

∴∴

Passenger Booking Arrangements by the

HAMBURG=AMERICAN LINE

Advertising for Zeppelin flights had already started in 1909.

the advice of his friends and had form-letters printed. But he still insisted that every inventor who called upon him should be told the reason for the refusal. He himself had known the life of an inventor, and he sought to make it easier for others whenever possible.

In the face of the incessant demands made upon him, Count Zeppelin finally retired to Italy, and his office forwarded only those matters with which they themselves could not deal. Among these was the impudent assumption of a wealthy merchant that His Excellency, to whom all was possible, would obtain for him a baronetcy in return for a contribution of a couple of hundred thousand marks toward the building of airships. Needless to remark, he had come to the wrong person. For this genuine nobleman was not impressed either by gold or rank. Alfred Colsman tells a very humorous story of how the Count proposed a mutually advantageous business arrangement to Sielken, an American coffee-king. 'Then you will participate in my airship construction, Mr Sielken.' 'And what would your part of the bargain be, Your Excellency?' 'I? Oh, I will drink a great deal of coffee.'

The miracle of Echterdingen relieved Zeppelin of his financial difficulties but he still had many other troubles. Phoenix-like, his new airship materialized out of the ashes of the old one, but there were many trials to be borne before the tenth Zeppelin, the *Schwaben*, piloted by Eckener, proved the practicability of the rigid principle. There was the LZ 5 which, after a 38-hour flight, was

LZ 5 was designed for military use. It was torn away from its moorings on 24 April 1910 and crashed as a complete wreck at Weilburg between Limburg and Wetzlar.

LZ 5 (Z II). LZ 5 was an experimental military Zeppelin which first flew 26 May 1909. It was carried away from its moorings during a storm and wrecked near Weilburg on 25 March 1910.

LZ 7 (*Deutschland*) first flew 19 June 1910. It was damaged beyond repair after crashing during a thunderstorm over the Teutoburg Forest on 28 June 1910. Pictured here is its successor, LZ 8 (*Deutschland II*).

LZ 8 (*Deutschland II*). This civilian Zeppelin saw its first flight on 30 March 1911.

awaited by whole Berlin, with the Royal couple at their head, but which Dürr, exhausted, had steered into a pear tree near Göppingen. Dürr ran away, and rumour had it that he had done himself some injury. But he had simply gone to sleep in a nearby cornfield; and he later brought the mended ship home on one motor. No more than a year later, the LZ 5 was wrecked near Weilburg; and in that same year the LZ 7 was wrecked in the Teutoburg Forest and the LZ 6 in its hangar.

The LZ 7 was the Delag passenger ship *Deutschland* and, carrying twenty press representatives from all the principal countries of the world, was to show the prowess of the Zeppelin airship. Dr Eckener was also on board, but, unfortunately, he was not in command at the time, and the ship suddenly flew down into a tree like a crow. Dr Colsman came out of the guest cabin, made his way forward through the passageway, and asked, 'When do we proceed?' Helmsman Marx, not in his best humour, growled, 'You'd better look at a railway timetable to find that out. The ship is done for.' 'Why, what do you mean?' the Director asked in dismay. 'Well,' said Marx, blinking shrewdly at him, 'ordinarily the Teutoburg Forest lies in Germany, but this time *Deutschland* (Germany) lies in the Teutoburg Forest.'

That was gallows' wit, but it helped us to get over the first shock. The ship was lost; and the new one which was built was wrecked while it was being launched. When this happened, Count Zeppelin went to Düsseldorf, and Captain

Deutschland II was caught by a strong crosswind while being walked out of its hangar and damaged beyond repair on 16 May 1911.

Hacker reported the accident to him. Not a word of condemnation fell from Zeppelin's lips. Consolingly, he replied, 'Well, we've learned something again. Apparently, this hangar is too small; we must build larger ones in future.'

While I was busying myself in Friedrichshafen with the dockyards, the LZ 98 was finished, and went through its workshop flights. At the end of April 1916, I delivered this new air-cruiser to Hanover, and Count Zeppelin was our guest on this 8-hour flight. In his honour, we detoured over the village of Zepelin, which is the ancestral seat of the family and lies on the Baltic near Bützow in Mecklenburg. Count Zeppelin had never been there before. 'You see,' he said to us, grinning, 'all that land below once belonged to my ancestors. But they drank and gambled it away.'

During this flight, the inventor of the rigid airship caught a cold, but that didn't interfere with his good humour. None of us knew that we were seeing him alive for the last time. One year later, on 8 March 1917, Ferdinand von Zeppelin died.

17

ZEPPELINS IN THUNDERSTORMS

ROM HANOVER WE made a side-trip to the naval airfield at Nordholz where there were half a dozen enormous double hangars, one of which was built on a turn-table. The navy had also built large repair-shops, a gas-works to supply hydrogen for the airships, and barracks quartering thousands of men. All the structures were of steel and brick, and they were constantly being enlarged and improved. The Navy Board had adopted the system of stationing a number of Zeppelins at each aerodrome. There was another base, fully as large, at Ahlhorn near Bremen, and two smaller ones at Wittmund near the Dutch border and at Tondern in North Silesia. Furthermore, there were various emergency landing-fields laid out along the Baltic coast so that the naval airships did not have to go far beyond their base of operations. Our LZ 98 was ordered to cooperate with the navy in raids on England.

During these raids, we often met heavy squalls and thunderstorms, and in one of these my army airship, the LZ 98, and the naval airship L 11 had the same exciting experience. I give my friend Schiller the precedence in narration:

We were homeward bound after a night attack on the industrial centres in middle England. Ahead of us, I noticed the lightning flashes of a storm, moving from the vicinity of Amsterdam toward the North Sea and bound to cross our path. We were still hoping to avoid it with the aid of a favourable west wind when the wind died.

The ship was heading toward a thick bank of clouds, and I changed course to avoid them. This caused me to strike stiff head winds which became stronger and stronger and killed our headway. The sea beneath us was covered with white foam. The storm increased in fury, the thunder rolled closer, and lightning struck horizontally over the ship, rendering the wireless apparatus useless.

The gusts came from all directions, dashing the vessel from side to side. The walkway swayed and trembled and the crew held on to the girders and supports in order not to be tossed out. Everyone was inside the ship except the officers on duty, who were at the navigating instruments in the control car, and the mechanics in the engine cars.

Our commander, Lieutenant-Commander von Buttlar, at first thought of turning back and running before the storm, but that would have carried us back to England and we had no desire to fight the enemy guns in addition to the elements. So we pushed on.

The man on the upper platform reported that it was raining in buckets. The pitching ship could not rise over the mountains of clouds looming up before it. With its nose sunk down, it dove into the darkness where lightning strokes flashed out at short intervals.

Then hailstones rattled on the dripping outer envelope, and the airship shuddered like an animal whipped by a lash. Sometimes it was tossed a hundred yards high and sank again two or three hundred yards before it steadied itself. Then a terrific bolt crashed by my ears, filling the inside of the ship with a blinding light. The man on the upper lookout post telephoned down that the muzzle of his machine-gun was spitting sparks. I climbed through the gun-shaft to see what it was all about. To my astonishment, I found the platform brightly illuminated. In the centre of this luminous circle sat the lookout, wet through to the skin, but sporting a veritable halo around his head. This extraordinary phenomenon is not unknown to mountain-climbers as well as sailors; it is called Saint Elmo's fire. The duralumin frame of the hull was charged with electricity and sent forth sparks at all connecting-points and corners. When we looked up out of the control car, we could see the sparks coming from all protruding objects. Wires and cables glowed with a bluish-violet fight; a wonderful sight, except that we were not exactly in a position to appreciate it. Our men were staggering like drunken tight-rope walkers on the narrow walkway. And with lightning flashing by every two minutes at arm's length, so to speak, our lives depended upon no hydrogen escaping from the gas-cells.

Neither I nor my comrades had ever experienced anything like this. Instead of descending as far as possible to escape the worst fury of the storm and lightning, we remained at 10,000 feet and were in a frenzy for three hours trying to keep the ship under control. Not until the break of dawn did the L 11 come out of the danger zone. The sun rose and quickly dried the soaking ship. We made our way home as fast as we could.

Meanwhile, the LZ 98 was again in Hanover, and the weather was bothering us, too. Stiff westerly winds down below, and storms up above, confined us to a modest patrol service over the North Sea. But no sooner was there a sign of improvement than I instantly thought of an attack on London. The take-off was scheduled for midday, and since the morning reports mentioned a probable storm centre forming over England, I decided to take advantage of the high pressure area between the two lows. I communicated by telephone with the Nordholz naval base, which sent five other airships along with us.

Soon after we left our hangar, we saw two naval airships taking off for Ahlhorn, but we lost sight of them later on. They were flying at a higher altitude and apparently had more headwinds. I remained at 500 feet, finding the air uncomfortably bumpy. A heavy mist clung to the earth, and the sky became filled with all sorts of unfavourable cloud formations.

Our course took us southward over Cologne and then on a detour of 225 miles around Holland. When we reached Belgium, we found the sky still more unfriendly and therefore stopped over at the Namur airport to obtain more complete weather reports. Meanwhile, night had fallen, and when no reports had arrived by morning, I went aloft again at 8.30, hoping that Namur and Ostend would wireless us the necessary information.

I took direct course from Ostend to Dover. Seventy sea miles from the coast we became aware of a bad storm coming up from the south-west, and we tried to race it. I hoped to reach Dover before it overtook us, in order to unload our bombs at the mouth of the Thames, or on Harwich, and then run before the winds. But the storm was faster than we thought, and it overtook us. I had just stepped from the chart-room into the control compartment when the machine-gunner on the upper deck reported that it was raining heavily. I still hoped to make it by putting the ship down to 3,300 feet. But already the rain was pouring down, and in the distance there was a flash of lightning.

'Altitude 2,000 feet, course north-west!' I ordered. A lightning stroke split the heavens above us, and was instantly followed by a deafening crash of thunder. The lookout called through the speaking-tube: 'Heavy rain, mixed with hail; lightning straight ahead.' The storm had won the race.

'Course east!' While the ship came around, the wireless operator stepped out of his cabin and handed me a report from the Namur station. 'Stiff, freshening south winds, later south-west and west storms. The navy has ordered the ships to return.' We had already taken the eastern course anyway, choosing the return as the better part of valour, in order to take off again as soon as the storm had abated.

Shortly thereafter we were under way again on a sultry night, and this time we struck a real British fog in which six other airships besides ourselves were endeavouring to hide. After a raid on Hull, I met another change of weather on the homeward trip. The warm air-currents coming from the continent create thunderstorms when they meet the colder currents over the sea; and I was, therefore, on the lookout for a surprise. In the pitch darkness I could not see the clouds; furthermore, we were already so close to the coast of Holland that I could not risk going down lower.

We were just climbing toward a cloud when, like an angry traffic policeman, it suddenly glared at us. Obediently, I was about to give down elevator when

Damage at Waller Street, Hull, 7 June 1915 resulting in one dead and fourteen houses damaged.

there was a blinding flash. Instantly, the control car was as bright as daylight, and the thunder sounded as if we were at the muzzle of a heavy gun. The heavens opened all their sluices at one time; the storm struck us from all directions. While we were moving the horizontal controls in order to dive as steeply as possible, I remembered the man on the top of the ship. Just then, he called down through the speaking tube:

> A lightning bolt struck the nose of the ship, thirty feet from my post. It almost knocked me down just as I was going to report that there were electrical discharges around me. Tongues of fire are licking around the muzzles of my machine guns, and around my head, too. And when I spread my hand, little flames spurt out of my fingertips.

Meanwhile, the LZ 98 had come down from 5,300 to 300 feet, and we were soon on our course again. But, as if that lightning stroke had been the signal for a general bombardment, the flashes now came down upon us from all sides. It was as if Satan had laid out a long fuse, and sparks and fire were running along it. In vain we searched the horizon for dark holes through which we could slip out of the storm zone. Only later, during the night, after following many serpentine courses, did we find a peaceful area between the individual thunder-squalls. Then we struggled towards our home base.

To the non-expert, it may seem well-nigh unbelievable that an airship filled with inflammable gas was not destroyed in such a storm; yet scientific research and dozens of carefully investigated cases show why it survived. Lightning, too, obeys the laws of nature. It is distributed only on the enormous surface of the metallic airship-frame which protectively encloses the gas-cells like a Faraday cage. Thus, as long as the airship pilot himself—and it lies entirely within his power—takes care that no inflammable gas forms between the cells and the outer envelope, lightning is no danger at all for a Zeppelin. When, at daybreak, we finally came out of the storm zone, all of us were tired, but we were absolutely hale. In Hanover, we inspected the ship. In the bow envelope, I found a number of small burns and holes marking the spot where the lightning had struck. The largest spot had the dimensions of a small pea, and the metal support at this point was somewhat melted, but that was all. We might not even have realized that the lightning had struck the ship if our lookout on the upper platform had not seen it with his own eyes.

Zeppelin victims looking at a fragment of a bomb mechanism.

18

LZ 98 Over London and the Loss of SL 11

A T THE BEGINNING of September 1916, the LZ 98 joined twelve other army and navy airships in a united action against London. Over the metropolis I made the unpleasant discovery that the English had still further improved their defence system and now sent veritable hornet-swarms of single-seater combat planes against us. Amid heavy losses of men and material, their fliers had learned to attack at night also, and their machine guns showered us with incendiary bullets. As long as an airship flew in the dark, it was almost invisible to the enemy; but once in the clutches of a searchlight, it could be seen for miles. In the protection of the night, the little combat planes stole unnoticed upon the enormous targets, which were at least a hundred times as large as they, and were often within shooting distance before the German, machine gunners could open fire. A single hit in one of the gas chambers sufficed to destroy the airship and its crew.

Nor did this new type of defence confine itself to London. Combat fliers were on duty all along the eastern coast of Britain, and others patrolled between Nieuport and Dunkirk to stop the airships on the way. We had to be careful, and we had to return before dawn at any cost. The LZ 88, Commander Falk, was attacked by enemy defence patrols on its way home, and only escaped destruction by diving into a low-lying cloud at the right moment and disappearing beneath its swifter opponent. The LZ 97, larger and of greater climbing power than its sister-ships, quickly rose to an altitude of 13,500 feet and its commander, Linnartz, was pleased to find that the pursuing fliers could not get to him.

If, during the latter part of the World War, comparatively few Zeppelins were shot down by airplanes, this is due to the fact that the climbing capacity of airships increased at a greater rate than did that of the airplanes. Airplanes, motors and pilots constantly reached greater heights, but Dr Dürr and his staff saw to it that the airship either retained its advantage in climbing ability or regained it in the next type. The greatest advantage of an airship, however, lies in its principle. Lighter than air because of its gas-content, it can remain aloft for days, while the flying machine, heavier than air, is entirely dependent upon its motor. If the English defence flier took off too soon, his gasoline supply might be exhausted before he came in contact with the invader; and if he started at the last moment, the airship would be out of his range before he could gain enough altitude to attack. Furthermore, it was dangerous for an aviator to go up during an attack on London; for he might be hit by his own artillery and, in the event of motor-trouble, he would be obliged to make a forced landing in the streets or on the roofs, which almost certainly meant death or serious injury.

So much the more is the performance of the English defence flier to be appreciated. At least, they made our raids more difficult and forced us to confine them to the darkest nights. These nights could be neither cloudless nor foggy, for the one delivered us inevitably into the hands of the searchlights and the other offered us no visibility in which to aim or get our bearings. We needed visibility and scattered banks of clouds in which we could hide from the searchlights, anti-aircraft batteries and pursuit fliers. And the nights fulfilling these conditions were exceedingly rare.

This was the situation when, on 2 September 1916, thirteen of us raided London. The course lay over Belgium and the sea, where, in order not to be burdened by the moisture, we had to avoid a number of rain squalls. When the LZ 98 arrived on the outskirts of the English capital, a few of her sister-ships were already in action. The dull crashes of the bombs answered the firing of the heavy guns, whose number and range had likewise been considerably increased. The whole endless sea of houses lay under a silvery fog in which rose up the incessant flashes of explosions and blazing fires. We saw these explosions, but

Caught and held by searchlights over London within range of incendiary flames.

we could no longer see the agents causing them; one by one they had disappeared in the mist. The conical rays of the searchlights passed through each other like bodiless ghosts, and thousands of bursting shells illuminated London like a display of fire-works. It seemed to us that we were sitting in the loge of a theatre, before us the brightly lit stage, and under us the darkened auditorium.

A whole hour went by before I found my opportunity to enter the city limits. Three times my ship had been caught by the searchlights, and three times I succeeded in withdrawing into a cloud before the 'Archies' found our range. Finally, some clouds passing at a 10,000-foot altitude, came to my aid. I zigzagged toward them, sailing from one to the other until we stood directly over the Thames. We dropped our bombs on the docks and then, protected by the nearest clouds, climbed to 14,000 feet. There, feeling ourselves safe, we curiously stuck our nose out to observe the result of our attack. Instantly the searchlights found us again. The shells fired at us, however, burst far below us. Undisturbed, the LZ 98 broke through the defence zone to the north-east.

I was in the chart-room bending over the maps to set our homeward course when Gemmingen let out a scream. I looked back in the direction from which we had come and I saw, far behind us, a bright ball of fire. Despite the distance, which I estimated at thirty-eight miles, we knew that the blazing meteor on the further rim of the city could only be one of our airships. As we later learned, Fate had overtaken Commander Schramm's SL 11, a rigid ship of the Schütte-Lanz type. The flaming mass hung in the sky for more than a minute; then single parts detached themselves from it and preceded it to the earth. Poor fellows, they were lost the moment the ship took fire.

We remained silent until it was all over, and then realized how easily the same fate could have overtaken us if we had not been fortunate enough to find clouds when we needed them. The clouds had begun to scatter during the latter part of the squadron attack, and the SL 11 had apparently remained visible for too long a time. As we subsequently learned, Lieutenant William Robinson shot down the SL after he had been in the air for almost two hours vainly attacking one of the other airships. His King soon afterward bestowed the Victoria Cross upon him.

The flames of the airship were visible forty miles away, and its fall was accompanied by the hurrahs of the spectators and the ship's sirens screaming in the harbour. The SL 11 crashed in the suburb of Cuffley near Enfield, and the wreck continued to burn for one and a half hours, its machine gun bullets exploding one by one.[17] When the fire was extinguished, only charred wood was found instead of the duralumin which was expected and it was deduced from this that the Germans were short of aluminium. But the satisfaction occasioned by this discovery was of short duration, for military experts explained that the wrecked airship was not a Zeppelin but a Schütte-Lanz, whose rigid frames at that time were still made of wood.

SL 11 shot down in flames over London.

The heavier parts of the SL 11 had buried themselves so deeply in the earth that they had to be dug out. In the morning, the bodies of the sixteen members of the crew were recovered. The *Star* printed a protest against burying the 'infanticides' with full military honours; but the English soldiers honoured not the fallen enemy, but the dead comrades. A colonel of the Royal Air Force headed the funeral procession as it went toward Potter's Field. A motor-truck carried the fifteen coffins of polished Japanese ash. The coffin of Commander Schramm was on a gun-carriage and bore a small silver shield with the inscription: 'An unknown German officer, Commander of a Zeppelin, brought down on 3 September 1916.' The Commander's coffin was borne by six officers of the Royal Air Force, among them Lieutenant A. de B. Brandon, who had received the Military Cross for bringing down a Zeppelin at the beginning of the year. During the burial, a combat plane of the same type that Robinson had used in the attack, cruised over the cemetery.

A tremendous crowd had gathered and hundreds of constables were called upon to prevent disturbances. Murmurs of protest were heard when the coffins were carried to the graves. But the majority of the spectators frowned at this and retained a respectful silence. Commander Schramm received a separate grave; the other bodies were placed into a common grave, coffin on coffin. After a short funeral oration by Reverend M. M. Handcock, the *Last Post* concluded the ceremony.

From the English newspapers we obtained, we read the reports of the funeral. Less detailed than these, however, were the reports of the damage which we had done. Still, a few bits of information seeped through the censor's net. In Dover, sixty houses were demolished, the docks were badly damaged in three places, and a warehouse was razed to the ground. In Norfolk and Suffolk, whole cities were so badly damaged that the inhabitants fled in a wild panic. London, with its comprehensive defence measures, seemed to them to be safest, and so they arrived by thousands with their travelling bags, crowding the hotels and raising the prices of foodstuffs.

But London itself had not been spared. The piers at Gravesend and Tilbury had been completely destroyed. The searchlight near the Woolwich Arsenal had been smashed to smithereens. Fires were raging along the Thames on the next morning. Marine traffic on the Thames and the Channel was completely interrupted for twenty-four hours, and foreign sailors were forbidden to leave their ships lest they see for themselves the terrific damage done by the raiders. In the city, the wrecked houses were shielded from curious glances by wooden barriers; but as a demolished house in Cockspur Street indicated, the German airships had pressed forward into the very heart of The City itself. The hospitals admitted many hundreds of people who had been injured by the bombs or who had received burns. Officially, the figures were 38 dead and 225 injured.

But the effect of our attack was most impressively characterized by neutral papers, which reported that a great many munitions factories were being transferred from the eastern coast of England to north Scotland out of the reach of German airships.

Nevertheless, our tragic experience prompted us to hold a conference, soon after our return, to decide upon a new course of action. We were unanimously of the opinion that the increased efficiency of the defence no longer permitted air raids on London at altitudes between 10,000 and 13,500 feet. At least 15,000 to 17,000 feet were necessary. But at the stage of development which airships had reached at that time, this would have meant a reduction of bomb-load from two tons to one ton; consequently the risks of a raid on London would scarcely have been worthwhile. Therefore, we waited until newer, more efficient airships were built, and meanwhile contented ourselves with other important objectives which had weaker defences. On a number of these bombing flights, however, we came close to London, each time vainly hoping that the weather conditions would be favourable enough for us to give the English a surprise by making use of our observation gondola.

At about that time the parachute was introduced for airshipmen also, in order to enable the crew to leap from the burning craft. But since the additional weight was at the expense of fuel and projectiles, we quickly abandoned them again and continued to leave the decision of life or death to our own skill and luck.

19

THE LOSS OF L 32, L 33 AND L 31

D URING MOST OF the raids on London, individual objectives, such as the Bank of England, were not clearly visible. We were obliged to determine their position from the maps or by other landmarks: the course of the Thames, the position of searchlights, and the situation of the anti-aircraft batteries. For this purpose, I used a special map of London. It was drawn according to information gathered by all earlier airship pilots, and it looked like an astronomical chart full of stars. The Thames was the Milky Way; the stars denoted searchlights, 'Archies' and everything else which was to be avoided or destroyed.

The question of the direction of attack was a problem in itself. The approach had to be made from a different direction than the flight over the metropolis, for it would otherwise have been too easy for the fliers and defence batteries to bring us down. Many Zeppelins that were shot down, or so badly damaged that they were wrecked on the homeward journey, had simply followed too close in the wake of the ship ahead.

In general it was advisable to set a course for London directly with the wind. The speed of the airship was thus increased by that of the wind and quickly brought us over the defence zone and out again on the other side. To cruise over the city, which was larded with cannon, would have been pure suicide. Therefore it was of vital importance to us to know how the wind would be blowing at a certain time and a certain height. We had to calculate this at least two hours before our arrival; that is, even before leaving the continent. For we could never be certain beforehand whether, when we were under way, we would be able to distinguish any landmarks for calculating the direction and velocity of the wind. Furthermore, we had to consider the position of the moon and choose the darkest time at night, between the setting of the moon and the rising of the sun, in order to cross the coastline, appear over London at the most opportune moment, and disappear again before dawn. The weather around us generally came from the west; but the enemy was in the west, and he was not so obliging as to supply us with weather reports.

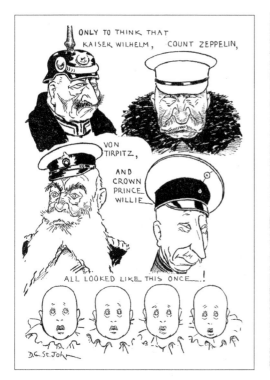

Above left: OUGHT WE TO GROW UP? *Punch*, 23 February 1916.

Above right: A German propaganda news-sheet.

On the night of 23 September 1916, a fleet of ten naval airships set out to raid England. Seven of them were older types and no longer quite up to the demands of an attack upon the capital. On the other hand, the other three, the L 31, L 32, and L 33, were new Zeppelins 650 feet long and containing 55,200 cubic metres of gas. Besides its own weight of 74,800 pounds and a crew, and 1,300 gallons of fuel, each of these airships could carry 9,240 pounds of bombs, and its six Maybach motors totalling 1,440 horsepower gave it a speed of 70 miles per hour. Its armament consisted of eight machine guns, four in the gondolas, three on the forward platform and one on the after platform of the ship's back. For emergencies, there were not only cork life-jackets and parachutes, but even two light life-boats. One hung under the belly of the ship between the forward engine car and the bomb-panel, and the other was placed on the forward platform. These life-saving devices, all things considered, were of small practical value, but they may have had some good effect upon morale.

In view of the more effective defence, we were no longer able to load the ships so heavily. The three new airships were therefore carrying a total of only six tons of explosive and incendiary bombs.

The panel of the electrical apparatus for bombing as in 1916 model Zeppelins.

The airship fleet passed the Dutch Islands in the North Sea and struck a westward course. The sky was painted with brilliant hues, the lower half suffused with red and yellow; but far off, beneath the play of colours, there was a black strip of land.

'Land ho!' All of the ten non-coms stationed on the upper platforms of their ships telephoned the information to their control cars. The Navigation Officers lifted their telescopes; out before them, in the last rays of the setting sun, lay Yarmouth. That was the signal for the ten Zeppelins to separate. The Commander of the L 31, Lieutenant-Commander Heinrich Mathy, later described that memorable flight.

> After nightfall, then, we flew over the English coast, the seven older ships turning northward, the three new naval airships taking course along the coast for the southern districts of London. The thermometer showed twenty-six degrees (Fahrenheit); pretty low for the crew of a military airship lacking conveniences, but welcome despite that. For with every degree the thermometer fell, the ship gained in climbing ability. On the upper platform, the machine-gunners had taken their posts and were keeping a sharp lookout for enemy fliers. In the darkness, the three naval airships lost sight of each other, and each was left to its own resources to act as an independent unit. From time to time I told my men what cities we were over, and each man marked the course on his map of England.
>
> The minutes stretched into hours. My Watch Officer reported a searchlight to the stern; it was evidently newly installed. I marked the discovery on my map and flashed the news out into the fog. Shortly thereafter my Radio Officer intercepted an English wireless message warning London of our approach. The

alarm was repeated by a number of stations. The effect was instantaneous. All the villages below us were immediately darkened, and the beams of huge searchlights shot upward to explore the sky. One of the searchlights, further away than the others, caught us. A series of thunderclaps from close by revealed an anti-aircraft battery. The L 31 banked sharply, the rays of the searchlight slid off her, and, although the 'Archie' continued to fire, the prey escaped.

At midnight, the three Zeppelins reached the city of London from different directions. The English could darken the metropolis as much as they liked, but they couldn't conceal the Thames. They even placed false streetlights in Hyde Park and similarly marked out whole city-districts on the outskirts. But the airship officers were not deceived; the course of the Thames betrayed the ruse.

I prepared for the attack. Almost the entire available water ballast was released in order to bring the L 31 as high as possible. A tug on a wire from the control car opened the sliding panels under the ship, where the bombs hung suspended side by side. The Watch Officer reported everything ready; the motors were running full speed ahead. In the dark sky, the searchlights crossed like bared swords.

My own experience—I was over London for the fifth time—had taught me that the capital had a weaker defence in the south than in the north and north-east. So I made a wide circle in order to come from the south and leave the city by the north. When, half an hour after midnight, we crossed the Croydon defence zone, the L 31 was caught in the merciless beam of a searchlight. But we outwitted the enemy. We dropped parachute flares, whose bright light made it temporarily impossible for the defenders to see the airship, and, in addition, confused them because they mistook the flares for the signals of an English flier. In such a case, the flares meant 'Cease firing.' At any rate, we had soon disappeared into the darkness again and we received no more fire until we began to bomb the city. But even then the searchlights were unable to find us. The L 31 laid a line of explosive and incendiary bombs right across London without suffering the slightest damage. This is only to be explained by the fact that the other two Zeppelins drew the entire attention upon themselves.

Suddenly, the sky burst into fire as if a stroke of lightning had split it apart. The L 32, commanded by Naval-Lieutenant Peterson, who was over England for the eleventh time, was overtaken by Fate. Peterson had described a narrower curve than we and crossed the Thames further east, where the defence was stronger. An English combat-squadron had climbed over the L 32 and sent phosphorus bullets into its envelope. We in the L 31 saw the ship catch fire. First the bow burned, and then the flames tongued over the whole envelope. The aft gondola broke off, and the wing cars followed. For eighteen terrible seconds the blazing ball hung like a fateful planet in the sky; then it burst asunder. A glowing mass with a tail of whirling flames fell like a comet on Billericay, east of London.

Millions of Englishmen witnessed the catastrophe, for the blaze was visible all over London and far into the countryside. The Britons, apparently so even-tempered and composed, broke out into frenzied cheers and danced like mad in the darkened streets. The ships on the Thames sounded their sirens. It was one o'clock in the morning, and noisier than on New Year's Eve.

Meanwhile, in Essex, at the scene of the crash, the fire department was attempting to recover the bodies and extinguish the flames of the airship, part of which hung in some trees. Two hundred yards away, covered by his grey army coat, lay the commander of the airship, Lieutenant Peterson. He must have jumped or fallen from the control car. The enemy was generous enough to accord him, too, a funeral with military honours.

The third ship of our naval trio, the L 33, under Lieutenant-Commander Böcker, had approached from the east and hovered over London parallel to the Thames. Hundreds of guns opened fire at it; but in the midst of a hail of bursting shells, Böcker steadfastly followed his course.

Now, his bombs were striking. Great fires sprang up under the airships and covered the city with a cloud of smoke that obscured the rays of the searchlights. Another searchlight groped through the smoke and illuminated the control car. Flaming incendiary rockets hissed by on all sides and the shells kept bursting closer and closer.

But the L 33 continued on its way. Over the eastern industrial quarter of the city, Böcker dropped the rest of his bombs. Factories blew up into the air, and flames leaped up to complete the work of destruction. Then a thin layer of clouds came to the aid of the hard-pressed ship. When the L 33 turned homeward, a narrow line of fire marked its pathway over the city. But the crew had no time to look backward, for an inspection revealed that the gas-cells were leaking. Böcker sent every available man inside the ship to repair the damage as well as they could; meanwhile, all unnecessary weight was thrown overboard. But, while it was still within range of the British guns, the airship continued to sink down, the few cells that remained unharmed scarcely sufficing to keep it aloft. After intense effort, the L 33 left the English coast at half past one in the morning, and began to struggle home. But soon Böcker was obliged to wireless that he could not even reach Holland. He determined to turn around and land somewhere in England. A few miles from Colchester he set the L 33 down in an open field, all twenty-two of the men jumped out and one of the officers shot Very lights into the hull. Despite every effort, however, the wreck could not be ignited, so that it remained practically undamaged in all vital parts.

Later on, the English used the structural part of the L 33 as a model for a reproduction of the German Zeppelin. In 1918, before the World War was over, they built the two rigid airships R 33 and R 34. In the following year, the latter was the first airship to fly the Atlantic in both directions; and the former served as an experimental ship for nine years, during which it once withstood a storm of 60 miles per hour.

But let us return to Böcker and his 21 men. Some fifty steps from their landing-place, the crew of the L 33 saw a modest farm-house. They approached it and knocked at the door, and when no one answered, they fired a few revolver shots into the air to attract attention. Then a man approached, but no amount of questioning could break down his stubborn silence.

Soon, however, a group of armed men approached, led by a village constable who carried a sword. They formed a semi-circle around the Germans and stared in astonishment at their sheepskins and leather jackets.[18] Böcker asked the way to the nearest village, and understood the answer more from the direction of their glances than from their gestures. He and his men then went off in that direction, grimly followed by the group of men.

At the entrance to the village the curious procession was met by a second group of armed men who appeared to be volunteer militiamen ordered out to defend the hinterlands. Perhaps the mayor himself was with the second group, for one of the men had an air of authority. Rifles were raised, bayonets sparkled, and a thunderous voice ordered, 'Surrender!'

The twenty-two Germans on the enemy island had no other choice but to submit to arrest. Böcker only requested permission to telegraph from the nearest post-office to an English friend in London, so that his wife would be informed that he and his men were safe. Then a military patrol took charge of the prisoners and led them to the various prison camps.

At the prison camp Böcker was visited by an English Air Captain with whom he had been acquainted before the war. The Englishman smilingly revealed that he had been in Friedrichshafen when Böcker's airship was in the dockyards, and that he at that time obtained some valuable information concerning the construction of the new type of Zeppelin. To confirm his statement, the spy revealed the exact whereabouts of the various airship commanders during his stay in Friedrichshafen. Böcker himself had, on a certain afternoon from 3.15 to 4.00 o'clock, dined at a table in the Bayerischen Hof at Lindau and had discussed with his First Officer the advisability of equipping the airship with new armament. The man had been eavesdropping from an adjacent table. The account was correct in every detail; we were entirely too naïve regarding the possibility of a bold espionage.

Thus, of the three new naval airships, only the L 31 returned to the Nordholz naval air station after the raid on London. The commander of the squadron, Lieutenant-Commander Mathy, could not be consoled in his grief for his fallen comrades. On the very next night, he raided Portsmouth, and a week later he set out for England with a fleet of ten airships. It was at the beginning of October, the visibility was poor and the weather was scarcely favourable, so the other commanders confined themselves to central England. Mathy parted from them in order to raid London, the grave of his comrades. His heavy bombs, each of which weighed 600 pounds, destroyed 300 houses in the northern part of the city. But near Potter's Field, exactly where the L 21 had gone down one month before, the L 31 was bracketed by 'Archies' and badly damaged. Crippled and out of control, it hung over the sea of houses as an English flier, Lieutenant Tempest, dove down from an altitude of 16,500 feet and shot it into flames. The burning ship broke into three parts which fell miles apart from each other. The commander and the entire crew were burned to death. The Royal Air Force buried them with military honours; and the grave of the commander bore the inscription: 'Commander Mathy. Fell in the line of duty, October 1, 1916.'

The squadron attack that night caused England severe losses. In London alone, the number of demolished houses was estimated at 160, the dead at 36, and the injured at 98. A railway station and a factory in the Midlands, a great munitions factory in Lincolnshire, factories for machines, armoured plate, shells and swords in Nottingham and Sheffield, all were damaged or completely wrecked by the heavy bombs from the German airships. Still, we had paid dearly for our success; for we had lost one of our most efficient and courageous airship pilots. The stories of the naval airships L 9, L 13, and L 31 are inextricably interwoven with the name of Heinrich Mathy. Lieutenant-Commander Mathy was brought down on his thirteenth flight against England.

Delighted Patriot (after three days' absence). 'Not much to fear from u-boats if we can grow food at this rate!' *Voice from, above.* 'Please would you throw over our little boy's Zeppelin?' *Punch*, 20 June 1917.

20

October 1916 to October 1917
A Year of Heavy Losses

URING THIS TIME, the weather was not favourable to us. Furthermore, the army airships which were sent out into northern France had to make a comparatively long flight, because they were stationed deep inside Germany in order to be out of the reach of enemy attacks by air. Much of their power was exhausted on the long flights before they could attack such cities as Boulogne, Étaples and Rouen. The navy, on the other hand, received airships of a later type, which, having a gas volume of 55,000 cubic metres, approximated the volume of the LZ 126 which was built for America after the war. With mixed emotions, we who commanded the outmoded army airships saw our naval comrades take off in weather which confined us to our hangars.

My LZ 98 was now stationed at Wildeshausen, near Bremen, far from the other army airships but hard by the naval air base. It thus annoyed me all the more to have to yield to the naval airships, and I therefore called upon my observation car to make up for our weakness. Disregarding its extra weight, we carried the observation car on board with us again. We had improved it considerably, but the steel cable remained a dangerously good conductor of electricity and it was for this reason that we did not use it during thunderstorms.

When we were returning from a raid on Rouen in October, 1916, we got into a thick fog over the coast of Holland. We lowered Gemmingen in the car to determine whether we were over land or sea. Just when I was beginning to fear that our observer would strike bottom, he reported water below him via the telephone, whereupon we took a somewhat more southerly course, until Gemmingen sighted land. We were then able to determine our position and complete the homeward journey without further difficulty.

But even the navy made use of older airships along with the newest types, and this circumstance was the cause of a double loss at a time when we were having great success. During one of the night-attacks on England (of which there were over one hundred), the German air fleet was caught in a heavy November fog. The L 34, Captain Max Dietrich, was just dropping bombs on West Hartlepool when a number of searchlights spotted him. Despite this fact, the artillery fire remained suspiciously weak, and that should have warned the airshipmen. For obviously the anti-aircraft guns were being held back to give the opportunity for an attack by airplanes. And sure enough, my friend Hans Flemming, commander of the L 35, which was flying nearby, soon saw the L 34 take on a reddish glow and burst into flames.[19] The English flier had taken off at the approach of the airship and had succeeded in attacking it with such speed that its machine guns could not hit him. The burning Zeppelin fell into the sea outside the harbour of Hartlepool.

A few hours later another ship of the squadron was shot down. The commander of the L 21, Naval-Lieutenant Frankenberg, after a fruitless search for objectives, had groped around in the fog and remained over enemy territory until just before the break of dawn. A few moments after he had left the English coast near Yarmouth and wirelessed the report of his return, he was attacked by a swarm of English aviators who had pursued him out to sea in the rising sun. The L 21, built in 1915, could not repulse airplanes constructed late in 1916, and thus fell a prey to their incendiary bullets.

At that time, the Imperial Navy suffered a series of additional losses. The L 36, under Commander Schütze, returning from a scouting flight in a thick fog, crashed to earth near home. The L 39, under Lieutenant-Commander Koch, was returning with four other Zeppelins after a raid on England and had to detour around a veritable deluge. The ship was driven southwards by the hurricane and finally arrived, of all places, over the French Headquarters at Compiègne, where, under the concentrated fire, it came down in flames no more than fifty yards from the German front.

The other four commanders reached Germany, but they had considerable difficulty in bringing their ships into the hangars during the furious storm. Captain Flemming, commander of the L 55, decided to fly 250 miles to Dresden, and landed his ship there with minor damages. The L 22 under my namesake, Lehmann, and the L 43, under Kraushaar, did not return from the scouting flight along the coast of Holland, and Strasser assumed from this that they had been surprised at low altitudes by English fliers. Actually, the L 22 was shot down by Commander Galpin. The Commander of the Airship Division thereupon prescribed a minimum altitude for all airships while flying over this territory.

One of the few people to live through a successful air attack on a Zeppelin is Naval-Lieutenant Otto Mieth.[20] He was the Bombing Officer on the L 48, a new ship of 55,800 cubic-metre capacity, when this ship, together with the L 42, under Commander Jahn, attacked London on 17 June 1917. On this flight the airship was piloted by Lieutenant-Commander Eichler; but Schütze, the former commander, was likewise on board. The L 42 succeeded in blowing up a munitions dump near Ramsgate. The L 48 was spotted by some twenty searchlights near Harwich, and the air around it was instantly filled with whistling shells, shrapnel and incendiary bullets. But the ship was not hit, and it dropped its bombs according to plan and departed from the zone of fire.

Crew of the L 39. This Zeppelin was destroyed by French ant-aircraft fire near Compiègne on 17 March 1917.

The firing grew weaker and weaker, the searchlights were out one after another, and the crew of the L 48 breathed with relief. Far behind them glowed the fires caused by their bombs; and the airship was already heading out to sea. Just then, it was found that the compass had failed. Instead of heading for the east, they had been going north, and valuable time had been lost. Furthermore, one of the forward motors had stopped, and the speed of the ship was retarded. Then, no sooner had the wireless operator sent out the report of the successful raid, than the ray of a single searchlight flared up and struck full on the hull of the ship.

A few moments later, the sentry on the upper platform reported 'Fire in the stern!' Mieth leaned out of the control car, looked backwards, and saw a reddish flame creeping toward him. He turned to the commander; but it was no longer necessary to report. Commander Schütze himself knew the meaning of that red glow; without losing his composure he said in a calm voice, 'Well, it's all over.'

The engines were still running, and the men in the engine car called through the speaking tube to ask whether to shut them off. The commander smiled bitterly; brave fellows, but it didn't make much difference now. The fire rolled forward from the stern, reached hungrily for the men fleeing through the walkway, swept on to the forepart of the ship and folded over the control car like a purple canopy. Black smoke filled the narrow space around the control stand and threatened to choke the men. One of them remembered the regulations on board ship and grumbled angrily to himself, 'No smoking allowed!'

The L 48 held an even keel for a few seconds, a flaming ball 10,000 feet above the silent English city. Then it broke asunder and fell stern foremost to

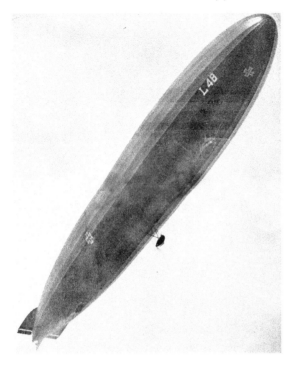

LZ 95 (L 48). As part of an attempted attack on London with three others L 48 became lost and was intercepted and destroyed by British fighters over sea near Great Yarmouth on 17 June 1917 crashing near Leiston. Three survivors; crew buried at Theberton, Suffolk

the earth. In the control car the men rolled about helplessly. Mieth remained in the wireless room until the blazing mass crashed into the earth with a terrific noise. He awoke in an English hospital, with a friendly voice asking, 'Do you want a cigarette?'

Then he was told that an English pursuit flier had approached the ship unobserved and shot a down. In the crash, the control car struck a tree and the wireless room was torn off. The radio mate's neck was broken, but Lieutenant Mieth got off with broken legs. Two other members of the crew were also rescued from the blazing ruins. One of them, Chief Machinist Ellerkamm, had fled up into the framework and, when he was thrown out, had extinguished his blazing clothing by rolling on the ground. The third man died of his severe burns.

When the English discovered how easily an airship could be shot down with incendiary bullets they introduced this method to the combats over the sea as well. Amphibians and flying boats were not dangerous for Zeppelins because it lay within the airship commander's power to stay beyond their reach. Therefore, the English fitted out airplane carriers, from whose runways fleet land-planes took off the moment an airship appeared.

Our navy entered the fourth year of the war with thirteen Zeppelins. On a beautiful summer morning, Lieutenant-Commander Dinter, who was on patrol with the L 23 off the Danish coast, sighted an enemy flotilla of light cruisers. He followed them at a moderate height and tried to discover their intentions.

He did not know that a combat plane of the latest type was on the fore-deck of one of the cruisers, and he did not see it take off because the air was hazy and the distance was too great. But after the L 23 had observed the English flotilla for about an hour, the tiny land-plane suddenly dove down upon it from the clouds, and a few minutes later only a few oil-spots and bubbles on the surface of the sea told the story of an airship destroyed by fire and water.[21]

The most unlucky day for our naval air fleet, however, was to be the 19 October 1917. In the morning, an order arrived from the Commander of the Airship Force. 'Prepare for raid. Take off at 12 noon. Details after completion of morning reports.' After a few bad weeks, the weather seemed favourable; all weather stations unanimously reported south-westerly to westerly winds at high altitudes. Only Bruges, the most westerly, and therefore the most important, weather station had not reported. As objectives, Strasser's orders had designated central England. The ships chosen to participate were: the L 45 (Commander Koelle) and L 54 (Baron von Buttlar) from the Tondern air field; the L 42 (Jahn), L 51 (Dose), and L 53 (Prölss) from Nordholz; the L 41 (Mauser), L 44 (Stabbert), L 46 (Hollender), L 47 (von Freudenreich), L 50 (Schwonder), and L 55 (Flemming) from Ahlhorn; and the L 49 (Gayer) and L 52 (Friemel) from Wittmundshaven.

Precisely at twelve noon, eleven German airships left their hangars and took off for England. The L 42 and L 51 could not leave the hangar at Ahlhorn because of the cross-winds. At about 6.30, at an altitude of 13,500 feet, the eastern coast came into view; and at the same moment, there were flashes from below. The enemy coastguard ships had discovered the approaching air squadron. The Zeppelins went up to 16,500 feet and crossed the coast-line. The first bombs fell near the mouth of the Humber. In reply, the searchlights flared up and the 'Archies' began to bark furiously. The raiders separated to attack the various objectives: Hull, Grimsby, and Sheffield.

Daylight had vanished, the moon had not yet come up, clouds obscured the visibility, and wireless messages from all the ships urgently requested reports of positions. Widely separated, the great grey bomb-carriers cruised over the island; and wherever the industrial centres were betrayed by lights or smoking chimneys, the explosions could be heard.

Individual ships cruising about uncertainly, happened to strike London. From an altitude of 21,000 feet, the L 45, under Waldemar Koelle, dropped its bombs on docks and factories. While the searchlights and combat planes searched the darkness for the invisible raiders, the L 45 drifted before a rising north-west storm and went out over the Channel, where the sole guiding points were the chain of searchlights to the north and the red flashes of the artillery battle in Flanders. The storm increased to a strength of 60 miles per hour; the Maybach motors were barely able to withstand it. The airship seemed to be nailed to the black sky. They descended then, hoping that the wind down below would be a little weaker.

Punch 27 June 1917.

LZ 100 (L 53) has the distinction of being the last Zeppelin destroyed in the war. It was intercepted and destroyed by a Sopwith Camel flown by Lt Culley RAF, who took off from a lighter towed by the destroyer HMS *Redoubt*, on 11 August 1918.

And then rocket-flares shot up from the patrol boats and destroyers, urging the combat-fliers upon the cornered prey. This danger forced the airshipmen to ascend to 20,000 feet. It was three in the morning, and for eight hours they had been on duty in the thin, icy air. The apparatus supplying their gasping lungs with liquid oxygen had been exhausted or was out of order, and the reserve bottles were of scant help. With frozen fingers, the mechanics fretted over the balking motors.

The main body of the airships found air-currents which made the homeward journey possible; but five ships drifted off toward France. The wireless communication with their home stations had long ago been severed. Now, the day broke and revealed them pitilessly to the enemy. A combat plane pursued the L 55 to 25,300 feet, forcing its commander, Lieutenant-Commander Flemming, involuntarily to establish an altitude record for naval airships. Blood ran from the ears, mouths and noses of the airshipmen; and vertigo attacked them one after the other. The water ballast in the emergency ballast bags turned to ice, and even the cooling water turned to ice in spite of the addition of alcohol. The gasoline supply was threatened. In vain Flemming attempted to reach the Ahlhorn air base by dropping all ballast and fuel. He had to make a forced landing near Tiefenort on the Werra; and the ship was lost.

Another vessel of the squadron, the L 44 under Stabbert, was brought down by planes near Lunéville while attempting to cross the enemy lines. The L 45, L 49 and L 50 remained over France at an altitude of 20,000 feet until their gasoline was exhausted. At eight in the morning, Koelle saw the city of Lyons at the junction of the Rhône and the Saône Rivers beneath him. He was still undecided whether to try to reach Switzerland, whose snow-topped mountains gleamed alluringly in the distance, or to drift southward and attempt to make Spain. Just then the Chief Machinist stumbled into the control car, reeling with exhaustion, and reported that the supply of gasoline would last only for another hour.

Heavy of heart, but conscious of his responsibility toward the sixteen men entrusted to his care, Koelle gave the order to descend. The L 45 sank slowly into the valley of the Durance. A small tributary, the Buëch, was almost dry and the receding water had exposed a number of small sandy islands. Toward these the tired helmsman set his course. The Watch Officer hurried from man to man, warning them under no circumstances to leave the ship until they received the order to do so. The gas valves were opened, the ship sank heavily to the sand-bank, breaking the gondola supports and bringing the envelope down over the men. The drag anchor was thrown overboard, and some of the men slashed the gas-cells while others destroyed the motors with their hammers.

A gust of wind gripped the wrecked ship from the port side and shoved it into the river, where a wing car was torn away by the boulders. With the remaining gondola, the hull rose and drifted another fifty yards. Then, as if she had thought better of it, the ship sank again and plumped down on another sand-bank. Only then did Koelle give the order to abandon ship. The crew acted as a landing party, commanded by the Watch Officer; the drag chain was pulled forward; and the monster bucked a few times and then lay still.

The commander and his helmsman were the last to leave the ship. Stationing himself at the stern, the helmsman aimed his rocket-pistol directly at the point where the bellying cells indicated the presence of gas. The green light hissed into the envelope, and, after a moment of breathless suspense, the flames tongued up, white smoke arose, and the L 45 blazed from stem to stern.

Nacelle rear of the army airship LZ 83 (LZ 113). It was launched on 22 February 1917 and survived 15 reconnaissance missions around the Eastern Front and the Baltic Sea; and joined in on three attacks dropping a total of 6,000 kilograms of bombs. In 1920 ordered to be transferred to France as part of war reparations.

Meanwhile, some country folk had gathered on both shores and silently watched the proceedings. Gendarmes on bicycles came up, automobiles roared, and a troop of Alpine Chasseurs arrived on the double-quick. The blazing ship reared up and struck against the rocks of the opposite shore. The commander expressed his gratitude to the members of the crew and they lifted him to their shoulders and waded across the river with him. Then, the awestruck crowd came to life, shouting threats and curses, and a few gendarmes and soldiers fired into the air. The seventeen Germans, so exhausted that they could hardly stay on their feet, shrugged their shoulders and surrendered.[22]

The fate of the L 49 was similar to that of its sister-ship. Only the crew had no opportunity to ignite their vessel, for they were instantly overpowered. The French captured the Zeppelin and later had all its details copied. The resulting design was later made available to the Americans, who used it in the construction of the naval airship *Shenandoah*.

The L 50 held out the longest. The airship cruised southward to Paris and then took an eastern course toward the French Alps. The crew hoped to reach Switzerland. They had already been in the air for twenty-four hours, at least ten of which had been spent at great altitudes, where they were obliged to make use of their oxygen tanks. The nervous tension and the extreme cold had rendered some of them almost helpless, and when the mechanics in the

LZ 96 (L 49) was forced to land near Bourbonne-les-Bains on 20 October 1917 and was captured almost undamaged by French forces. The design of LZ 96 influenced the design of the first American rigid airship, the USS *Shenandoah* (ZR-1) and the British R 38.

engine cars had exhausted their supply of oxygen, they simply lay there half unconscious while the engines ran untended. The officers and helmsmen in the control car economized on oxygen as much as possible, but they were consequently scarcely able to turn the rudder wheel. When a man suddenly remembered that there was a reserve cylinder of oxygen lying in the walkway, there was no longer anyone with enough strength to climb up the short ladder from the control car to get it.

Too exhausted to move or to eat the frozen provisions, the men let the ship drift along with running motors. At Dommartin it crashed against a mountain-peak. The mechanics in the motor gondolas were either unconscious or already dead, and the engines could not be stopped or reversed. The crash tore the control car and the aft engine gondola from the body of the ship. When the men, thus unexpectedly saved, extricated themselves from the wrecked gondolas, they saw the ship disappearing in the distance. The north wind drove the L 50 like a free balloon over the icy Alps. Again the ship struck a mountainside, and again it tore free and careened onward. Perhaps it went down in the Mediterranean. Nothing more was ever seen or heard of it.[23]

Bomb damage in Hull.

21

Zeppelins Cease Active Military Duty

AT JUST ABOUT this time, November 1916, I received orders to deliver the LZ 98 from the Wildeshaufen air base near Bremen to the newly constructed aerodrome at Kovno. The order was urgent. Russia was seething; two years of war had shaken the throne of the Tsar and a feeble push would overthrow him. That, we hoped, would relieve the Central Powers from military pressure in the east. And we were to give the deciding push; we were ordered to advance against Petersburg.

This mission brought us face to face with many difficult problems. The direct distance to Petersburg was 1,125 miles and could, of course, be covered by the LZ 98. But at least two-thirds of the route was over enemy territory, and even the longest night was not long enough to protect us all the way. Over the enemy positions, or the Russian part of the Baltic, we would inevitably strike daylight, and we would then require clouds to shield us. But clouds in this vicinity generally denoted adverse weather conditions and westerly winds which would hinder our return flight. A moderate east wind would have been ideal for our purposes, but this was generally accompanied by clear skies. Furthermore, we had to contend with Russian winter weather, which might even freeze our fuel. And since we had to carry sufficient bombs and ballast and our gasoline was closely calculated, every change in the weather placed us in danger of not being able to reach our own lines again.

At the beginning of December we made a practise flight to Mitau, on the route to Petersburg. We had been informed that the Russian army stationed in the swamps of this territory were unusually careless. We started from Kovno in the early forenoon in order to get over the lines right after nightfall. It was terribly cold, but we were more than satisfied, for the low temperature enabled us to take on a larger supply of gasoline. Nevertheless, we economized by flying with two engines. Half an hour later, I saw from the weather reports that a bad storm was coming up behind us. So we put about. A few days later, under the same conditions, we had to turn back again, for we always received our weather reports *after* the take-off. Then, because I could obtain the reports earlier there,

I flew the LZ 98 to the new naval hangar at Wainoden, in what is now Estonia. There, besides our own weather reports, we intercepted many of the Russians', whose code messages were always easily deciphered no matter how often they changed them. Even so, we got into bad weather again on the third attempt.

Worse luck befell the L 38, which was on the same mission. Commander Martin Dietrich, although he was just completing a long reconnaissance flight over the Baltic, impulsively decided to make a detour on the homeward journey and attack Petersburg. But south of Finland, an unexpected snowstorm covered the envelope with a thick layer of ice. That, in itself, would not have been dangerous, but they were forced to counteract the additional weight by an increase in motor power. Even then the fuel would have sufficed if the L 38 had not struck another snowstorm just two hours before reaching its hangar. The ship battled the storm and ice until the indicator on the sole remaining gasoline tank was almost at the zero mark. Then the commander determined at least to save his men. Slowly and majestically, as if only permitting herself a breathing spell, the L 38 came down in a field, without injuring any of the men. They attempted to hold the ship fast, but the storm struck it again and again, pounding it down on the frozen earth until it was completely wrecked.

The raid on Petersburg was postponed, and I surrendered the command of the LZ 98 to young Baron Joachim von Gemmingen, my comrade's nephew, who had been my First Officer at Wildeshausen. At Friedrichshafen, his uncle and I took over the newly built LZ 120, which was equipped with improved Maybach Motors, was built in streamline form and, although considerably more efficient, was lighter than the ships hitherto constructed. At Jüterbog, before taking the LZ 120 out against Petersburg, I experimented with a new type of radio-compass which enabled the ship to take its bearings by radio signals from land stations without betraying her own position. This method of taking bearings from the ship has been introduced everywhere today. In March, 1917, when we were again in Kovno loading the LZ 120 with seven tons of bombs destined for Petersburg, the Russian revolution broke out, thus forcing us to abandon our plan.

All in all, the role of the airship as a military weapon was over at this time. The development of air forces and defence batteries rendered it less and less useful over land, and it was replaced by the giant plane carrying heavy loads of bombs over the enemy positions at night. On 16 February 1917, the LZ 107 (Commander Rheinstrom), the last airship in the army service, raided Boulogne and made use of its observation gondola. Thereafter, all the army airships were dismantled with the exception of four, which the navy retained for patrol duty over the Baltic. My LZ 120 was one of these four.

Seerappen, near Königsberg, where the LZ 120 was stationed, was the home port of the Baltic Air Force. It was our duty to make daily flights to determine whether enemy forces were on the Baltic, to watch the Anglo-Russian submarine base in Finnish waters, and to search for mines and commercial ships off the coast of Sweden. Each ship was on duty for twenty-four hours before being relieved. But there were no really war-like incidents. One day, Prince Henry of Prussia, the Kaiser's brother, visited me on board and inspected the ship. Later, we sat at the window, looking at the sky and the deep blue sea as if we were on a pleasure cruise in peace-time. The quiet of the Baltic service also permitted us to make the control car and the crew's quarters more comfortable; we now had wicker chairs, pictures, tablecloths and sometimes even fresh flowers on board. And we utilized this period of calm by making all sorts of experiments. We improved the radio set and practised nautical astronomy as if it were a sport. And we spent many hours practising landing on the water. For this purpose, we waterproofed the gondolas, obtained life boats, and tested contrivances for producing water-ballast directly from the sea.

One night the conversation in the officers' mess turned on the question of whether it was not more advantageous from the military standpoint for an airship to remain out on patrol for a longer time—for instance, for a hundred hours or more. The hovering capacity of an airship is theoretically unlimited, but there were some doubts that the motors and crew could endure such a prolonged strain. Though the question popped up again and again, it remained unanswered, for no such endurance flight had ever before been attempted. Then, I decided to settle the matter, and within two days had equipped the LZ 120 for the test. After we had taken aboard 2,640 pounds of bombs; 6,160 pounds of arms, provisions and spare parts; and about 7,700 pounds of water-ballast, I found that, counting the crew of thirty men at about 5,500 pounds, we could still take on 37,000 pounds of gasoline and oil, which would be sufficient to run the motors, at reduced speed, for at least a hundred hours.

The crew consisted of six officers (myself as commander, Baron von Gemmingen as Observer, Lieutenant Schehl as First Officer, Lieutenant Buzilowsky as Chief Engineer, Lieutenant Bischof as Second Officer, and Lieutenant Bügel as Third Officer), four helmsmen, two radio operators, two Chief Mechanics, thirteen mechanics, two machine gunners and Professor Pohl, who was to take bearings with our new, suspended radio-compass antenna.

On 26 July 1917, a few minutes before midnight, we took off from Seerappen. The sky was full of stars, and the night was wonderful—but not for us. For with every foot we ascended, the air became warmer and the lift of our fully-loaded ship was correspondingly reduced; and although the motors were revving at top speed, we did not know whether, without loss of ballast, we could get over the flat hills encircling the airfield. We succeeded, but when we passed over the summit, we were not very high above the houses.

When we reached the open sea, I divided the mechanics into four shifts, and the rest of the crew into two shifts. Of the six motors, we used only three or, at most, four. The men who were off duty were sent to bed, but they retired only under protest, for everyone was anxious to know whether our attempt would succeed. During the first two days, the men on duty were relieved every eight hours and then rested for eight hours. On the following two days, I tried four-hour and then six-hour shifts. All of these methods proved to be practical.

Every man on board had been allotted his provisions for the duration of the flight. The rations consisted of potatoes, bread and bologna, a few hard-boiled eggs, bars of chocolate, and some pastry and biscuits. On the first day, however, we had hot frankfurters, a large kettle of pea-soup, and tea and coffee. There was no kitchen on board, but we had two ranges which were heated by the engines, and the control car was equipped with an electric stove on which we poached eggs and warmed coffee.

We cruised over the entire Baltic, in sunshine and rain, day and night. One of the motors ran so irregularly and with such vibration that the flange connecting bolts on the driving-shaft were neatly shorn off. Twice I had to stop and open the panel of the ship's hull to permit our Chief Machinist Grözinger, and his comrade Hölzemann, to climb out on the propeller block. With nothing under them but empty space, they slid to the end of the shaft and put new screws in.

On the afternoon of 29 July, when we were off the northern point of Oland Island, one of our lookouts thought he saw a submarine lying in the shoal water. We put about, but we found nothing. On the next day we sighted a number of sailing vessels off the south-eastern coast of Sweden. And later on, spying a number of wooden spars, we dropped four practise bombs and scored a direct hit on one of them.

But that was the only military action which interrupted the nirvana of our world-record flight. By removing the partitions, we had transformed the control car into one large room and furnished it as a mess-hall for eight men, complete with table, chairs and sofas. There were no radio concerts in those days, but I had a guitar, and others had harmonicas or music boxes. We played and sang whenever we were off duty; and the good-natured giant continued to carry us gently onward. At night we slept in our hammocks, Gemmingen forward in the quietest spot, and I close to the ladder leading down to the control car so that I could get down quickly in an emergency. Amid the anchor gear in the fore of the walkway, we had even installed a bathroom. There, every morning, I took a shower bath by standing in my rubber tub and pouring a bucket of water over my head. We were also able to take sun-baths when there was sun. The machine gun post in the stern of the ship was an ideal place for it. There it was calm and quiet, and even the thunder of the motors was heard only as a feeble hum. The platform on the top of the ship was equally recommendable for sun-baths except that the headwinds whistled through the windshield.

We were in constant wireless communication with the mainland, and we regularly received all the weather reports, so that we could prepare our own weather chart four times a day. Near the end of the flight, it became apparent that a storm-centre was approaching. And on the last night, just as I was reading the last of the five books that comprised our library, the ship began to rock slightly, and the Watch Officer reported strong freshening winds. After the strain of such an endurance flight, I did not want to fly the LZ 120 through a bad storm, and therefore turned full speed for Seerappen. At 4.40 on the morning of 31 July, the landing buffers again touched solid earth, exactly 101 hours after the take-off. We had used 34,750 pounds of gasoline and oil, and we landed with a useful load of 11,880 pounds which, converted into gasoline, would have made possible another thirty-three hours of flight. This successful attempt served to encourage another endurance flight which took place a few months later, and which deserves a position of honour in the annals of the World War.

22

ZEPPELINS IN THE BALKANS

T HE FAMOUS FLIGHT of the L 59, of which I am about to tell, takes us to another theatre of war: the Balkans. As early as the second year of the war, the Germans had established in the city of Timişoara an airship base complete with hangar, storehouses, wireless station and gas works; and it was from this point that the LZ 81, under Commander Jacobi, transported the German diplomats via Serbia to our Bulgarian allies at Sofia. At the beginning of 1916, the LZ 81 was replaced by the LZ 85. Its commander was Captain Scherzer, who had succeeded me in command of the *Sachsen* during Hindenburg's summer campaign against the Russians; and its First Officer was Lieutenant Nippe, formerly my wireless operator, who had also been my Bombing Officer on the *Sachsen* during flights over Belgium. Scherzer had as much luck as skill. He navigated the LZ 85 over the entire Balkans, and he once bombed the docks and warehouses of Thessaloniki, with such effect that his German comrades could still observe wide-spread fires for days afterward. And eighteen hours after the take-off, Scherzer was back in Timişoara, and the LZ 85 had not received a single scratch.

But Scherzer was not satisfied. He took out his maps and found that he could carry more bombs and less gasoline if, on the return flight, he made a detour over Bulgaria and a stop-over in Sofia. Thus when, on 17 March he attacked Thessaloniki for the second time, the damage he did was correspondingly greater, but since the thick clouds forced him to lower altitudes, his vessel was struck by shrapnel. In Sofia, where he made his stop-over, he could not procure sufficient hydrogen to replace the loss. Resolutely, Scherzer dismantled two of his four motors and had them sent back by train with the larger portion of his crew. He himself sailed the ship back to Timişoara.

Meanwhile, the German army was pressing far to the south, and Thessaloniki was attacked by our fliers so often that the Allies established an extensive defence system there. And when, on the night of 5 May 1916, the LZ 85 again appeared over the harbour, it was instantly spotted by a number of searchlights. I do not know at what altitude the ship was flying, but I know that Scherzer never flew high. Within a few minutes, the LZ 85 was so shredded by shells from the anti-aircraft batteries that its life's blood, its buoyant gas, was spurting from the cells. The ship rapidly lost altitude, and Scherzer could no longer make the German lines, which were only a few miles to the north. He was obliged to land in the middle of the swampland near the Vardar River.

The entire crew escaped uninjured from the ship, and they determined to fight their way through to the German lines. For days they waded from one swamp to another in their efforts to elude the enemy detachments. But the wrecked airship was too conspicuous, and it betrayed their whereabouts. Once found, the trail of the fugitives could not be lost again. Scherzer and his men were surrounded and though they defended themselves desperately they were eventually forced to surrender. I saw a few of them to speak to after the armistice when they were released from a French prison camp.

Towards the end of 1915, a second airship base, with a large hangar, a gas-works, an electricity plant and a wireless station, was erected in Yambol, on Bulgarian soil. This was done to defend Constantinople from possible attacks by the Russian Fleet in the Black Sea, to convoy the transports to the Turkish capital, and to guard the shipping lanes between Constantinople and Constanţa. This air station, no less than various others in the larger cities, was equipped with a radio compass; and after the defeat of Rumania, Bucharest was also supplied with such an apparatus.

At that time, the German Army Command already conceded Rumania's entrance into the World War and they were determined to anticipate her. Even before that, Yambol had served as the home base of the airships supporting our armoured cruisers *Göben* and *Breslau*, which had been taken into the Turkish fleet to compensate for the superiority in numbers of the Russian scouts and destroyers. In cooperation with the Turkish Battle Fleet, our airships searched the Bosphorus for Russian mine-fields and took part in raids which led them as far as Sebastopol and Batum.

The country town of Yambol lies well-situated in the valley of the Tundzha River; invariably the wind blew in the direction of the airship hangar. But our men were plagued by the gnats which gave many of them malaria; and the summer heat, which sometimes went as high as 105 (Fahrenheit) in the shade, was unbearable. Furthermore, they had difficulty in conversing with the Turkish and Bulgarian officials. For instance, it required a great deal of effort to induce the officials to expedite the delivery of our telegraphic weather reports, or even to deliver them at all. Even the code-word 'Osman,' which was used for the weather dispatches, was sometimes misunderstood. The telegram would come back with the notation: 'Addressee Osman Pascha not found.'

The first of our airship commanders to become acquainted with the Balkans was Commander von Wobeser. His vessel was the SL 10, one of those rigid airships of wooden construction which were built by Privy Councillor Schütte

at the Lanz Docks in Rheinau. With an overall length of 575 feet and a diameter
of 65 feet, it contained 38,800 cubic metres of hydrogen, carried 21 tons of
useful load including the 20-man crew, and attained a speed of 55 miles per
hour. In the midday heat of 2 July 1916, the SL 10 took off to lend a hand to a
German submarine lying off Sebastopol. The wind tore the ship away from the
ground crew, but Wobeser regained control and, despite defects in the wireless
apparatus and the two motors, set course for the Crimea, and returned to
Yambol on the next morning.

On 27 July, Wobeser prepared for a raid on the Crimean fortress of Sebastopol.
In order to take more bombs with him, he limited the crew to two officers,
three Chief Machinists, eight mechanics, two helmsmen and a radio non-com.
None of these seventeen men was to see his comrades again. When the SL 10
had not returned by the afternoon of 28 July, and no wireless report arrived
from it, the Varna air station sent out three amphibians to search for the lost
airship. But the search remained fruitless. A wireless message of unknown origin,
which was intercepted in a garbled form, mentioned a storm of 70 mph. It is
quite possible that the ship was caught in an electrical storm and lightning set
the wooden frame afire. A gasoline tank drifted to a beach on the south-west
coast of the Black Sea, and the body of the mechanic, Dahl, was washed ashore
on the Bulgarian coast on 1 September.

The LZ 101, under Commander Gaissert, replaced the ill-fated Schütte-Lanz.
This duralumin ship was more elongated than the streamlined form of the wooden
ship, and it was a bit speedier, covering the route from Bonn to Timișoara in
seventeen hours, and arriving in Yambol on the next day. A few weeks later, on
27 August 1916, Rumania declared war on the Central Powers; and on the very
same night, when the Rumanian troops were marching through the streets of
Bucharest, Gaissert flew over from Yambol and gave them their first foretaste of
the meaning of war. The black smoke from the petroleum refineries of Giurgiu,
which had been shot into flames by the Danube fleet, showed him the way; and
although the capital itself was darkened, a careless searchlight betrayed it when the
LZ 101 was flying overhead at 11,500 feet. Gaissert thanked them by unloading
one and a half tons of bombs over the military camp and the railway station.
Instantly, fifteen searchlights flared up, their rays groping toward the airship and
brightly illuminating the control car. Headwinds kept the ship in the same spot
as if it were anchored there, and it thus was a fine target for the anti-aircraft
batteries. The incendiary rockets were coming ominously close before Gaissert
moved away. Even the soldiers and policemen on the streets below were firing their
rifles and pistols at the enormous target. The Bombing Officer, however, proved
that he had better aim by dropping a heavy bomb on the Police Barracks and
sending it flying high into the air. Gaissert's daring exploit completely disrupted
the mobilization plans drawn up by the Rumanians; and during the next few
days, German planes completed the work begun so promptly by the LZ 101.

In September, Gaissert repeated his visit to Bucharest two more times and bombarded other important railway junctions, notably the station at Ploieşti. Under Lieutenant Wolff, the LZ 86, which replaced Scherzer at Timişoara, also attacked Ploieşti, but was completely wrecked during the return on the morning of 5 September. Wolff landed outside the airship base on difficult terrain, and tailwinds caused a crash that cost many of his men their lives.

The vacancy was filled by the LZ 81. Its commander, Captain Barth, followed in Gaissert's footsteps and bombarded Bucharest, which had meanwhile developed its air defence to a considerable degree. During the second raid, on 27 September 1916, the LZ 81 was spotted by a searchlight when it was at an altitude of 12,500 feet, and the batteries got the range. Though a hail of shells whistled around the Zeppelin, Barth grimly continued his bombardment. Meticulously he dropped his bombs on the objectives marked on his map. But when he left the zone of fire he found that the ship was leaking too badly to permit the return to Timişoara. He landed near Tulovo, in Bulgaria, where the lack of a ground crew forced him to have the ship dismantled. If an emergency troop with repair parts and gas had been stationed at the airfield for such cases, they would have been able to salvage not only the LZ 81 but many other ships as well.

After the loss of the LZ 81, the LZ 97 was sent to Timişoara, where it continued the raids together with the LZ 101, which was still at Yambol. Both ships bombarded the railway junctions of Ciulniţa and Feteşti; and they undertook their last attack on Bucharest in October 1916, shortly before the German army took possession of the city. Within three months after its alliance with the enemy, Rumania was in such a bad shape that there were few worthwhile objectives left for the Zeppelins to attack. Late in December, the LZ 101 raided the harbour and railway station of Galaţi; and at the beginning of 1917, our Zeppelins were obliged to apply themselves to new and more difficult tasks.

From its base in Hungary, the LZ 97 was ordered to raid the Italian harbours of Vlorë, (Albania), Brindisi, and Taranto; while the LZ 101, from Yambol, was to attack the English bases in the Aegean Sea, the islands of Lesbos, Lemnos and Imbros. Both ships were considerably hampered by the unfavourable weather conditions and the low clouds which generally hang over the Balkans during the winter. Consequently, the five distance flights and the other sorties which the LZ 97 made against Italy were navigational but not military successes. On a clear March night, when landmarks were visible at a distance of fifty miles, the LZ 101 raided the English base on the island of Mudros, destroying the docks and warehouses and returning with only a few tears in some of the gas cells.[24] And in April 1917, both Zeppelins were deflated for a thorough overhauling, and later were ordered back to Germany. The army did not require any more Zeppelins; and the hangars in the Balkans were occupied by naval airships.

23

L 59 TO AFRICA AND BACK AGAIN

Professor Dr Zupitza, Chief Staff Surgeon of the German Colonial Troops, who had been captured in Togo and exchanged during 1916, had learned that Lettow-Vorbeck's troops in our last remaining colony, German East Africa, were direly in need of medical supplies. It was his suggestion that the Colonial Ministry equip an airship and send it out to the aid of our East Africans, who were cut off from all supply. The Colonial Ministry passed the suggestion on to the Navy Command, which, however, only considered the plan when its practicability was proven by the L 16's provisioning of an ice-bound North Sea island and by my endurance flight with the LZ 120. Thereupon, the expedition to East Africa was approved, and I was entrusted with the preparations for it. I returned to Friedrichshafen for this purpose in September 1917, and there found the L 57 being outfitted for this special mission. Transferred to Jüterbog, the naval airship was loaded with medicaments and munitions for Lettow-Vorbeck and then, during a test-flight, was overtaken by one of the worst storms ever seen at that time of the year. The result was that after the landing, the L 57 could not be returned to its hangar because of the crosswinds, and since the modern methods of anchoring were at that time still unknown, the ship was badly damaged. The wreck was burned to prevent the secret of the planned expedition from becoming known.

Just at that time, at the dockyards in Staaken, near Berlin, a new Zeppelin of 52 tons dead weight and 1,200 horsepower was under construction. Within four days, this vessel, the LZ 104 (Naval number L 59), was enlarged to 68,500 cubic metres. The ship was so constructed that after its landing in East Africa as many as possible of its constituent parts would be suitable for use by our Colonial troops.

Thus, the cotton envelope of the vessel, which had a maximum diameter of 80 feet and was 750 feet long, was to be remade into tents and tropical uniforms. Sleeping-bags were to be cut from the gas-cell material and shirts from the linen partitions. The girders and struts of the duralumin frame were to be converted into portable, collapsible barracks and a wireless tower; the

LZ 104 (L 59). L 59 started out on a mission to resupply German troops in German East Africa, but turned back upon incorrect reports of a German surrender; nevertheless, the ship broke a long-distance flight record (6,757 kilometres) in 95 hours and 5 minutes. L 59 Caught fire and was destroyed during a raid on Malta on 7 April 1918.

five Maybach motors were to serve as motive power for the dynamos. The walkway was made of shoe-leather. And the antenna consisted of three wires each 400 feet long. In addition to its own weight of 65,000 pounds, the L 59 took on at Staaken and Yambol more than fifty tons of useful load, so that, at the take-off, the ship weighed 175,000 pounds. Besides the ship's requirements 48,000 pounds of gasoline, 3,350 pounds of oil, 20,150 pounds of water-ballast, 950 pounds of drinking water, and 1,550 pounds of preserves and other provisions—the cargo destined for General von Lettow-Vorbeck included 311,900 boxes of ammunition, 230 machine gun belts containing 13,500 cartridges, 30 machine guns, 9 spare gun barrels, 4 infantry rifles with 5,000 cartridges, 61 sacks of bandages and medical supplies, 2 hand-operated sewing-machines, 3 sacks of sewing equipment, mail, telescopes, spare gun-locks, bush-knives, and spare parts for the wireless apparatus. The bomb-release mechanism had been dismantled to economize on weight.

The crew consisted of twenty-two men. The commander was Lieutenant-Commander Ludwig Bockholt who at the beginning of the war captured an English fishing boat with the L 23, and later commanded the L 54 and the L 57.[25] As helmsmen, he was assigned Sergeant-Major Grussendorf, one of the Delag pilots, and Helmsman Wald, from the armoured cruiser *Göben*. Lieutenant Mass was Watch Officer, and Chief Staff Surgeon Zupitza made the flight as a guest. The Commissioners of the Imperial Navy Board, Dr Hugo Eckener among them, were on the delivery flight to Yambol. During the war, Eckener had been an advisor to the Commander of Naval Airships, Strasser, and had supervised the training of recruits, and he had been appointed technical advisor for this momentous flight. His genial personality and his intuitive knowledge of the peculiarities of aviation, had already earned him a reputation out of all proportion to his rank.

The crew of the L 59 thought the new airship was entering service in the Baltic region. And only after the ship took off from Staaken did they learn that the next stop was Yambol.

The air-cruiser made a false start on 13 November, but three days later, despite unfavourable weather reports and contrary winds, took off at 8.10 in the morning on its journey. The flight, however, was not under a propitious star. For reasons of secrecy, only a few official stations were informed of it, and so the appearance of an airship of unrecognizable nationality alarmed the Bulgarian port of Burgas. A naval flier cruised over the L 59 and, seeing that it was a German ship, returned and reassured his comrades. But later on the Turkish infantry was less discerning, and they enthusiastically shot at the airship wherever they saw it, boring five round holes in the gas-cells. Unable to bring the heavily laden ship up any higher, Bockholt was relieved when night came on. But then a thunderstorm formed over Akhisar.[26] The stern, its gas-cells leaking, began to sink, and the commander was obliged to give the order for the return. At midnight they passed Constantinople, and during the remainder of the night the L 59 flew through storm clouds. Just after daybreak, Bockholt landed at Yambol. The L 59 had been under way for thirty-two hours and had covered 900 miles.

Not until 20 November did the weather reports again favour the completion of the plan. The weather cleared up, and a ground wind blew from the north-east. In the higher strata there were north and north-east winds of more than 20 mph, giving the L 59 favourable tail-winds. Therefore, Bockholt and Dr Eckener decided upon a take-off the next morning at five o'clock.

The stars were still in the sky when we all gathered in the hangar. The slim airship lay bathed in the pale glow of the arc lights, and we all looked green and pale as corpses. We shook hands vigorously. The thermometer showed 32°, the barometer indicated 30 inches; nothing could have been better for the take-off of the heavily laden ship. Once more the gas hissed through the inflation tubes and into the cells. The motors were tested, warmed, and then turned off. The crew got on board, the ground crew detached the sand bags, and the ship was weighed off. Bockholt stepped out to join Eckener and me. 'Ship ready for take-off!' The whistle blew and the ground crew grasped the rails on the sides of the gondolas. 'Airship march!' We proceeded, and a flag indicated the direction toward which the L 59 was to be turned. Obedient as a good-natured elephant, the grey giant permitted itself to be led out of the hangar and set against the wind. Once more the Watch Officer on board weighed off, water spurted from the ballast tanks, and then the ship was so perfectly trimmed that the weight of one man would have sufficed to unbalance its 1,600 hundredweights. Bockholt shook our hands before he jumped into the control car. 'Haul in!' The hauling lines were unreeved. 'Up!' The bow lifted. The engine telegraph rang. 'Stern engines full speed ahead!' The propellers churned heavily at first, then faster and faster, until they appeared to be shimmering disks. Chief Staff Surgeon Zupitza waved from the control car and Grussendorf operated the helm. 'All engines ahead!' The ghostly form of the L 59 disappeared from view. The small group of German airship men stared mutely after this envoy of the Fatherland which was repaying loyalty with loyalty.

Even today I envy Bockholt and every one of his twenty-one men the rich experience of this flight over three continents, a flight which exceeds in audacity everything that much larger airships, with much stronger engines, have since then accomplished. The aim of the expedition, to bring relief to the German outpost in East Africa, was not achieved, and perhaps could not have been achieved at all. But the moral effect of a brave deed is not measured by success. And that applies to the heroism of our German East Africans who, undefeated, did not lay down their arms until the end of the war, and to the African flight of the L 59, the details of which the German people did not learn until many years afterwards.

After their return, the members of the expedition told the story of the flight, which I here repeat verbatim.

The L 59 first took course over Adrianople, cruised over the Sea of Marmora, and at two in the afternoon hovered 3,300 feet over the picturesque cliffs where, a few days before, it had turned back because of a storm. We were spared the Turkish rifle-bullets this time because all authorities had been informed beforehand. Over Smyrna, we cruised for some time while German planes made scouting flights to determine whether any enemy sea-forces or planes were lying in wait off Chios. But the enemy seemed to suspect nothing and the German airship left the coast of Asia Minor near Miletus, and at ten o'clock was over the island of Crete. The sky glistened suspiciously, and electrical disturbances affected the instruments. The north-east wind stiffened to a storm which soon overtook the ship. Encircled by lightning, the ship ploughed through the rain. Then the lookout cried excitedly through the speaking tube: 'Ship's afire!' Thank God, that was a false alarm; the streams of fire spurting from all the metal parts were St Elmo's fire. An aureole formed around the ship like a colourful wreath.

When the purple sun rose, the L 59 was out of the storm zone. The sun dried the ship and threw our shadow on the surface of the Mediterranean. Africa came into sight. At the gulf of Solum we reached the dark continent. The temperature suddenly rose to 68° (Fahrenheit), and the buoyant gas expanded and escaped through the valves. To equalize the loss of gas, we had to drop a ton of water-ballast. Africa soon proved to be more monotonous than the mobile sea; the endless yellow sand dunes of the Libyan desert ran on and on, only infrequently broken by small lakes from which wild ducks soared up.

The sunlight, reflected from the hot sand, hurt our eyes, and the sight of the Farafrah Oasis, with its gardens, pools and farms, was a blessing in that eternal similarity. Below us, a camel caravan flew apart in fright before the heavenly messenger. In the afternoon, there appeared before us the desert city of Dechel with its mosques and multi-storied stone houses. On the horizon the mountains rose like the towers of a fortress, and behind them flowed the mysterious Nile. Until now, everything had gone well on board, but then the gear-box of the forward propeller broke, and in the wireless compartment the operator began to fret over his receiving apparatus. A rose-red cloud approached from the Nile it was thousands of flamingoes who may have been frightened by the noise of our engines or simply searching for a place to settle for the night. When we crossed the Nile at the second cataract, it was already dark. We navigated by the stars and made a wide circle around Khartoum, for we did not wish to be seen by the English. Even at night, the thermometer showed 95° (Fahrenheit).

The operator was having no more trouble at this time and the receiver was working again. But when the non-com lowered the antenna for a test, he received, on the wavelength previously assigned to us by the German station at Nauen, a terse message from the Admiralty: 'Abandon undertaking and return stop enemy has occupied great part of Makonde highland and is already at Kitaugari stop remainder of troops attacking Portuguese from the south.'

This message had apparently been sent out more than once, and the wireless operator handed it to Mass, who decoded it and sent it on to the commander. Bockholt read it to his officers and placed the decision in their hands. Grussendorf and young Mass, son of a Westphalian preacher, were quite outspoken. If Lettow was in such great distress as the message indicated, then it was their duty to stand by him. But, Zupitza demurred, would they be able to find their compatriots in the infinity of the African bush? They might cruise for days and days, have to make a forced landing in enemy territory and present the enemy with the ship and its valuable cargo. Grussendorf expressed his willingness to bail out with a parachute before the landing and make certain whether they were in friendly or enemy territory. Bockholt shrugged his shoulders; even that would be useless if we were not able to find Lettow-Vorbeck's retreating troops, who had perhaps already crossed into Portuguese territory.

In point of fact, our East Africans were at this time forcing their way across the Ruvuma River. The L 59 had by then covered 2,800 miles, two thirds of the total distance, and if they had continued the flight, the crew would have witnessed the victory which General von Lettow-Vorbeck won from the Portuguese on 25 November 1917. On that day, with a handful of German colonials and black Askaris, he stormed the fortified camp of the Portuguese, of whom scarcely 300 escaped, killing more than two hundred, and capturing the rest.

But Bockholt was too much of a soldier not to obey the Admiralty's orders. Although everyone on board was against the return, emotional reactions carried no weight. The abandonment of the flight was a closed issue, and would very well have remained so even if Bockholt had known that the semi-official English message from the Malta wireless station, which had inspired the order from the German Admiralty, had falsified and exaggerated the situation. Malta itself involuntarily confirmed this fact in a later message intercepted by the L 59 during its return flight over the Mediterranean.

A captured German officer later reported that the English had sent out planes to shoot down the German airship as soon as it appeared over East Africa. We members of the expedition noticed nothing of the sort. Unchallenged, the L 59 turned homeward, slowed by head-winds and once forced down so deeply by an air-pocket that the little leaden weight on the end of the antenna trailed along the ground. We had to drop 11,000 pounds of ballast and cargo to regain altitude. The crate of wine and cognac, which we had wanted to empty with Lettow-Vorbeck, crashed down on the cliffs below us; the munitions exploded when they struck the ground. With great effort, we rose over the mountaintops, and during the night, the temperature fell from 90° to 23°. On the next day we received favourable winds from the stern. At nightfall, flying at an altitude of 6,500 feet, we sighted the searchlights of battleships cruising in the Mediterranean. Again we remained unobserved while crossing the sea. In the early morning of 24 November the European coast appeared upon the horizon. At sunrise, Crete lay below us. Cautiously, the L 59 rose to a 10,000-foot altitude, although it was really cold up there; the thermometer on board showed 27°, and the exhausted men, who had sweated for days in the Africa heat, now froze unmercifully. Over Constantinople, which we passed at ten o'clock at night, Bockholt wirelessed the report of his return. On 25 November 1917, at three o'clock in the morning, the L 59 was once more over Yambol. The wind was blowing cross-wise to the hangar, and we cruised until 8.15, when we were able to land.

Eckener had already left; but the others received us heartily and were delighted that we had come through the great adventure unscathed. Nevertheless there was an undertone of disappointment in their congratulations. Our smooth return was definite proof of the fact that the airship could have fulfilled the test demanded of it. In ninety-five hours of uninterrupted flight, the L 59 had covered 4,225 miles at an average speed of 45 miles per hour, and when we landed at Yambol its tanks still held eleven tons of gasoline and one ton of oil —fuel enough for sixty-four hours of flight and an additional 3,750 miles. The entire route we covered is approximately the distance between Friedrichshafen and Chicago.

Thus, as early as 1917, a German airship had already proved the practicability of international service between definite points.

On 21 December 1933, Karl Schwabe, the only German entrant in the International Egyptian Air Race, made a forced landing in the Dekhla oasis. Scratched on the wooden doors and mud walls of the huts in the desert village, he noticed the outline of a Zeppelin. When he visited the Bedouin sheik; he asked the meaning of those strange drawings, and he learned that they referred to a mighty sign which, as many years ago as there are fingers on both hands and toes on one foot, appeared in the heavens above the desert. The German Zeppelin which flew to Africa had become a legend and, out there in the desert, was worshipped as a harbinger of heavenly good-will.

A lucky escape in Hull; a Zeppelin bomb came through the roof, ceiling and floor without exploding.

24

THE LAST YEAR OF THE WAR

THE LATEST NAVAL Zeppelin, in which I accompanied the Acceptance Board from the dockyards at Friedrichshafen to the naval air station at Nordholz, was docked in the hangar, and I went over to the officers' mess to fortify myself for the return journey by rail. In the mess I met Dr Eckener and Commander Strasser, who was in command of all the naval airships. Strasser was sitting in a corner, thoughtfully playing with the glass of red wine with which he regularly concluded his meal and smoking the strong black cigar without which he was seldom seen off duty. He and Eckener were talking about the problems of the Battle of the Skagerrak, and the fifteen or twenty young officers around the table were listening with rapt attention. The orderly brought the commander a telegram. He read it and then glanced around the table until his eyes rested on one of the airship commanders.

'Prölss.'

'Captain?'

'Please come here. Would you be willing to undertake a 20-hour flight tonight?'

Prölss pulled out his watch. 'I can take off in fifty minutes, Captain.'

'Good, here are your orders.' Strasser handed him the telegram. Prölss read it, handed it back and saluted. 'Aye, aye, sir!' And he left the mess-room to inform his men.

This little scene held nothing new for me; I knew that every one of my comrades had to be prepared for flight at all times. But what I did not know was that Prölss had only two hours ago returned from a nine-hour flight through a heavy fog. His men, who now hurriedly replenished gas and gasoline, yearned for their beds, and their commander had not slept for thirty-six hours; yet they were all to be without sleep for another twenty hours. Not a muscle moved in his face when he received the orders from the Chief, who must certainly have had his reasons for choosing him particularly. In point of fact the Navy Board had expressly asked that one of the most experienced and skilful of the airship commanders be chosen for this mission of protecting a group of submarines engaged in a sortie and divert the attention of the English patrol boats from them. Prölss did not return from this flight until the following night, after he had permitted the English to chase him during the entire forenoon while the submarines got through unobserved along the Norwegian coast.

Such was the spirit behind our marine airships even during the last year of the war. The navy entered the fifth year of the war, 1918, with fourteen Zeppelins. Five days later four of them, the L46, 47, 52, and 58, and the Schütte-Lanz ship, SL 20, were destroyed at one stroke. The airships were lying inactive, and perhaps unguarded as well, in one single and two double hangars at the Ahlhorn naval base, when a number of violent explosions were heard. The officers rushed outside immediately but found only the blazing wrecks of the ships. Bravely, Flemming and von Schiller removed the bombs from their burning vessels. The circumstances of the catastrophe indicated sabotage; both double-hangars were 200 feet apart, and the single hangar was half a mile away from the others. In view of the swift sequence of explosions, a spreading of the fire was out of the question.

The navy instantly commissioned new airships and made all the more energetic use of those which remained. The Africa-ship L 59, was thoroughly overhauled in Friedrichshafen and, in January 1918, returned to Yambol. On 9 March it took off from that point for a raid on Naples. With motors dead, it drifted in the dark over the Albanian Scutari to the Adriatic, remained in the protection of a layer of clouds at an altitude of 6,500 to 10,000 feet over Italy, and at one o'clock on 11 March, was over Naples. The great city at the foot of smoking

Wreckage of airships and warehouses in Ahlhorn after the explosion and possible sabotage on 5 January 1918. Ahlhorn hangars exploded destroying five airships, killing 15 and injuring 134 people.

Vesuvius was brightly illuminated, and apparently had not been warned, when Bockholt, from an altitude of from 12,000 to 16,000 feet, dropped his bombs on the crowded harbour, the Arsenal, and the gas-works.

After the war, I happened to speak to an American officer who was in Naples that night. Frightened from sleep by the droning of the motors, the rattling of machine guns and the roar of the 'Archies,' the people fled panic-stricken into the cellars. Two of my friend's compatriots were riding in an open carriage when the first bomb struck. Horror-stricken, the coachman stopped his horse, jumped from the box, and crept under the wagon. All persuasion was futile; he refused to come out. The Americans had been in air-attacks on London and Paris and they had no intention of walking home. They took the reins and drove the carriage away, leaving the coachman lying face down in the road, numb with fright.

The L 59 dropped the main portion of its bombs over the Bagnoli iron works. Relieved of 14,000 pounds of bombs, the ship made the return flight without incident. The entire flight to the Gulf of Naples lasted twenty-six hours.

A few days later, on 20 March, the German air-cruiser carried the same load to Port Said. As during the African flight, the course was over Asia Minor. Bad weather delayed the L 59 in the Gulf of Adaja,[27] so that it did not reach Africa over Cape Brulus until three o'clock.[28] The delta of the Nile was covered by rain clouds, and stiff east winds prevented the ship from reaching Port Said before daylight. At five o'clock, no more than three sea miles from its destination, the L 59 was obliged to turn back, and spent the day over the Mediterranean in order to bombard Suda Bay, on the island of Crete, after nightfall. Rain squalls had made the ship heavy, and after sundown a snowstorm came up. To lighten the ship, Bockholt had 2,200 pounds of bombs dropped into the sea. Over the island of Serifos, the airship rose to 16,500 feet to avoid searchlights. When the ship came down lower over the Turkish mainland, our over-zealous allies fired at it; but their aim was so bad that they did no damage. Bockholt landed in Yambol after a forty-nine-hour flight. The L 59 had covered 2,400 miles at an average speed of forty-nine miles per hour.

Then the L 59's star sank; and on 17 April 1918, Fate struck. Once more the airship took off with a full bomb load, this time to raid the Malta base of the English Fleet. Naval-Lieutenant Sprender, commander of the German submarine 53 which was trying to break through the Straits of Otranto, sighted an airship at about eight p.m. flying 650 feet above the sea, but he was unable to determine its type or nationality. The submarine avoided an enemy destroyer and, shortly afterward, the Watch Officer noticed a bright light in the southern sky. He distinguished two distinct points of fire, close beside each other. The fire-balls sank, but the light remained visible for another twenty minutes, glowing beyond the dip of the horizon. A dull detonation was heard. At full speed, the U 53 sped fifty-five miles in the direction of the fire and searched the sea off Brindisi in vain. The famous Africa-ship with Bockholt and his loyal men burned and sank. The cause of the mysterious disaster was apparently an explosion on board.

The crash of the L 62, on 10 May 1918, remained equally enigmatic. When I was in Nordholz shortly afterward, I was told that the L 62 had been attacked by an English flying-boat about an hour before the disaster. The bold Englishman came close to Heligoland, was fired upon by destroyers and the airship, and was hit and forced down at sea. The German destroyers sped full speed toward the plane; but even before they came close, one of the fliers climbed out on the front motor and repaired it within a few moments. Before our destroyers knew what was happening, the plucky Englishman lifted his boat from the water and flew away.

It is not very likely that the loss of the L 62 was caused by this flying boat, as the English claim. For the airship was already behind Heligoland, on the return journey, when it burned in the air with its entire crew. Rather it is to be assumed that in this case also the explosion was caused by one of the fuse-caps, which always had to be unscrewed and stowed away while not in use.[29]

Soon after the L 59's African flight, I was ordered to Friedrichshafen to act as liaison officer between the navy and the Zeppelin Company; and the L 62 was one of the four new ships which I delivered to the naval acceptance board at the beginning of 1918. Friedrichshafen was operating at full capacity; at the Zeppelin docks where, at the turn of the century, only Dürr and a few others had been employed, there were now 1,600 technicians and mechanics and 12,000 men and women working in day and night shifts. The new air-cruisers searched the North Sea for mine fields, and two of them raided Hartlepool, where they proved that the English combat fliers were unable to reach their altitude. Strasser knew of this fact, but, wishing to convince himself, set out for England, on 12 April 1918 with five Zeppelins. One of the airships bombarded Birmingham, and another raided Wigan in Lancashire; and once again the English fliers were unable to climb to their altitude. Then the enemy avenged himself.

On 19 July, the airplane carrier *Furious*, convoyed by a fleet of light cruisers, brought a squadron of combat planes to within eighty sea miles of the Tondern airship base. Shortly after three in the morning, three planes, each loaded with two bombs of fifty pounds each, took off and bombed the great double-hangar at Tondern. The first squadron was instantly followed by a second, of four planes, under the command of Captain B. A. Smart, the famous aviator who, as early as August 1917, had brought down the Zeppelin L 23. Undisturbed by the vicious anti-aircraft fire and the fire from machine guns and rifles, he dived down on the next hangar, scored a direct hit with his second bomb, and then returned to the airplane carrier, which he reached with his last drop of gasoline. One of his comrades was shot down, another fell into the sea, and three lost their way and were forced to land near Esbjerg, in Denmark; but the surprise attack was a success, for the L 54 and L 60 were destroyed in their hangars.[30]

The loss was made up by the new type of ship, L 70, which I turned over to the navy in June 1918. This was the fastest airship we built during the war. It was 62,200 cubic metres in capacity, and its seven Maybach motors easily developed a speed of eighty miles per hour. During the test flights it reached almost ninety miles per hour. Lieutenant-Commander Lossnitzer, who had followed me in command of the LZ 120, was appointed commander of the L 70.

Commander Strasser was on board when, on 5 August 1918 the L 70, together with four other Zeppelins, took off for a squadron attack on the munitions factories of England. The L 65 (Commander Dose) and the L 53 (Commander Prölss) reached Cromer shortly before nightfall. As we later learned, the English had assembled a total of thirty-three planes to prevent the approach of the German airships. The L 70 was at 17,300 feet when it was sighted by a plane of the new DH 4 type. The pilot succeeded in climbing just as high as the airship, and then attacked it from the front. A stream of incendiary bullets spurted from its machine gun into the nose of the ship, which instantly caught fire. The wreck fell into the sea near Wells. With the commander and his entire crew, Peter Strasser also was killed. Thus, the airship fleet lost its Commander, a man of great military talent, the very soul of duty. Admiral Scheer, Chief of the High Seas Fleet, honoured him with the words:

Pater Strasser (1876-1918). In September 1913, Strasser took command of the Naval Airship Division (*Marine-Luftschiff-Abteilung*). Airships were as yet an unproven technology and Korvettenkapitän Strasser became the new naval airship chief after his predecessor, Korvettenkapitän Friedrich Metzing, drowned in the crash of the very first naval airship, the L 1.

LZ 112 (L 70) was a tragedy for the German authorities as on its last flight on 5–6 August 1918 it has on board Fregattenkapitän Peter Strasser, Commander of the Navy Airship Department. It was intercepted and destroyed over North Sea by British de Havilland DH-4 flown by Major Egbert Cadbury with Captain Robert Leckie as gunner.

As Commander of Airships, Peter Strasser took the airship, created by Count Zeppelin's inventive genius and grim persistence, and with unfaltering spirit, despite all reversals, moulded it into a formidable offensive weapon. The spirit which, during the many attacks made with this weapon, he inspired and maintained, has now been glorified by a hero's death over England. As the inventor, Count Zeppelin, will live in the memory of a grateful German people, so will Commander Strasser, who led the airships to victory, live, never to be forgotten.

One week later, Prölss was likewise brought down. He had just gone out over the sea with the L 53 when he sighted an English flotilla steaming against the wind under the protection of a smoke screen. Prölss followed it, not knowing that this was precisely what the enemy desired. For the English had built a number of special barges equipped with runways for small fast planes. These barges were towed out into the North Sea as close as possible to the German airship bases and, when an airship appeared, they were set into the wind to enable the fliers to take off. Prölss, who kept a safe distance between his ship and the enemy flotilla, did not see the combat-flier start. The Englishman swiftly climbed to an altitude of 20,000 feet and, by a circuitous route, got between the Zeppelin and the sun. The lookout on the airship's back did not sight the plane until it was diving toward the hull, which was 650 feet long and offered an excellent target for the incendiary bullets. In the next instant, the L 53 caught fire and fell into the sea, a blazing torch.

In Friedrichshafen at that time, the L 71, the first ship of a new series, had just been completed. It was instantly returned to the dockyards, where it was enlarged to 68,000 cubic metres and lightened by one motor, so that with a speed of eighty miles per hour it could nevertheless rise to 25,300 feet. Thus, the airship was again made superior to the plane in climbing ability. But for how long? When the war began, we generally flew no more than 3,500 feet above the earth; in the third year of the war, scouts and combat fliers met above the heights of Mont Blanc; and near the close of the war, fliers and airshipmen, bundled in furs and artificially protected from asphyxiation, were out-climbing each other at Mount Everest altitudes.

The adjustment to the conditions of the rarefied air created the high-compression airship motor, and to decrease wind resistance, the later types had their outside cars and engines removed to the interior of the ship. The rebuilt L 71 was again delivered to the navy, and the L 72 was under construction while the L 73 and L 74 were laid on the ways. Simultaneously, we worked on the plans of two more highly developed types. The L 75 was to contain 75,000 cubic metres of gas. Its eight motors were equipped with compressors and, at an altitude of 25,000 feet, were to give the ship a nominal speed of ninety miles per hour. The second type under consideration bearing the dock-number L 100, was to have the same speed and climbing capacity as the L 75, but was to be considerably larger, and protected from incendiary bullets by a protective gas-cover. But the collapse of the Central Powers intervened, and put a stop to our plans for a considerable length of time.

An image from a popular magazine showing Zeppelin destruction as propaganda.

25

Post-war Events, 1919–1921

T HE ARMISTICE FORCED Germany to surrender her fleet to the Allies. And since the airships were considered a part of the naval fleet, we had to settle accounts on this basis.

During the World War, Germany had fifty airships in service with the army and seventy-eight with the navy. The army airships, thirty-four of them Zeppelins, undertook 232 military flights; and in 111 raids dropped 132,700 pounds of explosives over Russia, 98,300 over France, and 80,500 over England which with flights over other countries made up a total of 311,500 pounds. Seventeen army airships were destroyed by the enemy, two of them by anti-aircraft guns; eight were wrecked; and the remaining twenty-five, among them fourteen Zeppelins, were outmoded by technical advancements and were consequently dismantled. Fifteen officers and fifty engineers, helmsmen, mechanics and machine-gunners were killed in their airships.

Of the seventy-eight naval airships, sixty-five were Zeppelins, nine were rigid airships of the Schütte-Lanz type, three were non-rigid dirigible balloons of the Parseval system, and one was a semi-rigid balloon of the Gross-Basenach type built by the Military Commission of Prussia. Fifty-two naval airships were lost, among them nineteen with the entire crew and twenty-four without any sacrifice of human life. In six cases the crews were captured, and in three they were interned on neutral territory. Forty officers and 396 deck officers, non-coms and crewmen of the naval airships were lost during the war. In all, our naval airships undertook 1,148 scouting flights and 200 raids, the latter mainly against England. Eighty-five of the entire 1,348 flights were carried out by army airships in the naval service.

The English themselves admitted after the war that a single bombing attack on London destroyed property to the value of more than 30,000,000 marks; one can judge from that the extent of the entire damage inflicted. Five hundred anti-aircraft guns and at least twelve Air Squadrons with a hundred fliers had to be retained at home for air defence. False and genuine alarms again and again caused whole cities and industrial districts to cease operations. In constant fear

Youthful Patriot. 'Take away the night-light, Mary. I'd rather risk the dark than attract a Zeppelin.' *Punch*, 1 March 1916. German propaganda made much out the fear of Zeppelins in England, but it was still a subject suitable for a cartoon.

Old Lady, 'Ah, it'll take more than preaching to make them Zeppelins repent! *Punch*, 23 February 1916.

of an air attack of great proportions, England kept an army of half a million men on the island.

We were more than satisfied with the military performances of our airships, and we looked upon it as self-evident that the technical developments made during the war would be used for the good of peaceful world traffic when the war was over. As early as December 1918, Baron Gemmingen and I attempted to carry out the wishes of old Count Zeppelin by preparing for the first transatlantic flight of an airship.

At the time of the Armistice, the last airship destined for the German Navy was still in the possession of the Zeppelin Company. If the Armistice released the navy from its contract, then, according to our understanding of the matter, there was nothing to prevent our using the L 72 to carry out our plan. Basing our plans on our experiences during the endurance flight over the Baltic, we intended to set course for New York and return without either landing or refuelling. Since the L 72 had been built as a war craft and not a commercial ship, it could carry sufficient fuel to cross the Atlantic in both directions, under normal weather conditions. To prevent the French and English from thwarting us, we kept our plan a secret. We intended to fly over the English Channel at night, or sail around the British Isles to the north, and we did not want to wire for permission to fly over American soil until the day before we reached it.

After long deliberation, the Zeppelin Airship Company gave its consent to the undertaking, which I was to command. I at once prepared the L 72 for its transatlantic flight, for it was the beginning of March, 1919, and we had to hurry to take advantage of the first good weather. But since our undertaking was not meant to satisfy our own ambitions, but to re-establish Germany in the eyes of the world, it was necessary to inform the government of our intentions. And from that time on, we met with more and more difficulties. No official bureau would assume the responsibility. They feared that the Allies would take reprisals; that the French, for instance, would occupy Friedrichshafen and confiscate or destroy the dockyards. Even Count Bernstorff, the former German Ambassador at Washington, could not conceal his forebodings. He said:

> If you had made the transatlantic flight before America's entrance into the World War, you would have aroused more enthusiasm than the arrival of the commercial submarine *Deutschland* in Baltimore. But since then, the two nations have opposed each other on the battlefield. Consequently, you cannot count on a friendly reception in America, and you will more than likely aggravate the situation rather than improve it.

We did not disregard these obstacles, but we banked on the enthusiastic reaction to the deed. The navy had cancelled its contract, and therefore if the L 72 flew to America the entire affair was the concern of a private company.

In April 1919, the airship was prepared to take off. In order to take along the rows of gasoline tanks placed along the walkway, I had denied myself an equivalent weight in water-ballast. We had built in a workshop, and a mess-room for the officers and crew. The sides of the engine cars could be swung open, so that we could make repairs, if necessary, even while we were under way. The gas leads were ready to inflate the hydrogen as soon as permission to start arrived from Berlin.

One morning, when I arrived at the dock, a telegram was handed to me. It was from the government in Berlin, forbidding the L 72 to take off. No reason was stated for the refusal, but I later learned that the Inter-allied Commission was behind it. In some way—treason was cheap amongst us at that time—the Commission had learned of all the particulars of our plan. Why the Allies opposed an undertaking which was intended to blaze the path for peaceful international transportation I only learned eight weeks later, when the English rigid airship R 34 was the first to fly the Atlantic.[31]

While I was still equipping the L 72 for the trip to New York, the commander of the sister-ship, L 71, had been working on a similar plan. To show the world what a Zeppelin could do, Lieutenant-Commander Martin Dietrich intended to cross the Atlantic and then continue his flight beyond New York until the last gasoline tank on board was emptied. Then, he intended to land the ship and moor it to a tree or an emergency anchor. The entire crew was prepared to go through with it, but when Dietrich applied to Berlin for permission, the answer he received was no different from mine. The government, they said, was in enough difficulties without burdening itself with additional ones. Besides, the airship question was finished once and for all.

The example of the crews of the German High Seas Fleet, who sank their ships at Scapa Flow to avoid surrendering them to the enemy, was followed by the crews of the German naval airships. On the same day the German warships sank off the Orkney Islands, the naval airships L 14, L 41, L 42, and L 65 were destroyed at Nordholz, and the L 52 and L 56 at Wittmund. While the ships hung empty in their hangars, the crews carried their tools past the firemen as if to their usual work. Instead, they loosed the wire cables and chains on which the airships hung, and the navy hulls crashed to the ground into a confused heap of girders and struts which were irreparably damaged.

The Allies avenged themselves not only by demanding the surrender of the nine remaining naval airships, but also by attempting to deal a death blow to German airship travel. Dr Hugo Eckener had returned from the naval base at Nordholz to Friedrichshafen in order to arrange with Baron von Gemmingen and General Director Colsman the conversion of the Zeppelin Company to a peace-time basis. For the Delag, he ordered two passenger airships with which to resume the flights between German cities, just as they had been made before the war. The *Bodensee* and the *Nordstern*, with 20,000 and 22,500 cubic metre capacities, were no larger than my old *Sachsen*, but their carrying capacity and speed were once again as great. During the test flights, the *Bodensee* reached a speed of 83 miles per hour, and in the autumn of 1919 made 103 flights within 98 days. During this time, she visited Stockholm, and the deep impression produced upon the people of Sweden seemed to open new markets for German aviation which at that time was hard-pressed both commercially and politically.

The Svenska Luft Trafik Aktiebolaget in Stockholm communicated with us through its Director, Captain Lenn Jacobson; and in July 1920 I was sent to Stockholm to confer with him. The Swedish Parliament seemed to be willing to approve a government loan for the establishment of an airship base in the capital. The plan, according to Eckener's suggestion, was for the Svenska Luft Trafik and the Delag, in joint operation, to cover the Stockholm–Berlin–Friedrichshafen route with two commercial airships flying on a two-day rotating schedule. The Swedish Company was to order from the Zeppelin Company a ship of the *Bodensee* type, but of 32,000 cubic metre capacity, and was also to buy from the Zeppelin-Hallenbau in Berlin a wooden hangar designed by Engineer Baron von Schleinitz. Besides contributing an airship, the Germans were to place at the disposal of the company the large hangar at Friedrichshafen-Löwenthal and—for short stop-overs—the hangar at Berlin-Staaken. In addition the Svenska Luft Trafik planned a shuttle schedule of Dornier flying-boats between the Swedish mainland and the island of Gotland.

Sweden, which had maintained its neutrality in the World War and given us many indications of its friendship and sympathy, was thus the first land to extend a helpful hand to a Germany defeated. For while I was still nego-tiating in Stockholm, the new regulations of the Inter-allied Commission had entirely changed the picture of the situation. On 9 August 1920, Major-General Masterman, chairman of the commission, informed the Aviation Peace Commission of the Defence Ministry that 'all naval and military hangars and

LZ 120 (D I) *Bodensee* before reconstruction. LZ 120 commenced life with DELAG until 1921. It was then ordered to be transferred to Italy as part of the war reparations. It arrived in Rome from Staaken on 25 December 1921 and was renamed *Esperia*.

buildings for airplanes, amphibians and airships must be dismantled or destroyed by 15 February 1921, according to the protocol signed at Spa on 9 July 1920.' The dismantling and destruction were to begin at once, with the exception of those hangars whose maintenance was sanctioned for international commercial traffic (one airship hangar each in Nordholz, Seddin, and Löwenthal) and those assigned to the allied powers. France was awarded the six hangars at the Ahlhorn air base, Italy one each in Ahlhorn and Seerappen, and Japan one in Jüterbog.

Not satisfied with the radical extermination of our military craft, the Inter-allied Commission four days later ordered the dismantling of all German airship hangars in municipal or private possession. That sealed the fate of another seventeen hangars and workshops, which, for the most part, had already found other use. The industrial concerns housed therein were obliged to close, and the unemployed workers increased the gravity of the internal situation.

Fortunately for us, an international air system, such as that contemplated by the Allied Powers, simply did not permit the exclusion of the most central land in Europe, and therefore the Commission had to make exceptions in the destruction of the commercial hangars. Both large airship hangars in Staaken and Löwenthal, including gasometers, were permitted to remain; only their compressors and steel containers for hydrogen were to be destroyed. At the main dockyards at Friedrichshafen we were permitted to retain the old hangar, dating from 1909; and though the large construction hangar was to be dismantled, we were left with construction hangar No. 1, which was only fit for a small ship.

At once, Eckener made efforts to save Count Zeppelin's life-work. But at the beginning it seemed as if even he would be frustrated by the hate-psychology which existed for years after the war. Despite all pleas that the large construction hangar was indispensable, we received no satisfaction. The Allies made no secret of the fact that they wished to deprive us of the means of building still larger airships in the future. Only Eckener knew that patience meant victory; and he proved to be right.

As early as the end of 1919, the sister-ship of the *Bodensee* was completed and ready to enter service as the *Nordstern*. Then came an order from Berlin confining both ships to their hangars until further instructions. We were dismayed. And we soon learned the meaning of that terse order. Both vessels, although they were commercial airships built after the war and by private enterprise, were to be surrendered to the Allies with the military airships. The Inter-allied Commission based this demand upon the contention that Germany was obliged to indemnify the victorious powers for the naval airships destroyed by their crews on 23 June 1919.

The victorious powers, it seemed, intended to make use of Zeppelin's invention, at our expense. They wished to enlarge their own air fleets and at the same time prevent Germany from developing her airship travel. The attempt failed, as it had to fail, because the appropriation of our latest type airships

LZ 121 (D II) *Nordstern* (North Star). This Zeppelin was intended for regular flights to Stockholm, but it was ordered to be transferred to France as part of the war reparations and renamed *Mediterranée*.

forced their new owners to skip over stages of development which we had gone through in the hard school of the World War. The lack of practical experience in construction and operation of dirigible airships sealed the fate of the ships and their owners.

After the war, the French airship fleet consisted of a couple of old dirigible balloons of the non-rigid principle which were no longer in service, and of two new ships each of the Nieuport-Astra and Zodiac type, which were of 10,000 and 4,000 cubic metre volume respectively. To these were added, as France's portion of the spoils, the 62,000 cubic metre L 72 which, though it was intended for the German navy, had not yet been accepted and thus rightfully was still the private possession of the dockyard; the LZ 113, which was somewhat smaller; and the 22,500-cubic-metre passenger ship *Nordstern*.

The L 72 (dockyard number LZ 114) was delivered in June 1920, from the Friedrichshafen docks to Maubeuge and, after being re-christened *Dixmuide*, made a series of long flights over the Sahara and the Mediterranean under the command of Lieutenant-Commander Du Plessis. On an endurance flight from 25 to 30 September 1923, the air-cruiser remained aloft over the Mediterranean for 118 hours and 41 minutes and covered 5,000 miles. With this performance, the claim to fame for the longest flight of an airship became France's instead of Germany's; and it was not until November 1935 that it returned to Germany. For six years I had held the record set with my LZ 120, and another twelve years were to pass before I regained it with the LZ 127, the *Graf Zeppelin*, the story of which opened this book. Just a quarter of a year after its record flight, the *Dixmuide* plunged into the sea near Sicily during a thunderstorm and went down with the entire crew of fifty men. There were no witnesses to the disaster, and its causes are unknown. Although it was suspected that explosive gas had been ignited by lightning, it seemed that the air cruiser lost its bearings in the heavy weather and first crashed against a mountainside. The LZ 113 was dismantled by the French, who did not seem to know what to do with it. The little LZ 121, named *Nordstern* by the Delag and *Méditerranée* by the French, was damaged during its first launching from its new hangar and, after being repaired by German mechanics, undertook a flight to Rome and served as an experimental ship until 1927.

On 20 August 1920, the naval airship L 61, commanded by Reserve-Lieutenant Heinen, made a stop-over at the Löwenthal airship field on its way to Italy. The Italians rechristened the L 61, *Italia*. 'The *Italia*,' a report states, 'on one of its first flights, literally threw itself at the feet of the King with its motors wide open.' A number of the crew were killed, and the airship was completely wrecked. On 1 December 1920, the last naval airship crew ceremoniously hauled down the war flag from my LZ 120. The ship was inefficiently hung up in its hangar by the Italians and consequently collapsed. On the other hand, the little *Bodensee*, re-named *Esperia*, took part in many Italian manoeuvres and stood the test excellently. But Italy preferred its domestic types for the requirements of the navy, army and colonies. They had small semi-rigid dirigible balloons for coastal service and a few pressure balloons of the volume of my pre-war *Sachsen*. After another unsuccessful attempt with a new ship of 42,000 cubic

LZ 114 (L 72). *Dixmude* from the leading gondola, over Lindau 9 July 1920. In 1920 the L 72 was ordered to be transferred to France in the context of war reparations and handed over on 9 July 1920 and renamed *Dixmude*. It made a world duration record flight of 118 hours. It exploded off the coast of Sicily during a thunderstorm in December 1923, killing all aboard.

metres, the two famous pressure balloons *Norge* and *Italia* were constructed. In May, 1926, the semi-rigid *Norge*, with its designers Amundsen and Colonel Nobile, crossed the North Pole and in seventy-one hours covered the 2,625 miles from Spitzbergen to Alaska. Two years later, when Nobile attempted to repeat this splendid performance with the *Italia*, the ship failed him. Amundsen, conqueror of both poles, disappeared during the plane search for the lost airmen, and Nobile fell into disfavour and was deprived of his General's rank. This drove him to Russia; and not until we made our polar flight were we again to meet the man who had many times visited us in Friedrichshafen. Using Nobile's principle, Soviet Russia ordered Engineer Wusskin to build a semi-rigid airship of 38,000 cubic metre capacity. But nothing has been heard of this ship as yet.

The third airship of the Nobile design, which was delivered to Japan, crashed during naval manoeuvres. At the Japanese Naval Ministry it was openly admitted that only large rigid airships were suitable for scouting duty in the Pacific Ocean area. In the partitioning of the German naval air fleet, Japan had been allotted the L 37, which was dismantled in Sedding and reassembled in the hangar shipped from Jüterbog to Kasumiga-ura. Adhering to its usual policy, Japan wished to stand on its own feet even in the matter of airship building. Captain Jamamoto and Commissioner Takata turned to us for construction plans and instructors for the training of personnel, and when nothing came of this they confined themselves to the shipping of the vital structural parts of the dismantled cruiser to Japan.

Like Japan, Belgium, which had been promised the L 30, contented itself with the delivery of vital structural parts; and the SL 22, dismantled, served the experts of the victorious powers in the practical illustration of the various patents.

At that time, England was the only country building rigid airships of the German type. Most of them were based on the Zeppelin design, but the R 31 and R 32 were based on the Schütte-Lanz principle. The R 33 was a successful copy of our L 33 which the English had captured. When it was dismantled in 1928, it had served for twelve years, and it was the first airship from which planes took off. In July 1919, the R 34, under Major G. H. Scott, who was later to be our guest on the *Graf Zeppelin*, crossed the Atlantic Ocean from the Scottish coast to Mineola (3,600 miles) in 108 hours, and made the return flight from New York to Pulham (3,575 miles) in 75 hours. Our naval cruisers L 64 and L 71, which a civilian crew had delivered to Pulham, were to be rebuilt, as they said, for mail and passenger service to Egypt. When the R 34 made an emergency landing at Pulham, the L 64 had to be removed from the hangar to make room for the damaged ship. That night, a storm came up and tore the Zeppelin from its moorings, driving it nine miles. There the L 64 was wrecked and had to be dismantled. The L 71 likewise had to make way for an English cousin and was dismantled in her hangar. The R 38, a large airship, 725 feet long and with a capacity of 75,000 cubic metres, which, as the ZR

II, was destined for the American navy, collapsed over the Humber during her test-flight on 23 August 1921, killing forty-four Englishmen and Americans.[32] This horrible catastrophe caused the English to interrupt their construction of rigid airships for many years.

Throughout the swift and tremendous development of their airplanes, the Americans could not be dissuaded from continuing to build small blimps for patrol service and pleasure and advertising flights. A semi-rigid military balloon, the *Roma*, which they received from Italy, was burned in February 1922 when it struck high-tension wires near Hampton Roads. On the other hand, the *Shenandoah*, 690 feet long and with a capacity of 60,845 cubic metres, copied without our assistance from the construction of our L 49, upheld itself, despite certain weaknesses of construction, until September 1925, when it was destroyed because of a technical oversight and an error in navigation. To economize on the costly helium gas, they had closed off a number of gas valves.

Of the confiscated German air-cruisers, the United States wanted none; but an American airship officer visited the dockyards at Friedrichshafen and carefully, scientifically, examined everything there was to be seen. He came again, often, until he finally revealed that he was authorized to place an order for a Zeppelin. The only condition was that the price must not be exorbitant and that the commission be kept a secret until the airship flew to America. One conference followed another and we generally met in Switzerland.

It was said that the Treasury Department of the United States had sent half a million dollars in gold to Koblenz, where, at the headquarters of the American Army of Occupation, it was being held in readiness for the responsible agent. We had agreed upon an airship with a gas volume of 100,000 cubic metres and the contract was ready to be signed, when the secret leaked out in Paris. The French Ambassador to Washington protested that the state of war between Germany and America was not officially terminated; and thus the Americans were obliged to withdraw a contract which would have assured the continuance of the German enterprise and would have accelerated the development of international traffic by a few years.

At the Paris Conference, Germany had offered to replace with new ships the naval Zeppelins which had been destroyed by their crews. The American industrialist, Vissering, who in 1919 had made a flight with us and since then has been a loyal adherent of our cause, persuaded President Harding, who was his personal friend, to press America's claims at the Conference. The United States then demanded, in place of the two naval airships which had been granted them, a doubly large airship of 100,000 cubic metres gas content. At the Paris Conference, however, America's suggestion met with little sympathy; even then, the Allies were unwilling to permit the Americans to have a larger airship than they themselves had. There was a compromise, and the volume of the American airship was reduced to 70,000 cubic metres.

USS *Shenandoah*, (ZR-1) under construction at Lakehurst.

USS *Shenandoah*, (ZR-1) under construction. It had been manufactured in Philadelphia and sent to the US Naval base at Lakehurst for assembly.

ZR-1, a 2,115,000
cubic foot rigid airship,
was fabricated at the
Naval Aircraft Factory,
Philadelphia and
assembled at Naval
Air Station Lakehurst.
She first flew in early
September 1923. During
the final four months of
1923 and the first weeks
of 1924 *Shenandoah* made
several flights around the
eastern United States.

Shenandoah photographed
at Lakehurst, 1923. On
3 September 1925 USS
Shenandoah encountered
violent weather over
southern Ohio, broke up
in flight and was a total
loss. Fourteen of her crew
died in this tragedy.

Das Amerika Luftschiff
LZ 126 (ZR-3) under
construction.

The cost of this airship was charged to reparations, and the new ship, bearing the dock number LZ 126, was registered as the ZR-3 for the American Navy, which rechristened it the *Los Angeles*.

In the LZ 126, we had our wish; now we could show the Americans what an airship of German construction, under expert command, was capable of doing.

Das Amerika Luftschiff LZ 126 (ZR-3) under construction.

26

The Trans-Atlantic Voyage
of LZ 126

O UR CENTURY HAS been called the technical age. It has also been called the age of abbreviation. Time is money, the American says; to decrease time means to save money. From the commercial standpoint, airships and airplanes were invented only to cut down distance.

The airship itself was obliged to submit to abbreviation even in its designation. Germany says LZ when it means (Luftschiff Zeppelin) Zeppelin airship; our Navy was content with the still shorter 'L.' America uses ZR, which means Zeppelin Rigid. The construction numbers on the English airships were simply prefaced by an R.

The *Shenandoah* was the first American airship. The German Reserve Lieutenant Heinen, who owes his practical experience to the *Hansa* before the war and the *Bodensee* afterward, and whom we last met during the delivery of the naval air-cruiser L 6 to Italy, once saved this ship by bringing it back to its mast after a storm had torn it away and threatened to destroy it.

The American Navy Board wanted to order the second airship from England. During the test-flights, the R 38, or ZR II, proved to be too slow and her motor-power was appreciably increased. But the construction was not equal to this additional strain, and thus caused the disaster which I mentioned in the previous chapter.

The ZR-3, then, was finally ordered at the only place where the technical conditions necessary for its construction existed—the Zeppelin Airship Company in Friedrichshafen. The order was charged to reparations, which means that Germany had to pay for it. Under the circumstances, this was the best solution, for the government would otherwise have had to pay three million gold-marks in cash as indemnity for the American claims, and this way the money remained in the country, created employment during bad times, and kept the Zeppelin Company from closing down entirely.

Until then, 115 airships of the Zeppelin type had been built. The ship destined for America bore our construction number LZ 126. The construction department of the dockyard, under Ludwig Dürr's supervision, designed the ship in an ideal

Das Amerika Luftschiff LZ 126 (ZR-3) in flight. After it was delivered to the United States it was renamed *Los Angeles*.

stream-line shape. The duralumin body consisted of twenty-two longitudinal girders which were connected and stiffened by wired frame girders and unbraced intermediate girders. The gas-cells, made of special gas-cell fabric, were placed between the wiring of the ring girders. The outer cover of the ship's body was made of impregnated cotton fabric. The control system in the stern consisted of unbraced fins or stabilizers with pairs of elevators and rudders.

Besides the control car, which was rigidly constructed into the body, the ship had five engine cars suspended on struts.

Each of the five Maybach motors developed 400 horsepower. With an overall length of 670 feet and a maximum diameter of 92 feet, the LZ 126 contained 70,000 cubic metres of buoyant gas capable of lifting a total weight of 182,600 pounds (including 41 tons of useful load). The maximum speed of the ship was 79 miles per hour, and its travelling speed 68.

Throughout the years when no contracts were forthcoming, the dockyard had taken to manufacturing aluminium pots and similar small items, but with the construction of the new airship, the workshops came to life again.

For the first time since pre-war days, the workshops on the Bodensee were again the goal of thousands of travellers and spectators, who looked with astonishment at the wonderful flying ships. In the summer of 1924, the LZ 126 was completed and began its workshop flights. These were made not only to test the construction, the wireless apparatus and other equipment, but also to familiarize the crew with the ship and its peculiarities.

The radio room on LZ 126.

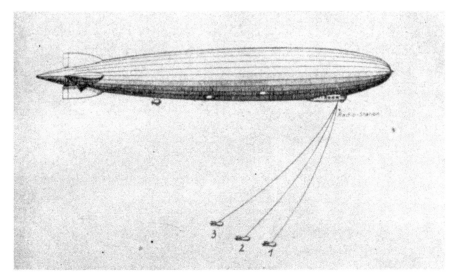

The antennas for LZ 126.

In the belly of LZ 126 *Los Angeles*, showing partly inflated gas cell.

The Acceptance Board of the US Navy had arrived in Friedrichshafen and a swarm of American newspapermen followed in their footsteps, cabling long reports for every edition of their papers and outdoing one another in new sensationalisms. As may easily be imagined, the pipe-dream of every newspaperman was to make the flight with us. Weyer, correspondent for the International News Service, and the cameraman, Varges, of the International Newsreel, besieged Dr Eckener for permission to accompany us. Eckener shrugged his shoulders and said he had no authority; they must turn to their own Navy Board which had contracted for the ship. This advice, which was not meant in earnest, tied the newsmen's hands completely, for they knew only too well how hopeless the attempt would have been. Military affairs are no joking matters even in America, and although according to the terms of the peace treaty, the ZR-3 was not a war vessel, since Germany was forbidden to export war materials, the ship was a training ship of the American Navy, and civilians had no business aboard it.

By the time the test-flights and preparations were completed, October had arrived and it was high time to take off for the United States if we did not want to be caught in the severe autumnal storms and fogs. We loaded the airship with thirty tons of gasoline, which was sufficient for seventy hours at full speed or a hundred hours at reduced speed; and we took on, in addition, two tons of oil and 3,300 pounds of water-ballast. The crew consisted of twenty-eight men; and no less than five of us possessed our masters tickets as airship pilots, namely: (besides Commander Dr Eckener, and I as his alternate) Hans Flemming, who died of cancer in 1935, and of whose war exploits this book has revealed a good deal; Lieutenant-Commander Hans von Schiller; and our comrade from the *Bodensee*, Anton Wittemann.

The take-off was scheduled for the early morning of 11 October 1924. When Flemming weighed the ship, a mysterious excess load disturbed him. 'The vessel is tail heavy,' he grumbled; and ordered the stern searched. The investigation brought to light two familiar faces: those of the newspaperman, Weyer, and the cameraman, Varges. They had put on work shirts and slipped through in these clothes, hoping to defeat their rivals by stowing away on a transatlantic flight.

As much understanding as Dr Eckener had for the assignments of the press, and as willing as he was to cooperate with them for the good of air travel, he did not care for pranks which might jeopardize the safety of his ship and the success of the flight. The police were notified to keep their eyes on the two smart Americans until the LZ 126 took off.

In vain, the two men tried to shake off the two plainclothes men shadowing them. They took a taxi and drove to the lake. The officers resolutely followed in a second car. The trip went on through Vorarlberg and into Switzerland. In Arbon, the Americans stopped and went into a tavern to have their lunch. The pursuers stopped and waited.

The two men inside seemed to be relishing their meal, for they were taking their time. The officers suddenly became suspicious and went inside to have

LZ 126 leaving Friedrichshafen 12 October 1924.

a look—and found that their slippery birds had flown. The artful dodgers had gone into the tavern and, without stopping, had gone right out the back door. They had caught a steamer long ago, and were probably already back in Friedrichshafen, perhaps concealed once more in the huge belly of the airship! The dutiful officers perspired anxiously. But there was no need for the telephoned warning. Since the disagreeable incident, the hangar and the ship were so closely guarded that the stowaways couldn't possibly get into the ship again.

Yet, if they themselves were not permitted to make the flight, they determined that something belonging to them should be on board. The cameraman rushed to his hotel-keeper. 'Mr Hauber, I need a bird!' The hotelman politely asked what kind of bird was required. 'No matter! A crow, a canary, or anything else you can get me!' The hotelman thought for a moment. Then he remembered that a friend of his in Stuttgart had a friend who bred canaries. So they ordered a canary by telephone and it arrived by Special Delivery and was presented to the airship. All manner of gifts had been received—flowers and musical instruments from the aesthetic, cakes and wine from the materialists, mittens and earmuffs from solicitous housewives and their fond daughters, advertising material from shrewd businessmen but a living thing was not yet among them. Hans Flemming, who had charge of the weighing and launching of the airship took care of the tiny passenger and gave him a place on the electrophone near the observation window. Ariel Varges and his colleague, Weyer, were delighted; they had their news sensation! 'The first bird to fly the Atlantic as a passenger!'

But the start of the LZ 126 was delayed for another twenty-four hours. The wet fog lying over the Bodensee weighted the outer envelope of the airship so heavily that 4,400 pounds of fuel would have had to be unloaded to bring the ship into aerodynamic balance. Furthermore, we would have struck contrary winds over Biscay, and we might have been forced to detour through the Rhône valley and over the Mediterranean to Gibraltar. For these two reasons, Dr Eckener set the take-off for Sunday morning.

Outside, it was still dark, when we took our posts, and the hangar was flooded with the ghostly green light of the arc lamps. We twenty-eight Germans were joined by the four members of the American Commission: Captain George W. Steele, Commander Jacob H. Klein of the naval air station at Lakehurst; Major Kennedy, the observer for the Army; and Lieutenant Commander Sidney Kraus, the youngest among them. They had their own roomy cabins, but they generally remained in the control car and proved to be good fellows.

On 12 October 1924, at 7.30 in the morning, the LZ 126 rose from German soil. The crowd of people, who had surrounded the landing-field since the grey of dawn, spontaneously broke out into the German national anthem. '*Deutschland, Deutschland, über alles!*' were the last words we heard before leaving our native land.

The weather forecast for the first half of our transatlantic flight was favourable. Over Europe and the west coast and out beyond the Azores there lay a high-pressure area. First, however, we met fog over our native Bodensee. We went to 1,750 feet, and the white vapours clouded around us. We went to 2,000 feet—nothing but fog. The altimeter gauge showed 2,250 feet, and there was still nothing to be seen. Twenty-five hundred feet—and a general sigh of relief; the sun broke through the screen of fog and the Alps gleamed in the light of the new day.

Between the Alps and the Black Forest, the LZ 126 followed the course of the Rhine. At eight o'clock we were over Basle, which we were better able to guess at than see; the Swiss, who had been waiting since early morning for our appearance, heard only the drone of our motors.

The next 450 miles led straight through France. We had permission to fly over it, but we had to avoid Forts Belfort and Besançon according to regulations. The sun shone and now the air was clear. Their memories of the horrors of the war and of our airship raids were too fresh for the French to greet our passing with any signs of rejoicing. In the meanwhile they have become accustomed even in France to the sight of a German passenger airship, and they regard it no differently from a mail plane or a train.

The wind came from the south-west, and the ship rocked in the air which had been unevenly warmed by the sun. The wooded mountains of the Côte d'Or lay only a little below us. The question was whether it would not be wiser to veer to port and take the route over the Mediterranean. But Dr Eckener remarked, 'Perhaps the ship is just cutting a caper in the presence of Burgundy and its exquisite vintage.'

Captain Hans von Schiller, our Navigation Officer, was also our Quartermaster; the navigator, Hans Ladwig, was his assistant and our cook. Our first lunch in the air, 2,550 feet over France, was quite sumptuous: turtle-soup, Hungarian goulash with peas and carrots, and pudding and coffee. The shifts had been divided into two watches of four hours each. Before the second change of watch, on the Greenwich meridian, the clock was set back an hour, for we were moving westward. The men on watch were already anticipating their feast, but they had to remain on duty another hour. Meanwhile, the town of Cognac conjured up all sorts of exciting visions. At the next watch, the change of time was compensated for.

Thus, instead of one o'clock, it was twelve o'clock when the fine line of the coast came into view. Railway lines cut through the forest which sloped softly to the fruitful land at the mouth of the Gironde. A flotilla of coastguard ships were anchored near the beach. The ocean sparkled in the light of the sun.

Our hearts beat faster. It was a solemn moment when the LZ 126 left the European mainland to trust itself to the infinity of the Atlantic for the next few days. Before us, a west wind came up and blew against us. But one of the great advantages of airships is that they can choose their own routes.

We crossed the Bay of Biscay, which at first belied its reputation of being the storm-corner of Europe. But just as we were preparing to apologize, she betrayed her bad character. At about seven o'clock a stiff south-west wind came up, and the horizon became spotted with rain clouds. The ship heaved and forged heavily ahead. Near Cape Ortegal we swung the rudder around and flew parallel to the Spanish coast. The sun went down into the sea, and then the full moon played like a searchlight over the picturesque rocky coast and enchanted us with magical effects.

The steamers and the coastal vessels under us seemed to regard the airship as a fantastic apparition. By Morse-code and signal lights, they asked us more than we could answer.

At eight o'clock we passed Cape St Vincent, the landmark by which we had set our course. The gusts, which made their appearance in a series close to the Spanish coast, and which sometimes attained a velocity of 30 to 35 miles per hour, continued to shake us for a time. At eleven o'clock, however, the wind veered to the west, and we came out of the depression.

LZ 126 *Los Angeles* leaves the coast of Europe for America.

Through the night the wind blew evenly from the north-west and the north. Our flying speed, which for a time had fallen to 35 to 40 miles per hour, now rose again to 55. In the morning, after our watch as we sat at breakfast—Café complet, as in the best Swiss hotels—the freighter *City of Boston* under way from New York to Port Said, passed below us. It was obvious that they had never heard of us at all, for they wirelessed in astonishment, 'Who are you? Where are you going?' We told them, and continued the conversation for fifteen minutes, during which we learned what we wanted to know. From the bearings thus determined, it appeared that, during the night, we had had a position-error of only 15 miles. We again resumed the exact course.

On the second midday—sea travel creates an appetite, and next to the problems of navigation the question of food was the most important on board—we had bouillon in cups, ham in Burgundy sauce, pudding and coffee. But our five Maybach motors consumed more than we thirty-two people and a canary—680 pounds of gasoline per hour. Thus, the ship was consequently 17,600 pounds lighter, and we rose to 5,000 feet to release 8,000 cubic metres of hydrogen.

It was just about noon when San Miguel, the first island of the Azores group, appeared on the ocean five miles ahead. We made for the Island of Terceira, whose great cliffs are mantled with thick vegetation. Tongues of land covered with carefully fenced squares of produce pushed out into the sea. We followed the white highway to the little bishopric of Angra, where, from a low altitude, we dropped two mail bags containing our greetings to our dear ones at home. We did not carry Portuguese stamps on board and we trusted to the generosity of the finder to mail our letters and cards—if he didn't prefer to keep them as souvenirs of the first flight over the island.

We saw the islanders running helter-skelter below us as if they hoped to come closer to the fabulous monster of the skies; then a thick layer of clouds came between us. The summit of Pico Alto—the highest point of the volcanic Azores whose nine islands rise a sheer 13,500 feet from the sea—lay truncated on the clouds.

Again we were surrounded by the infinity of heaven and sea. The weather reports indicated a depression forming off the Newfoundland Banks, and smaller disturbances from there to Bermuda. But we did not notice them; we had beautiful, clear weather; but the south wind freshened and veered to the south-west. At nine o'clock, its velocity rose to 17 to 20 miles per hour, reducing our speed to 45 miles per hour. We had now been under way fifty-five hours and still had ten tons of fuel.

The US Navy had ordered the cruisers *Detroit* and *Milwaukee* to stand by during our crossing. Our intercourse with them was bad, however, because of the static. The Atlantic was a deep blue with sea-weed floating on it like islands. It was so humid on board that we worked in our shirt-sleeves. The freighter *Robert Dollar*, with the white dollar sign on its black smokestack, was literally run over by the LZ 126. Clearly, we recognized the Captain and helmsman on the bridge, and the sailors staring from bow and stem.

At about this time we met strong breezes from the south-west, which retarded our progress, and indicated that we would strike strong headwinds on the route to New York if we remained on our present course. My watch was from midnight until two o'clock, and Dr Eckener discussed with me our course of action in case we continued to be without weather reports because of the static. We decided to keep our course until eight o'clock in the morning; if, by that time, conditions had not changed, we could sail around the low pressure area which was approaching from the south-west, but of whose extent and path we could learn nothing. I tried to get some sleep then, but it was too warm. As early as five in the morning, Flemming, who was on duty after me, changed course to the north-west, basing his action on the last weather report from the Cape Race wireless station. For the south-west winds had increased to 37 to 45 miles per hour and we could strike eastern winds further up north. Soon afterwards, the weather reports were received. The cruiser *Detroit*, from its position near Cape Race, reported south-east winds; and the *Milwaukee*, 300 miles south-east of that position, reported more southerly winds. From this we unmistakably recognized the position of the low pressure area and the advisability of flying around it. Dr Eckener instantly ordered the change

Anton Witteman, Navigator; Dr HugoEckener, Captain; (looking at the camera) on board LZ 126 *Los Angeles*, 1924.

of course to the north-west, and thus, favoured by the wind, our ship sped on at a rate of 105 miles per hour. To release gas, we climbed to 8,300 feet, high over the layer of clouds.

At eleven o'clock in the forenoon, the wind slackened and finally died down altogether. A quarter of an hour later it again became noticeable, but this time from the south and south-east instead of the south-west. The calculations were correct; we had won our game. Taking course almost exactly with the direction of the wind, the LZ 126 began to make 90 miles per hour.

But gradually the wind turned from the east to the north-east, and we got into fog banks spreading off Newfoundland. At two o'clock we were deep in a thick fog. For a few hours we climbed to 5,000 to 6,650 feet and once more saw the sun.

Then we sank into the pitch darkness again, for we had to descend almost to the surface of the angry sea in order to ascertain the direction of the wind. The thermometer dropped from 77 to 41 degrees. A bitingly cold storm blew at 60 miles per hour from the north-east. The vessel creaked and groaned under the strain but it proved the strength of the German construction a single torn wire was all that the storm achieved. Later, the moon peeped down at us from between the racing clouds. After three hours, the storm abated.

Lights blinked from the depths, and we determined our course from them finding our speed to be 72 miles per hour. Thursday night at 10.18 we sighted the light of Sable Island. We had reached the American continent! We exchanged our marine maps for land maps, and tried to conceal our excitement from each other. But now we know how Christopher Columbus and his crew felt when, on the night of 12 October 1492, the lookout on the *Pinta* sighted land.

The storm had abated, but another, worse than the first, lay in wait for us. A hurricane of wireless congratulations and inquiries crowded the weather reports off the air. Then we began to suspect what was in store for us on the mainland and we prepared ourselves for the landing. In the pressure of duty, we had had scarcely enough time to shave, and the plentiful supply of water had been used only for morning washings.

Flemming and I were just emptying one of the caviar boxes which had been presented to us, when at 4.15 a.m. New York time, the roaring motors of the German airship woke the inhabitants of Boston. The metropolis seemed like a diamond-merchant's show-case, with innumerable lights gleaming below us.

Three hours later, we were over New York. The tremendous city with its stone forest of heaven-raking skyscrapers made a deep impression upon us. We steered for Long Island, crossed the little towns strewn along the shores, and then followed the course of the East River, and circled the Statue of Liberty while all the sirens in the harbour howled their welcome toward us. Then we cruised over the city, flying here and there over Broadway and the Battery. Shrill factory whistles spat out white clouds of steam and from the roof-tops great crowds of people waved a greeting. In the narrow stone canyons of the streets, omnibuses, trolley-cars and automobiles stopped, the passengers rushing out to stare raptly into the sky. The sun rose and painted a halo around the 'Queen of the Air' as the Americans called the Zeppelin.

Over Brooklyn and the Lower Bay, we took course for Lakehurst. A squadron of planes from Mitchell Field gave us an escort of honour. Masses of people had assembled from far and wide for our arrival; two football games were cancelled because of us. Thousands of autos, whose owners had spent the night waiting, lined the edge of the landing-field.

It was 9.05 o'clock when Lakehurst came into view. The 400 men of the ground crew were waiting. From a height of 50 feet, the landing cable was dropped. It was plain that the soldiers and ground crew had had plenty of practice; the landing manoeuvre was executed as precisely as it was at Friedrichshafen. The *Shenandoah*, the ZR-1 of the American Navy, was at this time on a long flight in California.

At 9.37 New York time the gondolas of our airship touched American soil. The LZ 126 had made the flight from Friedrichshafen to Lakehurst, 5,030 miles, in 81 hours and 2 minutes. The average speed for the flight was 62 miles per hour.

Officers of the army and navy were the first to greet us, but almost immediately we heard some German voices. Our compatriots couldn't resist coming to meet us. The first man to jump from the ship was Commander Klein, who wished to embrace his waiting wife, but he instantly found himself surrounded by reporters. 'It was a magnificent flight!' he cried, and pushed through the crowd toward his wife. Captain Steele then climbed out and greeted his wife and his eighty-year-old mother, who had come all the way from Indiana to meet him.

Then Eckener stepped out. The crowd, which had been gazing at the 'great silver fish' with mute astonishment, then gave three cheers for the ship and its crew. There was such shouting and hurrahing that we couldn't hear ourselves talking. We still had to dock the ship, but when it was inside the enormous hangar, there was no longer any escape from the crowds of interviewers, photographers, cameramen, reporters, autograph collectors and souvenir hunters. Our provisions of zwieback, cake, chocolate, apples and small cheeses were distributed in a few minutes.

Heaps of telegraphic congratulations came in. President Coolidge sent a long message to Dr Eckener.

I congratulate you on the successful completion of your transatlantic flight on the great airship which you have brought from Germany to the United States. This was not only a brilliant feat—more than that, it was a trail-blazing exploit and proved as never before the ability of lighter-than-air craft to make long-distance flights with considerable quantities of freight and passengers. It gives me and the people of the United States great pleasure that the friendly

Guests of Henry Ford. *From left to right:* Meeting with Henry Ford. From left: Hans-Curt Flemming; Ernst Lehmann; Dr Hugo Eckener; Hans von Schiller; Henry Ford; unknown; Paul W. Litchfield (president of Goodyear Tire & Rubber Co.)

Lehmann besieged by the American press.

relations between Germany and America are reaffirmed, and that this great airship has so happily introduced the first direct air-connection between the two nations. I hope that you will feel at home in the United States and that the splendid service you have rendered by delivering this airship will remain a proud satisfaction throughout your entire life.

Even our native Germany echoed our success. Carl von Wiegand, the Chief Correspondent for the Hearst Press, reported the wave of enthusiasm that swept Germany. The cities and towns were decorated with flags, the church bells rang, and the left and right wing newspapers united in acclaiming our flight, through which, as Wiegand said, 'Germany has rehabilitated herself in the eyes of the world.'

Dr Hugo Eckener in the United States, 16 October 1924.

27

THE FORMATION OF THE
GOODYEAR ZEPPELIN COMPANY

THE DELIVERY OF the LZ 126, which the American authorities re-christened the *Los Angeles*, by no means concluded our stay in America. According to contract, nine members of the crew remained at Lakehurst to familiarize the US Navy's airmen with the ship and its operation. These were Airship-Captain Hans Curt Flemming, Navigation Officer Walter Scherz (who later returned to Friedrichshafen and was fatally gassed while inflating a free balloon), Helmsmen Ludwig Marx and Albert Sammt, Chief Engineer Gustav Belser, Chief Mechanics Emil Grozinger and Hermann Pfaff, Mechanic E. Martil, and Sailmaker Ludwig Knorr.

Knowing that the LZ 126 was safe in Flemming's hands, Dr Eckener and I set forth to complete the great task which he had set as his life's goal—the inception of a regular transatlantic airship service. Considering Germany's post-war financial condition, there was no hope of achieving this goal through our own resources. We were depending upon American capital and cooperation.

The prospects were more favourable than ever. Our ocean flight had proved beyond the shadow of a doubt that the Atlantic was no longer an obstacle even for a comparatively small airship. The Goodyear Tire and Rubber Company at Akron, Ohio, had had a good deal of experience in the building of small non-rigid ships and was inclined to consider the construction of larger types.

The negotiations during the year before had already led to the founding of the Goodyear Zeppelin Company which made use of the Zeppelin Company's patents and its Chief Constructor, Paul Weeks Litchfield, was chairman of the American Zeppelin Company. After long preparation, the *Akron* and the *Macon*, of which we shall hear more later, were built at the Akron dockyards.

The intervals between these difficult negotiations were more than occupied by an endless series of banquets and celebrations which were held in our honour and which we could not avoid. And these festivities were not solely occasions for honouring us personally; they were politically significant indications of friendship which contributed to clearing the international atmosphere of the after-effects of war-psychosis.

Los Angeles in Panama, 1929.

The plethora of festivities makes it difficult for me to keep them apart in my memory; and it would be unjust to recall one and omit others. But in order to give the reader a picture of the American scene, I shall let my notes speak for themselves of those exciting weeks.

On the afternoon of 27 October 1924, I left Akron, where I had business with the Goodyear Company, and drove to Cleveland, where I called for Eckener. He had come from New York via Niagara Falls, and he and Flemming and Schiller, who were with him, had been feted during the entire week. We then drove back to my quarters in Akron, at the Portage Country Club. Eckener had a bad cold and went to bed soon after dinner. I remained up for a long time while Flemming and Schiller told me about New York.

On one night the entire crew of the LZ 126 had been invited to the Capitol Theatre, where they showed a newsreel of the *ZR-3*. When it was over, a spot-light was directed at the loge in which Eckener and his men were sitting. A storm of applause broke out, and the 3,000 people of the theatre stood up and sang first the German and then the American national anthem. It was the first time since the war that the German anthem had been sung in public.

Indeed, our entire undertaking—actually, since the beginning of the test-flights, but more than ever here in America—had political significance. The Americans spoke more of how our flight had served Germany than of the flight itself. In fact, all the diplomats and speeches could not have done as much for the improvement of Germany's political situation, and especially for its relations with America, as we had unintentionally done with the flight to

America. Eckener was even called 'Germany's greatest and only diplomat.' In his replies to the many speeches made before German-Americans and German organizations, he did have to be very diplomatic in order not to spoil the good impression made upon the Americans. His breakfast with General Dawes, originator of the Dawes plan, was widely commented upon in newspapers in America and throughout the world.

On Tuesday, 28 October, we had a conference with Litchfield, and then drove to a banquet at the City Club in Cleveland. The opening of this affair was repeated at all the luncheons and dinners we attended during the following few days. There was always a room with a great many narrow tables at which the crowd was seated. At the end of the room on a small platform stood the speakers' table, with places for the chairman and the guests of honour. Eckener, with me beside him, was always seated next to the chairman. Flemming and Schiller, when they were along, sat at the wings. The main difference between our customs and those of America is that in America the guests must entertain those who organize the affair while with us it is exactly the other way around. First the chairman would speak, introducing us individually. Which meant that we had to rise and bow, being greeted by applause, as if we were actors. This was generally followed by one or more speeches in English, after which Eckener spoke in German, his speech being translated sentence for sentence by me, or by Schiller or Flemming, who had composed a sort of standard talk for such occasions.

On the other hand, Dr Eckener and I, because we never had time to prepare, always spoke extemporaneously. And this was least convenient for me; for interpreting was bad enough, but in this case I had to arrange my speech according to what Eckener had said, taking care that I never repeated what he had said nor contradicted him. Then, after the conclusion of the chairman's speech, the other diners formed a line and we shook hands with them until our fingers were numb. And then, after all this was over, they came back again with menus which they wanted us to autograph.

We didn't rise from the table at the Cleveland City Club until three o'clock. Nevertheless, Eckener, who had the grippe and a fever, accepted the invitation of a German-American architect. And this celebration was a regular drinking-bout, replete with German student songs—the Mayor of Cleveland, and many other German-Americans were present—and when we broke up, it was six o'clock, and we hurried back to Akron.

Our attorney, Carpenter, who had come from Philadelphia to be present at the meeting of the Board of Directors of the Goodyear Company, was already waiting for us. Until late that night, we talked with him, and on the following morning he and Mr Vissering discussed the supplementary contract between the Goodyear Zeppelin Corporation and the Luftschiffbau Zeppelin-gesellschaft. The Board of Directors met at eleven o'clock. The meeting settled the conditions of the contract between the two companies and furthermore approved a plan which called for the construction of an airship of 150,000 cubic metres. When the new Board of Directors was elected, Dr Eckener, Mr Vissering and I were voted in. After lunch at the Goodyear Casino, there were additional conferences until nightfall. Then we had dinner with ladies at the University Club, where Eckener and I spoke, and later attended a large public meeting at the Goodyear Theatre. The auditorium was jammed; Litchfield and the other officials took their places with us on the stage. After many speeches, Eckener and I were called upon. Afterward, Litchfield unexpectedly asked the audience to question Eckener, who, speaking imperfectly and with only a small vocabulary, pushed the whole matter off on me. So for half an hour I had to stand up and reply to the questions asked me, and some of them were disconcertingly difficult.

We returned home at 11.15 o'clock; the train for Detroit left at 12.30. So we packed and went to the station, and spent the night in a Pullman. We arrived in Detroit at eight in the morning. At the station we were met by the inescapable hordes of photographers and reporters and a reception committee of the Detroit Aviation Society. We had been looking forward to a quiet breakfast, but that was out of the question. The committee had reserved a suite of rooms at the hotel, and a tremendous community breakfast-table was already waiting in the private dining room.

First of all we were photographed again and again before the hotel, then we were permitted to breakfast with the inquisitive newspapermen. After that we motored out to inspect the Packard automobile factory, where new airplane motors were demonstrated. Then we went through the Ford factory with Mayo, Ford's Chief Engineer, who took charge of me for the rest of the day. After luncheon at the Detroit Athletic Club—with the usual speeches—we were taken to Dearborn where Ford lives and where he has a large experimental workshop.

Ford received Eckener, Mayo and me in his private offices and he entertained us so long that the others had to wait for an hour. I liked the old gentleman; he has a really fine, good face. Later, Mayo invited me to come to Detroit again; and Ford asked me to advise him on the purchase of an airship mooring-mast which he wished to present to the city of Detroit. Then Ford himself led a large group of us through the workshops.

By that time we were due for another dinner, which the Detroit Aviation Society held in our honour. There were many speeches, and the public again was permitted to ask me a lot of questions. At nine o'clock we proceeded to the Harmonia, a German organization where we met up with another banquet and an octet. And they had beer for us, good beer, so we remained there until eleven o'clock and only left when it was time to board the express for Chicago.

We arrived in Chicago at seven in the morning and were met by reporters, photographers and a delegation from the German clubs. Eckener was ill and had slept badly, but there was nothing else for him to do; he at least had to speak at the hotel—and then Vissering and I did the rest for him. Vissering drove us both to his home in Kenilworth. We visited the president and the faculty of the University, and the Professor of Germanic languages reminded me that in the summer of 1914 he had made a trip on the *Sachsen* with me from Leipzig to Dresden.

On the next day, our attorney, Carpenter, appeared again to discuss some business with us. At one o'clock, we had an appointment with the Mayor of Chicago. But he was not there, and we had no time to wait, for at 1.30 we were due at the great banquet given by the combined German Clubs of the city. We went to the Mayor again, who was present this time and apologized profusely. Afterward we conferred with our attorney, and in the evening we accepted the invitation of a German-American hotel-owner.

I had to leave before the end of the meal to catch my train and was back in Akron the next morning. There I worked all Sunday and Monday on calculations of the cost and estimated income of airships and airship lines. Then I went back to Chicago where the contracts were signed and the Illinois Association of Commerce gave us a luncheon. To the newspapers, it was a great sensation that 1,160 of the most important businessmen in America were present; even Lloyd George had only had 40 more.

Despite two invitations to lunch (Monday at the Deutscher Verein in Milwaukee, Tuesday at the German Lincoln Club in Chicago), Dr Eckener was well again. We therefore obliged the son of our host, Vissering, by visiting his fraternity house. For hours we told the boys of our experiences, of German Zeppelins and of Germany and they were a grateful and appreciative audience.

A few days later we met Mr Dawes, took an express for New York, which we reached after a 24-hour trip, had a conference with some people interested in airship lines, travelled on to Washington and there spoke to Admiral Moffat and Secretary of State Wilbur about the acceptance date of the LZ 126, which was set for 10 November. In the national capital, society women, who were just carrying on a drive for the Red Cross, abruptly appointed us honorary members and photographed us on the steps of our hotel. The pictures were used in newspaper publicity. That same night we travelled back to New York and Dr Eckener took some time off to answer some of his personal letters, of which he had a drawer-full.

Meanwhile, what with travelling and conferring, banqueting and delivering speeches, half of November had gone by. Dr Eckener left me to continue the affairs he had begun, and returned to Germany. We had hammered the first breach in the wall of obduracy presented by the Allies now we had to set aside those paragraphs which were hindering us from cooperating in the peaceful development of world aviation.

28

LZ 127 Graf Zeppelin

An autumnal frost had come upon the Bodensee. The sun rose over the valley of the Rhine and serenely lifted its rays toward Säntis. The lake lapped at the piers, and the black smoke flags of the steamers waved long and low. At the station, on the walks, and in the village streets there was an unusual air of excitement; motorcycles outroared the automobiles bearing foreign licence plates, and all vehicles were heading for the dockyards.

But the portals of the Zeppelin Airship Company, through which two hundred thousand visitors had passed during the construction of the LZ 127, were now closed. The tension heightened in the vicinity. Waterproofs, knapsacks, climbing sticks, Parisian silk stockings, American knickerbockers and vagrants' packs—the whole crazy-quilt world gathered in thousands and thousands around the fence-work of the dockyards. A common expectancy levelled all social and national differences; the same benches, stones and fields offered themselves to the poor and rich, the young and old; the same village inn supplied them with beer and hot frankfurters; and a quick rain fell derisively on the entire crowd.

All this—eyes, gestures, words—indicated that an airship was going up. These words have a magical effect, a dazzling sound, and they lure to the closed portals a group of people who come from the five lands bordering the lake. The inconveniences of the long wait in the sun and rain, which made them martyrs to their enthusiasm, gave their small reward an additional value, and we suddenly understood the festive mood in the open amphitheatre. For this performance was one of the rarest treats of our century. The *Graf Zeppelin* was to make its flight across the ocean.

We were followed by envious glances when the doors opened to admit us. The hangar, bursting full of airship, looked grey in the dim light. The smooth sloping lines of the hull threw bright silver reflections on the confusion below a feverish crowd of men like ants attacking a dead caterpillar. The enormous body of the new ship seemed to defy the laws of gravity; it weighed 129,800 pounds, and yet it seemed weightless even before the buoyant gas raised it. The gas hissed through tubes which writhed with the pressure. The ice-crystals

LZ 127 *Graf Zeppelin*
under construction.

melted from the pipes and evaporated in steam. Like God's apprentice, midget man was blowing breath into his gigantic creation; the gas hissed through the umbilical cords into the huge body.

The limp gas-cells of goldbeaters' skin, which hung inside the airship between the braced ring-frames, blew up slowly. The fabulous hollow space with its filigree of struts and bracing wires was no more; the taut cells bore down on the walkway, leaving only enough room for the drainage canals, through which excess gas could escape upward from the automatic valves. The quantity of hydrogen which this 105,000-cubic-metre ship consumed was almost inconceivable. If the watchman at the dockyards were permitted to illuminate his entrance-way with the gas-content of the LZ 127, the light would still be burning in the year 2400.

Up a shaft larger than the ventilating shaft, Sailmaker Knorr climbed to the back of the ship to check the manoeuvring valves. A stairway led from the service walk to the lower walkway which lay parallel to it like a street running through the ship. Between the service walk and the main walkway hung the cells for fuel gas, which was the most important improvement on the new Zeppelin and, from the third flight on, fed the five Maybach motors. Thus, two-thirds of the gasoline tanks in the girders served only as safety reserves or as additional ballast to the water-bags and emergencies which the airship command could empty by operating a valve on the control panel.

In the narrow walkway under the arch of struts there was a restless continuous activity—steps, shouts, knocks that seemed futile and unnecessary. As if in a mine, the mechanics swung into the side shafts and dove through a hatch into free space. Themselves paunchily enclosed under the great belly of the airship, the five engine cars, with the propellers as tailfins, hung like five baby whales swimming beneath the mother-whale. By flowing freely between the cars and the ship, the air-currents prevented escaping gas from reaching the motors. For days and weeks, the motors, each developing 530 horsepower, had roared from the testing-blocks in the nearby factory; now they lay waiting for their hour of resurrection.

Once more I checked the gasoline tanks which were lined up on both sides of the walkway, and then went on to the storerooms, the crew's quarters and, finally, the control car. The latter was so large that naïve visitors, not seeing the forest for the trees, often mistook it for the entire airship. The cabins on both sides of the middle walkway, the spick and span kitchen with its wind motor to supply it with the necessary electricity, the square dining-room with its furnishings of rare wood and its wide observation windows—all were empty. In the wireless cabin the operator turned the generator impeller which created the current for the wireless apparatus, and swung it outboard to check it. The six-tube receiving set was capable of operating on wave-lengths from 415 to 85 feet; the two 100-yard antenna wires, with their little Zeppelin-shaped weights, lay rolled up beside it.

LZ 127 *Graf Zeppelin* landing at Friedrichshafen.

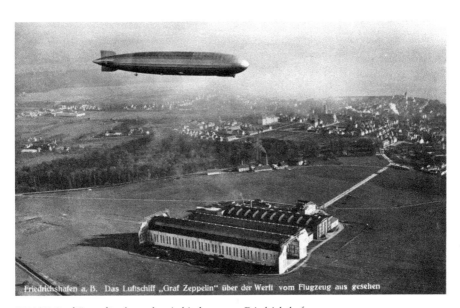

LZ 127 *Graf Zeppelin* above the airship hanger at Friedrichshafen.

In the Navigation room, Navigation Officers Wittemann and Pruss—both with airship captains' tickets—leaned over their maps. In this new type of ship, which, like the reflections of a steamer on the water, carried its superstructure on its bottom, the control room was up forward. The frame-work of struts cut an inclined cross through the front field of vision. Along the row of oval windows were the stands with the helm wheels, the manometer, the switchboard for the operation of the gas-cell valves and water-bags, engine telegraphs, board telephone for the transmission of orders, the megaphone and the signal apparatus. His blue seaman's eyes sparkling, his cap covering his rich blond hair, Eckener leaned overboard to give his orders. The young helmsman at his side was his son; the other two were commanders of Zeppelins during the World War: Lieutenant-Commander Hans Flemming and Hans von Schiller, both of whom are already known to my readers.

Four years had passed since our first flight to America in a Zeppelin airship of German origin. In these four years a great many things had changed. The Allies had rescinded the regulations which had throttled Germany's commercial aviation—our American flight contributing to this sudden about-face. We were again permitted to build efficient airships, and the German people, grown poor in money and ideals but retaining their faith in their own future, once more gave us the means of continuing the late Count's work. The national fund which united the name of the inventor, Zeppelin, with that of his successor, Eckener, made possible the construction of the first great commercial airship, the LZ 127 which was outfitted as an experimental ship and on 9 July 1928, was christened *Graf Zeppelin*.

The builders and the public expected this ship to prove the suitability of large Zeppelin airships for overseas traffic. We airshipmen did not need this proof, because twenty-five years of experience with 116 airships of the same type of construction had convinced us of the correctness of our calculations and technical conclusions. But we knew that before a sound commercial enterprise could be established, we would have to convince financial circles by a conclusive demonstration.

Although the airship was equipped for transporting mail, passengers and cargo, it had been designed and built merely for a series of demonstration flights over great distances.

Since we could not beforehand determine either the exact nature of these demonstration flights or the points between which they would be made or the sort of cargo we would carry, the airship was a sort of compromise in design. It was neither a genuine passenger airship, for there were accommodations for only twenty travellers, nor a mail airship, since it was not fast enough for that purpose but it had just enough of the qualities of both to carry out all the necessary demonstrations. Principally, it was designed to have a large radius of action, a good average speed, and a surplus of efficiency for extra safety on the longest flights and in the worst weather conditions.

The controls of LZ 127 *Graf Zeppelin.*

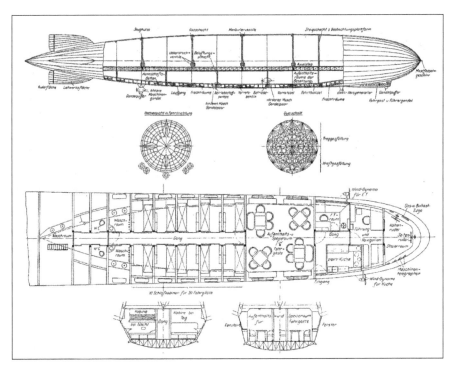

LZ 127 *Graf-Zeppelin*, diagrammatical plan.

But there was something else which influenced the design. Even the largest of the Zeppelin Company's hangars in Friedrichshafen was not large enough to permit the construction of a ship of such dimensions as the designers would have chosen to fulfil all the conditions mentioned above. In other words, the measurements of the hangar limited the size of the ship, and its proportions, especially the relation of the length to the diameter. Therefore, it was necessary to find a compromise between the largest possible volume commensurate with lifting capacity and the best possible streamline form for speed. This compromise proved to be to the disadvantage of the speed factor.

The final specifications of the airship, which were conditioned by these considerations, were an over-all length of 790 feet, a maximum diameter of 102 feet, and a maximum height of 112 feet. In cross-section, the streamlined form of the hull was a regular figure of twenty-eight sides, and the ship had a total gas volume of 105,000 cubic metres. The useful load under normal atmospheric conditions, i.e., the entire weight which the LZ 127 was capable of lifting from the earth, was 132,000 pounds. After deducting the weight of the fuel, the crew, etc., from this figure, the airship was in a position to carry a load of 15 tons, or twenty passengers and 26,400 pounds of mail and freight, over a distance of 6,250 miles and at an average speed of from 60 to 70 miles per hour.

The ship's hull consisted essentially of a rigid frame of longitudinal and cross pieces which, laid end to end, would be ten miles long. The frame was entirely covered on the outside. The covering consisted of an especially strong and light cotton mixture protected by several coats of varnish and metal powder. The entire covering then received a finishing coat of paint to attain the greatest possible smoothness and the least possible frictional resistance in the air. The gleaming silver colour of the outer envelope gave the impression of a metal hull, and the suggestion has often been made that envelopes actually be made of thin layers of metal instead of cloth, which is generally supposed to be an inferior material. In reality, however, there is scarcely a better material for the special requirements of an airship than the combination of cloth, paint and metal, and there is practically nothing to be gained by the use of metal, which, even at minimum strength, would be heavier than other materials and would entail the sacrifice of vital characteristics of the rigid principle. The major advantage of a metal hull would be protection from the actinic rays and heat of the sun, both of which have an undesirable effect upon the inside of the airship, but this protection is gained just as certainly, at a minimum sacrifice of weight, with the cloth-and-metal combination.

The progressive efforts of the designers, and the compromises necessitated by the limitations of the overall dimensions, forced them to seek improvements and new ideas with which to increase the efficiency of the airship beyond anything hitherto attained.

The metal supports of the frame were of duralumin, which is fundamentally an aluminium and copper alloy and combines the durability of ships' steel with only a third of its weight. Though of the same weight, the material was twenty per cent stronger than that used in the construction of the ZR-3. A basis for the evaluation of its structural strength may be obtained from the fact this enormous and entirely rigid metal creation was the size of a large ocean liner and weighed, including its coverings, cells, motors and furnishings, no more than a small tug-boat.

The inside of the ship's hull was divided into seventeen compartments, each containing an individual cell for the buoyant gas. These divisions served the same purpose as the water-tight bulkheads of a sea-vessel. It is almost impossible to conceive of an accident which would force an airship to come down upon an undesired spot, such as the middle of the Atlantic Ocean.

On the underside of the hull, a sort of corridor ran through the entire length of the ship, from the foremost point of the bow to the stern-most point of the tail. This main service walk made it possible to reach all parts of the ship. The various service rooms distributed throughout the length of this walkway consisted of spaces for gasoline tanks, oil tanks, ballast tanks, motor supplies, provisions and general supplies, and the accommodations for the crew. There were many spaces provided for the storage of freight, so that it was always possible to stow the cargo according to the demands of the trim of the ship, and, if necessary, to shift it.

At certain points along the main walkway, other walks branched out at right angles, permitting access to the engine cars on the side of the great hull. Besides these walks, the *Graf Zeppelin* had still another, which likewise ran through the length of the entire ship. This was placed high above the main walkway, close below the axis, and it was therefore called the axial walk. Its main purpose was to serve as a walk from which all the gas cells could be instantly inspected and reached for purposes of repair. The *Graf Zeppelin* was the first ship to have such an axial walk, an additional advantage of which was to reinforce all the sixteen cross-sections and contribute to the solidity and safety of the ship.

There was, however, another improvement in the new airship. The arrangement of the gas-cells was different. Instead of gasoline, which hitherto had been used exclusively, the motors of the *Graf Zeppelin* burned a fuel which was carried on board in a gaseous state. In order to make room for this fuel-gas inside the ship, the size of the gas-cells in the twelve largest sections was reduced, so that together they required only two-thirds their former space and left place for twelve additional cells in which the fuel-gas could be stored.

The introduction of this gaseous fuel was an entirely new departure, bringing with it a whole series of advantages. Before, when an airship came back to land after a long flight, it had an excess of climbing power which resulted from the consumption of gasoline during the flight. This surplus lift had to be counteracted before the landing, either through the release of large quantities of buoyant gas or the taking on of ballast during the flight from the surface of the water, or by the production of ballast from the exhaust gases of the motors. All these methods were used and are still used with satisfactory results, but there are still many drawbacks, such as the waste of buoyant gas or the loss of carrying ability and speed because of the ballast production apparatus. Since the fuel-gas weighed the same as air, it made no difference in the lifting power of the ship whether the fuel was on board or not, whether the gasometers inside the ship were empty or full, or whether the airship was just taking off for a long flight or was returning from a voyage of many days' duration. This was the third improvement on the *Graf Zeppelin*.

The fourth improvement was the absence of heavy supplies of gasoline, which usually placed considerable strain on the frame of the airship. On its Atlantic crossing, the ZR-3 carried a total of thirty tons in gasoline tanks, alone equivalent to the weight of a small locomotive hung up inside the frame. One can just imagine the inclination of this weight to tear loose from the airship when both are being shaken by a storm, and one can easily realize the gain in safety resulting from the absence of such massed weights.

The fifth improvement, which was likewise connected with gaseous fuel, consisted of a minimizing of the fire hazard as compared to the operation by gasoline, for the combustion range of gasoline vapour is considerably greater than that of the mixture of fuel-gas and air.

The sixth and most important improvement in the *Graf Zeppelin* resulted from the fact that by using gaseous fuel it was possible for the airship to carry a larger supply of motive power on board than would have been possible with the use of liquid fuel.

In itself, gaseous fuel is neither a new nor an unusual discovery. Actually there are a great number of fuel-gases or gas mixtures which can be obtained from natural sources or produced fairly cheaply. The common characteristic of all such fuel-gases is that they are hydrocarbon gases of medium weight and that they have approximately the same weight as air.

Even the idea of using gas as fuel for airships is not a new one. A German inventor, Paul Hänlein, who built an airship in 1872, realized that the buoyant gas (which in his ship happened to be coal gas) could also be used as fuel for the motors. Since then, attempts have been made to use hydrogen, the modern buoyant gas, for the same purpose, but the construction of a practical hydrogen motor is still an unsolved problem.

29

THE USE OF FUEL GAS

I N A WELL-ORDERED state it is hardly possible just to build an airship and put it into service; the LZ 127 was licensed by the Defence Ministry, just as its successors the LZ 129 and LZ 130 are under the administration of the National Air Ministry created by the Third Reich. Even during the first work-shop flight, the Air Ministry had certain doubts about the use of fuel-gas, and so when, on 18 September 1928, the *Graf Zeppelin* took off under Eckener's command for its maiden flight, its motors were still powered by a gasoline-benzol mixture. The flight lasted three hours and fifteen minutes, and it was so satisfactory that the 3,500-mile test-flight was undertaken on the following day. I draw upon Engineer Karl Beuerle's notes to refresh my memory:

When, at 7.30, Dr Eckener, entered the hangar beaming like the rising sun, the *Graf Zeppelin* was ready for the take-off. Quickly it was undocked, and set off in the direction of Zürich.

During a tour of the passenger quarters I saw our guests, various representatives of the German and American press, diligently at work. At first glance one would have thought this was a race, so quickly did the pencils fly over the paper. An especially sly gentleman, off in a single cabin, had armed himself with a portable typewriter and worked away so furiously that I timidly withdrew and closed the door behind me.

The mist became thicker, and we sped on over Thurgau, accompanied by one of our small brothers, a Klemm-Daimler ship, which soon fell behind. But another convoy remained steadfast; our shadow rushed over the green fields, gardens, hills and villages, always by our side. Incidentally, it was an excellent means of gauging our own speed. Stopwatch in hand, we measured the crossing of a certain specific point. The length of the ship, divided by the time in seconds, gave the speed.

Everyone was looking ahead to see when Zürich would become visible. Suddenly, as in a theatre, the curtains parted and below us lay the first large city to be passed on our trip. Groups of people waved up at us in frantic greeting. We made three trips over the city and Lake Zürich. Then we passed over Waldshurt, along the Upper Rhine toward Basle. Here another convoy came alongside, a trim little plane from which a camera was cranked at us.

Another inspection tour through the ship showed me that there was hard work going on not only in the cabins, but also in the walkway, where experiments and calculations were being made. The whole web of structural girders was being carefully examined for their reactions during the flight. Specialists were making tests of the air currents in the walkways and searching for traces of gas—one of the most important researches, for the Traffic Ministry's permission to use fuel-gas was dependent upon its outcome.

The telephone in the walkway rang. 'Two photographers who have permission to take pictures in the ship and from the engine cars would like to be conducted into one of the wing cars.' A delicate undertaking when one considered that these neophytes had to be taken down the steep ladders, where the air current was strong. But with assistance from above and below, the thing was done, with only the loss of a photographic plate whose traces we later discovered on the propeller of the rear gondola.

Meanwhile, we had flown over Freiburg, whose cathedral tower, circled by swarms of pigeons, stretched up toward us in a greeting. We went on. Ahead of us, a black misty cloud heralded Mannheim and Ludwigshafen, Captain Lehmann's birth-place. What a smoky forest of chimneys! The inhabitants of our industrial cities should take an airship flight every month to pump clean air into their lungs; they ought to build an airship just for that purpose.

To see the occupied territory at least, we made for Mainz, but avoided the actual border of occupation. Then, hard to starboard along the Main, toward Frankfurt. Plane loads of newspapermen and photographers greeted us. All Frankfurt seemed to be waiting for us, for we saw groups of people everywhere, and autos and street-cars stopped on the streets.

Since we were using gasoline, we had in the meantime become light, and over Darmstadt we had to rise to release gas. Slowly a white mist veiled the landscape; forests and fields and cities became smaller; and the tiny earth-dwellers disappeared entirely.

Then we came down again. Like the eye of a projector in a cinema, the scene widened and the people and objects grew larger and became visible once more. Now, the dark shadow of the airship flew over the Castle of Heidelberg.

A few planes coming toward us indicated that we were already expected in Stuttgart. At reduced speed, we flew slowly over the last resting place of old Count Zeppelin.

Then the last portion of our flight began, and we had to get back to the engine cars. We had to make calculations at top-speed and determine the length of time required to bring the ship to a stop after the motors were cut off. At 5.29, the *Graf Zeppelin* was again on solid ground.

Six days later, the third test-flight. Command: Lehmann. Purpose: technical experiments.

We were to determine the radius of turn of the ship and ascertain at what rudder-angle we came out of the turn and into the straightaway again. Assuming that the ship is forced to fly low, either over level land where there are church-spires, lofty buildings, chimneys and the like, or in some safer valley, the pilot must always know how quickly and with what radius of turn the ship will obey the rudder. This knowledge is likewise important in landing, to permit the pilot the appropriate approach run. On our experimental flight we made the necessary calculations by camera-shots and bearings taken from above, combined with compass readings, and then had these bearings checked by theodolites from below.

In addition, we ascertained the climbing capacity of the ship with all or individual motors. On long flights, this   knowledge enabled the pilot to equal-ize, without losing gas or ballast, the severe fluctuations in temperature caused by the change from day to night. The evening cold decreases the climbing capacity of the ship. Therefore, in order to maintain its static equilibrium, it must release ballast. Inversely, during strong sunlight, the ship becomes lighter and, to retain its static equilibrium, must release gas. These static differences are dynamically equalized by the ship's command by flying the ship in an inclined position; when the ship is heavy, the nose is pointed up, and when the ship is light, the bow is held down. With the aid of kiting forces, which are considerable even at small angles of inclination, several thousand pounds can be counteracted and retained. This dynamic pressure enables the airship to continue its flight even with a defective gas-cell and repair it while under way. Incidentally, we tested the excess-pressure valves on the individual cells to see that they were operating correctly.

The calculation of the climbing capacity goes hand in hand with that of the greatest possible speed of descent. During the descent of the ship, the gas con-denses and its volume is rapidly reduced, so that if the ventilating apparatuses did not permit air to enter the ship quickly enough, there would be danger that the higher pressure outside would cause the ship's frame to collapse.

As an additional experiment, we took radio-bearings through the various stations. For flights during fog or other unfavourable weather, the radio direc-tion-finder is one of the most important means of determining the course of the airship. When the human eye finds no more points to check, and an astronomical fix is made impossible by the clouds, the radio, the electrical ear, must and does help.

The bearing is taken with the aid of a radio-loop. In getting a bearing on a given station, one determines a minimum or a maximum volume of sound, depending upon whether the loop is parallel or perpendicular to the particular station. Let us assume that an airship has been flying for hours in a fog over

France and would like to know its position. The radio operator chooses two widely separated stations, in this case Friedrichshafen and Norddeich. He calls one of these stations and asks for radio signals. The operator on the airship sets his radio loop by the signals of the station called. If he is exactly on bearing, he then reads on the dial of his loop, which has the same divisions as a ship's compass, the position of the signalling station in relation to the ship, and he transfers this reading to his map; that is, he marks on the map the reverse direction of that read from the signalling station and draws a line toward the approximate position of the ship. If he then repeats this process with the second station and draws the second bearing on the map also, he will have two lines which intersect. If the airship calls upon still a third station, any miscalculation in the first bearing will be corrected. These radio bearings are so exact that, on test-flights over the Bodensee, the airship could be directed toward the landing-field from the enclosed radio-compartment.

For navigation over the sea, we also tested flares to be used in taking bearings. These are made buoyant by air-chambers and have a special compartment containing a bag of calcium-phosphate mixed with calcium-carbide. The calcium-phosphate ignites when it comes in contact with water, and the mixture produces a bright light and a heavy cloud of smoke, both of which are visible at great distances. By taking a bearing on this floating point on the water, the pilot of the airship can measure the drift, calculate the strength and direction of the wind prevailing at the time, and correct his course accordingly.

On our fourth experimental flight we had on board, besides representatives of the government, men well-known in science and aviation: from Germany, Oskar von Miller, the founder of the Deutsches Museum, who used the radio on board to tell the people of Munich his impressions of the flight; from England, Squadron-Leader Booth, who two years later flew the R 100 across the Atlantic, and Major Scott, who, in 1919, with the R 34, was the first to conquer the Atlantic Ocean and who met a tragic fate in 1930 when he commanded the R 101; and from America. Commander Rosendahl, commander of our LZ 126, rechristened the *Los Angeles*.

On the previous day we had filled two of the fuel-gas cells with Blaugas to see what effect this would have upon the cells. Even during the first test-flight, when we used gasoline, we had occupied ourselves incidentally with the question of this Blaugas which, in case of a cell or tubing leak, would, because of its specific weight (equal to air), be likely to spread in the walkway unless it was sufficiently counteracted by ventilation. But on this day we were really going to test it. At 8.05 in the morning, motor No. I was changed from gasoline to gas. The alteration was effected exactly according to plan, just as we had done it on the blocks. Willingly, even with visible appreciation, the motor accepted the new food and quietly continued functioning. Report to the control car: 'Everything O.K.' Nobody was surprised.

As had happened with the ZR-3, we had for weeks been receiving hundreds of letters begging us to fly over certain localities, even particular houses. If only we could have fulfilled all those requests. But at least we did everything humanly possible. Then, the flight through Germany, the last flight before our ship to America, was begun.

At 7.05 we went aloft into the warm air, which our airship tolerated only unwillingly. Some must have thought our take-off somewhat dangerous, for we pulled ourselves up slowly, foot by foot, over the trees and electric wires until we took course for Ravensburg.

Northward to Ulm, whose cathedral pointed out the direction. Shortly after Ulm, motor No. I was changed to gas.

At 9.10, through the breaks in the clouds, a large city appeared below us: Nürnberg. The pea soup fog became thicker and thicker, and from the rear gondola I could no longer see the forward wing car. Reports from Berlin indicated that the weather was bad there, too. Eckener made a quick decision and turned off westward, hoping that the weather at the capital would improve, for we wanted to congratulate Hindenburg on his birthday.

We went westward, toward Würzburg. Heavy rain-clouds came toward us and it became stormy; earlier flights had accustomed us to this around Spessart. I went through the dining-room. How quickly men become accustomed to the unusual! Tired of looking out the window, two passengers sat at a table quietly playing a game of chess.

Now we moved further, over Frankfurt, along the Taunus, toward Wiesbaden. We had to take this route because there was bad weather to the north.

From Neuss we heard the dull ringing of the Cologne Dome, singing its brassy songs to us in welcome. Then Düsseldorf was below us. This city presented the Count with his first hangar and from this point the memorable flights of the first passenger airships were carried out. Our convoy of planes had grown to seven. One of the planes flew over our ship despite strict orders forbidding it. According to regulations, they were to remain at least 1,700 feet from the airship in order not to endanger us.

We flew over another group of industrial cities, and then, in the twilight, headed toward the border of Holland. The Dutch cows were apparently frightened by the airship. Like their German sisters, they scattered in all directions when we approached. The typical Dutch landscape, with its straight canals and dikes, slowly disappeared in the twilight. At 6.45 we passed Rotterdam. The illuminated city was a beautiful sight to behold; we Germans could not yet afford such things.

For the first time since the war, a German airship again approached the English coast, but with peaceful intentions. We cruised over the cities of Lowestoft and Yarmouth, and then turned to meet the German ship *Cap Arcona* which greeted us with a searchlight.

During the night, we rose to 8,500 feet to release gas. A wonderful starry sky spread over us. At 2.58 we flew over Bremen. Then we changed course toward Flensburg to pay a visit to Dr Eckener's birthplace. Over the empty harbour of Kiel the sun came up. In the harbour of Hamburg there was an air of activity; it was plain that Hamburg's commerce was rising again.

Ahead in the sun, we could see the roofs of Berlin. But when we came closer, the capital, despite the beautiful clear morning, again wore its cap of mist. At Nauen, the first planes came toward us, singly at first, then in groups. The air was alive with them. First our course took us along the Linden to Wilhelmstrasse, to present the President with a great bouquet of flowers which we dropped by parachute. We received Hindenburg's reply during the homeward journey.

We flew over Leipzig, Dresden, Chemnitz, Nürnberg, and at last returned home to Friedrichshafen. We were in the air 34 hours and 30 minutes, and covered 1,950 miles.

Dr Hugo Eckener, (1868–1954), was the manager of the Luftschiffbau Zeppelin during the inter-war years, and also the commander of the famous *Graf Zeppelin* for most of its record-setting flights, including the first airship flight around the world, making him the most successful airship commander in history. He is pictured here in 1929. He was an anti-Nazi who was invited to campaign as a moderate in the German presidential elections. He was blacklisted by the regime and eventually sidelined.

30

THE FIRST TRANSATLANTIC FLIGHT
OF THE *GRAF ZEPPELIN*

T HE GERMAN FLIGHT was the prologue to the *Graf Zeppelin*'s great demonstration flight to New York. The Traffic Ministry, which had made the new construction possible by contributing 1,100,000 marks, now gave another 500,000 marks to insure the airship and its crew and carry out the test-flights. But the money was not sufficient to finance the American flight. Eckener decided to take on paying passengers.

Chief Correspondent Karl von Wiegand, of the Hearst Press, secured the press-rights for America, and Scherl and Ullstein obtained them for Germany; two American and two German journalists, two painters and two photographers made the crossing. One of the two painters was a Flensburg compatriot of Eckener's, Honorary Professor Dr Ludwig Dettmann, who drew a picture map of strong, colourful impressions of the trip. His artistic eye and skilful hand revelled in the eternally changing play of colour, light, air and water.

Two Americans, Dr Reiner, an industrialist who also owned a factory in Chemnitz, and Gilfillan, a financier living in Switzerland, paid 3,000 dollars each for cabins. Additional offers had to be rejected because of lack of space, although a rich Russian offered us the same sum, passionately assuring us that he was not a Bolshevik.

The government sent a Senate representative along, and the Traffic Ministry sent three men, namely: Ministerial Director Dr Brandenburg, a meteorologist, and a Fellow of the German Research Institute for Aviation.

The Telefunken-Gesellschaft and the Zeiss Company permitted us to experiment with shortwave sets and optical instruments. The Allianz Insurance Company sent along one of its Directors to determine the safety factor in airships with a view toward reducing the insurance rates which were still extremely high.

The guests invited to make the flight were Count Brandenstein-Zeppelin, son-in-law of the old Count, Colonel Herrera, head of the Spanish Airship Company Colon, who was making efforts to establish a South American line, and Commander Rosendahl.

Altogether there were twenty passengers and forty men of the crew, besides

Dr Eckener as Commander, Flemming, von Schiller and me, and the Watch Officers. As to mail, we had on board 66,000 letters and cards each franked with two- or four-mark stamps; the commemorative stamp issue was in great demand at the Post Office Department. We had valuable freight on board, too, and we again had our lucky canary.

Storm reports from the Atlantic prompted us to delay the departure for one day. The take-off, which Schiller commanded, was set for the morning of 11 October 1928.

When the airship was ready to be brought out, we found that the only woman passenger, Lady Drummond Hay, the journalist, had not yet finished her toilette and was not present. Breathlessly, she arrived with her colleague, Karl von Wiegand. Since the entrance stairs had already been removed, she was lifted on board through the door of the gondola and was no sooner there than she cried out the gondola window, 'For goodness' sake! My coat!' The ship's command was gallant enough to send a fast auto to the hotel to fetch the coat; and finally, the colossus, directed by Schiller's whistle, was set in motion by the rope spiders and trolleys.

At 7.55 the *Graf Zeppelin* rose from the earth, circled over the village and, flying at a low altitude in order not to lose gas, took course for Constance and the Rhine. Over Basle, two Swiss planes escorted us on our way.

On the other side of the border, they were replaced by two French military planes which convoyed us past the forbidden zones. This time, we did not cross France in a straight airline to the west, but made a detour through the valley of the Rhône although this increased the route by 1,250 miles. The regular weather reports had indicated that we would find more favourable flight conditions further south than we would have in the northern zone.

We sailed by the bright white chain of Alps, and at midday we were over Lyon where an airplane climbed up toward us. The earth was a burning brown; the past stared up at us from the ruins of the amphitheatres of Arles; the surf decorated the coast of the Mediterranean with a white ruff.

The Pyrenees were off to starboard; our mail-bag sank down toward the million lights of Barcelona. In the clear bright night, the mountains of Spain looked as cold and unreal as a lunar landscape. Still in darkness, we passed the Rock of Gibraltar at 5.18. The searchlight of the Ceuta lighthouse wandered in a restless circle.

The sun rose and poured its fiery rays on the endless ocean. A symphony of yellow and blue formed around the dark shadow of the airship. The clock was set back an hour. Up to this point we had flown with gasoline but now the motors were changed to gas, of which we had 25,000 cubic metres on board, enough for 120 hours.

Twice during the course of the morning we came across the German trade flag; the first steamer was sailing between Hamburg and South America, the second to East Africa. Almost all the ships on the normal route between the English Channel and Newfoundland reported 'Wind 9.' On the island of Madeira, however, where we set our clocks back for the second time, the sun was shining.

When at nightfall my watch was over, it was so humid in my cabin over the control car that I could not sleep. The south wind was warm and moist. Coming eastward over the Azores, the secondaries of a low pressure area poured in buckets over the outer envelope, and in the morning we sighted severe storms. The very first gust, apparently because it was incorrectly parried by our helmsman, who was still inexperienced, knocked the coffee-cups from the breakfast table and tossed our lady involuntarily into the painter's lap.

Shortly afterward, the Chief Machinist on duty came running through the walkway. The lower covering on the stabilizer had ripped loose, and the shreds were snapping in the wind. The engines were stopped. Every additional moment increased the damage. There was a call for volunteers. Helmsman Engineer Knud Eckener, Engineer Albert Sammt, Chief Helmsman Ludwig Marx, Navigator Hans Ladwig, Chief Engineer Wilhelm Siegle and Chief Mechanic Karl Beuerle relieved one another in assisting the Ship's Inspector, Ludwig Knorr. Supplied with tools and held by ropes, they climbed into the inside of the fin, which was partly open below them, and made their way along the girders like seamen swaying on the yardarms in a storm. They tore off the flapping shreds, tied the ends tight, spread some blankets over the damaged portion, and secured the whole thing with cord. Meanwhile, more rain squalls had set in, burdening the ship so much that, deprived of the aid of the engines, it began to sink.

Flemming was on duty in the control car. Observing the sinking of the ship, he turned to Dr Eckener. 'We've got to do something. We must start the engines.' Eckener knew that his son was among the half dozen men outside on the swaying duralumin girders, working desperately to repair the damage; he also knew that the increased wind-pressure might toss the men from the ship. But not a muscle moved in his haggard face, when he curtly ordered: 'Start engines!' The group of workers in the stern were withdrawn from the fin, and the ship resumed flight and regained altitude. Then the motors were stopped again, and the work continued. This procedure was repeated until the men had satisfactorily bound together the torn pieces of the cloth and made the stabilizer safe.

This battle with the elements took place exactly in mid-ocean. To strain the damaged fin as little as possible, we flew at half speed, and Eckener prudently asked the US Navy to have a torpedo-boat stand by—a precaution which later proved to be unnecessary and was countermanded. Unfortunately, thousands of well-intentioned messages of congratulation hindered us even on this flight. A radiogram from South America belatedly warned us of the bad weather, and Eckener laconically wired back: 'Thanks for warning, we've just had the weather.'

A mission was undertaken to repair the fin and a small team of riggers set out across the top of the Zeppelin in the late night storm to reattach the canvas and restore control to the captain. It was an extremely dangerous mission and it took place thousands of feet above the raging North Atlantic, during the repair process the Zeppelin's engines were turned off although this caused the airship to slowly descend, twice during the process the engines had to be powered up to push the ship back up to a safer altitude whilst the men on top held on for their lives. It is hardly surprising there is slight camera shake.

By then we had reached the vicinity of the Sargasso Sea, where islands of yellow weeds floated below us. The tail winds had veered to the northwest, and our progress toward the Bermuda Islands was retarded. It was dark again when we reached the city of Hamilton. The storm howled, and like a steer with its head lowered, the ship pushed on against it. At two in the morning, I was relieved at the control stand, where Eckener had watched for twenty-seven hours. He, too, lay down for a short nap.

Another dark night in the squally Gulf Stream weather, flying between monstrous black clouds, and then the coast of America rose out of the bright morning, a dark yellow stripe in the grey-green sea. A US Navy amphibian looped-the-loop in greeting. At eleven o'clock we flew over the beach, and at 12.28, convoyed by planes and welcomed by sirens, we dropped a floral wreath over the capital for the President of the United States.

City followed city, and between them lay the country towns with their square streets and identical little houses: Baltimore, Philadelphia, New York. The impression was stronger than it had been the first time. When we headed for the Statue of Liberty, we almost recoiled from the terrific din which rose up toward us. There was so much tooting, howling, shouting and whistle-blowing that our engines seemed mute beside it. Among the planes, I noticed a German Junkers with the word 'Hurrah' painted on its side. The North German Lloyd had painted a message on its roof, 'Welcome, *Graf Zeppelin*!'

On the 15th of October at 5.38, we landed in Lakehurst. Cross-winds prevented the immediate docking of the airship, and we moored it temporarily. It was berthed in the hangar some hours later. During the second half of the trip, we had been flying at reduced speed, and thus our flight had lasted 111 hours and 44 minutes in covering 6,200 miles. Journalists, photographers and cameramen crowded around us with Health, Customs and landing officials.

The emotion that gripped America was very much different from that of years before. Then, it was really only German Americans who fêted us; the rest of America welcomed the American naval airship ZR-3, and regarded the conquering of the Atlantic as a technical demonstration and a sporting proposition. This time, however, they stretched out a friendly hand, honouring, in the enemy of yesterday, the friend of today. When, at two at night, we were brought to New York in autos, and appeared in the restaurant of the Warwick Hotel, we were instantly recognized by the guests and received with spontaneous enthusiasm.

The official reception took place in the forenoon. The army of private autos which had been driven out to Lakehurst for our landing, moved toward New York, where our crew had been brought by steamer and train. Autos decorated with flags drove us up Broadway to City Hall. The masses of people went mad with enthusiasm; factory sirens were blowing, locomotive and steamer whistles shrilled out; the automobiles blew their horns, and a veritable storm of confetti and paper streamers fell from the windows of the skyscrapers. At City Hall, Mayor Walker bade us welcome.

For three days there was a stunning profusion of banquets, receptions, teas and dinners. We could not refuse any of them for our voyage again took on a political importance which quite overshadowed our worry about the proper maintenance of the airship, left to the Watch Officers and Engineers on duty. On the occasion of our arrival, the President of the United States and the President of Germany exchanged cordial telegrams, and then Coolidge received Dr Eckener and his officers at the White House in Washington. While we were talking to him, the door opened, and Mrs Coolidge asked permission to listen to the story of our odyssey. At night, every important naval, military and political personage in the United States was at the German Embassy.

The Zeppelin fever had gripped entire America. Even certain sober persons were not entirely untouched by it, namely, those very persons whom we needed to establish a regular airship service. American financial circles seemed inclined to invest a few dollars in this new and interesting venture, but they first demanded a great many thoroughgoing explanations. During conferences

Ernst Lehmann, Hugo Eckener, Hans Flemming, President Calvin Coolidge and Navy Secretary Curtis Wilbur at the White House, 16 October 1924.

with leading bankers in New York and Akron, where President Litchfield of the Goodyear Zeppelin Corporation had invited us, Eckener suggested a joint operation of four great airships, and he estimated the necessary capital at fifteen million dollars. But since the financial backers themselves wished to make certain investigations they first founded the International Zeppelin Transport Corporation, whose experts undertook extensive and precise researches into the entire problem of airship transportation. Meanwhile, the navy board of the USA had become aware of another possible use for the airship, namely, the military. Not without justification, the airships seemed to them to be the perfect scouting weapon for a land lying between two great oceans. The orders which the American Zeppelin Company later received were issued by the Navy Board of the United States. They actually left the German company out in the cold—to the detriment of both, as later events were to prove.

Meantime, the damaged stabilizing fin was repaired by the civilian personnel of the naval air station. The *Graf Zeppelin* was supposed to make a side-trip to Cleveland, St Louis, and Chicago, but this was cancelled in view of the bad weather.

When Eckener returned from a visit to Chicago, he found the airship ready for the take-off. Hydrogen and 27,000 cubic metres of American gasoline were taken on, and to this we added fifteen tons of Gasoline-benzol, three tons of oil and six tons of water-ballast. Forty-eight bags of mail and 331 packages were stored in the cargo rooms with a bale of cotton which was to be auctioned off at the Bremen stock-exchange for the benefit of our crew. The canary remained behind as an immigrant, and was replaced by a chow, which Helmsman Sammt took under his charge.

Of the twenty-five passengers, a few had made the trip over. Our lady remained in America to lecture about her voyage; and we instead received another paying woman passenger, Mrs Clara Adams. Five of her American compatriots had also secured passage through the Thomas Cook agency, paying 3,000 dollars each. Again the demand was greater than the supply. One prospective passenger offered a thousand dollars to anyone who would give up his ticket. And in the fact of this attractive proposition, business triumphed over pleasure; the buyer flew with us, the seller remained behind.

We almost left another passenger behind, too. Mr Joseph Jessel, dissatisfied with the hot dogs at Lakehurst, drove his family to Lakewood. On the return trip, they met with an accident, and Jessel and his mother were injured. But the mother herself begged the son not to abandon the flight because of her; and with his injuries well bandaged, Mr Jessel boarded the airship.

When the *Graf Zeppelin* was just about to start, Jessel's private secretary rushed to the entrance-platform, threw her arms around unsuspecting Knud Eckener's neck and kissed him 'in the name of all the women of America!' Blond Knud had been a hero since the day he repaired the damaged fin in mid-ocean. Fortunately, he inherited some of his father's qualities, and he bore his fame with equanimity.

On 29 October, at 1.55 in the morning, the airship began its return trip over the Atlantic, this time taking the shorter northern route, where a number of surprises awaited us.

The sea of light over New York showed us our way, and the Statue of Liberty lifted her burning torch toward the proud ship. The sirens howled again, but by the time the sleeping metropolis was awakened, we were already out over Long Island. Nantucket fell away behind us and, as the moon paled before the rising sun, we were out over the ocean once more.

Schiller, making an inspection trip through the ship, discovered a stowaway, whom he brought to the control car. The boy, not yet nineteen years old, had sneaked in at Lakehurst and hidden in the mail-compartment of the ship.[33] It was said that this had been prepared by the American press as a little surprise for us and their readers. The blond boy, wearing a blood-red shirt, and with a toothbrush as his sole piece of luggage, was pitifully hungry and cold. Since we could not throw him overboard, Eckener made the best of a bad situation. The adventurer was placed in charge of Flemming, who sent him to the steward to help wash the dishes and sweep out the cabins. The press had its sensation; and more was radioed about the stowaway than the real sensation which awaited us off Newfoundland.

The *Graf Zeppelin* flies over New York.

It was midday. The diners inside the ship were enjoying the food prepared by the new cook whom we had borrowed from the North German Lloyd in New York. We had chicken soup, chicken, vegetables, and gooseberry cake or fruit. The young dog, however, devoured the newspapers, either because of his vanity, since they made mention of him, or because he liked the taste of them.

At this moment of calm, the ship suddenly reared up violently. Heavy rains pattered down on the outer envelope and the wind changed in one swift motion from north-west to south-west. We of the ship's command knew what this meant; we were passing a squall front, a sign that we were flying into a low pressure area. At first we remained low over the sea, flying at the rate of 100 miles per hour, but when we approached Newfoundland, the thick fog forced us up over a layer of clouds.

The changes of watch were arranged as on the trip across; day-shifts of four hours and night-shifts of three hours. But I do not believe that a single one of our men slept during the turbulent night that followed this calm day. It was the worst night an airship ever lived through, not excepting the years of the war. Whoever lived through that night now knows what an expertly constructed airship, in skilful hands, can endure. Experienced airshipmen and helmsmen were at the control-stand, and Eckener is a commander the like of which the world has never seen. During this night, when the hurricane almost tore the light, but well-made ship apart, I became convinced that the Zeppelin of today need fear no storm on any part of the earth.

The fog banks which always lie off Newfoundland forced us high into the clouds, and for a few hours we had no opportunity to determine our course or the direction and strength of the wind. Thus, we hardly noticed that above us a storm from the south-east was racing along at a speed of 80 and sometimes 115 miles per hour, that is, at a rate far swifter than the *Graf Zeppelin*'s own speed. Consequently, the ship was forced off its course, which should have taken it south of Newfoundland, and driven north; and a short time later, when the veil of clouds parted, we were no little surprised to find ourselves over the islands north-east of Newfoundland. That would have meant very little to us if the hurricane, in passing over the islands, had not broken up into thousands of air-currents which hour after hour continued to hammer at the ship. But Eckener knew what to do. The motors were set at half speed, for it was wiser to yield, and the rocking of our airship diminished. The main force of the gale was broken. But naturally we scarcely moved from our position, and it was almost daybreak before we were able to push out of the storm-centre, which had delayed us almost half a day. We changed course to keep our bow into the wind, marking time, so to speak; but we were still being driven to the north-east. The *Graf Zeppelin* rolled and heaved like a sea-vessel; in the black sea below us, the waves were high as houses, and half a dozen icebergs floated by.

The radio operator received a message from the *Mauretania*, which was south of us. The wind velocity there was 8 (about 50 mph), and all the passengers on the liner were sea-sick. We expected an improvement, and tail-winds, at the break of day. At midday, the sun pushed through, and the sea became comparatively calm. An English steamer gave us its position, which coincided with our calculations. A cable-steamer sent its boats out to work. And our engines, which had bucked the changing squalls for so long a time, were stopped one at a time for rest and inspection.

The weather map, which was worked out at night, indicated another low pressure area north of Ireland. We avoided it by taking a southern course and heading for Biscay. Our passengers, meanwhile, were dancing with the only woman on board.

At midnight, we again changed course and headed east. At three in the morning the clock was set ahead for the third time. Everything had become light, and a rainbow haloed us as if the heavens were bestowing a laurel wreath upon the ship. We accepted that as a happy omen and took time out to devour the cake which was presented to us in America. Even our stowaway and the dog received their share. But below us, the sea was still raging, and later, when Dr Eckener leaned out of the window, a freak gust blew away his well-known blue naval cap.

The sea traffic became livelier, and fishing steamers were dancing on waves far higher than they. The lighthouses blinked off the French coast, and at 5.10 we passed the mouth of the Loire. Later, it became hazy, and only once could we recognize a large city below us—Dijon. Fog concealed the rest of France, and when it parted again, there was water below us once more, the Bodensee, our homeland.

For technical reasons and in consideration of the waiting crowds and the photographers, we made three great circles before descending to the dockyards. At seven in the morning, on 1 November 1928, the handling lines dropped. The *Graf Zeppelin*, with sixty-four persons on board and a service load of 88,000 pounds, had covered the 4,560 miles of the return flight with an average speed of 63 miles per hour, in 71 hours and 51 minutes.

Thirty-thousand people, summoned by fireworks, surrounded the enclosed dockyards; and in response to the general demand, General Director Colsman permitted the doors to be opened, letting in a jubilant crowd. The church-bells rang; and once more the *Deutschland* hymn was sung spontaneously. After that, the band played the *Star Spangled Banner*. The Traffic Minister was lifted into the control car, and was the first to congratulate us in the name of the government. The President's congratulations arrived by radiogram. The next ones on board, soon after the airship was brought into the hangar, were two customs officers; their visit was a mere formality. But the American Consul from Stuttgart was waiting at the stern exit with two policemen to take charge of the stowaway.

That night, during a modest celebration at the Kurgarten Hotel, Eckener carefully poured oil on the all too high-breaking waves of enthusiasm by announcing that a passenger service to North America required stronger and larger ships than the *Graf Zeppelin*. Later, the honours and congratulations poured in. Three colleges, Freiburg, Heidelberg and Karlsruhe, presented Eckener and Dürr with honorary degrees.

Most of the American passengers soon left for Berlin where they could telephone to their relations at home. Mr Jessel quickly completed his business in dress models, and then retired to a Berlin hospital to have his injuries attended to.

Five days later we were in Berlin with the airship. For the 500-mile trip to Staaken, we required 7 hours and 27 minutes; that is, our average speed was 67 miles per hour. But during the last part of our flight, our speed rose to 112 miles per hour. The gusty winds and the roaring crowd of enthusiastic people endangered the anchored vessel; later, at night, the wind died, and the great silver fish gleamed in the bright glare of the searchlights.

At midday we made our entrance—I can use no other phrase for it, immodest as it sounds—into Berlin. Heerstrasse, Charlottenburger Chaussee, Linden and Wilhelmstrasse were thickly crowded with men and women and especially children, who had been given the day off and shouted happily at us. In the palace of the President, we were received by Hindenburg. The President shook the hands of Eckener and the officers, had each man of the crew presented to him, and even singled out Dr Dürr, who designed the LZ 127, and Dr Maybach,

Above left: Clarence Terhune is led away by a policeman.

Above right: Ludwig Dürr, (1878–1956). After completing training as a mechanic, Dürr continued his training at the Königliche Baugewerkschule. From 1899 Ludwig Dürr worked for Ferdinand von Zeppelin. After assisting in the construction of the first Zeppelin airship, the LZ 1, he himself began to construct airships and lightweight construction parts. All of the following Zeppelin designs were the work of Ludwig Dürr. He remained with the Company until the end in 1945. He is photographed on 1 November 1928.

who constructed the motors, for special recognition. He also greeted the three American naval officers. Hindenburg wore the black frock of civilian attire, and he seemed to have grown old, but his glance was clear and his bearing was that of the old soldier. I was touched by the memory of that hour in Lötzen, when for the first time I had stepped into the presence of this great German.

The President addressed us as follows:

> That it is a great pleasure to see you, gentlemen, the builders, commanders and crew of the *Graf Zeppelin*, I need not indicate in words. It is a great satisfaction to me to learn to know you all personally, and to tell all of you with what avidity I followed your flight, and how pleased I was over your splendid performance. All of us, the entire German people, sent our prayers and good wishes with you on your flight. The heart of all Germany beat proudly for the airship, especially during the days of uncertainty and the dangerous hours of storm.
>
> In this new airship, in its glorious flight through storm and fog, over continents and seas, the Fatherland saw a superb German achievement. I am certain of speaking in the name of the entire German people when I express my deepest and most heartfelt gratitude to all those who worked with head or hand in the creation of the airship and piloted it safely through storm and

danger. You have in the best sense of the word completed a national exploit. The hearty reception which the *Graf Zeppelin* received from the American people is bound to make good neighbours of peoples separated by oceans. May the German Airship Company, and you, gentlemen, continue to have success always!

Dr Eckener made a suitable reply, thanking the President for his kindness and good wishes.

Eckener remained in Berlin to confer with the government officials, and I flew the *Graf Zeppelin* from Staaken to Friedrichshafen. There, after a last flight of a few hundred miles, the airship was placed in its hangar for its winter's sleep and a thorough overhauling.

31

THE FIRST MEDITERRANEAN FLIGHT
OF THE *GRAF ZEPPELIN*

WHEN THE GREAT feats of the LZ 127 are spoken of, the general public usually remembers only the transoceanic flights, and entirely forgets the flights to Holland, England, Iceland, the North capes, Spain, the Balkans, Moscow over the North Sea, the Baltic, the Arctic Ocean and the Mediterranean. I must deny myself the pleasure of telling about each of these trips individually, but I can illustrate all of them by an account of the first Mediterranean flight, making use of Flight Engineer Beuerle's notes.

Months had passed since our two-way crossing of the Atlantic, and the *Graf Zeppelin* had been overhauled and thoroughly inspected by officials of the Deutschen Verlagsanstalt for Aviation both in the hangar and on short test flights. Certain improvements were made, such as replacing the cotton covering of the stabilizers with stronger linen, and rebuilding the crew's sleeping quarters in the walkway.

The completion of these alterations was the signal for the beginning of flights on a grand scale, the first of which was to be to the Orient. For weeks, the world press had been preoccupied with the airship and especially with this momentous project. The entire world was even playing a guessing game about whether or not we would be permitted to fly over Egypt.

On Sunday, 24 March 1929, the ship was reported 'Ready' for the first Orient flight, with mail compartments and passenger cabins entirely occupied. There weren't even enough cabins for the twenty-eight passengers, and a few had to be accommodated in the rebuilt crew's quarters in the walkway.

As often before, the weather was tricky. Although the rain stopped, it was replaced by a north-east wind, the sort that always made our launching difficult. We had to stand by to get the ship undocked during a lull.

Our ruse worked. The take-off was scheduled for 12.50 a.m., and at 12.55 we were once more in the air. Over the lake, we headed for Constance and toward the Mediterranean, following the same route we took during the trip to America.

The fog became thicker and thicker, so that it seemed ill-advised to take the airship further south into the valley of the Rhône, in the mountainous regions of France. Therefore, in the vicinity of Lyon, Dr Eckener slowed down to wait for daylight. And at daybreak, the fog disappeared.

By 8.45 we had reached the Mediterranean, and we crossed Marseilles at a great altitude. The harbour swarmed with ships. In the middle of the city, looming high on a bare cliff, stood a lonely church with a large gilt figure. An island was almost hidden by a solid mass of birds flying hither and thither in fear of the great stranger hovering above them. Soon thereafter we observed the antics of dolphins or porpoises. Singly and in groups they leaped from the water, their silver bodies showing clearly against the blue of the sea.

We set course for Corsica and descended to 650 feet to check our altitude; that is, to determine our flying altitude by Echolot and thereby ascertain whether the barometer was rising or falling and regulate our instruments accordingly. Lady Drummond Hay absolutely insisted upon getting into an engine car, and she finally obtained the permission. With a little help and a great deal of courage, she made it. For more than a half hour she endured the roaring motors, and then she smilingly ascended the ladder and climbed into the ship. Good girl! But even after that she was still restless. And since there was nothing to be seen below, she helped the ship's mailmen stamp the airmail postcards.

At 12.39 we passed the northern point of the island of Corsica, and ahead of us lay the island of Elba, covered by a queer cloud formation. Then we flew with a west wind along the Italian coast, and over old Ostia toward Rome, which we reached at 3.45 o'clock. With a direct course for the Vatican, the *Graf Zeppelin* flew over Rome, greeting the King and Mussolini, who, depressed by Nobile's failure, not so long ago had ordered the Italian airship fleet destroyed as obsolete.

It was a pity, but our next goal, Naples, was concealed in mist. An ocean steamer was just leaving the harbour. Vesuvius had donned a colossal cap of smoke. Behind Sorrento, a few mountains, only 4,600 feet high, were heavily covered by snow, a rarity for this locality and that particular time of year.

We steered straight across the mainland toward the eastern coast of Italy. At nine o'clock we passed over a large, brightly illuminated city of Catanzaro. The fog-banks now became so thick that sometimes the lights on the gondolas became invisible. Suddenly, as if it had been cut off, the pea-soupy fog ended. Before us there appeared a ghostly wall, good enough for a stage set, and its frightful formations were repeated below us. We were again over water, and the clouds were being reflected in the bright moonlight.

In the morning, we left the north-eastern coast of Crete and flew eastward toward Palestine. Light winds, which continued to come more and more from the stern, accelerated our flight.

At 4.15 in the afternoon we reached Haifa. Palestine, the furthest point of our flight, lay at our feet, and the city stretched outward into the bay. The neat red-brown houses were of Turkish style of architecture. On a field below us stood a landing-crew, and in great white letters the word 'Welcome' was visible on the ground. In the vicinity of Caesarea a nomad tribe had pitched their tents, and further south another tribe lived in red earthen huts.

Then, as in Haifa, the close-pressed houses lay beneath us again; we were over Jaffa. The Arabian quarters formed the centre of the city, crowded house on house in close terrace-formation. Since the Levantine twilight was falling quickly, lights flared up here and there, accentuating the artistry of the setting.

Our route led inland toward El Ramleh, where our mail was to be dropped. The receiving station gave the Morse signal with a searchlight. When we replied that we were ready, we headed for the field, and the first mailbags of the German Imperial Post Office swayed slowly to earth in a little parachute, a greeting from the Occident to the Orient.

Onward we flew, towards Jerusalem. Unfortunately, we were a few hours too late. Even while we were approaching, the full moon rose red as blood and threw its magical light over the city. We could do nothing but make a few turns over the holy place and thus extend our greetings. From below, we must have looked like a fiery chariot.

At a low altitude we flew over the Dead Sea, where we dropped an incendiary bomb into the water to check the wind. In the full moonlight, we flew only 500 feet over the level of the sea. Since this sea is 1,300 feet below sea level, we were flying 800 feet under the surface of the Mediterranean.

At 6.10 in the morning, we were in Athens. The houses were built so that we could look into almost all of them from above. The Acropolis was clearly visible. Around Athens, all the high peaks were covered with snow. Increasing head-winds and reports that the weather conditions were not much better in the Black Sea region, caused Dr Eckener to make the return trip over the Adriatic. At midday we entered the Straits of Otranto, a sacred place, for there lay the men of the L 59, the Africa-ship.

At a 5,000-foot altitude, we pushed northward between the Velebit Mountains and the Dinaric Alps. In a dark, stormy night we flew over the mountains which were still heavily clad with snow. At 2.55 o'clock we were over Vienna. Slowly, we cruised over the brightly lit city. A few searchlights groped upward, but could not reach us. Through a nasty rain we returned to Friedrichshafen. In 81 hours and 28 minutes we had covered 5,000 miles, fully as many as the distance to New York.

This first Mediterranean flight found such favour that it was repeated a month later. Shortened to 3,400 miles, the second flight was made in 56 hours and 53 minutes. On the third flight, in April 1931, we landed in Cairo. The enthusiasm of the Egyptians knew no bounds and the fire department had to be called out to use their hoses in protecting the airship from the crowds. The *Graf Zeppelin* circled the pyramids and the old and new sciences took each other's measure. From Cairo I piloted the airship on a flight over the Holy City of Palestine, while Eckener, Flemming and one watch of the crew remained behind for a banquet with the German, English and Egyptian officials. Over the grave of the Redeemer we reverently sank the prow of the ship. German, Swiss, Spaniards, Englishmen and Egyptians enjoyed this pilgrimage, during which, in a flight of 5,600 miles, were touched fourteen lands and three continents. There were many more of these Mediterranean flights, some of which were round-trips from Friedrichshafen without intermediate landings, and others which made landings in Mediterranean countries, such as Italy and Spain.

I want to tell another little story, about a landing in Seville, because it indicates the spirit which existed between the crew and the officers where duties permitted it. It was about Eastertime, and we had again landed in Seville. King Alfonso XIII, who was still ruling at that time, was on the field with the royal family and wished to inspect the ship. He was very much interested in it, and once before, after the world flight, I had had to tell him a great deal about it during an audience in Madrid.

Now, he was coming along the landing-field, and I was still trying to get a clean collar on. Naturally, the collar button broke. I rushed into the radio cabin and said, 'Dunke, take off your collar. I need the button.' Our radio operator, Chief Inspector Dunke, had mild doubts about my sanity, but he rose quickly and handed me the button. Then I heard Flemming, who was on watch in the control room, call out, 'The King will be here soon!'

I: 'Delay him for a minute!'

Flemming: 'Schiller! Delay the King!' Schiller, who was on watch at the entranceway, alertly commanded, 'Steps away!' Then, although it was not at all necessary, he had the ship hauled back and forth until I had won my battle with the obstreperous collar-button. Then the stairs were replaced and the King was permitted to enter.

Then the following incident took place. Flemming was on duty in the control car when Ernest, the little second steward, reported in beautiful Swabian, 'Mr Flemming, there's a dame in the kitchen. She says she's the Queen.' And it was.

By mentioning the Mediterranean cruise, I anticipated the events that preceded it. In May 1929 we were to repeat our flight to North America, but an incident of a technical nature, which we could not reckon with, forced us to make an emergency landing in southern France and at one stroke placed a doubt upon everything we had hitherto achieved. Much has been whispered about the mystery of Toulon; in reality, however, it was nothing more nor less than the result of torsional vibrations which caused crankshaft cracks, and this had always been a frequent and never entirely clarified occurrence even in aeroplane

Graf Zeppelin Jerusalem, 26 April 1931.

Graf Zeppelin over the pyramids, 1931.

motors. The technical shortcoming, once recognized, was done away with once and for all, and the research instruments and methods discovered at that time are now at the service of aviation as a whole. Our official accident-report of the damage, which conceals nothing, follows:

The airship *Graf Zeppelin* took off on 16 May 1929, at 5.58 o'clock in the morning for a flight to Lakehurst. On board were eighteen passengers, forty-one crew, 650 pounds of mail and 2,530 pounds of cargo.

At about ten o'clock we reached the Rhône Valley. The wind, which until then had been west-south-west, now swung to the north and remained steady, so that for a time a tailwind of 38 miles per hour was measured. At midday, we passed the coast at Le Grand du Roi and took course for Barcelona, which we reached at 2.42 p.m.

One hour earlier, engine No. 3 (starboard stern) was cut off, since its crankshaft had broken at the second cylinder. The ship's command debated whether, under these conditions, the flight should be abandoned. But since there were no general conclusions to be drawn about the rest of the engines from the breaking of one crankshaft and the weather conditions were such that the flight over the Atlantic could be undertaken even with the four remaining engines, we continued on our way.

At 6.25, at 38 degrees 31 minutes North and 0 degrees 33 minutes West, we had to stop Engine No. 5 (starboard fore) also, since the No. 7 governor arm had broken. Thereupon, we instantly put about.

Although we carefully nursed the motors, our tailwinds gave us a comparatively good speed, and at 10.34 o'clock Barcelona was on the beam bearing. Shortly thereafter, a northern wind set in and during the night, sometimes reached a velocity of 55 miles per hour. But despite the failure of the two starboard engines, the ship rode calmly and responded easily to the rudders. At 7.46 o'clock, on 17 May, we crossed the coast at Sainte-Marie. But since we had to reckon on mistrals in the Rhône valley, we remained west of the Rhône.

For a time, the ship's speed over the ground fell to five miles per hour. Therefore, we tried to do better at a higher altitude. But since at 5,300 feet the wind velocity was 55 miles per hour, equalling the speed of the ship, we descended again. At midday, the wind died down somewhat, and our speed over the ground increased to 20 miles per hour. Above the heights of Montelimar, we took a more easterly course, heading toward Friedrichshaften via Lake Geneva.

At 2.15, shortly after changing course, the No. 7 governor arm on engine No. 2 (port stern) broke off. Five minutes later engine No. 1 (middle engine) stopped—governor arm No. 3 had broken. The ship's speed through the air fell to 25 miles per hour, and it was impossible to continue the homeward journey against a wind still blowing at 30 miles per hour. There was no alternative but an emergency landing on a suitable field, in order to finish the return flight after the repairs, or when the wind died. First, to get out of the strong winds, we turned out of the valley of the Rhône and into a side-arm of the valley of the Drôme.

Even with the one remaining motor, the ship answered the helm. Near Saillans, a short distance from the end of the valley, we were to land at a place which had seemed suitable from above. The preparations for the landing were made, and the ship was to come down slowly and then be secured to trees by means of the landing ropes.

But during the approach to the landing-place, we found that a strong gusty wind was blowing along the ground also. Consequently we went up again, turned in the narrow valley and sought for another, calmer spot. But since we were unable to find an appropriate spot, we once more left the valley of the Drôme and dropped a message for the garrison at Valence to prepare troops for a landing.

But while we were slowly getting out of the valley, we saw that we could not reach Valence because of the strong head-winds. We then turned toward the Riviera, where we hoped to find calmer weather. During the flight there, we received a radio from the French Air Minister, which offered the French airship bases for an emergency landing. The naval airship base at Cuers-Pierrefeu, near Toulon, was on our route, and we immediately set course for it. When we reached Cuers at 8.15 o'clock, we found a landing-crew of forty-five waiting for us. The landing took place without any difficulty.

The German commercial airship found safety in a modern French hangar. From Friedrichshafen, replacement motors arrived by rail, were assembled and brought us back home, where we set to work to determine the cause of the accidents.

As fatal as the cancellation of the second Atlantic flight at first seemed to be for our commercial traffic plans and our financial prospects, the accident brought its blessings too. France, which hitherto had tolerated rather than welcomed us, had found the opportunity to prove its nobility, and this opportunity was grasped willingly by everyone from the Air Minister to the last soldier in the landing-crew. Furthermore, this magnificent gesture had considerable influence upon public opinion and contributed no little to the subsequent improvement in relations.

The second blessing was derived from the safety of the airship, which seemed again and again to be placed in doubt because of accidents in other countries.

Two years after this journey, when I was returning from Brazil on the *Graf Zeppelin*, I flew up the Rhône, and showed my collaborator the route we took through the rectangular corner of the wide, stony Drôme Valley. He shook his head in astonishment. 'I am aware that you must have escaped the mistral with your one remaining motor, but how in the world did you ever get out of this mouse-trap?'

Many people asked us the same thing and said it was a mystery that we came out of the valley and got to Toulon at all. The answer is simple and unequivocal; the very fact that the flight was broken off proved that the ship's command could retain control under all circumstances and that a skilfully piloted airship could get out of a critical situation even with only a minor portion of its motor power.

Many people were needed to hold down LZ 127 *Graf Zeppelin*.

32

THE ROUND THE WORLD VOYAGE

T HE SET-BACK, FOR which we were not to blame, was made up for. More
than that; that which had been the aim and object of the abandoned flight
over the Atlantic, now became incidental child's play. Between 1 and 10
August 1929, the *Graf Zeppelin* flew to Lakehurst and back simply to fetch
the passengers for the world flight, which the Americans began from Lakehurst
and the Germans from Friedrichshafen.
Crew of the *Graf Zeppelin*, world tour 1929.

There was a five day rest in the home port, and then the *Graf Zeppelin*
continued on its trip around the world. On 15 August 1929, at 4.35 in the
morning, the ship took off with a crew of forty-one, twenty passengers and
880 pounds of mail. The passengers were representatives of the press, films,
government and army, including a few civilians, Germans, Americans, Japanese,
a Swiss, a Russian, a Frenchman, a Spaniard, and an Australian. Once again,
Lady Drummond Hay was the only woman on board.[34] Her small black
kitten, which died in Japan, was our mascot. One of the most interesting of the
passengers was Sir Hubert Wilkins.[35] Mr Leeds, who married Grand Duchess
Xenia of Russia, stared thoughtfully at the representative from Soviet Russia;
I don't think they would have understood each other even if Mr Karklin had
spoken a language other than Russian.

We set course over Leipzig, Berlin, Stettin, Danzig, and Königsberg. So many
good wishes and prayers accompanied us! For it was not only our little dockyard
affairs we were furthering this time, it was all Germany's affair.

On the next morning, when I was hurriedly breakfasting between my stretch
of duty and a four-hour nap, we were already deep in Russia. What a great
contrast there was between this gigantic, desolate land brimming with treasures
and the neat, economically divided German countryside. We saw people staring
up at us as if they were turned to stone; and others ran at the sight of us, fleeing
with the cattle that stampeded in fear.

Vologda, where some thirty golden church cupolas stood up in the midst of a
great many wooden houses, was the first Russian city which we saw by daylight,

Crew of the *Graf Zeppelin*, world tour 1929.

Grace Marguerite Hay Drummond-Hay, Lady Hay Drummond-Hay, (1895-1946). She was widowed in 1925, and later lived with fellow journalist Karl Henry von Wiegand, (1874-1961). They are photographed here together.

Hubert Wilkins, (1888-1958), photographed shortly before his death.

and it was indicative of its kind. The Russian geographer spoke to Eckener, to me, and to Schiller; and though we did not understand him, we suspected that he was inviting us to Moscow—an invitation which the government soon thereafter confirmed by radio. But we could not accept if we wanted to fly through to Tokyo; we had to take advantage of the tailwinds and remain on the straight airline without deviation or halt. We therefore politely declined. We later learned that they were quite disappointed in Moscow; there, as in many other places, they could not realize our successes were the result of never exceeding the limits or violating the laws of science.

The forests stretched off toward the Urals, behind which lay the terrible desolation of the tundras of Asia. Our newspapermen worked feverishly on their portable typewriters while the other passengers spent their time dancing. In my free time, I got out my 'seaman's piano,' the large accordion which substituted for the cello when we were under way, and played excerpts from *Die Meistersinger*.

We flew over Siberia day and night, seeing swamps, forests and streams, but not one city, hardly even a person. It was a benumbing yet somehow great impression; it can best be expressed by the word — 'monstrous'!

Only when we were on the Lena River did we again strike a city: Yakutsk. We dropped a wreath for the German prisoners of war who were buried in Siberia. A mailbag was dropped overboard—when would the mail reach its addressees from this remote locality?

Meanwhile, radio-communication with the outer world had long since ceased. There was some anxiety for our safety, and we were reported lost. We ourselves were much relieved when our radio officer, Dunke, and his radiomen, Speck and Freund, finally received weather reports from a Japanese station. The reports were satisfactory—remarkable as that may sound—for they mentioned a typhoon passing along the eastern coast of Japan. The Japanese Frigate-Captain Fuijiyoshi, who had had a great deal of experience in the typhoon service of his country, proved to be invaluable.

The Stanovoi Mountains, which cut off the view of the sea, proved to be many hundreds of feet higher than the maps indicated; luckily, we had clear weather, so that we could choose the easiest route through the valleys and between the mighty naked peaks with a minimum loss of altitude and gas. The Okhotsk Sea on the other side received us with a wet cold fog. When, near Port Ayan, the fog dispersed, the vast extent of the Pacific Ocean was spread in an endless blue-green mass beneath us.

The expected typhoon brought us a night of storm, rain and strong tailwinds, and carried us over the Tartar Sound, along the coast of Sakhalin. And on the next morning, over the Island of Hokaido, we saw our first Japanese, who were literally hidden under their wide-brimmed, pointed straw-hats. How refreshing this was after Siberia; all the islands were neatly divided into rice fields, gardens and clean houses. Instantly, this pleasing order formed a bridge of sympathy between us Germans and the sons of the Far East.

On 19 August, at 2.45—Central European Time, which our clocks had naturally abandoned a long time ago—the German airship *Graf Zeppelin* flew over the city-limits of Tokyo. In ninety-nine hours we had covered a stretch for which the Siberian Express required five times as long. And the steamer trip from Germany to Japan takes forty-two days.

From the bird's-eye view, Tokyo looked like a modern American metropolis around which were pressed thousands of villages. The village-like outskirts were the old city, which rejuvenates itself and remains unchanged through all earthquakes. We avoided flying over the Imperial residence, for, according to Japanese customs, it would have been disrespectful. We steered over the lively harbour of Yokohama and over the naval base at Ksumiga-ura, where the former German airship hangar had been rebuilt.

The colourful clothes and the bright paper and silk parasols of the Japanese made a delightful wreath around the landing-field. The white clothes in the crowd marked the members of the German colony, who had come from all parts of Japan to see with their own eyes this flying bit of their homeland.

After the LZ 127 had landed and was in the hangar, we were welcomed with Japanese speeches and Japanese beer and the happy laughter of fifty thousand

The wireless station at Nauen, Germany which received all of the messages from the *Graf Zeppelin*. 'All the latest devices of radio-land are in service in this huge wireless station at Nauen, Germany. Radio messages sent from the *Graf Zeppelin* on its epochal flight around the world passed through the receiving apparatus shown in the photo above.'

spectators. Eckener replied in German, which was then translated into Japanese, and we were escorted to autos and driven through a landscape that seemed fabulously strange and yet somehow familiar. 'I keep pinching myself on the arm,' said Hans von Schiller softly, 'to make sure I'm not dreaming.' For my part, I didn't have to pinch myself; I was quietly reckoning, and noted with satisfaction: 'World flight, first stretch Friedrichshafen-Tokyo: distance, 7,030 miles; time, 101 hours and 49 minutes.'

The kindly hospitality of the Japanese host has no equal in the world. The whole country outdid itself in expressions of friendship which were not meant for us alone, but for the land we represented. Our hearts were warmed; but we were also warm in a different way. We had come from Siberian cold, against which our leather jackets and furs had been woefully inadequate protection, into the Japanese summer at its hottest. '105 in the shade,' gasped my neighbour at a tea house while he poured one bottle of beer after another into himself and only perspired the more.

The tea house, with geishas and everything that goes with them, was the site of the official reception, and here Dr Eckener, who sat with folded legs on a silk cushion, like the others, was presented with a number of gifts.

I cannot deny myself the pleasure of telling another amusing story, which I am sure Dr Eckener will not take amiss, because it so neatly shows Flemming's sense of humour.

After the landing in Tokyo, and before disembarking from the ship, Eckener had to change his clothes hurriedly. In the darkness of the cabin, his foot caught somewhere, and he tore a big hole in one of his stockings. Naturally, he just stepped into his shoes and later came on to dinner.

Flemming and I were with him when he stepped out before the brightly illuminated entranceway of the tea house, where our hosts were already waiting for us in gala dress. In the background of the sparkling lacquered floor stood a whole row of geishas, wearing beautiful colored robes—and all the people, hosts, guests and geishas, were walking around in their stocking feet! According to Japanese custom, shoes are never worn in the house—much less real boots—and so we, too, in friendly and courteous pantomime, were requested to take ours off.

The gracious geishas approached and kneeled to untie our laces when Flemming and I noticed that Dr Eckener suddenly remembered something. He began to shift nervously from one foot to the other. First we heard him murmur and then grumble, and finally he declared loudly and categorically, 'I won't take my shoes off.'

While our hosts and the geishas laughed courteously, and blankly, he took Flemming and me off to a corner and explained the situation. Then, in a deep calm voice, Flemming said, 'All right, Doctor, we'll all three of us keep them on and simply explain that it's against our religion to take them off!'

We got by with this explanation, for the Japanese had meanwhile observed our reluctance, if not the reason for it, and they came to our assistance with large woollen sacks, which were pulled over our shoes and gave us wonderful elephantine feet. Then we were permitted to participate in the festivities.

At another dinner, Eckener was presented with an ancient sword of honour, and the entire assemblage broke into laughter and applause when he buckled it on immediately. Then the charming geishas placed delicate cups and saucers on the table and served tiny portions of bouillon, chicken, rice, salad, raw meat and a number of other foods which we uncertainly attempted to lift with chop-sticks. Our efforts again caused laughter among the Japanese, but not the offensive sort; rather an infectious laughter, in which we Germans heartily joined.

On 22 August, at four in the morning, the flight was to be resumed. But as the ship was being brought out, the trolley guide stuck to the rail, and although Captain von Schiller, who had charge of the start, acted instantly, he was too late to prevent the rear engine car from striking and bending three of its struts. That meant repairs, and a whole day lost.

An echelon of Japanese naval fliers escorted us out over the Pacific. When they had turned around, another echelon was released from on board the *Graf Zeppelin*, namely, four carrier-pigeons which a Japanese journalist had taken along as couriers, and which Commander Rosendahl carefully loosed from the stern.

During the first night, we sneaked up on a typhoon in order to take advantage of its tailwinds, and in storm, rain and lightning, we passed through its southernmost secondary.

Somewhere in the Pacific we crossed the international date line, and we thus had the 24th of August twice. For forty hours, the fog obscured everything, but after that, the Pacific Ocean became blue and clear, and we sighted the California coast just off San Francisco. Our blind navigation had proved to be more accurate than our wildest expectations. On the afternoon of 25 of August, we flew over the Golden Gate and the city of San Francisco amid the howling of thousands of ship's sirens. Hundreds of planes circled our ship while we made a trip over the skyscrapers. Dr Eckener, who had not been well during the last few days, again appeared in the control car. His happiness over the successful completion of the second part of the journey helped to renew his strength. Darkness fell while we flew along the coast and over the fabulous castle of the newspaper king, Hearst. Then we made our way over Los Angeles to the airship base.

Los Angeles, too, is a metropolis, and Hollywood is merely a sort of suburb. The German members of the film colony literally pushed the enthusiastic Californians out of our way. Our stay was short, but it was lively from morning to midnight. The weather was excellent, but for that very reason proved to be unfavourable for the lift of the ship during the take-off. A dozen members of the crew were sent ahead to Lakehurst by plane in order to lighten the ship, and we limited our ballast and fuel to the barest necessities. Even so, the *Graf Zeppelin* rose sluggishly from the earth and just managed to get over the high tension wires which ingeniously surrounded the flying-field.

The trip across the continent was likewise difficult for headwinds delayed us. We reached Chicago just before twilight, and millions of hands waved to us from the skyscrapers, the streets, and the shores of the lake. We passed Cleveland and Detroit during the night; swaying from the Cleveland mooring-mast, bathed in the rays of spot-lights, hung the *Los Angeles*, which we had delivered five years before and whose commander was our guest, Rosendahl.

On the next morning, New York lay before us, and we landed at Lakehurst; for our Americans, the world flight began and ended here. In 21 days, 7 hours and 12 minutes, including all stops, the *Graf Zeppelin* had circumnavigated the globe.

We had sworn to take no more part in festivities, excepting the quiet marriage of our flight-comrade, Wilkins, to the pretty actress, Suzanne Bennett.[36] But try to keep such a vow when America is in a mood to celebrate! There were parades, a triumphant procession from the Battery to City Hall, a banquet at the Hotel Astor, and a profusion of private invitations between our business conferences. Additional business negotiations kept Eckener in the United States.

He turned the command over to me and I brought the *Graf Zeppelin* back over the Atlantic to end the world flight at Friedrichshafen. In place of the passengers who disembarked, we had fourteen new ones, among them two women and a gentleman who was caught smoking off in a corner. The other passengers would have liked to throw the culprit overboard. I could not put him in irons, but the unanimous contempt of the other passengers during the rest of the voyage was punishment enough. If he had waited a few years, he could have satisfied his desire to smoke on the LZ 129.

After our landing, and a great reception in Friedrichshafen, the record was complete.

Airship *Graf Zeppelin* left Friedrichshafen on 1 August 1929, at 3.30 in the morning, and landed on 4 September, at 8.19 in the forenoon, after completion of the world flight. Within this one month, it covered the following distances:

Friedrichshafen—Lakehurst, 5,220 miles in 95 hours and 22 minutes at an average speed of 54.8 miles per hour.

Lakehurst—Friedrichshafen, 4,415 miles in 55 hours and 2 2 minutes, at 79.7 miles per hour.

Friedrichshafen—Tokyo, 7,030 miles in 101 hours and 49 minutes, at 69.1 miles per hour.

Tokyo—Los Angeles, 6,033 miles in 79 hours and 3 minutes, at 76.3 miles per hour.

Los Angeles—Lakehurst, 3,015 miles in 51 hours and 57 minutes, at 58 miles per hour.

The *Graf Zeppelin* over Chicago, 28 August 1929.

The *Graf Zeppelin* at Lakehurst 29 August 1929.

Graf Zeppelin with a 1929 Packard at Lakehurst.

Graf Zeppelin draws a crowd at Friedrichshafen.

Lakehurst—Friedrichshafen, 5,298 miles in 67 hours and 31 minutes, at 77.8 miles per hour.

Altogether, in six stages, about 31,250 miles (exactly 31,011), or 5,968 miles more than the distance around the earth at the equator.

This was the first flight around the world by an airship and according to weight carried and distance travelled, it was the greatest performance of any aircraft to date.

An advertisement for the Hamburg-Amerika Line.

33

GRAF ZEPPELIN FLIES TO SOUTH AMERICA

A YOUNG GERMAN IN Recife de Pernambuco, Roland Lütjohann, presented me with a beautifully bound book describing the reaction of Brazil and its German colonists to the first visit of the *Graf Zeppelin* to South America. I quote the report in the first part of his book:

On 4 April 1930, the SS *Sachsenwald* arrived in Pernambuco and unloaded the materials for the erection of an anchor-mast and a gas factory for hydrogen. In Giquia, outside the city, the government had opened a field which was eminently suitable for landings and whose dimensions were 660 by 1,000 yards. The government also assumed the entire cost of erecting the tower and the requisite buildings. Camp dos Affonsos, the field at Rio de Janeiro, is much larger, but the wind conditions are not as suitable and thunderstorms are more frequent there than in Pernambuco where the favourable trade winds cause no difficulties in landing. Rio de Janeiro could not decide whether to erect a mooring-mast. Eight days before the ship was due, it was naturally too late, and so it happened that the capital of the country only had the pleasure of greeting the *Graf Zeppelin* for a few hours on this first trip.

But even in Pernambuco the completion of the field was being delayed. Though the gas factory was built and the foundations for the tower were sunk by 13 May, the mooring-mast itself was erected only a few days before the arrival of the Zeppelin. The landing-crew were quartered in barracks which housed the wireless and radio stations as well as the press-room. Glass bottles filled with Pyrofax were lined up beside the hydrogen plant. Two pipe-lines led to the mooring-mast one of them was to convey the pure hydrogen to the airship, the other was for the hydrogen-and-Pyrofax mixture, which formed a kind of Blaugas. There were also stands for the spectators.

Fourteen days before the flight, there was an unprecedented demand for the special issue of stamps. Mail arrived from the entire world, from Germany and North America, from Capetown and Canada and many other lands, addressed not only to the Herm. Stoltz Company, the Condor Syndicate representative, which was entrusted with the details of the flight, but also to the banks, which received large sums of money with the request that the accompanying self-addressed envelopes be mailed with the Zeppelin stamps on them. Thousands of letters were posted in Rio de Janeiro for this purpose.

Various towns along the coast sent telegraphic requests to the German Consulate and the Pernambuco newspapers asking that the airship be routed over their localities. From the time of the take-off from Germany, on Sunday, railway trains arrived from inland, thickly crowded with people who wished to be present at the first landing of an airship in South America. All the hotels in the city were filled up, and still the telegraphic reservations continued to pour in. The hotel-keepers took advantage of the situation and the prices were raised. The visitors' tickets to the airship were raised in price, too, but the demand continued to increase. The dry-goods stores sold cloth with which to make the German flag. The whole affair assumed the importance of the political rebellion in Princeza, which sowed the seed of the October revolution. In one breath, the editorial offices were asked: 'Has Princeza surrendered? Has the Zeppelin arrived? On Sunday, thousands of people visited the airship base, and on the next day Giquia was in utter confusion.

The Director of the Weather Bureau in Rio de Janeiro ordered the radio stations Fernando do Noroñha and Olinda, in the state of Pernambuco; Ondina and Amarina in the state of Bahia; and Cabo Frio in the state of Rio de Janeiro, to supply the airship with hourly meteorological reports which were checked by the central office in Rio. The last editions of all the daily newspapers printed warnings that all fireworks were forbidden in order to avoid an accident. In Brazil, the setting off of fireworks and rockets plays an important role in all celebrations, even church festivals. And last but not least it was pointed out again and again that fliers who took off to greet the airship were forbidden to approach closer than 500 yards.

The Condor Syndicate had prepared a number of planes in case some of the passengers wished to visit the capital of Brazil during the three day stop-over in Pernambuco. As in Lakehurst, replacement motors were prepared for emergencies. General Alberto Lavenere ordered 300 soldiers of the 21st Scouts to aid in landing the airship under the command of Naval Engineer Besch who erected the mooring-mast.

The daily newspapers published enthusiastic articles praising the German people as 'a race of Titans, of admirable energy and astonishing capabilities. Not yet recovered from the effects of the World War, it developed an activity which has enthralled the entire world and which deserves the highest praise. Hail to the fearless conquerors of space!'

At one o'clock on 22 May, the *Graf Zeppelin* passed the Island of Fernando do Noroñha and reported: landing at six o'clock. Then began a veritable migration toward the airship base; in autos and on foot, in trains and electric cars, the crowds hurried to the landing field, where, besides the ground-crew of 300 soldiers, some 240 civil policemen, 100 horsemen and 70 firemen were called out to clear the field. In the grandstand were the State President and the Governor, the President of the Senate, the Minister of Finance, the Minister of Agriculture, other high officers and the members of the German colony as well as the Consuls from all countries. When night fell, three searchlights were turned on.

The sky was clear and starry. Suddenly a siren howled in the distance, and then a neighbouring factory joined in. There, off in the distance—was that a star or the Zeppelin? And then the ghostly ship drew over the field, vanished to the south, and reappeared in the west. With throttled motors, the ship hung in the air, then the nose sank, the ropes were dropped, and the ground-crew took hold. The *Graf Zeppelin* had landed in Pernambuco. The band played the German anthem, and the acclaim knew no bounds. Everyone rushed toward the colossus, crowding close together to see this *bicho*, this wonderful animal at close range.

The first passengers landed amid the loud applause of the spectators whose enthusiasm exceeded all bounds when Commander Dr Eckener and Captain Lehmann appeared in the grandstand. The German national anthem was played again by the Brazilian Battalion Band, and the Brazilian national anthem followed. Brazil honoured German inventive genius, German efficiency and German courage!

This report refers to our first visit to South America, which occurred during the course of a so-called triangular flight. It lasted from 18 May to 6 June 1930, was divided into seven stages, with stop-overs in Seville, Pernambuco, Rio de Janeiro, Lakehurst, and Seville, and covered a total of 18,460 miles.

We left Friedrichshafen with twenty-two passengers and a crew of forty-three. Since rain made the ship heavy, we operated the motors on gasoline, which relieved us of 880 pounds every hour. The mistral helped us southward toward the Mediterranean at a rate of 125 miles per hour. But since we had to wait for the cooler hours of the evening before landing in Seville, we cruised over Morocco and Tangiers.

In Seville, the *Graf Zeppelin* spent the night on the stub mast. We did not strike the expected north-east trades until we had passed the Canaries. Over Cape Verde, we dropped some mail. The doldrums brought us cloudbursts of rain, and the Equator brought the neophytes their first equatorial baptism on board an airship. Near Fernando do Noronha, the outpost of South America, the sea became bright blue and transparent as glass. Schools of flying fish leaped up and fled before the sharks speeding like torpedoes through the water.

After sixty-two hours, we landed at Recife de Pernambuco, and at midnight continued the trip along the Brazilian coast.

Three views of the dining room on the *Graf Zeppelin*.

During this flight we struck tropical rain squalls of such severity as we had never before experienced. Our good *Graf Zeppelin* came through them without a drop of help from the ballast-tanks. At Bahia we were greeted by fire-works and sirens and the whole population waved to us. Until daylight, we cruised off Rio de Janeiro, hovering over the huge hills around the bay, one of the most beautiful places in the world.

After a one hour stop-over, while the ship and crew were enthusiastically acclaimed, we retraced our path to Pernambuco. At night, we circled over the German steamer *Cap Polonio*, whose band could be heard playing the German national anthem. In salute, we dropped bomb-flares ahead of the ship's bow. It was a strange and fascinating night-scene.

At the anchor-mast in Giquia, the tropical rains weighted the ship with 8,800 pounds of moisture, thereby delaying the trip to North America for half a day. Via Natal and the Lesser Antilles, we steered for Cuba. Since the weight of the rain had forced us to leave four tons of gasoline behind us in Pernambuco, and the weather conditions were threatening, we had to forego our scheduled visit to Havana, much to the annoyance of a few unreasonable passengers and the understandable disappointment of the Cubans.

That night, off Cape Hatteras, the *Graf Zeppelin* once again pushed through a so-called front-line in which the stormy winds changed from south-west to north-west within a few seconds. On the morning of 31 May, we crossed the coast near Atlantic City and landed at Lakehurst. Late at night on 3 June, we took off again. This time we went over New York, flying so low that the Woolworth Tower and the Singer Building were 160 feet above us. Our return trip was made via the Azores. Seville, 3,900 miles from Lakehurst, was reached in 61 hours and 24 minutes.

The last stage of the great triangular flight brought us two more battles with the elements. In the Straits of Gibraltar, the rain and wind struck us furiously; and just before reaching Bourg, while we were pushing through a storm centre, great black hail-clouds tossed the ship 1,000 feet high, only to drop it down 1,150 feet shortly thereafter. At night we were safe home again in Friedrichshafen.

In practical results, the triangular flight was of great significance for it was decisive in the formation of the first transatlantic airship line which first flew to Pernambuco and then to Rio de Janeiro.

The service has been operating all these years without cancellation, incident or accident. Only once the *Graf Zeppelin*, weighted by rain, came down somewhat short of the landing field in Giquia, much to the consternation of a negro who was just making coffee in his hut. Two members of the crew jumped overboard and carefully extinguished his hearth-fire with his hot coffee. The *Graf Zeppelin* carried the traces of this landing back to Friedrichshafen in the form of slime on the control car and the stern.

The *Graf Zeppelin* entering the harbour of Rio de Janeiro, 25 May 1930.

In October 1933, for the termination of the yearly programme, we repeated the triangular flight, but this time with an average speed of 65 miles per hour for the 21,000 mile stretch. We took course over Gibraltar and along the African coast to the Cape Verde Islands. The north-east trade winds served as tailwinds and increased our speed to 115 miles per hour. In the early morning of 17 October, we reached Recife de Pernambuco. After one day of rest to replenish gas, fuel and food supplies, we continued on to Rio de Janeiro, exchanged passengers and mails at the airship base sixty miles from the capital and then turned back again to Recife.

On 21 October, the *Graf Zeppelin* again left the mooring mast at Giquia and took a northern course. Over Natal Dr Eckener dropped a wreath on a parachute in memory of the first Brazilian aviator, Augusto Severo.[37] In the Amazon territory, great streams of brown fluid spread wide into the glassy sea which gnawed perpetually at the rim of the jungle. In the flat swamps, we clearly saw numerous alligators, who ducked their heads and fled before the unknown enemy flying above them. At night, we flew over Devil's Island upon which we looked down in horror. Over Guiana and Venezuela, with their sugar cane plantations cut into squares by irrigation ditches, we flew toward the green island of Trinidad which greeted us in all its unbelievably colourful beauty.

The Antilles, on the other hand, received us discourteously with bad weather, and in view of the weather, which was streaked with lightning, Dr Eckener abandoned the proposed flight over Haiti. We followed the coast to the passageway

Augusto Severo
de Albuquerque
Maranhão,
(1864–1902),
a pioneer of
airship design and
construction.

Dirigível *Bartolomeu de Gusmão* designed by Augusto Severo de Albuquerque Maranhão in Brazil. It was destroyed in March 1894 by a gust of wind.

between Cuba and Haiti and from there took course for Florida, landing at Miami. We were received there by a great procession and the Mayor presented us in the name of the city with a large field for a future airship base. Our next stop was Akron, home of the Goodyear Company, in whose great airship hangar, 1,000 feet long and 300 feet wide, the *Graf Zeppelin* found plenty of room beside the smaller American ships. At Chicago, Dr Eckener, accompanied by the German Ambassador, Dr Luther, visited the World's Fair while I brought the ship back to Akron and made a side trip to Canada.

On the return trip from Akron, we flew over the White House in Washington to pay our respects to President Franklin D. Roosevelt. As we had done from the South Atlantic to the North American continent, we now spoke via short-wave to Europe. But strong headwinds delayed the flight. After landing in Seville, we arrived in Friedrichshafen on 2 November.

How the performance of the Zeppelin is judged by an expert who made the triangular flight, may be seen from the following report by Lieutenant-Colonel Breithaupt, Referent for Airship Affairs in the German Air Ministry.

Not once on the long flight did the ship fail in any part, and at times it was subjected to strains which must be admitted to be extraordinary. Whoever experienced the critical moment off the notorious Cape Hatteras, when in a depression the wind veered from SSW to NE, or nearly 180 degrees, within

Graf Zeppelin flies over the Capitol.

a few seconds, and the ship quivered and heaved and strained; whoever experienced the squall strains on the westerly slope of the French Alps south of Bourg, when hail-stones as large as hazelnuts struck down like drum-fire on the hull, and at an inclination of 13 degrees the ship was tossed up 1,000 feet and descended again at a rate of thirteen feet per second—whoever experienced these things must have learned to have unfaltering confidence in the ingenious construction of a Zeppelin.

At no time did I observe anxiety in the passengers. An elderly American woman said to me, 'I shall use only airships as soon as the regular service is available, for I don't get sea-sick on them.' The passengers indicated their confidence throughout the entire flight by their unconcerned actions which were entirely like those of passengers on a large ocean liner. They played bridge or chess, and among other things developed an interest in the course of the flight. The ship's command had obligingly permitted them to enter the control car at certain specified times, and this indubitably contributed no little to the comforting of the timid, for it proved that the command had nothing to conceal.

Like the ship itself, the Maybach motors had proved their value during the world flight. Now they had undergone another test of their efficiency. Not once during the 275-hour flight did they cause trouble. One became so inured to the steady sound of the engines that even small deviations from the usual 1,380 to 1,400 revolutions were instantly noticeable. This outstanding performance is due in part to the excellent crew, but it is a definite proof of superior type and material. No wonder the Americans used Maybach motors for their large airships.

The skilful piloting of the ship, especially during difficult landings on dark nights, on unfamiliar fields and with entirely unpractised ground-crews, excited the general admiration of the spectators on land and on board, and especially that of the American experts, who certainly were qualified to make critical judgments.

The mere appearance of Dr Eckener, who was always the essence of serenity, instilled confidence in all the passengers. He would sit or stand calmly at his open window, observing the clouds and the weather, at his post day and night. The Watch Officers, Lehmann, Flemming and Von Schiller alternately piloted the ship, and Dr Eckener issued only the fundamental orders. He knew how to instil confidence in his crew by trusting them and holding them responsible for the performance of their duties. The officers knew their ship and knew how to handle it in all circumstances—that was the consensus of opinion of all the travellers on the Zeppelin.

The Navigation Officers and Helmsmen were matter-of-fact and confident in fulfilling their duties, whether they were making astronomical calculations, wind measurements or entering the weather reports on the map. The same confident sense of duty inspired the mechanics who tended their engines and religiously controlled their service. Day and night, one met men in the corridor inspecting the frame or the gas-cells, re-pumping fuel or climbing into their engine cars to relieve the watch. Each knew his duties exactly; one saw nothing of orders being given; and the complicated management of the vessel was ideally regulated.

At the same time, it must be remembered that during the first fourteen days, the ship was always moored in the open, and the crew seldom had a chance to rest even in port, for there were always numerous things to be done, especially since the rains and winds in Pernambuco required redistributions of the weight and the turning of the ship. This flight placed unusual demands upon the physical endurance of the entire personnel.

Graf Zeppelin flying over Wembley Stadium in London during the 1930 FA Cup Final, 26 April 1930. Arsenal beat Huddersfield Town 2–0.

34

THE SUPERIORITY OF GERMAN AIRSHIPS

VERYTHING THAT OLD Count Ferdinand von Zeppelin prophesied for his airships came true or was exceeded. Perhaps the reader will recall that in the summer of 1910, Count Zeppelin, together with Prince Henry of Prussia and the meteorologist, Hergesell, sailed for Spitzbergen on the Lloyd-steamer *Mainz* in preparation for a Polar flight with the airship. The World War intervened, the old Count died, and Nobile pushed north to the Pole in a semi-rigid airship, crashing when he attempted to repeat the performance. Amundsen, his companion on the first flight over the pole, was lost when he went up in a plane to rescue Nobile.[38]

From the first, we ourselves, as well as the German and Russian explorers on board the *Graf Zeppelin*, had no intention of rediscovering the North Pole. It was our self-imposed object to photograph and measure the swampy, icy coastland between Franz Josef's Land and the North Siberian Islands, to survey the meteorological conditions in the Arctic, and to search for new land further eastward. The airship and its crew were equipped for this purpose. We lacked neither polar clothing, nor kayaks and sleds, nor emergency rations and fire-arms in case of a forced landing and a trip over the ice. The scientific leader of the expedition was the Russian Professor Samoilovitz, who in 1928 rescued a part of Nobile's men with the ice-breaker *Krassin*.

Count Zeppelin named a lake in the Cross Bay region 'Lake of the 24th of July' because that was supposed to be his lucky day. Twenty-one years later, on 24 July 1931, a ship, bearing the inventor's name, took off under Eckener's command for a voyage of exploration to the Arctic. After landing in Berlin, at the mooring mast in Staaken, the *Graf Zeppelin* 'set off over Gotland, Reval, Helsinki and Narva to Leningrad.

In Leningrad we left everything contributing to the comfort of the passenger airship. From then on we ate off cardboard plates and swept our own cabins. All available space and the saving in weight was utilized to carry the scientific paraphernalia for radio, photography, geodesy, meteorology and magnetometry.

Soon after leaving Leningrad, we were over forestland; on the rivers, wooden

Umberto Nobile 1926 with dog Titina.

rafts floated toward the White Sea; and in certain places one could not see the river for the trees. Archangel is an important source of wood. The Barents Sea was free of ice and, in the Arctic night, which was as bright as day, it gleamed in a flat green colour. For us newcomers, it was a curious thing to see the sun shining at midnight, spilling an unreal yellow light over a sea of ice-floes.

Off Franz Josef Land, the Russian ice-breaker *Malygin* was waiting for us. Aided by two-way radio signals, we set course for it. When later in the afternoon of 27 July, we met the Russian steamer in a quiet bay on Hooker Island, the evening sky, if one can call it that, displayed a wonderful variety of colours. The *Graf Zeppelin* descended slowly and floated on its bumper-bags between the drifting ice-floes while a boat put out from the *Malygin*. A man wearing a fur cap stood up in the stern, and through my binoculars I recognized Nobile, whom destiny had placed into the hands of the Russians after the crash of his second polar-ship, the *Italia*.

When the boat came alongside our control car, we handed out the mailbags and photographs intended for the steamer. The hand of his polar comrade, Ellsworth, who was a member of our party, was stretched out to Nobile. Both were visibly touched, and the rest of us also felt the tragedy of the Italian with whom we had had so many technical discussions in Friedrichshafen. Since then, Lincoln Ellsworth had undertaken an audacious and successful polar flight to the Antarctic, had been lost and almost abandoned, but was found again and rescued.[39] A few months before, I had visited him at his Castle Lenzburg, in Switzerland, when he had told me in detail of the preparations he was making for his polar flight. Verily, we are living in a lively epoch.

The ice-floes were coming closer like curious polar bears, and Eckener became worried because the bumper-bags on which we were floating could not stand much strain. We took quick leave of Nobile and the Russians and continued the flight along the coastal islands of Franz Josef Land. We found that Gamsworth Island and Albert Edward Island, all maps to the contrary notwithstanding, were absolutely non-existent. North of Franz Josef Land there was nothing but pack ice. Professor Moltschanov, an exceptionally brilliant Russian savant, and a very quiet, likeable man, zealously sent his pilot balloons into the stratosphere.

We took an easterly course for Nicholas II Island, now called Northland. Glacial peaks almost 3,500 feet high reached up over the sea of fog. Then we sighted unknown islands. But the continuance of the exploration was forestalled by the heavy fog. We therefore steered southward to the Taimyr Peninsula, where herds of wild reindeer fled before us, and where we measured Taimyr Bay and found hitherto unknown mountains. Later, at the mouth of the Yenisei, we dropped mail and packages of newspapers over the Dickson radio station. The six men who composed the station stood before their modest huts and looked longingly toward us as we turned west, back to inhabited land and civilization.

Lincoln Ellsworth, (1880–1951), photographed with Edward H. Smith (*right*), July, 1931.

The only other American on the Arctic flight was USN Lt-Cmdr Edward H. 'Iceberg' Smith, USCG. Smith was an expert on ice conditions.

The *Graf Zeppelin* crossed the Kara Sea, and set course for the great double islands Novaya Zemlya, whose stone mountains and glacial-slides fall thousands of yards into the sea. Guillemots, resembling the penguins of the Antarctic seas, waddled on the cliffs, and gulls filled the air like snow-clouds. Then at last we were again back on our old route, Barents Sea; Archangel, Leningrad, Berlin, Friedrichshafen. We had not needed our sleds and weapons.

It is not my place to judge the scientific results of our Arctic flight. We were demonstrating that the airship was capable of operating in all zones, the cold as well as the hot; and that, especially in the polar region, it could fulfil the necessary tasks in as many days as steamers and dog-sleds had heretofore required years.

To meet the objection that not only the semi-rigid *Italia*, but also great airships of the newest type have proved failures, I must explain the catastrophes which caused England and America temporarily to abandon the construction of additional airships.

Encouraged by the performance of the two German Zeppelins, LZ 126 and LZ 127, England used government funds to construct the R 100 and the R 101. We saw these experimental ships not only during the *Graf Zeppelin*'s trips to England; for our construction-department at Friedrichshafen had unselfishly advised both the English and the Americans, and our engineers, as well as Dr Eckener, were sent to Cardington. We were not concerned with our own personal gain, but the knowledge that the general progress served each of us individually.

The R 100, a vessel of 140,000 cubic metres, with Rolls Royce motors of 4,200 horsepower, proved to be too heavy. It was destined for shuttle service between England and Canada, but it completed only a single round-trip over the Atlantic course. The R 101, with a 141,000-cubic-metre capacity, had its passenger space, like the LZ 129, inside the ship, and it also was one of the first airships with heavy oil engines.[40] It was intended for service to India, but crashed shortly after its take-off on 5 October 1930, in Northern France, with a loss of forty-six lives, among them, its designer, Lieutenant-Colonel Richmond; the Commander, Major Scott; the Minister of Aviation, Lord Thomson; the chief of the civil aviation, Sir Sefton Brancker; airship Captain, Lieutenant Irwin; and Squadron Leader Johnson.[41] The only ones saved were the radio operator, who was thrown out, and a few mechanics, over whom a water-ballast tank burst.

We had been on a flight to Saxony and had just landed in Leipzig when we heard the terrible news. Dr Eckener instantly made efforts to obtain further reports and be on hand for the newspapermen. The English government later invited him to take part in the investigation.

In determining the cause of the disaster, the official report mentioned the following points:

The R 101 in flight. When built it was the world's largest flying craft at 731 feet in length, and it was not surpassed by another hydrogen-filled rigid airship until the *Hindenburg* flew seven years later.

The R 101 crashed on 5 October 1930 in France during its maiden overseas voyage, killing 48 of the 54 people on board.

To equalize the greater weight of the heavy oil engines, which were calculated to develop 3,300 horsepower, and also because the ship itself was heavier than had been expected, the R 101 was subsequently enlarged by a middle-section of 84 feet. The position of the gas-cells was later altered to increase the buoyancy, and they were no longer arranged to prevent friction and chafing against the frame-work. Leakage caused an excessive loss of gas even during the test-flights. At the start of its flight to India, the ship was loaded to capacity and, soon thereafter, was additionally burdened by a rain-squall. A cell in the upper part of the bow of the ship, having been previously damaged by chafing, must suddenly have ripped under the gas-pressure. Because of the considerable loss of gas in the fore-part of the ship within a few seconds, the bow could not remain high, and the ship consequently ran nose-down into the flat forest-land near Beauvais, in the vicinity of Paris.

In America, the Goodyear Zeppelin Corporation, using the patents acquired from the Zeppelin Airship Company, later built the two 184,000-cubic-metre naval airships, *Akron* and *Macon*. Their most striking innovation was the enclosing of the engine cars in the body of the ship. On the night of 4 April 1933, the *Akron* went down in a stormy sea. Of the crew of seventy-three, only three escaped with their lives, among them, First Officer Wiley, who was later given command of the newly completed sister-ship, *Macon*. Among those lost were Admiral Moffat, Commander of the American Naval Air Fleet, and Commander MacCord, of the *Akron*.

USS *Macon* under construction. (ZRS-5) was built for scouting and served as a 'flying aircraft carrier', designed to carry biplane parasite aircraft, five single-seat Curtiss F9C Sparrowhawk for scouting or two-seat Fleet N2Y-1 for training.

USS *Macon* in its vast hangar.

USS *Macon* at Moffett Field.

On 13 February 1935, the *Macon* became tail-heavy and came down during a severe storm off the California coast. Warships steamed to the rescue, and saved eighty-one members of the crew, but two men were lost through their own carelessness. The repetition of the accident under almost identical conditions supports the assumption that, exclusive of the matter of ship's command, there was a structural deficiency. In comparison with our Zeppelins, the reinforcements of the sterns and fins of both American airships were weakened through the economizing of cable-braces and especially through the absence of the cruciform girders which, in Dürr's ships, support the stabilizing and rudder surfaces; and the ships were consequently unable to withstand the excessive strain.

The LZ 127 withstood without damage a hurricane in the Atlantic and severe tropical storms in the South Atlantic. Because of the accidents to foreign airships, the Zeppelin Airship Company decided to complete at once its newest type of ship, instead of the LZ 128, which had already been designed.[42] The LZ 129 and the LZ 130 are considerably stronger in engine-power and construction.

The USS *Macon* over San Francisco shortly before the disaster.

35

THE LUXURIES ON THE *HINDENBURG*

'**O**H, I BEG your pardon,' an ambitious young woman said as I stood at the control-stand of the LZ *Hindenburg*, 'but I'd like to know whether you sell student-tickets at reduced rates on the new airship? I'd like to go to New York to study.'

It is astonishing how rapidly the human being can accustom himself to change. What was a miracle yesterday, becomes a habit today. Radio-telephony is as customary as television will be tomorrow. And aviation, the recently realized dream of the centuries, is but another means of transportation.

When the airships of the Zeppelin type, the R 34, the LZ 126 and the LZ 127, crossed the Atlantic for the first time, the whole world was electrified. The conquering of the ocean seemed a heroic adventure. But only a few years later, an old woman and an entire family, including children, trusted themselves to the LZ 127 for the trip to America. The regularity and dependability with which the *Graf Zeppelin* completed its schedule year after year on the Friedrichshafen–Rio de Janeiro route, completely obscured the fact that this airship was originally supposed to serve only for a series of demonstration flights.

The *Graf Zeppelin* proved to be equal to the demands made upon it by the South American route which was favoured by the trade winds. Of twenty-five mail and passenger flights from Friedrichshafen to Rio de Janeiro, twenty lasted from 90 to 99 hours; only five were somewhat shorter or longer. Of twenty-three flights from Rio de Janeiro to Friedrichshafen, fifteen lasted between 100 and 110 hours; two were a bit longer, and six were shorter.

Over the North Atlantic, however weather conditions were much less stable; unforeseen thunderstorms, squalls and fogs delayed us and forced us to round-about routes which added a thousand or so miles to our flying-distance. As the LZ 126, the American naval airship ZR-3 *Los Angeles*, had covered the distance to Lakehurst in eighty-one hours, at an average speed of 62 miles per hour. For the same distance, with unfavourable weather conditions, the LZ 127 once required 111 hours, and another time ninety-five hours, averaging 55 miles per hour.

As a rule, the return flight over the North Atlantic in the eastern direction is more likely to be favoured by the wind; on four flights from Lakehurst to Friedrichshafen, the *Graf Zeppelin* required 71, 55, 67, and 87 hours respectively, and 102 hours for the flight from Akron to Friedrichshafen. The average speed for these flights fluctuated between 58 and 80 miles per hour. Until now, the averages for the flights to North America are ninety-six hours for the trip over, and seventy-six hours for the flight back. The return flights to Friedrichshafen have required twenty hours, or almost a full day, less time.

Even shortly after the first North American flight of the *Graf Zeppelin*, Dr Eckener publicly admitted that this otherwise outstanding ship was not efficient enough to maintain a regular mail and passenger service over the ocean. The inferences to be drawn from that were self-evident: larger and stronger commercial airships had to be built for this purpose. The previous government was not blind to the need for such new airships, but used the financial predicament of the nation as a pretext, and thus, valuable years were lost until the new government completed the first large new-type airship and placed another under construction.

The founding of the German Zeppelin Yards relieved the Zeppelin Airship Company of its freight and passenger operations and permitted it to return to its original functions as a construction company.[43] To the German airship hangars at Friedrichshafen-Löwenthal and Rhein-Main, near Frankfurt am Main, were added one in Rio de Janeiro, for the South American service, and a private hangar in the USA for the North American service.

The new vessels of the *Hindenburg* type have a nominal volume of 190,000 cubic metres. With a length of 825 feet, they are only 35 feet longer than the *Graf Zeppelin*, but they have a maximum diameter of 137 feet. While, as we know, the LZ 127 represented an obligatory compromise dictated by the limited dimensions of the hangar, the LZ 129 made use of all the advancements in streamline form although it was about the same length, it contained almost double the amount of buoyant gas used in the *Graf Zeppelin*, and it was therefore capable of lifting about 220,000 pounds of useful load in addition to its own weight. 1,750 express locomotives could have been placed inside the airship which, when empty, weighed no more than one of them. The motor-power, increased to 3,400/4,200 horsepower, raised the nominal speed of the LZ 129 to 86.5 miles per hour and during the work-shop and test-flights, it effortlessly attained an average speed of 85 miles per hour.

The excess power decreased the flying time so that the duration of the flights to North America was reduced by one third. As the first model of a new type, the LZ 129, too, was actually only an experimental ship, and the flights to North America were made to determine the conditions upon which depended a regular airship service with the United States.

Since, besides mail and cargo, the LZ 129 and LZ 130 each were to carry fifty passengers to and from America, the technical improvements were not solely of a navigational nature, but took into account the safety and comfort of the travellers. At bottom, of course, every improvement in navigation signifies an improvement in the flight altogether. If the steering controls are more effective, the stabilizers, gondolas and inner rooms are not subject to vibration, the braking length is shortened, and the heavy oil motors operate more economically—these improvements are all to the benefit of the passenger.

With the transition to the heavy oil engines, the LZ 129 now avoided that fire hazard which, although it never once appeared during a quarter of a century of airship operation, nevertheless still played an important part in the imagination of the travelling public. Furthermore, in order to do away with this fire hazard entirely, the new commercial airship could be refilled, in America, with helium, which is not inflammable, more expensive and somewhat less buoyant; and only the centre cells would carry hydrogen for release in the air. And then the acceptance board made no objection to permitting a smoking-room to be built into the *Hindenburg*.

This fulfilled a pipe-dream of many Zeppelin travellers, and was part of a plan to offer the passengers the conveniences and freedom of movement which could be enjoyed on an ocean liner. By transferring the passenger rooms to the inside of the ship, designer Dr Dürr was able to enlarge them to four times the size of the one on the *Graf Zeppelin*. The double row of cabins, on an upper A deck and a lower B deck, were connected by a stairway and formed the backbone of the spacious social rooms. There was a dining salon, a writing and reading room, a bar and a smoking lounge, and the social rooms had a promenade deck on both sides, from which the traveller could see the panorama of the world passing below him. Professor Breuhaus, the decorator of the ship stated:

> The most important task of interior decoration was to permit the greatest possible vision in all the recreation rooms. We had to devise a new form for rooms and windows and abandon all previous methods. In the LZ 127, the passenger compartments were in the gondolas and were easily adaptable to the aerodynamic form. But in the LZ 129 everything, cabins, corridors, dining-room, smoking-lounge, kitchen and baths, had to be removed to the bowels of the ship.
>
> Actually, I am an exterior architect. But I maintain that the genuine architect must create entire buildings, including the interior. Therefore, I am grateful for every opportunity to act as an interior decorator and especially to solve unusual problems. I have outfitted Pullmans, ocean liners and airplanes. I assisted in the equipping of the training ship *Gorch Fock*, and the German Imperial Navy commissioned me to decorate the aviso *Grille* and the armoured ships *Admiral Scheer* and *Admiral Graf Spee*. And in all these vessels, I learned to make use of even the minutest spaces.
>
> Thus, I was well prepared when I received the commission to decorate the guest rooms of the LZ 129. And yet all this experience was not very helpful. I

was required to combine the conveniences of a first class hotel with those of a small ocean liner, and install them by magic in the round body of the airship. For this hotel of the air, which had to be a hostelry, an express vehicle and an observation train all in one, there was no model. Even the interior decoration of airplanes offered no guiding points, for planes were too small to give a basis of comparison; more than that, they are built according to heavier-than-air principles. In a plane, one is not so hampered by weight calculations. As light as possible and as sturdy as possible was the cry which the gentlemen of the Airship Company always repeated. Naturally all the walls and floors were made of the light metals and woods which the Zeppelin yards had long ago tested and approved. To insulate the rooms against heat and cold, a number of special materials were placed at our service. But despite these materials, the results were always too heavy. And the same with the furniture.

I even made a number of models of the chairs to be used in the various rooms to test them for stability and weight, until there was no longer any criticism of them. Yet, the chairs, like all the other furnishings, were to be the epitome of comfort, for the *Hindenburg* was to serve mainly as a passenger airship to America. We had to have cabins for fifty passengers. Each was to have two beds, one above the other, as they are placed in Pullmans, and each was to have hot and cold running water. Imagine the pipes required for this purpose alone. Heating pipes, fortunately, were done away with because all the rooms were electrically heated. Since families sometimes travelled together, two cabins and a foyer could be combined into one separate apartment.

All the social halls were equipped and furnished in the most modern manner. From the writing room, a private mail tube led to the post room and conveyed the letters directly to the cancelling machine. The kitchen, which was on the lower B deck, had all the apparatuses used in hotel kitchens, including an electrically operated oven, and connected with the dining room by an elevator.

The bath-rooms presented an individual problem. For practical reasons, they were located on B deck. Now, an airship carries a large amount of water, which is used as ballast. Therefore, the waste-water from the cabins and baths could not be dropped or the ship would become too light. Thus, we had to build a large apparatus on the back of the airship to catch rainwater and replace the loss of ballast.

All these technical arrangements, together with the walls and the furniture, could not exceed a certain specified weight. Yet everything had to be fireproof. Thus, we first used cellophane in the observation windows, but later replaced these with an entirely new material, Plexiglass. But we saved weight on the wall decorations more than anything else. Everywhere, except in the smoking room, these consisted of airship cotton, a very thin, light, but tightly woven material. The floors were made of light metal and were covered with rugs. As a precautionary measure, the walls of the smoking room were covered with leather, and the floor was made of impregnated wood. A part of the floor was utilized for window-space; a little balustrade was constructed so that the passengers could lazily lean over and look directly down to earth.

One demand which was made by the American passengers, I was reluctant to meet: that there be a piano in the salon. To me, a piano is an earthbound instrument which does not rightfully belong in an airship. Furthermore, even the smallest available model exceeded the permissible weight. But we had one made of light metal, and on the first North American flight of the *Hindenburg*, this unique Blüthner piano, which weighs only 112 pounds, was found in the lounge.

The LZ 130,[44] the sister-ship of the *Hindenburg*, shows a number of improvements in its interior decoration. Thus, the wash-rooms are no longer on B deck, but are placed between the sleeping cabins. The guest rooms are made of latticed duralumin. The magic wand of the interior decorator touched all the various objects, and they became light. Even Arpkes pastel-like wall paintings of

The LZ 129 *Hindenburg* featured the first piano ever to be carried on a passenger aircraft. To meet the weight constraints, the Zeppelin company commissioned the piano making firm of Julius Blüthner to create a lightweight aluminium alloy piano, and the Julius Blüthner Pianofortefabrik created a small grand piano that weighed only 162 kg. Zeppelin chief designer Ludwig Dürr standing, at right of photo, Professor Franz Wagner at the piano, Captain Ernst Lehmann to Wagner's right.

airships took the place of walls. Hundreds of industries and trades in Germany made every effort to extend themselves to satisfy the exacting passengers, who demanded comfort in addition to miracles. The radio set communicates with land from the middle of the Atlantic. Gas-filled life-rafts made of watertight cell-material are provided to calm the fears of the timid.

The sleeping quarters and mess rooms for the crew lie further to the stern, inside the ship; the officers' mess is in the lower deck, beside the kitchen. The flying hotel for a hundred persons also demands personnel and provisions. The Chief Steward is surrounded by a general staff of two cooks, a bar-tender, stewards for tables and cabins, and will perhaps later have a stewardess. The storage rooms on the airship hold 5,500 pounds of fresh meat and chicken, 220 pounds of fish, 330 pounds of delicatessen, 440 pounds of butter, cheese and marmalade, 800 eggs, and 440 pounds of preservers and iron utensils. Of beverages, there are 33 gallons of milk, 250 bottles of wine and liquor, and a like amount of mineral water, in addition to 55 gallons of mineral water for the crew.

But there are heavier objects than salad and cheese on the LZ 129. The water-ballast alone—which had to be emptied in 48 seconds, if necessary—weighed 22,000 pounds. Mail and freight weighing 44,000 pounds could be carried, and the twenty-five tanks for the four Daimler-Benz engines were filled with 137,500 pounds of fuel oil. At the average nominal speed, this suffices for 100 hours of flight over 8,000 miles.

Except for the service personnel, the crew of the *Hindenburg* is no larger than that of the *Graf Zeppelin*. As commander, I had three additional airship captains, Pruss, Sammt and Bauer; the *Graf Zeppelin* was commanded by Captain von Schiller, who was assisted by Captains Wittemann and Ladwig.[45] Two German airships and two German airship bases were now in the service of world traffic.

36

THE TRIUMPHANT ELECTION TOUR
OF THE FATHERLAND

O N 4 MARCH 1936, at 3.19 o'clock, the LZ 129, the first of the two giant airships destined for transatlantic service, began its workshop flights. On board were eighty-seven people; namely: Dr Eckener, chairman of the Zeppelin Airship Company, which had built the ship according to Dr Dürr's plans and under the supervision of Engineers Knud Eckener, and Sauter; Lieutenant-Colonel Breithaupt, Airship Referent for the Ministry of Aviation; the eight airship captains of the Deutsche Zeppelin Reederei; forty-seven members of the crew; and thirty employees of the dockyards. The airship had not yet been named; the six intertwining rings of the Olympic insignia were painted on both sides of the shimmering hull.

A last weighing of the huge body; then the command, 'Airship march!' Stern foremost, the LZ 129 was pulled out of the east door of the construction hangar by rope-spiders and trolleys, and, upon a bell signal from the control-stand, was let loose. Amid the shouts of the spectators on the field, the giant airship lifted itself into the air. At 300 feet the starboard and port motors began to turn over. I was agreeably surprised at their silent operation; we in the control car scarcely heard them, and there was no vibration at all in the passenger quarters.

The second pleasant discovery was made when we tested the control capacity. Since the LZ 129 was of entirely different dimensions from the LZ 127, the rudder had to be differently constructed. Cruising over the Bodensee, we made tests and found that the LZ 129 steered just as well if not better than the *Graf Zeppelin*. In this connection we checked the reversing of the motors and propellers and gauged the deceleration distance of the ship. And when we landed at 6.25 o'clock, we were more than satisfied with the results obtained.

On the next day we went aloft again while the ground fog was still rising from the dockyards. This time there were ninety people on board, among them Lieutenant-Colonel

Breithaupt and Commander Peck of the US Navy. At 8.53, the command was given to 'Up Ship!' After a few turns over the lake, during which we made various types of calculations, Eckener decided to pay a call. A radio-telegram notified Mayor Fiehler and we arrived punctually, at 12.30, over Munich. From there we took course up the Isar toward the chain of Alps gleaming white as sugar in the distance, turned over Bad Tölz and steered toward Augsburg, which likewise welcomed us jubilantly.

We also tested the electric kitchen; there were meat and sandwiches for breakfast, and Hungarian goulash for lunch. In the radio cabin over the control-stand, our operators continued the tests which they had begun with Norddeich on the day before. Chief Inspector Speck reported:

> We first dialled the set to 17-70 metres and then raised a number of American coast stations. On wave-length 24, we succeeded in communicating with the Chatham station. We introduced ourselves: 'This is the LZ 129, making second test-flight and testing apparatus.' Hello, this is Chatham; we hear you clearly and thank you for the call,' was the answer. The same attempt was later made telephonically.

After an eight-hour test-flight, the LZ 129 came down to its hangar again.

These two first flights were widely commented upon in the foreign press. The English were openly enthusiastic. 'Since no Zeppelin,' wrote the *News Chronicle*, 'will ever again be used for military purposes, everyone can congratulate Germany on her phenomenal success with the new airship!' And the *Daily Telegraph* pointed out the admirable tenacity with which the German designers had held fast to the determination to make airships serviceable as express transports for long distances.

> The designers have established the correctness of their contentions; the new Zeppelin was really built to be a ship of the air, and the world can have only good wishes for the airship on its mission of peace.

That France did not at once give us the permission to fly over its territory—though we had had the permission before was due to the tense political situation in those eventful days.

The third-test flight of the LZ 129 was a sort of public flight, and the members of the proving-ground committee took part in it. We landed after three and a half hours in a pouring rain. The ship was officially approved for the transportation of passengers, and it entered the service of the Deutschen Zeppelin Reederei under my command. Principally to make further experiments with the radio-compass and subject the fuel-oil engines to a prolonged test, I undertook a thirty-hour flight which carried us through the Allgäu to Tegernsee and Chiemsee, from there down the Inn and past Braunau, across through Bavaria and back to the Bodensee. At night we crossed over Ulm for the second time, flew over Munich and Augsburg, and then circled over the Bodensee. The weather was partly fair and partly cloudy; at 8.27, despite the strong east wind, we landed at the dockyards to take on fifteen engineers of the docks and the DVL.

In the meantime, the *Graf Zeppelin* had awakened from her winter sleep and was thoroughly overhauled in the nearby hangar. Thus, on 23 March, both ships could take off together for the first time. LZ 127, which was entering its eighth year of operation, was commanded by Schiller, and had twenty-four passengers on board. On the LZ 129, no less than 101 passengers were entrusted to my care, among them Carl Christiansen,[46] Police Chief of Magdeburg and one of the officials of the Deutschen Zeppelin Reederei; representatives of the government; a number of officers; and a group of newspapermen. From this flight, the LZ 129 no longer returned to the hangar at the Zeppelin Company's dockyards, but to the large hangar in nearby Löwenthal.

This press-flight was a forerunner of the Germany flight which for the first time in history saw the airship used as a means of propaganda and a voting place. Four days and three nights long, from the 26 March to the night of 29 March when 99 per cent of all Germans voted for Adolf Hitler, the LZ 127 and LZ 129 remained uninterruptedly in the air. On the starboard and port sides of the bow of the LZ 129 was painted in large letters: *Hindenburg*. In the inner body of the ship was a large radio and loudspeaker for the broadcasting of election speeches. From a release mechanism in the stern, little parachutes carrying millions of leaflets fluttered down to the millions of voters below us. Representatives and guests of the government propaganda bureau, the Air Minister, the Minister of Transportation, party members, and officers of the Air Force, altogether eighty people, made this four-day flight with us. One cabin was reserved for the two women on board, the secretary of the Zeppelin Company, Count Zeppelin's 78-year-old niece, and the sister of my dead war comrade, Baron von Gemmingen.

An incident, meaningless in itself, which took place during the launching of the *Hindenburg* from the Löwenthal hangar, and which was very like that which happened to the *Graf Zeppelin* during the world flight at Kasumigaura and Los Angeles, and to the American airships *Los Angeles* and *Akron* in Lakehurst, accidentally presented a proof of the dependability of the new type of airship. The unpractised ground crew tore the steel spiders which held the stern of the ship, and a gust of wind, blowing at a thirty-five-degree angle to the hangar, pushed the stern fins to the earth and bent them. The bent pieces were partly sawed off in the air and the job was completed after the landing; the fin was pasted together without having the slightest effect upon the steering capacity of the ship. Furthermore, after the completion of the Germany flight, the *Hindenburg* made the flight to Rio de Janeiro with the truncated rudder and had no trouble despite the detour we had to make around France.

The *Graf Zeppelin*, which had started off ahead of us and was waiting for us over the Bodensee, received my orders to continue without us. Captain von

Schiller and I communicated via radio-telephone, though it may seem unusual to the layman that this conversation between two commanders who could see each other was made through the radio station at Norddeich. Thanks to the head start which the *Graf Zeppelin* had, Schiller visited Stuttgart and Munich and was already on his way to Silesia when we reached Saxony via Nürnberg and Bayreuth. Over Chemnitz and Dresden we got into a real pea-soup fog and were unable to see anything. Even our searchlight, with its one and a half million candlepower, could rarely pierce the clouds and strike a patch of earth. The *Graf Zeppelin* had no better weather. At 10.25 p.m. Schiller radioed me:

Up to 1935 DELAG (*Deutsche Luftschiffahrts-Aktiengesellschaft*), was the only airline using Zeppelins. It was founded on 16 November 1909 and operated Zeppelin rigid airships manufactured by the Luftschiffbau Zeppelin Corporation. Hugo Eckener, chairman of Luftschiffbau Zeppelin had the temerity to indicate a desire to run against Hitler in the 1932 presidential election. Further, when Eckener later resisted the new Nazi government's efforts to use Zeppelins for propaganda purposes, Reich Minister of Aviation Hermann Göring insisted that a new agency be created to extend Party control over LZ Group. A personal rivalry between Göring and Propaganda Minister Joseph Goebbels also played a role. To complicate matters further, the Luftschiffbau was a loss-making concern and needed cash investment, in particular to complete construction of the *Hindenburg*. Deutsche Zeppelin-Reederei was therefore incorporated on 22 March 1935 as a joint venture between Zeppelin Luftschiffbau, the Ministry of Aviation, and Deutsche Luft Hansa. The LZ Group's capital contribution came primarily from its two airships LZ 127 *Graf Zeppelin* and LZ 129 *Hindenburg*, the latter of which was not yet complete on the date of incorporation. The first chief executive officer of DLZ was Ernst Lehmann, author of this book and Hugo Eckener was appointed chairman, a nominal position he accepted because it left him with a degree of influence over the Zeppelins. In this manner, the Nazis side-lined Eckener, who was effectively replaced by Lehmann who was more supportive of the Nazi cause. This photograph is the Deutsche Zeppelin-Reederei office in Frankfurt.

'Bautzen, Görlitz and Hirschberg unseen. Course Breslau. Altitude 3,000 feet. Suggest abandon Silesian flight. Course Landsberg—Pomerania— East Prussia.' I replied: 'Suggestion OK abandon Silesian flight. Course Landsberg—Leba. We abandon simultaneously, and await you between Leba and Tilsit.'

At two in the morning we reached the Pomeranian coast of the Baltic. The cloud bank ended at Stolp. The route led over the Gulf of Danzig, the Kurische Nehrung and the Kurische Haff to Tilsit. The sun rose like a flaming ball. At about six o'clock the Memel River came into sight. Great expanses of land were inundated; forests and fields and villages were under water. At 6.15 we reached Tilsit, the eastern border of Germany.

A radio message informed me that the *Graf Zeppelin* was in the vicinity. Our flight went over Stallupönen, Trakehnen and Gumbinnen. At 7.30 our companion-ship appeared. The two giants of the air met over Insterburg, where most of the inhabitants were standing on their roofs. The *Graf Zeppelin* circled over us and then took her place behind.

Together we flew to Königsberg. The airships made two wide circles over the city while the march tunes sounded from the loudspeakers. At midday we were in Allenstein and shortly thereafter over the national monument at Tannenberg. The LZ 129 visited the last resting-place of the victor of Tannenberg, whose name it bore.

Our ship turned and took a direct course for the monument. The motors were set at half-speed, and when we were exactly over the spot, they stopped entirely. Almost immobile, the giant airship hovered over the towers while the Deutschland Song was sung by the crowds below and the occupants of the ship up above.

Soon thereafter we passed Neudeck, where Hindenburg lived and died, and later we flew over Marienburg. At 2.30 we reached Danzig, and the sirens on the ships in the harbour and the factories along the shore howled up a welcome. Banners swayed from all the roofs, the streets and even the gas-works. Twice we circled the Marien Church, and then departed.

The sky and the sea were deep blue when the LZ 129 and LZ 127 turned to the coast to cross the Gulf of Danzig and reach Pomerania. At four o'clock we had land under us again and flew toward Stolp. Over Stolp, Schievelbein and Stargard we flew toward Stettin, where we cruised about for twenty minutes. In contrast to the day before, the visibility was excellent. Over the Bodden, the lights of the Greifswald Oie flashed out. After Rohstock came Lübeck with its innumerable lights. Torch parades moved through the streets. Over Neumunster and Schleswig we set course for Flensburg, to get to Hamburg by way of Kiel. If Kiel, with its searchlights, its festive illumination and its gaily decorated houses left a deep impression upon us, then Hamburg was an almost fabulous sight. The whole city was illuminated, an endless sea of lights stretching almost as far as the eye could see. A symphonic greeting arose from the whistles of the locomotives and the fog-horns and sirens of the ships in the harbour. For an hour we cruised over the city, greeted everywhere by deafening 'Heils!' Then we parted; and the *Hindenburg* spent the night hours over the North Sea.

At four in the morning we flew to Heligoland, and at six to Wyk on Föhr, the home of Chief of Police Christiansen, who was on our ship. The little town was given an early morning concert. Shortly thereafter, we flew over the Wattenmeer, a group of shallow coastal bays, from which land was being reclaimed for settlers and farms.

Over Cuxhaven the flight continued to Bremerhaven, where we exchanged greetings with the *Europa*, the sister-ship of the *Bremen*. The sky was deeply overcast, and the rain streamed constantly over the window-panes. But the enthusiasm could be dampened by no mere rainfall. As in Oldenburg, we received a hearty reception in Bremen, which we reached at ten o'clock. Thousands and thousands of our countrymen waved from the roofs and the streets. We flew low under the clouds, so that we remained visible at all times.

Soon after 11.30 we passed Osnabrück and took course for Münster. The fog was so thick in this region that we could hardly see. We made a short spurt and were soon above the comparatively thin strata of fog and, from time to time, were able to see through it. Up there, we had sunshine, and it looked as if the weather was improving.

Shortly before Münster, the *Graf Zeppelin* pushed by us out of the clouds. Since early morning it had flown a different route, so that our compatriots in lower Saxony might at least be partly consoled for our absence.

The *Hindenburg* came out of the clouds and in a few seconds descended from 2,200 to 1,000 feet over Münster. After Bielefeld we flew over Minden, and we visited Hanover and Brunswick before we reached the high-point of that day's flight, the capital.

At 4.30 we passed over the Olympic Village. The *Graf Zeppelin* flew from Staaken to join us. We were just flying over the landing field when I received a telegram from Der Führer.

> I thank the crew and passengers of the *Hindenburg* and the *Graf Zeppelin* for the greetings sent me from the Tannenberg Memorial. I reciprocate them heartily and wish you further good flights. Adolf Hitler.

We flew over Spandau and could see far off towards Potsdam. The sports field lay below us. A few minutes passed, and we were over the Brandenburg Tor, past the Reichstag and the Siegessäule. The school-children of Berlin were gathered in the Lustgarten, and the square before the Castle was a single black mass. Both airships stopped their motors for a minute and flew low over the Lustgarten to greet Berlin's enthusiastic children. The houses of the capital resembled a sea of flags. The greater portion of the Berliners were on the streets, and others waved from the windows and roofs. The Kreuzberg resembled an ant-heap. The great ship circled around, and squads of planes took off to fly over and under us.

Over Potsdam and Sansouci we made a side-trip to Magdeburg. President Christiansen delivered a special greeting to his Magdeburgers through the loudspeaker. After Dessau and Bitterfeld, we flew over Leipzig. Tens of thousands of people were gathered in the streets, and shrill shouts of welcome rose up to greet us.

Adolf Hitler had just begun his last great appeal when we left Leipzig and took course again for Berlin. During our second visit, both the giant airships were spotted by searchlights. The correspondent of the DNB wrote:

> Words cannot describe the scene. The capital was illuminated, the stores and buildings were lighted up, and a dozen searchlights groped in the sky and first caught the *Graf Zeppelin* and then the *Hindenburg*, while flares burned brightly like enormous red torches all over the field.

Again separated from the *Graf Zeppelin*, the third night brought us over Erfurt, Kassel and Paderborn to Wesel, on the Dutch border. In the night sky, the swastika flamed on the tower of the Schwanenburg Lohengrins in Cleve. Our music awakened Düsseldorf. At nine o'clock we again met the *Graf Zeppelin* over the Ruhr. We visited Essen, Dortmund, Bochum, Witten and all the many cities in the industrial district, where an endless forest of foundries and smelteries were now permitted to smoke once again. Through the mountainous region we flew to the Wupper Valley where the suspension railway seemed to rival us.

While we flew to Aachen over Gladbach-Rheydt, the preparations for the voting were being made on the stern promenade deck. A cell-wall was put up and covered by a large linen cloth. Beside the voting booth, the voting-captain had opened his office. 'District—Airship LZ 129, *Hindenburg*,' the sign said.

At nine o'clock we cruised over Aachen. Shortly thereafter, the voting began. The latest issue of the ship's newspaper appeared with the last appeal made by Der Führer from the Cologne Fair Hall. In half an hour, the LZ 129 voted; 104 eligible voters on board, 104 votes for Der Führer.

We circled high over the Cologne Dome. Around us fluttered the parachute flags dropped from the ship. Fireworks thundered from the banks of the Rhine, and the swastika flew from the castles. We made a side-trip to Bad Ems, in honour of a veteran of the old Zeppelin garde, Albert Gross, who made the first flight of the first Zeppelin, and who was now spending his last days in the beautiful resort.

From Koblenz, we followed the winding Moselle, with its many castles, deep valleys and sunny vineyards. Trèves and the Saar region were our destinations.

At one o'clock we were over Saarbrücken. Over Kaiserslautern the flight took us back to the Rhine and past Mainz. In Frankfurt am Main, the *Hindenburg*

Workmen standing on factory roofs at Wuppertal-Barmen to see the *Graf Zeppelin*.

visited the new airship base at the meeting of the North-South and East-West autobahns. The airship hangar there was 937 feet long, the largest one in Germany. The hydrogen is delivered by direct pipe-line from the I. G. Farben to Frankfurt. Professor Knapp-Darmstadt, the creator of the Frankfurt airship base, was a guest on board the *Hindenburg*.

We followed the autobahn. Behind Darmstadt we were greeted by the mountains with all their blossoming glory of fruit trees. We visited Mannheim and Ludwigshafen which were covered with flags and banners.

Our last stop was Stuttgart, which had been passed over at the beginning of the Germany flight. Soon the Bodensee was in sight again, and at six o'clock, the *Hindenburg* was down in the Löwenthal hangar. Half of Friedrichshafen appeared to welcome us home. We were in the air for seventy-five hours and covered 4,110 miles. The *Graf Zeppelin* landed at 6.40, having covered 4,375 miles.

It is easy to believe that we airshipmen, during the three or four days of the flight through Germany, slept even less than our guests who considered every hour in bed a wasted one. The appearance of our airship was always the signal for a spontaneous outburst of enthusiasm, for the ship was a symbol of freedom to the German people. The acclaim of millions of people drowned out the sound of our motors.

37

CROSSING THE EQUATOR AND MY AUTOBIOGRAPHY

AT THE INCLINED observation window on the promenade deck, a woman shuddered. What was that? It was a sound dull as the distant thunder of a cannon.

But the fifty guests in the dining-room were not disturbed. They had entirely forgotten that the small, neatly decorated tables and the comfortable chairs were on an airship. The cover of the menu showed an etching of a German airship over the skyscrapers of New York, and inside, heading the list of foods, were the initials of the German Zeppelin Company. In his native language, each traveller read what the prodigal ship's kitchen offered for that day. A white-haired, red-cheeked American recited, 'Beef Consomme, Cold Capon, Virginia Ham and Tongue, Potato Salad, Cheese and Crackers, Sherry Netherland Cake, Coffee.' He had just come from the smoking room after a strong Cuban Cigar and a glass of light Rhine wine. The clatter of the cutlery and the subdued conversations in German, English, Portuguese and Spanish overtoned the hum of the ventilators ceaselessly sucking in the hot tropical air. Neophytes are inclined to confuse this noise with the droning of the engines and the humming of the propellers, although these are even less audible within the ship than the engines of an ocean liner to a passenger on an upper deck.

The woman at the observation window was so fascinated by the miracle of flight that she did not eat with the others, but stood there revelling in the swift-changing impressions of space: the course of the sun, the blue ocean with its white-capped waves, dolphins, spindle-like sharks, and giant rays, the shadow of the ship which expanded or contracted depending upon the altitude of the ship and the position of the sun, and the smooth snow-like expanse of clouds, inviting the dreamer to step out and walk upon them.

But once more, and this time unmistakably, the woman was roused from her dreaming. Even the people at the table became aware of it and looked up attentively. The Chief Engineer and the crew came running excitedly down the main stairway. The Officer on Duty barred their way.

'The ship is being held up!'

'Held up? In the middle of the Atlantic? By whom?'
There was a net, spread out from East to West
Which caught the ship; and then, from out the blue,
Strange figures boarded us, who now in wrath
Do rant and threaten and demand their due!

A net? That could only be the Equator. Neptune, God of the Sea, was exercising his lawful prerogatives. Already he was entering in person, heralded by the Wind God, Æolus, and his retinue of Tritons blowing conch-horns. And not even the smartest salute could protect the Watch Officer from his wrath.

Perhaps you thought it easier to escape
By riding o'er the sea instead of on it.
I sent my warning flash,
And you but higher flew.
I sent my good Æolus;
You held your course despite the winds he blew.
Until my equator caught your keel
And like a lasso fastened hard upon it.

Mighty Monarch, forgive us.
'Twas carelessness and not our conscious will.
For whether in storm or rain or calm,
Our ship speeds onward still,
And in the thundering of our motors,
Never a call can find us,
But echoes silent in the wind behind us.

His Majesty weakened. Mercy should temper justice if each neophyte crossing the line for the first time recognized his empire by receiving the Equator-baptism. And the romantic woman no longer complained of the lack of genuine romance. As one of the neophytes, she was benevolently sprinkled with water and received from bearded Æolus an Equatorial passport valid forever:

We, Æolus, Hippocrates' son, friend of the immortal gods, rightful ruler of the air, the winds and the trades, the monsoon and the calm, do graciously confer upon the earth-born neophytes on board the airship our permission to cross the Equator by air.

On the Equator-pass, with a signature betraying Dr Eckener's brother as the artist, there was an etching of Neptune rising from the Atlantic, and Æolus, enthroned upon a cloud with his bellows, stopping the airship at the line.

What a few years ago was still Utopian, today becomes an everyday reality. The commercial airship, with a volume of 190,000 cubic metres and lifting power of almost 440,000 pounds, 830 feet in length and 135 feet in height, does not even bow before the dimensions of the largest ocean liner. It bridges the gap between the sea-vessel and the flying boat, for with its speed of 80 miles per hour it is faster than the one, and with its 8,000-mile cruising-radius and 90-ton useful load it is superior to the other in buoyancy and useful lift. The airships adhere to their schedules; the flying time between America and Europe is shortened between two and three days; and the gods of the sea are called upon only to fulfil the desire of the passengers for romance. The *Hindenburg* was in operation.

It was no time at all before people looked upon an airship crossing in the same light as an ocean liner voyage. Even when the LZ 129, *Hindenburg* still lay unfinished in her hangar, American newspaper syndicates had already reserved their places for the flight to America; and the smaller *Graf Zeppelin*, in its seventh year of operation, was sold out for all its flights to and from South America.

Of the passengers carried over the Atlantic, one third were of the most varied nationalities and professions: businessmen, industrialists, farmers, doctors, artists and journalists. Once twenty-two passengers represented eleven nationalities. During the inspection of the German autobahns, thirty different nationalities were represented by thirty-five guests. Transportation and aviation experts personally inspected the only airship service in the world: Ministerial Directors Brandenburg and Ritter, and Minister Hergesell, son of the meteorologist for the Air Ministry; Director Wronsky for the German Lufthansa; General Director

A passenger relaxing in a day cabin on board the *Graf Zeppelin*.

Dorpmüller for the German National Railways; Commander Booth, of the dismantled English airship R 100, for the Royal Air Force; Commander Peck, and Lieutenant-Commanders Shoemaker, Cochrane, Kenworthy and Orville for the US Navy; Colonel Herrera for the Spanish-Argentine Company, Colon. Among many other air-travellers were Sir Hubert Wilkins, the polar explorer and Lauritz Melchior, the Metropolitan Opera tenor.

The freight list on the airships is of the most varied sort. Valuable animals especially are entrusted to the airship service: gorillas, chimpanzees and other monkeys for scientific research and zoological gardens, guinea pigs, queen bees, canary birds, breeding and carrier pigeons, and pedigree dogs. A young Brazilian equestrienne used the *Hindenburg* for the transportation of a fine Trakehner she acquired in Germany. But on the other hand, we were obliged politely to decline to transport a grown elephant which an Indian Maharaja presented to the King of England.

Since cargo, no matter of what kind, was billed at the rate of 10 marks per kilo from Friedrichshafen to Rio de Janeiro, and on the Friedrichshafen–Lakehurst route at a dollar a pound, the freight service was limited generally to the transportation of highly valuable goods of small weight. The booking-office listed, among many other things, chemical preparations, medicaments, dyes, special parts of machines and automobiles, film copies, radio tubes, lamps, important documents, rare orchids and roses, and also bathing suits, children's clothes, rabbit-skins, confections and bottled mineral water. On the first South American flight of the *Hindenburg* an Opel cabriolet, bearing the Jubilee number 500,000, was carried in the frame-work. On the return trip of its second North American flight, the *Hindenburg* carried Captain Haizlip's speed-plane, in which he and his wife wished to tour Europe; and on the following flight to South America there was a sport-plane, destined for Rio, in the freight compartment.

Our main source of income, however, is derived from mail charged at the rate of forty cents per half-ounce: letters, cards, printed material, samples and packages. As I mentioned at the beginning of this book, the airships divided the service with the mail planes of the German Lufthansa, and together we carried many millions of letters across the ocean.

Thanks to the smooth cooperation of the German Lufthansa, the Deutscher Zeppelin-Reederei and the Condor Syndicate, or, in other words, the cooperation of fast Heinkel planes, tri-motored Junkers Ju 52's, Dornier-Wals from the catapult ships *Ostmark*[47] on the African coast and *Westfalen*[48] off Fernando do Noroñha, as well as the Zeppelin airships, Condor flying boats and Condor airplanes, this overseas service functioned as dependently as any railway mail-system.

With the first regular passenger flight of the *Hindenburg* I intended to end this book which tells of war-times, of defeat and victory, and of the disappointments and triumphs of the Zeppelin airship. The new chapter dealing with the introduction of a merchant marine of large airships into regular world traffic, rightly belongs in another book. But before I lay down my pen, it is fitting that I should introduce myself.

I was born in 1886 in Ludwigshafen on the Rhine, opposite Mannheim. My father was a chemist and supervisor of the Badischen Anilinfabrik, now a major division of the I. G. Farben; my mother was the daughter of former Mayor Schäfer from Diez on the Lahn.

I was brought up amid sulphuric acid and Pfälzer wind, was graduated in 1904, and soon thereafter went to Kiel as a so-called Marine-baueleve, for even when I was fourteen I had decided I would be a builder of ships. Possibly a Holstein grandmother was responsible for that.

But when the *Stosch* went aground on the African coast, losing its propeller—it was a sail-boat with auxiliary motor—and bending its rudder-post, and I was ordered to determine the extent of the damage, the decision was made.

Soon afterward I went to the Berlin-Charlottenburg College to study ship-building and marine engineering.

In 1912, after six years of experience in regattas and making sea-voyages with sail-boats, I passed my examination and became a certified Engineer. Meanwhile, I had been on warships in fleet manoeuvres and had been made a Naval Reserve Lieutenant. Then I entered the Imperial Dockyards at Kiel as a naval engineer.

I was quite dissatisfied with the career of a government employee when I received an inquiry from Dr Eckener, who was looking for a pilot for the airship *Sachsen*, then built for the Delag. His conditions fitted my case so well that I applied a short time later and was accepted.

Ernst Lehmann in his uniform as part of the crew of the training ship SMS *Stosch*.

In the spring of 1913, I began to learn airship piloting under his supervision, and in the fall I was given command of the *Sachsen*.

In the winter of 1913–14, I was already aiding Dr Eckener in training the first officers and crews of the newly organized Naval Airship Division. During the first half of 1914, I made a great many passenger flights with the *Sachsen* in order to earn as much money as possible for the Delag. In the summer of 1914, the war began and my record goes as follows:

1914   Commander of the Army airship *Sachsen*; raids and scouting flights over Belgium, England, France, Russia, the North Sea, and the Baltic.

1915   Commander of the Army airship LZ XII.

1916   Commander of the Army airships LZ 90 and LZ 98.

1917   Commander of the Army airship LZ 120.

1918   Director of the Zeppelin Co.'s construction department and agent for the Zeppelin Airship Company in Friedrichshafen (development, demonstration and delivery to the naval authorities). Baron von Gemmingen Director of the Zeppelin Company.

1919   Preparation for the flight to America with the L 72. Plans for future North Atlantic service. (Flemming commander of the Bodensee.) Founding of a Spanish research line: Seville—Buenos Aires.

1920   Six months in Sweden, calculating cost and income of an airship line from Stockholm to Friedrichshafen to the Mediterranean.

1921   Four months with Flemming in North America, negotiating for an airship line New York—Chicago.

1922   Negotiations with USA and England concerning North Atlantic Service schedule. Founding of the Spanish airship Service Company, Colon; Seville—Buenos Aires.

1923   Founding of the Goodyear Zeppelin Corporation. I went to Akron, Ohio, as 'Vice President in charge of Engineering.'

1924   After the death of Gemmingen, Dr Eckener becomes Director of Zeppelin Company. From April to October, I was in Friedrichshafen; in October, I was second in command of the LZ 126 (ZR-3) on its flight to America.

1925   Founding of the US Airship Transport Company indefinitely postponed because of the crash of the US Navy's *Shenandoah*.

1926   Plans for US Navy airship in Akron.

1927   Back in Friedrichshafen as Dr Eckener's assistant.

1928   Flights of *Graf Zeppelin* began in fall; by end of 1935 the *Graf Zeppelin* had made 505 flights.

1936   April; Business manager of the Deutschen Zeppelin-Reederei, Berlin, Friedrichshafen.

Ernst A. Lehmann at his desk, 1 July 1929.

In command of the airship *Graf Zeppelin* from 18 September 1928, to 10 December 1935:

Dr Eckener	133 times
Captain Lehmann	272 times
Captain Flemming	34 times
Captain von Schiller	27 times
Captain Wittemann	23 times
Captain Pruss	16 times
	505 flights

The airships I commanded were:

Viktoria Luise and *Hansa*	20 times
Sachsen	550 times
Z XII	127 times
LZ 90	20 times
LZ 98	50 times
LZ 120	28 times
Bodensee	3 times
LZ 126 (ZR-3)	5 times
Graf Zeppelin	272 times
	1,075 flights

Added to this, since 4 March 1936, the flights of the *Hindenburg* to South America and the ten round-trip flights to Lakehurst during the summer of 1936.

38

THE FIRST TRANSATLANTIC CROSSING
OF THE *HINDENBERG*

OR 1936, THE Deutschen Zeppelin-Reederei had long planned to introduce two airships into the South American service and develop a closer
cooperation with the German Lufthansa and the Condor-Syndicate in
the passenger and mail transport inaugurated by the *Graf Zeppelin* between
Germany and the South American countries.

Accordingly, during the spring of 1936, the *Hindenburg* operated along with
the *Graf Zeppelin* on a fourteen-day schedule to Rio. On 31 March 1936, with
a crew of fifty-three and thirty-seven passengers, we took off for Brazil. I took
course over Stuttgart, Frankfurt am Main, Cologne and Rotterdam. At 10.30
o'clock we crossed the Dutch border in hazy weather; and at midday, just when
our guests were in the dining-room relishing young fat geese, we flew over the
North Sea and into the Channel.

In Biscay that night we struck a storm which our passengers slept through;
they learned the news while they were at breakfast the next morning. On the
third night we crossed the equator; but Neptune and Æolus were considerate
enough to wait until daylight before coming aboard with their baptismal certif-
icates. Over the accustomed landing-field in Pernambuco, we dropped our mail
via parachute. On the morning of 4 April we landed on the new airship field
at Santa Cruz, where a broken cable had rendered the mooring-mast useless
and we went into the hangar under our own power. A special train brought the
passengers to Rio de Janeiro, thirty-five miles away, where the people outdid
themselves in tokens of friendship and admiration.

On the return flight, I purposely steered into a rain front. The ship's back
had a drain on both sides, through which rainwater ran into the ballast-tanks.
In this simple manner we obtained six tons of water and counteracted the
weight lost through the consumption of oil by the motors. Over Africa, one
of the heavy oil motors broke down, and as strong head winds were reported
from Biscay and the Channel, I radioed for and received permission from the
French government to fly through the valley of the Rhône. On 10 April, at 6.35
o'clock, we landed in Löwenthal after a voyage over ten countries and three

continents, during which we covered 13,500 miles in 216 hours of flight. Our average speed was 62 miles per hour; off Bahia we made 110 miles per hour.

The *Graf Zeppelin*, which relieved us for the next two flights, completed its 112th to 115th ocean crossings. The list of our passengers remained colourful enough, for the following nationalities were represented: German, Austrian, Danish, Dutch, Italian, French, English, Australian, Brazilian, Argentinian, Chilian and American.

Between the South American flights, the *Hindenburg* made some demonstration flights to Lakehurst. Through these we endeavoured to prove, and did prove, that by using sufficiently large and sturdy airships a regular service could be maintained over the North Atlantic route.

Our four engines were overhauled at the Daimler-Benz factory in Untertürkheim and tested in a nine-hour workshop flight before I decided to start on the first North American flight on the evening of 6 May. Besides our old friends—Mr Leeds and Sir Hubert Wilkins, and their wives, Mrs Clara Adams, Lady. Drummond Hay and Carl von Wiegand, and a total of twelve women—we had with us Dr Lewald, chairman of the German Olympic Committee; State Councillor Dr Krebs, mayor of Frankfurt am Main; Dr von Böckmann, of the German Short-Wave Corporation; Commander Peck, of the US Navy; and Director Fickes and Engineer Dick, of the Goodyear Zeppelin Corporation. In freight, we carried 200,000 letters and 3,300 pounds of cargo—Rheinwein, Bavarian beer, 60 pounds of asparagus, and films and other things. Since the flying base at Rhein-Main lies only 350 feet above sea level, the *Hindenburg* could lift 13,200 pounds more than she could at the Friedrichshafen base, which is situated 1,000 feet higher.

The *Hindenburg* rose at 9.30 o'clock and disappeared into the night sky. Again the spectators spontaneously sang the German national anthem. Down the Rhine, we took course over Cologne and Holland and out over the Channel. The English coast gleamed in the morning sunlight. Over the Atlantic Ocean the wind blew north-north-east, and we flew at 80 miles per hour. Six hundred sea miles from Ireland, we met the *Europa* of the North German Lloyd and a few hours later passed the French express-liner *Champlain*. At night, the passengers gathered in the lounge to hear the first concert ever given on board an airship. The Dresden pianist, Franz Wagner, played on the concert piano, whose manufacturer, Dr Rudolf Blüthner, was on board. And on the next morning, in the same room, services were held by Father Paul Schulte, the 'flying missionary.'

When our passengers emerged from their cabins that morning, none of them knew that during the night we had come through a heavy rainstorm. We did not complain about such weather, for it filled our ballast-tanks with 11,000 pounds of rain-water and thus saved us a great deal of gas. At midday, two icebergs drifted by below us, and to please our passengers we went down to 500 feet and flew over the larger one, which loomed a good 175 feet above the surface of the sea.

The promenade deck on the *Hindenburg*.

During the entire flight we were in constant wireless contact both with the Old and the New World. The Reichsrundfunkgesellschaft and the National Broadcasting Company had representatives on board and broadcast reports to all the receivers throughout the world. When in the grey morning of the third day of flight we were flying over the ship lanes near Long Island, the famous American war ace, Captain Rickenbacker,[49] who had flown out to meet us, radioed the news of our arrival, and newspaper extras were on the streets of New York in no time at all. The radio representative of the DNB reported:

On board the passengers are already speaking of the moment when they must part. And that moment is approaching at a speed of 70 miles per hour. America has prepared a magnificent reception for the airship, as is revealed by the thousands of telegrams that have been received on board. That the North American route has developed in due course from an experimental stage to the point of an accomplished fact, seems to be established beyond doubt.

Indeed, the technical picture is overpowering. Whoever has stepped behind the little door separating the back of the stage from the pit is overcome by the impression. It is false to imagine the inside of the airship as crammed with swollen gas-cells. One can see a great part of the frame-work, which is covered with a steel-blue protective coat of paint. With its ribs and struts it seems like a cathedral. While one ponders on this impression, one remembers that this cathedral is speeding along 3,000 feet over the sea. The men of the crew, for whom the narrow blue-painted gangway has become a second home, radiate calm assurance. They never once doubted that the Atlantic could be conquered. The *Hindenburg* is the result of thirty-six years of airshipping, and its crew is too. These men understand without being told, and their duties are completed without delay or nervousness. They have all tinkered with the mechanisms and the paraphernalia, and they have rejected whatever was unsatisfactory. They have rejoiced over a successful technical innovation. And already they are dreaming of an entirely new airship beside which the LZ 129 will be a mere experiment.

The passengers didn't show up so well in this accounting. They hovered between nervousness and phobia. Even though they were offered what no transatlantic service ever offered them before—a crossing without seasickness. Not a spoonful of soup was spilled during this flight. Everyone was able to enjoy the beauty of the sea without being obliged to submit to the sea's humours.

We had a triumphant flight behind us. In the sixty hours we had crossed the North Atlantic, for which crossing the best steamship time from Bremen to New York was 5 days and 17 hours. Since the departure from Friedrichshafen, we had covered 3,800 sea miles at an average speed of 75 miles per hour. The engines worked exceptionally well. At about five in the morning, we reached New York. As we approached from the east, the great city still lay in sleep. It was the silent hour between day and night.

Slowly we glided over the sparkling ribbon of the East River. The lights of the bridges were reflected by the water. Then the first siren howled up beneath us. And in a moment all the steamer whistles, all factory whistles, all the horns and steam-whistles of the ships in the bay, joined in. But this was only a sample, for now we were over Manhattan, and the giant ships added their voices to the primitive concert which filled the air around us.

An interior view of the *Hindenburg*.

Sky-dining-room, Dr Eckener presiding.

Passengers in the dining room of the *Hindenburg*, April 1936.

Slim and brazen, a pillar reached up through the dark, seeming almost to touch the airship: that was the Empire State Building. While we stared at it, our eyes dropped to the yawning canyons and the stalagmites of smaller buildings. A veritable hurricane of sound blew around us. The propellers of planes suddenly roared around us and escorted us on our way. A strong searchlight beam leaped up from the *Bremen*. And beside this one, a second beam rose toward us, that of the Statue of Liberty.

The wide arms of the river, the gigantic houses and streets, remained behind us, and we took course for Lakehurst. In New Jersey, we sighted the *Los Angeles*, which once carried us over this same route, fastened to the mooring mast. Our former LZ 126 had left its hangar to make way for its big brother. We were over Lakehurst. On the wide field, detachments of sailors were waiting for us. The ship descended, the handling guys dropped, and the men caught them up.

The landing crew at the bow proved to be too weak, and Dr Borchers, our General Consul in New York, and about fifty journalists, ran forward and helped to fasten the *Hindenburg* to the mooring mast. It was 6.08, New York time, when the two landing wheels of the German airship touched American soil; and twelve minutes later she was in the hangar.

For the flight from Friedrichshafen to Lakehurst, the LZ 129 required 62 hours and 38 minutes, the fastest Atlantic crossing of an airship on the east-west route, thus beating that of the LZ 126 by some 18 hours and 36 minutes.

The four planes of the American Coast Guard, which escorted us from New York, left us to a swarm of naval planes. Fourteen passenger planes of the American Air Lines transported the spectators to Lakehurst and now stood prepared to carry our passengers back to New York. A giant transport plane flew off with a few of our airship passengers towards California, stretching the Europe–North America route to San Francisco. But before they could disperse, the passengers had to submit not only to passport and customs examination, but also to the interrogations of the newspapermen.

That night, a special plane brought Dr Eckener and me to New York, where the Deutsch-Amerikanische Handelsgesellschaft gave us a dinner at the Waldorf Astoria Hotel, in the grand ballroom. The whole place was decorated with flags, bunting and banners, and the two national flags, the Stars and Stripes and the Swastika. Thousands of beautiful evening gowns and white-ties. The balconies were crowded with people looking down on the gathering.

The mood of the entire affair was feverish, and all the assembled people applauded when the guest of honour appeared. Ambassador Dr Luther, Dr Eckener and I were greeted most enthusiastically, as was Commander Rosendahl, the Commander of the Naval Air Station at Lakehurst. Before the speeches began, the lights were turned out, and a spotlight illuminated the large heap of ice-cream, presented by the Association of German Bakers. This was followed by a parade of fifty waiters with uplifted ice-cream dishes.

The *Hindenburg* passing the Empire State building.

The press reception for the *Hindenburg* on its first US landing.

Then the toastmaster, without whom an American banquet seems to be impossible, began his duties. He first introduced Dr Luther. The Ambassador pointed out that the event being celebrated by this banquet was the result of the cooperation of Germans and Americans, and spoke of the commercial significance of a fast service between the two continents. Undersecretary of State Johnson intimated that considerable support might be expected from the American government.

Then Commander Rosendahl expressed the wish that he might one day visit Friedrichshafen as the Commander of an American airship. Dr Eckener, in his address, voiced the same hope.

This banquet was concluded by a ball, which was arranged by a group of German-Americans, and it was the occasion of my second speech. I expressed my thanks for the magnificent reception and the generous assistance of the officials. By train, Dr Eckener and I travelled to Washington, and accompanied by Lieutenant General von Bötticher, visited Secretary of State Hull, Secretary of Commerce Roper, Admiral Standley, and other prominent officials, and were then received at the White House. Once again, the President of the United States revealed the most profound interest and promised to furnish everything necessary for a regular airship-service between Germany and the USA.

Meanwhile, Captain Pruss had prepared the LZ 129. Eckener and I returned to Lakehurst, and the ship was undocked in the dark. Old and new passengers, fifty-five in all, including a woman of eighty-six, a man of seventy-three and a boy of thirteen, came aboard. About 155,000 letters and 2,640 pounds of fast-freight were loaded in the compartments. At 4.27, Central European Time, the *Hindenburg* took off from Lakehurst. Exactly one hour later, we passed New York amid the clamour of the sirens.

The thirteen-year-old boy was named William Sharke and belonged to the American Boy Scouts. He sat opposite his grandmother at the observation window, a crumpled autograph book pressed against himself, a rubber ball in his pocket; and in their excitement and delight, neither the boy nor his grandmother noticed that he was sitting on the large chocolate egg which had been presented to him as a 'bon voyage' gift.

When we left the American coast, we flew into a thick fog, through which the sun could not penetrate. We did not succeed in getting into the west wind until the next day. The wind tore the clouds and shoved at our ship. In vain the black shadows on the sea tried to keep up with the airship. At night, we sighted the Scilly Islands at the entrance to the English Channel. We had required 39 hours and 51 minutes from New York to the coast of Europe. A female passenger, an Englishwoman, was called by telephone from London; within ten minutes the connection was established, and both voices were clearly heard. As I learned from our Chief Radio Operator, Speck, our station on board was using two sending and receiving apparatuses day and night and wirelessed no fewer than

35,000 words! At night we took course over South England and Holland, and then up the Rhine, and at sunrise were over Frankfurt.

The landing manoeuvre was directed by Major Baron von Buttlar Brandenfels, whom my readers will remember having met in earlier chapters of this book. At 5.41, the *Hindenburg* was safe on the mooring-mast. The stern car rolled on the rails and aimed the ship toward the hangar, whereupon it was towed inside by the trolleys.

Music accompanied our arrival in the hangar, our new home. Hitler Youths surprised our young American Boy Scout by addressing him in English. State Councillor Dr Krebs became our host instead of our guest by inviting us to the Römer at eleven o'clock. Frankfurt was proud of our airship, and joyous crowds surrounded us everywhere. By covering the route from Lakehurst to Friedrichshafen in 49 hours and 14 minutes, the LZ 129 had beaten the LZ 127's record by 6 hours and 9 minutes.

The happiness of our German compatriots was expressed by a telegram from Chancellor Hitler. In Berlin, where I went for one day, the Chief of the Foreign Press, Dr Hanfstangl,[50] gave a banquet in honour of our first North American flight, and his speech praising the friendly relations between Germany and the USA was greeted with loud applause by the American correspondents. The House of Representatives in Washington received a petition, inspired by our success, which requested that the *Los Angeles* be placed in service again.

During our trip to North America, the *Graf Zeppelin*, under Schiller's command, had completed another flight to Rio, had returned to the Friedrichshafen dockyards for a minor repair and, three days before, had once again left for Rio with twenty passengers. At this time, the LZ 127 had covered a total distance of 970,000 miles.

When the *Graf Zeppelin* was approaching Cape Verde on the return from Brazil, the *Hindenburg*, again under way for North America with forty passengers and 286 pounds of freight, was just taking course north of the Azores. This time, because we received fewer reports from steamers, we went through four storm centres and a thunder-squall, and the head-winds, which sometimes reached forty-five miles per hour, made our trip last 78 hours and 27 minutes. Nevertheless, we adhered to our schedule by not entering the Lakehurst hangar, but taking on fuel and provisions at the anchor-mast and flying on again that night.

The wind, which had hindered our flight across, aided our return, our fastest to date—45 hours and 42 minutes. On the morning of 23 May, 1936, we landed in Rhein-Main; and on the evening of the 25th, we took off again with forty passengers and 200,000 letters for Rio de Janeiro. After the return, the *Hindenburg* flew to its home base at Bodensee before undertaking the next North American flight.

We made eight more regular flights to Lakehurst during the summer and after establishing the North American service, in November the *Hindenburg*,

The *Hindenburg* in flight.

with Captain Pruss in command, made four more trips to Rio de Janeiro. The seven South American flights made by the *Hindenburg* in the spring and fall of 1936 rounded out the year's programme for the *Graf Zeppelin*. For the summer of 1937, no less than fifteen flights on the South American route and eighteen on the North American have been scheduled for the *Graf Zeppelin* and the *Hindenburg*.

The *Hindenburg* made the trips from Frankfurt to Lakehurst in an average of 63 hours and 42 minutes; the trips from Lakehurst to Frankfurt were made in 51 hours and 46 minutes; the average speed was 81 miles per hour. The fastest speed was 188 miles per hour, with stern winds. The number of the Atlantic travellers increased to 3,530 from 841 in the preceding year. In addition, 66,000 pounds of mail and cargo were carried. Many pieces of mail bore, besides the airship's stamp, the strange mail stamp 'Zepp'; they were sent by philatelists from the little Virginian town Zepp.

On the third US trip the *Hindenburg* carried back home Max Schmeling who, because of his victory in the ring over Joe Louis, received an enthusiastic ovation upon his arrival in Frankfurt. Schmeling later returned to New York on the *Hindenburg*. After landing in Lakehurst, the *Hindenburg* started, with sixty invited passengers, on a sightseeing tour over Philadelphia, Baltimore, Washington and some of the larger cities of New England. The newspapermen, because of the passengers carried on this trip, called it the 'millionaires' trip,' and they took my picture with Nelson Rockefeller and Winthrop W. Aldrich. The ninth and next-to-the-last North American trip of the year 1936 was under the personal command of Dr Eckener.

The establishment of regular transatlantic lines closes that chapter in the development of airshipping which I should like to call historical. The fight to conquer the air has ended in the defeat of the elemental forces of Nature. The era of inventions bows to the era of transportation. If airshipping has finally

Two photographs of the *Hindenburg* over Lower Manhattan.

been established, it signifies more than the technical success—a triumph of perseverance. The readers who have followed me through the chapters of this book know that Zeppelin's cause seemed lost on three different occasions, only to rise three times phoenix-like from the ashes to resurrection all the more magnificent. And each time it was the united will of a nation which came to the aid of an inventor's life-work. The National Fund after Echterdingen, the Zeppelin-Eckener Fund after the war, the founding of the Deutschen Zeppelin-Reederei by the Third Reich, all three are linked like the Olympic rings and forge the chain of development until it is indestructible.

World traffic via airships has begun. By the expansion of weather-service on land and sea on the one hand, and the increased safety, comfort and practicability of airships on the other, it will spread out over all the seas and continents. The world should be grateful to Germany as the trail-blazer.

The *Hindenburg* at Lakehurst.

39

THE LAST FLIGHT BY COMMANDER CHARLES E. ROSENDAHL

L ATE ON THE afternoon of 6 May 1937, while engaged in the landing operation at the US Naval Air Station at Lakehurst, New Jersey, with dramatic suddenness and without warning the airship *Hindenburg* burst into flames, settled to the ground and was there consumed by the fire of her own hydrogen. Thirty-six persons perished, among them Captain Ernst A. Lehmann, author of the previous chapters of this book and world-renowned leader in airship development and operation. It is with full realization of his prominent place in lighter-than-air history that this unhappy chapter is added to his book.

For certain details prior to and during the last flight, acknowledgment is made to Leonhard Adelt who, with his wife, was a survivor of the *Hindenburg* disaster.

During the early months of 1937, both the *Hindenburg* and the *Graf Zeppelin* had been thoroughly overhauled and groomed for further conquests. As the beginning of the 1937 schedule approached, the *Hindenburg* made several European flights. During these, Major-General Ernst Udet of the German Air Ministry conducted experiments of hooking his airplane onto the *Hindenburg* and being launched from it in flight.[51] Although the utility of such complementary uses of the airplane with the airship had been demonstrated for years by our American naval airships, Udet's experiments with the *Hindenburg* represented the first practice of this kind with commercial airships. Lehmann himself was one of the principal backers of this project, realizing fully the great advantages it can afford even in commercial airship operation.

There followed a round trip to Rio de Janeiro on which that patriarch of airships, Dr Eckener, beloved, admired and respected by the entire world, went along to participate in the formal opening of the new airship terminal facilities at Rio. Upon the *Hindenburg*'s return to Frankfurt, all attention was concentrated on the opening of the 1937 service over the North Atlantic and the eyes and minds of all concerned were magnetically drawn westward to Lakehurst.

Following negotiations through the usual official channels, the Navy Department of the United States had issued a permit for use by the *Hindenburg* of certain airship facilities at its airship base at Lakehurst that were not being

LZ 129 *Hindenburg* with RD 4 over Lakehurst May 1936.

used by American airships. The permit was granted in return for payment to the United States for all services received by the *Hindenburg* at Lakehurst and a disclaimer of expense or risk on the part of the United States. The approved schedule comprised eighteen round trips between Frankfurt and Lakehurst from May to November. The American Zeppelin Transport Incorporated were to act as General Agents for the Deutsche Zeppelin Reederei, owners and operators of the *Hindenburg*, and the Hamburg American-North German Lloyd organization were the General Passenger Agents. From experience gained in 1936, the preparations and details for handling all pertinent matters on this end of the route had been carefully worked out, and a very successful season was anticipated by all concerned.

The coronation of King George VI of England and the Paris Exposition were drawing-cards that resulted in a complete sell-out of accommodations for the first eastbound trip of 1937, for the schedule would have permitted arrival of *Hindenburg* passengers in Europe well in time for the coronation. It had been planned also to bring the coronation films to this country on the second trip of the *Hindenburg*.

The take-off of the *Hindenburg* for the first scheduled North Atlantic flight in the 1937 series took place on 3 May at 8 p.m. Central European Time, from the new Rhein-Main World Airport, in ideal weather conditions. On board were thirty-six passengers representing five nationalities. The Danish Minister of Transportation, who was to have made the trip with one of his officials, had to cancel his reservation at the last moment. In command of the ship was

Captain Max Pruss whose airship experience dates back to the world war; in his crew were included two other captains, Albert Sammt and Heinrich Bauer. As Director of the Deutsche Zeppelin Reederei, Captain Lehmann came along on this 1937 inaugural trip; also Captain Anton Wittemann of the *Graf Zeppelin*. Although the normal crew of the *Hindenburg* was about forty, a considerable number of younger airship men was carried in addition for training purposes, bringing the total crew up to sixty-one. Among them were Dr Rudiger, the first doctor ever to be carried regularly in the crew of any commercial aircraft, and the first airship stewardess, Mrs Imhof. There were, then, ninety-seven persons on board the *Hindenburg* on this trip.

Within a short time the city of Cologne was reached, the shadowy outline of its famous cathedral silhouetted against the city's lights. The course then proceeded as customary via Holland to the North Sea; there thunderstorms over the Channel made it advisable to detour to the north. For a while the weather remained unpleasant but not severe, with bad visibility; neither the French nor English Coasts were sighted. Over the ocean the ship took a course somewhat more northerly than that generally taken by steamers at this time of the year. On the afternoon of 5 May, the coast of North America was first sighted near Newfoundland. Large horseshoe-shaped ice fields pushed their way into the sea and closer to the shore numerous icebergs of varied and fantastic forms floated about. For the benefit of the passengers, the ship flew low over the crystal-like, glittering ice forms.

Now the ship's course was changed to a generally southerly direction, passing the lighthouse at Cape Race and several lonely coastal cities. As had been experienced on practically the entire trip, head winds persisted, now blowing at 45 to 50 miles-per-hour velocity at flying levels. However there was no turbulence during the flight, merely the slowing down of the ship's speed over the surface because of opposing winds. It was noon on 6 May before Boston was reached; by three o'clock the ship was over New York City and then soon headed southward for the vicinity of Lakehurst. Although the scheduled time of arrival set many months in advance had been 6 a.m. on 6 May, the prevalence of head winds had caused Captain Pruss to radio that he would delay the landing time until 6 p.m. that day. Hence although the ship arrived over the Lakehurst field at about a quarter past four, no attempt was made to land before the announced time of 6 p.m. since the arrangements necessarily involved not only the ground crew at a designated time but also all those officials who are customarily associated with the official entry of a foreign commercial vessel.

Meanwhile, a weather 'front' accompanied by rain and thunderstorms was moving in from the westward. Cruising in an area a few miles south and south-east of Lakehurst, the *Hindenburg* awaited the passage of this front at Lakehurst, then proceeded westward coming in behind the front. Although the ground crew stood in readiness at six o'clock, heavy rain and a thunderstorm made it advisable for the ship to stay clear until the weather improved. As the thunderstorm passed and the rain practically ceased, I sent a radio message to Captain Pruss recommending that he come on in and land. Hence, at about 7 p.m., Eastern Daylight Saving Time, the *Hindenburg* came into view and passed over the station on a northerly course at an altitude of 500 to 600 feet to have a look at surface conditions. The ground crew consisted of some ninety Navy enlisted personnel together with a proportionate number of naval officers, and 138 civilians recruited from the vicinity, practically all of whom had at one time or another been employed at the station and hence were familiar with airships and their landing and mooring. After circling, the *Hindenburg* came back over the station, adjusted her trim and static conditions by valving hydrogen and dropping ballast in perfectly normal fashion, headed into the wind, descended to about 200 feet altitude, backed down on her engines to check the headway of the ship, and at 7.21 dropped her manila landing ropes to the ground. It was raining almost imperceptibly and while the light of the sinking sun was dimmed by the overcast cloud condition, the weather was definitely improving.

On board, all members of the crew were at their landing stations, eager to land and re-service their proud ship and be off again on schedule eastward over the Atlantic. In the passageways near the gangway, the passengers' baggage had been assembled ready to be passed out immediately upon reaching the ground. In the spacious lounge rooms near the open observation windows, most of them on the starboard side with their passports and papers ready for examination there by the boarding officials, were crowded nearly all the passengers trying to recognize friends on the ground and watching the landing operation.

The ground crew at once grabbed the ship's landing lines, connected them to corresponding ground lines and began the operation of hauling them taut as the first step in the landing manoeuvre. From the very nose of the ship, the steel mooring cable by which the ship was to be pulled in to its connection on the mooring mast, began to make its appearance. Following the passage of the thunderstorm, the wind had become light and variable, scarcely two miles-per-hour velocity on the surface and only some six knots at the ship's altitude; the direction there was some 90° different from that on the surface. Before the slack of the landing ropes could be taken in by the ground crew, a light gust from the port side caused the ship to move very very slowly to starboard and also gradually tightened the port manila landing rope.

At 7.25, or just four minutes after the landing ropes had been dropped, I saw a burst of flame on top of the ship just forward of where the upper vertical fin attaches to the hull. It was a brilliant burst of flame resembling a flower opening rapidly into bloom. I knew at once that the ship was doomed, for nothing could prevent that flame from spreading to the entire volume of hydrogen with which she was inflated. There was a muffled report and the flames spread rapidly through the after quarter of the ship. In the control room,

These two images are exactly the same photograph, but exposed differently when printed they each show subtle differences of detail. The photograph was take a few seconds after the spark had ignited the gas and when *Hindenburg* is adjacent to the Lakehurst mooring tower.

the officers were not aware that anything was wrong until they felt a shudder through the ship that reminded them of the snapping of a landing rope, but a quick glance assured them that it was something else. As the stern section of the ship lost its buoyancy in the fire, it began to settle to the ground on almost an even keel, ablaze throughout and sending huge pillars of flame and smoke to great heights, particularly as the fuel oil began to burn.

As the stern settled, the forward three-quarters of the ship, still having its buoyancy, pointed skyward at an angle of about 45°. Through the axial corridor of the ship, in reality a huge vent extending along the very central axis, the flame shot upward and forward as though it were going up a stack. Although the travel of the flame was actually progressive, it spread forward so rapidly and so quickly encompassed the entire length of the ship that to some it may have seemed almost instantaneous. The forward section was not long in following the stern to the ground, and within less than a minute from the first appearance of the fire, the ship had settled, not crashed, on to the ground and lay there writhing and crackling from the hottest flame that man knows.

The feelings of those on the ground are difficult to describe. Visitors who stood in the assigned visiting space several hundred yards away were stricken dumb or fled in horror at this amazing spectacle. In order not to be caught under the burning ship, the ground crew were ordered to run from the immediate vicinity. But even before the ship had touched the ground, they had dashed back to effect such rescues as might be possible. In the ground crew were many men who were not only acquainted with many of those on board the ship but were also familiar with the parts of the ship where passengers and crew were located. To such places they went immediately. On board the ship there was little time for warning or help. Some were surprised in their cabins or at their posts of duty and never knew what overtook them. Others heard shouts from within and from without the ship to jump through the windows and many of the survivors got out by this method. At first glance, it seemed impossible that human beings could come out alive from such an inferno. As I stood off to one side, spellbound by this most unexpected tragedy, I saw the flames eat rapidly along the fabric sides of the hull greedily devouring the illustrious name 'Hindenburg' letter by letter.

It is unfortunate that most of the passengers were gathered on the starboard side and that they and perhaps others on board did not realize that the wind on the surface was blowing directly onto the port beam and hence was driving the flames to starboard. Realization of this fact might have saved a few more lives. I do not recall when I have been so startled as when I saw Chief Steward Kubis, Watch Officers Ziegler and Zable, and several others, suddenly emerge from the burning mass of wreckage totally unharmed. There were of course some miraculous escapes, not all of which will ever be recorded. One of the elderly women passengers, as though led by a guardian angel, left the ship by

Hindenburg just after bursting into flames. The landing crews are running to safety.

Hindenburg slow sinks towards the ground as it loses buoyancy, the hull has buckled.

Hindenburg hits the ground stern first and collapses as hydrogen flames burst out of the bow.

the regular hatchway with the calmness of a somnambulist, receiving only minor burns. Others hearing the call to them to jump, went through the open windows and were then led to safety. Mr George Grant, a British shipping man, escaped without a single scratch or burn by jumping through a window, and then as he was picking himself up to run away from the fire, suffered the great misfortune of having another person leap from the same window and land squarely in the middle of his back injuring him severely. Probably the most miraculous escape was that of Werner Franz, a 14-year-old cabin boy. As he jumped through a hatch in the bottom of the ship and reached the ground, the searing flames began to choke him. Just at that moment, a water tank opened up immediately above him discharging its entire contents upon him and bringing him to his senses. Just then he spied an opening in the wreckage free from flames, worked his way through it and emerged into the open air from this fiery furnace totally unharmed and thoroughly drenched. Another who escaped without injury was Captain Anton Wittemann. Nelson Morris, an American passenger and an experienced airship traveller, jumped through a window on the starboard side and then with his bare hands snapped the red hot structural members about him as though they were twigs and fought his way clear of the burning wreck with only minor burns.

Those in the control car, as had every member of the crew, stuck to their posts in accordance with the highest traditions. As the forward section of the ship settled to the ground, it rebounded slightly from the resiliency of the forward landing wheel. Then and only then came the word 'Now everybody out.' There had been plenty of quick thinking in the control car during those seconds of descent. The normal impulse would have been to drop water ballast to ease the impact of the ship with the ground, but those in the control car in an instant decided not to drop it but to let the weight of that water remain in the ship as long as possible to bring the burning hull to the ground in the shortest space of time. In my opinion, this was one of the outstanding events in the whole disaster.

Captain Pruss was badly burned, but not so badly as Captain Lehmann who nevertheless was able to stagger away from the ship. Largely because there were many tons of fuel oil still remaining on board, the fire raged for more than three hours despite the efforts of all available fire-fighting apparatus.

Thirteen out of thirty-six passengers perished or died subsequently from injuries; of the sixty-one crew members twenty-two fell victims to this awful fire and one civilian member of the ground crew died of burns. To anyone having seen the tragedy, it seems remarkable indeed that out of 97 persons on board, 62 of them or nearly two-thirds have survived.

Sad as was the loss of every one of them, no loss will be more keenly felt in the airship world than that of that outstanding pioneer Ernst Lehmann who succumbed to burns.

It is almost impossible to recount the many deeds of heroism performed in the emergency by members of the armed services and civilians alike. The period immediately following the settling of the ship to the ground was one of individual initiative; no orders had to be given as to the rescues. We shall probably never know all of the individuals deeds within the ship itself, particularly on the part of those who perished. One event, however, cannot pass without mention. On board the ship returning from a visit abroad were Mr and Mrs John Pannes, he having been for many years an official of the Hamburg American-North German Lloyd Steamship interests in New York City. As the ship neared the ground, someone shouted to Pannes to jump through the open window; but glancing about for Mrs Pannes to go with him, he did not find her and would not go without her; both perished within the ship.

Requests for medical assistance had gone out quickly from the Air Station since our own Dispensary, of limited size and facilities, could hardly cope fully with the unanticipated volume thus thrust upon it. Quickly doctors and ambulances came from every direction. Fire-fighting departments, American Legionnaires, Sea Scouts, members of the C.C.C., soldiers, sailors, members of the civilian ground crew, all pitched in despite great danger to themselves in effecting rescues, in attempts to subdue the blaze, in caring for survivors and those who had perished. Within a few minutes the clearing of the station of sightseers was under way. The response to this emergency was inspiring

Forward keel provisioning hatch through which Werner Franz escaped.

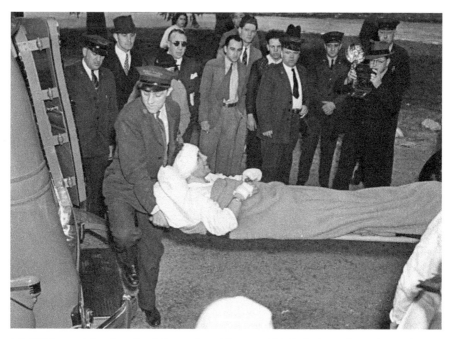

Adolf Fisher, an injured mechanic is transferred from Paul Kimball Hospital in Lakewood, New Jersey, to an ambulance going to another area hospital, on 7 May 1937.

proof of the readiness with which many agencies of mercy and assistance can be mobilized at such a crisis.

As the ship approached for the landing, I had stood on the ground below running over in my mind the many topics which I wanted to discuss immediately with Captains Lehmann and Pruss relating to the season's operations just beginning. The 1936 season of the *Hindenburg* had been so outstandingly successful as to merit and receive the applause of the entire world. German airship construction and operations were being expanded greatly. All of us engaged in airship development had high hopes that 1937 would more firmly establish the airship in its proper permanent place in the realm of transportation. But now through the medium of fire, man's greatest foe as well as his great friend, the mighty airship on which we had pinned our immediate hopes, lay there in the dusk an utter wreck. There has been and will continue to be many a conjecture as to what caused the disaster. This much must be definitely recognized however. The *Hindenburg* arrived in perfectly normal condition, made a skilful and normal approach, and was being landed in an entirely normal way. In my opinion, there was nothing wrong whatsoever within the ship until the fire broke out.

In other words, the *Hindenburg* was not lost as a result of any weakness or defect in the airship as a type, but, as in the case of many steamers, airplanes and other instruments of transportation, fell prey (through its own hydrogen) to fire and fire alone. Had the *Hindenburg* been inflated with helium, no such disaster could possibly have occurred.

The situation presented by the loss of the *Hindenburg* was an unprecedented and involved one. Here was a foreign ship of commerce, stranded on American soil and at a Naval Station, her passengers of many nationalities. The heartrending task of identification of those who had perished was performed at a board composed of sufficiently diverse representatives to insure the satisfaction of all concerned. The United States Department of Commerce appointed a Board of Investigation consisting of three members, Col. South Trimble, Jr, Mr Dennis Mulligan, and Major R. W. Schroeder, and made available to them a number of technical advisers from various walks of life. The German government sent to the United States a commission of six distinguished aeronautical experts that included Dr Hugo Eckener, Dr Ludwig Dürr, Lieutenant-Colonel Joachim Breithaupt, Dr Gunther Boch, Professor Max Dieckmann, and Dr Friedrich Hoffmann. Sitting together, this joint investigating body heard much testimony from numerous witnesses and survivors, and questioned scientific experts of various categories. Many letters and reports from eye-witnesses and others were read and studied. From photographers both professional and amateur came a wealth of motion and still pictures for examination by the investigators; but unfortunately not a single photograph has turned up to show the first appearance of fire. To ignite or explode the hydrogen in the ship from other

Surviving members of the crew are photographed at the Naval Air station in Lakehurst, New Jersey, on 7 May 1937. Rudolph Sauter, chief engineer, is at centre wearing white cap; behind him is Heinrich Kubis, a steward; Heinrich Bauer, watch officer, is third from right wearing black cap; and 13-year-old Werner Franz, cabin boy, is centre front row. Several members of the airship's crew are wearing US Marine summer clothing furnished them to replace clothing burned from many of their bodies as they escaped from the flames.

Customs officers search through baggage items salvaged after the disaster.

than premeditated or deliberate causes, would require escaping hydrogen or a free mixture of hydrogen and air, and a spark or flame as the igniting agency. Theories advanced included snapped wires, broken structure, disintegrated propellers, lightning, sparks from a motor, St Elmo's fire, the whole range of electrostatics, and even the phenomenon of catalysis.

But as the world knows (the investigation into this disaster having been in open sessions), definite evidence to pin the cause of the fire conclusively on any of these agencies was lacking nor could it be shown that there was free hydrogen or any dangerous mixture of hydrogen and air present.

While one shrinks from the thought of ascribing the disaster to sabotage, nevertheless until and unless the cause of the disaster can be definitely attributed to natural phenomena, sabotage still remains in the picture as a possible cause. Every effort will continue to be made in attempting to solve this mystery. Immediately upon its return to Germany, the German technical commission announced that it had been unable to ascribe a definite cause for the disaster; and the German government just as quickly directed the Commission to continue its studies. Scientific tests and experiments of many kinds are being continued in Germany and in the United States as well, in the effort to pin this mystery down to a definite cause. In the United States, as this is being written, the Investigating Board has not yet concluded its study of the testimony and evidence, and consequently has not rendered any opinion.

But from this mass of testimony and evidence, one conclusion can be clearly drawn—one repeatedly expressed in both German and American airship circles and now clearly established to the world. It is that for use in lighter-than-aircraft, hydrogen as a lifting medium, at least for peace time purposes, is a relic of the past, and that the entirely safe helium gas is now recognized as the salvation of airships.

The morning following the accident I went to see my friend Ernst Lehmann as he lay in the hospital not suffering particularly though badly burned. We had a rather extended conversation and then to permit him to conserve his strength, I departed intending to return in the afternoon as the medical pronouncements were that his chances for surviving were at least even and that the crisis would not be reached for at least three days. But his injuries were worse than had been diagnosed. In what therefore turned out to be practically his last conversation on the subject, I discussed with him the future of airships. Although completely baffled over the possibility of any natural phenomena having caused the loss of the *Hindenburg*, Lehmann told me of his still firm conviction that the airship will go on. No words were wasted in agreeing, however, that the salvation of the type lies in the employment of helium.

And so, I, too, am convinced that the *Hindenburg* disaster is not by any means the last chapter in the story of lighter-than-air craft; it is rather a turning point. Hitherto, lasting success with great rigid airships has been accomplished

Fritz Deeg, (1912–1990), steward on the *Hindenburg*. The day after the fire, Fritz Deeg, along with fellow steward Wilhelm Balla and Chief Engineer Rudolf Sauter, had the unenviable task of trying to identify bodies of those killed in the fire.

Two men inspect the twisted metal framework of the *Hindenburg*.

largely by German genius. Now has come a providential opportunity for the United States to play an active and leading part in the development of the safe airship. It is most deplorable that it should take such a tragic event as the loss of the *Hindenburg* with thirty-six lives to make an apathetic world 'airship conscious' and 'helium conscious' but this it has done. From knowledge of its existence previously confined mainly to students, helium has now become a by-word with all who are interested in the realm of aeronautics.

Occasionally the world hears of efforts to 'fire-proof' hydrogen but no successful and practicable solution seems to be in sight. But, as with many other natural resources, nature has blessed the United States with a practically inexhaustible supply of helium, and so far no other nation has found enough helium within its boundaries to warrant production. With this abundant world monopoly of helium thus thrust upon us, the future of dirigibles throughout the world now rests squarely upon the shoulders of the United States. The availability of helium at economical prices is dependent solely and simply on its production in quantity. Reliable reports emanating from Washington indicate that those in high authority are willing that the world may share in our bounteous helium supply for scientific, humanitarian, and peaceful commercial purposes.

In Friedrichshafen, Germany, the cradle and proving grounds of so many airships, there now nears completion the LZ 130, a sister ship of the *Hindenburg*. It seems certain that this ship will never feel the upward surge of hydrogen but will float in oceanic skylanes only through the medium of helium. That its performance may be reduced somewhat from that of a similar hydrogen-inflated ship is part of the price we must pay for the element of safety; nowhere in nature does man get something for nothing, and safety many places in life is a relatively dear commodity. German airships have proven the type entirely practicable; American helium and co-operation can make safe airships available for the benefit of all mankind. From the ashes of the *Hindenburg* and from American resources and co-operation will arise tomorrow's safer airship.

And so the sacrifice of those who gave their lives in the *Hindenburg* has indeed not been wholly in vain. They have startled the world into recognition of the airship. And once again there is demonstrated that through international cooperation and understanding the advances of civilization are most surely and quickly consummated. May the success of the newest German Zeppelin as part of an expanding world airship program mark the triumph of the ideal to which such men as Ernst Lehmann have given their lives.

In New York City, funeral services for the 28 Germans who lost their lives in the *Hindenburg* disaster are held on the Hamburg-American pier, on 11 May 1937. About 10,000 members of German organisations lined the pier.

Germans give the Nazi salute as they stand beside the coffin of Capt. Ernest A. Lehmann during a funeral service held on the Hamburg-American pier in New York City, on 11 May 1937.

ENDNOTES

1. Baron Max von Gemmingen, (1862-1924), volunteered at the start of the First World War. As he was past military age he become general staff officer assigned to the military airship LZ 12 *Sachsen*. He was the son of Wilhelm Friedrich Karl von Gemmingen and Eugenie Graffin von Zeppelin, nephew of Ferdinand von Zeppelin and brother of Karl Moritz Friedrich von Gemmingen-Guttenberg and Amalie von Gemmingen-Guttenberg.

2. Flight Sub-Lieutenant Reginald 'Reggie' Alexander John Warneford, VC, (1891–1915) of No. 1 Squadron Royal Naval Air Service managed to bring down Zeppelin LZ 37 over St Amandsberg near Ghent during the night of 6–7 June 1915. The family of Oberleutnant Kurt Ackermann erected a memorial in the Western Cemetery in Ghent and Oberleutnan Otto Van Der Haegen and Kurt Ackermann were reburied at the monument in 1916. On 17 June 1915, Warneford received the award of Légion d'honneur from the French Army Commander in Chief, General Joffre. Following a celebratory lunch, Warneford travelled to the aerodrome at Buc in order to ferry an aircraft for delivery to the RNAS at Veurne. Having made one short test flight, he then flew a second flight, carrying an American journalist, Henry Beach Newman, as passenger. During a climb to 200 feet, the right-hand wings collapsed leading to a catastrophic failure of the airframe. Both were thrown out of the aircraft, suffering fatal injuries.

3. Air Vice Marshal Reginald Leonard George Marix CB DSO, (1889–1966) was a British pilot with the Royal Naval Air Service. He is credited with being the first pilot to destroy a Zeppelin, when in 1914 he bombed the airship sheds at Düsseldorf. Marix joined the RNAS in 1912 and was one of the early naval aviators, gaining his aviator's certificate in January 1913. On 8 October 1914 he was one of three Sopwith Tabloid aircraft that attacked the airship shed at Düsseldorf. Marix dropped a bomb from 500 feet onto the shed and succeeded in destroying Zeppelin LZ 25 of the Imperial German Army, the first recorded destruction of dirigible by an aircraft. In 1916 Marix was testing an aircraft near Paris when it broke up in mid-air injuring him and he had to have his

left leg amputated. Although no longer an active flyer he moved across to the
newly formed Royal Air Force in 1918. During the Second World War he rose
to the rank of Air Vice Marshal and retired in 1945.

4. Friedrich Christiansen, (1879–1972) was a First World War seaplane ace who
claimed shooting down twenty planes and an airship; thirteen of those victories
were confirmed. In 1922 Christiansen was active again in the merchant marine,
as ship's captain. He continued in this pursuit until 1929, when he was employed
as a pilot by the Claude Dornier Company. In 1930, while with Dornier, he flew
what was at the time the largest seaplane in the world, the Dornier Do X, on
its maiden Atlantic flight to New York. In 1933, Christiansen's distinguished
career eventually led him to being called to a post in the Reich Aviation Ministry.
In 1936 he was promoted to Generalmajor and in 1939 General der Flieger.
During the Second World War, he was the commander of the Wehrmacht in
the Netherlands. After the war Christiansen was arrested for war crimes. On
2 October 1944 he had ordered a raid on the village of Putten in Gelderland,
the Netherlands, in retaliation, after one of his officers, a Leutnant Sommers,
was killed there by the Dutch resistance. When he heard about the actions
of the resistance near Putten, Christiansen is reported to have order several
members of the civilian population to be shot, the village was burned, and 661
of the males of the town were deported to labour camps, the vast majority of
whom never returned. Christiansen was sentenced to 12 years imprisonment
in 1948 in Arnhem for war crimes but was released in December 1951. He
died in 1972.

5. Kapitanleutnant Heinrich Mathy, (1883–1916), achieved a rare accolade
during the First World War; he was one of very few Germans whose names
were household words in Britain. During the 'Zeppelin Scourge' of 1915 and
1916, Mathy was known and feared as the most daring and audacious of all the
Zeppelin raiders. Mathy was an exceptional naval cadet and achieved command
of his own ship earlier than was usual in those days. Having been selected for
a possible Naval Staff role, he spent two years at the Marine Akademie and it
was during his two summers there, 1913 and 1914, that he was able to fly in
Zeppelin airships. At the beginning of 1915, at the insistence of Peter Strasser,
(Führer der Luftschiffer), Mathy was transferred to airships and took part
in his first raid on England a few days later, on 13 January, being forced to
turn back on this occasion because of bad weather. Later, however, he flew on
several raids over England, usually over Northern England. On 8 September
1915, Mathy's L 13 caused great damage by fire to the central area of London
itself, and further damage was caused when Mathy returned to the capital on
the night of 13–14 October. By the summer of 1916 Mathy, in command of
the new ship, L 31 was ready for more attacks on London. He attacked on the
night of 24–25 August 1916, again causing considerable damage. The L 31 was
damaged on landing on this occasion and while it was grounded for repairs,

news came in that the British had, for the first time, managed to shoot down an airship by using incendiary bullets. Mathy and the L 31 attacked London for the last time on the night of 1–2 October, 1916, to be shot down in flames by 2/Lieut. W. J. Tempest. The ship fell just outside Potters Bar, to the North of London. Mathy's body was found some way from the wreckage of the ship, half-embedded in the corner of a field. His last act had been to leap clear of the falling inferno rather than wait for the crash. According to some accounts, he lived for a few minutes after striking the earth.

6. Kapitänleutnant Claus Hirsch was the commander on the L 10. Officers on the bridge of SMS *Deutschland* at Altenbruch saw the disaster and wrote in the War Diary: '15.22: L 10, about Cuxhaven, apparently destroyed by lightning.' The event was also observed from Cuxhaven as well as by soldiers on the shore batteries.

7. Horst Julius Freiherr Treusch von Buttlar-Brandenfels, (1888–1962), was a Zeppelin commander. Buttlar-Brandenfels was awarded the Pour le Mérite on 9 April 1918 for his service as the commander of Zeppelin L 54. Other awards were Iron Cross 1st and 2nd class, (1914); Knight's Cross of the Order of Hohenzollern with Swords (9 October 1916) and the Hanseatic Cross of Hamburg. During the Second World War he was the commandant of Frankfurt Airport.

8. Hans von Schiller, (1891–1976), was a well-known Zeppelin commander. Born in Schleswig-Holstein, Hans von Schiller joined the navy at the beginning of the First World War. He volunteered for Zeppelin service and was active on numerous raids against Britain from a base at Tonder in Denmark—now the site of the Zeppelin museum. After the War, Hans continued his career with the Zeppelin company and was on board Zeppelins for flights to the Arctic and the journey to circumnavigate the world (1929). He captained many flights to the USA and South America until the Lakehurst disaster in 1937 brought this travel to an end. It was only because of a delay in Rio that he was unable to reach Friedrichshafen to join the last flight of the *Hindenburg*. During the Second World War he was promoted to Oberstleutnant. Von Schiller went on to write several books on Zeppelin flight.

9. The floating wreck of the airship L 19 (LZ 54) was discovered by a trawler, the *King Stephen* of 162 tons, commanded by William Martin (1869–1917). The crew had sighted distress signals during the night and had spent several hours steaming towards them. Clinging to the wreck were the airship's crew of 16. The normal complement of a P-class Zeppelin was 18 or 19, but Zeppelins flying on air-raids often flew short-handed, with two or three of the least needed crew-members left behind in order to save weight. The fishing-vessel approached and Kapitänleutnant Löwe, who spoke English well, asked for rescue. Martin refused. In a later newspaper interview he stated that the nine crew of the *King Stephen* were unarmed and badly outnumbered, and would have had little chance of resisting the German airmen if, after being rescued, they had hijacked

his vessel to sail it to Germany. Ignoring the pleas for help, promises of good conduct and even offers of money, Martin sailed *King Stephen* away. He later said he intended to search for a Royal Navy ship to report his discovery to. However, he met none and the encounter with the L 19 was only reported to the British authorities on his return to the *King Stephen's* home-port of Grimsby.

10. After the crash of the L 15 (LZ 48) in the Thames estuary on 31 March 1916 Joachim Breithaupt became a prisoner of war. After the war he became an official in the Air Ministry and rose to become head of the airship division. He was one of the German officials who went to the USA in 1937 for the enquiry into the *Hindenburg* disaster.

11. Kapitänleutnant Franz Stabbert had captained L 7, 1915; L 20, L 23, 1916; L44, 1917. The event referred to took place in May 1916. The L 20 (LZ 59), running low on fuel, made a forced landing off the coast of Norway near Stavanger. The crew destroyed the airship. 16 were captured, 3 died. Kapitänleutnant Stabbert escaped six months later. He was killed in action on 20 October 1917 when L 44 (LZ 93), driven south to France by a heavy storm was shot down over Lunéville.

12. The Battle of Jutland 31 May–1 June 1916.

13. Ferdinand Adolf Heinrich August Graf von Zeppelin, (1838–1917) was the founder of the Zeppelin airship company. In 1855 he became a cadet of the military school at Ludwigsburg and then commenced his career as an officer in the army of Württemberg. In 1863 Zeppelin took leave to act as an observer for the northern troops of the Union's Army of the Potomac in the American Civil War. Later he travelled to the Upper Midwest and on reaching St Paul, Zeppelin encountered German-born balloonist John Steiner and made his first aerial ascent with him. Many years later he attributed the beginning of his thinking about dirigible lighter-than-air craft to this experience. In 1890 Zeppelin was forced to retire from the Army with the rank of Generalleutnant. After his resignation he devoted his full attention to airships and hired the engineer Theodor Gross to make tests of possible materials and to assess available engines for both fuel efficiency and power-to-weight ratio. After many years of development and experimentation, actual construction started on the first successful rigid airship, the Zeppelin LZ 1. On 2 July 1900, Zeppelin made the first flight with the LZ 1 over Lake Constance near Friedrichshafen in southern Germany. The airship rose from the ground and remained in the air for 20 minutes, but was damaged on landing. After repairs and some modifications two further flights were made by LZ 1 in October 1900, however the airship was not considered successful enough to justify investment by the government, and since the experiments had exhausted Count Zeppelins funds, he was forced to suspend his work. Zeppelin still enjoyed the support of the King of Württemberg, who authorised a state lottery which raised 124,000 marks. A contribution of 50,000 marks was received from Prussia, and Zeppelin raised the remainder

of the necessary money by mortgaging his wife's estates. LZ 2 was started in April 1905. It was completed by 30 November 1905, when it was first taken out of its hangar, but a ground-handling mishap caused the bows to be pulled into the water, damaging the forward control surfaces. Repairs were completed by 17 January 1906, when LZ 2 made its only flight. It was not a success and had to be dismantled. The success of LZ 3 later in 1906 produced a change in the official attitude to his work, and the Reichstag voted that he should be awarded 500,000 marks to continue his work. However the purchase by the Government of an airship was made conditional on the successful completion of a 24-hour trial flight. Knowing that this was beyond the capabilities of LZ 3, work was started on a larger airship, the LZ 4. This first flew on 20 June 1908. The final financial breakthrough only came after the Zeppelin LZ 4 was destroyed by fire at Echterdingen after breaking free of its moorings during a storm. The airship's earlier flights had excited public interest in the development of the airships, and a subsequent collection campaign raised over 6 million German marks. The money was used to create the 'Luftschiffbau-Zeppelin GmbH' and the Zeppelin foundation. LZ 3 was later officially accepted by the Government and on 10 November Zeppelin was rewarded with an official visit to Friedrichshafen by the Kaiser, during which a short demonstration flight over Lake Constance was made and Zeppelin awarded the Order of the Black Eagle. Ferdinand Graf von Zeppelin died in 1917 and thus did not see the later triumphs of the commercial Zeppelins *Graf Zeppelin* and the death of the airship with the disaster of the *Hindenburg*.

14. Ludwig Dürr, (1878–1956), entered the Imperial German Navy in 1898, but was discharged at the end of the year. In 1899, Ludwig Dürr commenced work for Ferdinand von Zeppelin. After assisting in the construction of the LZ 1, he himself began to construct airships and lightweight construction parts. All of the subsequent Zeppelin designs were the work of Dürr. He was appointed technical director in 1915 and remained employed by the Zeppelin company until its dissolution in 1945.

15. August von Parseval, (1861–1942), was a pioneer airship designer. In his early life he joined the Royal Bavarian 3rd Infantry Regiment Prinz Carl von Bayern, and interested himself with ballooning and aeronautics. In Augsburg he met August Riedinger and also came to know his later partner Rudolf Hans Bartsch von Sigsfeld, with whom he developed *Drachenballons*—balloons used for military observation. In 1901 Parseval and Sigsfeld began building a dirigible airship, but Sigsfeld died during a balloon landing in 1902, resulting in suspension of work until 1905. With improvements in engine development his designs were licensed to the Vickers company in the UK. Up to the end of the First World War 22 Parseval airships—both non-rigid and semi-rigid—were built. The Parseval-Siegsfeld '*Drachen*' Kite Balloon was used extensively by German forces in the First World War.

16. The Crown Prince had wired: *Halte Ihnen nach wie vor die Stange. Wilhelm.* The Kaiser sent a message to the Crown Prince: *In Zukunft hältst du gefälligst den Mund and nicht die Stange.*

17. On 3 September 1916 the army Schütte-Lanz airship SL 11 was shot down and crashed in Cuffley during an aerial bombardment intended for London. Lieutenant W. Leefe Robinson, the pilot who shot the airship down; he was awarded the VC.

18. The L33 (LZ 76) commanded by Kapitänleutnant der Reserve Alois Böcker arrived over the East End dropping bombs on Bromley-by-Bow, Bow and Stratford. These set fire to a timber yard, an oil storage tank and demolished a row of houses killing six people and injuring another twelve. The Black Swan pub was destroyed, killing four customers. After it turned to head back home an anti-aircraft shell fired from Bromley exploded inside the L33, but did not ignite the hydrogen. The crew dropped water ballast then drifted east, losing 800 feet of altitude each minute. An airborne RFC pilot, 2nd Lt Alfred de Bath Brandon, MC, had previously shadowed the airship, and attacked it with several drums of Brock-Pomeroy ammunition but with no seeming effect, however this may have further reduced the hydrogen by the additional bullet holes in the gas sacks.

19. Hans-Curt Flemming, (1886-1935) was a Zeppelin commander. He participated in the Battle of Jutland in 1916 on the cruiser SMS *Stettin*, and then went on to serve as commander of naval airships L 25 (LZ 58), L 35 (LZ 80), L 55 (LZ 101) and L 60 (LZ 108). On 20 October 1917, as commander of L 55 returning from a raid on Birmingham and London to the home base in Alhorn he reached a record height 7,600 m. After the war Flemming commanded airships in civil service in Germany, the United States and South America. In October 1924 he was the right-hand man to Dr Hugo Eckener during the flight of LZ 126 from Friedrichshafen to Lakehurst, New Jersey. The peak of his career was taking command of the LZ 127 *Graf Zeppelin*. It was under the command of Hans Flemming on 19 December 1934 that LZ 127 reached the record of a million kilometres in the air. During his career he participated in the round the world voyage of 1929 and the Arctic voyage of 1931.

20. Bombenoffizier Otto Mieth, watch officer aboard airship L 48 (LZ 95) on 17 October 1917, wrote in his memoir that at 15,000 feet: 'We shivered even in our heavy clothing and we breathed with such difficulty in spite of our oxygen flasks that several members of the crew became unconscious.' As soon as the ship dropped its bombs on Harwich, 20 or 30 searchlights converged on the intruder. Guns fired from the ground, and in an instant the ship was ablaze. 'I heard the man next to me say, "It's all over," and I sprang to one of the side windows to jump out, the thought of being burned alive was so horrible. At that moment the ship's skeleton collapsed, the gondola swung over and I fell into a corner with others piling on top of me. I felt flames against my face and

I wrapped my arms against my head, hoping the end would come quickly. That was the last I remember.' When the ship's metal frame hit the ground it telescoped, breaking the fall. Mieth surmised afterward that the pile of comrades on top of him had shielded him from the flames. English soldiers heard his groans and pulled him from the wreckage—he was one of the very few men to survive the downing of a Zeppelin.

21. L 23 (LZ 66) was destroyed on 21 August 1917 by 2nd Lt Bernard A. Smart flying a Sopwith Pup launched from a platform on the cruiser HMS *Yarmouth*. Smart later took part in the Tondern raid flying from HMS *Furious* which destroyed L 54 (LZ 99) and L60 (LZ 108).

22. Commanded by Waldemar Koelle, L 45 LZ 85) ran out of fuel on 20 October 1917 and was destroyed in a forced landing near Sisteron, France, the crew being taken captive.

23. L 50 (LZ 89) ran out of fuel on 20 October 1917 and, after the control car had been torn off as a result of an attempt to crash the airship to prevent it falling into enemy hands near Danmartin. The L 50 rose to 23,000 feet which was 3,000 feet too high for the French planes to shoot it down. She was last seen over Frejus heading out to the Mediterranean. Years later some fishermen claimed to have seen the L 50 come down around 100 miles south-east of Frejus, but there were no survivors.

24. This is almost certainly the port of Moudrus on the island of Lemnos.

25. Ludwig Bockholt, (1885–1918) was commander of several Zeppelins. He commanded L 23 (LZ 66) from 30 March to 13 June 1917, but passed over command before this airship was destroyed on 21 August 1917 by 2nd Lt Bernard A. Smart flying a Sopwith Pup launched from a platform on the cruiser HMS *Yarmouth*. Bockholt then commanded several other Zeppelins, and finally L 59 (LZ 104). L 59 started out on the mission to resupply German troops in German East Africa, but turned back upon (false) reports of a German surrender in East Africa; nevertheless, the ship broke a long-distance flight record (6,757 kilometres in 95 hours and 5 minutes). Bockholt died on 7 April 1918 when the L 59 caught fire for unknown reasons and crashed over the Strait of Otranto during a raid on Malta.

26. Lehmann says 'Aka Hisser' but it seems likely that he meant Akhisar in Turkey.

27. It is not clear where the Gulf of Adaja is.

28. Cape Brulus is El Brulus, on the Egyptian coast to the west of Port Said.

29. L 62 (LZ 107) crashed north of Heligoland on 10 May 1918. The British authorities claim it was shot down by Felixstowe F2A flying-boat N4291, flown by Capt. T. C. Pattinson and Capt. T. H. Munday. It is interesting to read Lehmann's comments.

30. The Tondern Raid. 19 July 1918. It is interesting that Lehmann credits Captain Bernard Smart with the successful hit. The mission was code-named Operation F.7. The Camels flew from the deck of HMS *Furious* between 03.13 and 03.21. The

first flight consisted of Captains W. D. Jackson, W. F. Dickson and Lieutenant N. E. Williams; the second of Captains B. A. Smart and T. K. Thyne and Lieutenants S. Dawson and W. A. Yeulett. Thyne was forced to turn around with engine trouble and ditched his aircraft before being recovered. The first three aircraft arrived over Tondern at 04.35, taking the enemy by surprise. There were three airship sheds, codenamed by the Germans as 'Toska', 'Tobias' and 'Toni'. Toska, the largest one, was a double shed and housed the airships L 54 (LZ 99) and L 60 (LZ 108). Tobias contained a captive balloon and Toni was in the process of being dismantled. The first wave of aircraft focused on Toska and three bombs hit the shed and detonated the gas bags of L 54 and L 60, destroying them by fire but not causing them to explode and destroy the shed. Another bomb from the first wave hit Tobias shed and damaged the balloon. The second wave destroyed the captive balloon. Despite the loss of the two airships the Germans suffered only four men injured. During the attack ground fire was directed at both waves but the only damage was an undercarriage wheel shot off a Camel from the second wave. Williams, Jackson and Dawson, in the belief that they had insufficient fuel to reach the British squadron offshore, headed for Denmark and landed there. Dickson, Yuelett and Smart flew to sea to find the British ships. Dickson ditched at 05.55 and Smart, having suffered engine trouble, at 06:30. Yuelett was not heard from again and his body was recovered later.

31. Captained by Major George Herbert Scott of the RAF, the R 34 left East Fortune at 01.42 a.m. on 2 July 1919 and arrived in Mineola, Long Island, New York at 09.54 a.m. on 6 July 1919 covering a distance of about 3,000 miles in 108 hours 12 minutes flying time. He then made a return trip to England, thus also completing the first double crossing of the Atlantic.

32. R 38 was destroyed by a structural failure while in flight over the city of Hull. It crashed into the Humber estuary on 23 August 1921 killing 44 out of the 49 crew aboard.

33. Clarence Terhune, (b. 1899), was a golf caddy from St Louis, Missouri. Clarence was always on the move seeking new escapades. He stowed away on trains, ships, and crashed major sporting events until he found out the Germans were flying a giant airship to America. Against all odds he evaded the tight security of the hangar and managed to get on board.

34. Grace Drummond Hay, née Lethbridge, (1895–1946), was the widow of a British diplomat, Sir Robert Hay Drummond-Hay. As a journalist for the Hearst press organization, Drummond-Hay made her first Zeppelin flight in October, 1928, when she was chosen to accompany five other reporters—including her companion and Hearst colleague Karl von Wiegand—on the first transatlantic flight of the *Graf Zeppelin* from Germany to America. As the only woman on the flight, Drummond-Hay received a great deal of attention in the world's press. In March 1929, Lady Drummond Hay and von Wiegand were once again aboard *Graf Zeppelin*, for the ship's 'Orient Flight' to Palestine. Later in 1929,

the Hearst organization co-sponsored *Graf Zeppelin's* historic Round-the-World flight, and their reporter Lady Drummond-Hay was once again a passenger. She was the only woman among the 60 male passengers and crew, which again included her companion von Wiegand. Drummond-Hay's presence on the flight, and her reporting as the ship circled the globe, garnered tremendous attention in the press. Lady Drummond-Hay and her partner Karl von Wiegand were in the Philippines when the Japanese invaded the islands in 1942, and both were interned in a Japanese camp. Although Drummond-Hay survived the war and returned to New York, she died of coronary thrombosis in early 1946 as a result of the extremely harsh conditions she had suffered at the hands of the Japanese.

35. Sir George Hubert Wilkins, (1888–1958), was an Australian polar explorer, ornithologist, pilot, soldier, geographer and photographer. As a teenager, he moved to Adelaide where he found work with a travelling cinema, to Sydney as a cinematographer, and thence to England where he became a pioneering aerial photographer while working for Gaumont Studios. His photographic skill earned him a place on various Arctic expeditions. In 1917, Wilkins returned to Australia, joining the Australian Flying Corps in the rank of Second Lieutenant. Wilkins later transferred to the general list and in 1918 was appointed as an official war photographer. In June 1918 Wilkins was awarded the Military Cross for his efforts to rescue wounded soldiers during the Third Battle of Ypres. After the war he was involved in several polar expeditions, and latterly was financed by William Randolph Hearst. Wilkins continued his polar explorations, now flying over Antarctica in the *San Francisco*. He named the island of Hearst Land after his sponsor, and Hearst thanked Wilkins by giving him and his bride a flight aboard *Graf Zeppelin*. He is best known for his *Nautilus* submarine expedition. In 1931, largely finance by Hearst, he leased an ex-war US submarine, renamed it *Nautilus* and set off to explore the waters of the North Pole. The expedition was beset by failures, but did gain much useful scientific data and he was able to prove that submarines were capable of operating beneath the polar ice cap, thereby paving the way for future successful missions.. Badly damaged, Wilkins eventually gained permission to sink the submarine off Norwegian waters. Wilkins died in Framingham, Massachusetts in 1958. The US Navy took his ashes to the North Pole aboard the submarine USS *Skate* on 17 March 1959.

36. On 15 April 1928, only a year after Charles Lindbergh's flight across the Atlantic, Wilkins and pilot Carl Ben Eielson made a transarctic crossing from Point Barrow, Alaska, to Spitsbergen, arriving about 20 hours later on 16 April, touching along the way at Grant Land on Ellesmere Island. For this feat and his prior work, Wilkins was knighted, and during the ensuing celebration, he met an Australian actress in New York, Suzanne Bennett who he married on 30 August 1929. She died in 1975, and her ashes were scattered at the North Pole from USS *Bluefish* on 4 May 1975.

37. Augusto Severo de Albuquerque Maranhão, (1864–1902). In 1880, Severo travelled to Rio de Janeiro and began his engineering studies at the Polytechnic School. Motivated by the work of aero-station inventor Para Julio Cesar Ribeiro de Souza, who presented an airship project to Brazilian Polytechnic Institute in 1881, Severo began to take an interest in flight, carrying large soaring birds and building small models of kites, one of which called *Albatross*. In October 1892 the Government provided financial aid to Severo and the commission of his design was given to the Lachambre company in Paris which specialized in building balloons. After several experimental dirigibles were tried out, a new aircraft, *Pax* was built in France capable of holding 2,500 cubic metres of hydrogen, and was 30 metres in length and 12 in diameter. Tests were successfully performed on 4 and 7 May 1902. On a flight on 12 May *Pax* climbed to 400 metres and then exploded violently and the two crew members—Severo and Sachet—died in the crash. The remains of the airship fell in the Avenue du Maine, Paris. The *Pax* disaster had a huge impact and further development ceased. The configuration proposed by Severo, a blimp semi-rigid, was revolutionary and influenced the development of airships in the following decades.

38. Roald Engelbregt Gravning Amundsen, (1872–1928), was a Norwegian explorer. He led the Antarctic expedition (1910–12) that was the first to reach the South Pole, on 14 December 1911. In 1926 he was the first expedition leader to be recognized without dispute as having reached the North Pole. He is also known as having been the first to lead an expedition to traverse the Northwest Passage (1903–06) in the Arctic. He disappeared on 28 June 1928 in the Arctic while taking part in a mission to rescue Nobile by plane. Umberto Nobile, (1885–1978), was an Italian aeronautical engineer and Arctic explorer. Nobile was a developer and promoter of semi-rigid airships between the two World Wars. He is primarily remembered for designing and piloting the airship *Norge*, which may have been the first aircraft to reach the North Pole, and which was indisputably the first to fly across the polar ice cap from Europe to America. Nobile also designed and flew the *Italia*, a second polar airship; this second expedition ended in a deadly crash and provoked an international rescue effort. He was eventually rescued and lived to the age of 93.

39. Lincoln Ellsworth, (1880–1951), was a polar explorer from the United States and a major benefactor of the American Museum of Natural History. Ellsworth accompanied Amundsen on his second effort to fly over the Pole in the airship *Norge*, designed and piloted by Umberto Nobile, in a flight from Svalbard to Alaska. On 12 May 1926, the Geographic North Pole was sighted. This was the first undisputed sighting of the area. Ellsworth made four expeditions to Antarctica between 1933 and 1939, using as his aircraft transporter and base a former Norwegian herring boat that he named *Wyatt Earp* after his hero.

40. R 101 was built in 1929 as part of a British Government programme for airships capable of service on long-distance routes within the British Empire. When

built it was the world's largest flying craft at 731 feet in length, and it was not surpassed by any other hydrogen-filled rigid airship until the *Hindenburg* flew seven years later. It crashed in France on 5 October 1930 during its maiden overseas voyage, killing 48 of the 54 people on board. Among the deceased passengers were Lord Thomson, the Air Minister who had initiated the programme, senior government officials, and almost all the dirigible's designers from the Royal Airship Works. The crash of R 101 effectively ended British airship development, and was one of the worst airship accidents of the 1930s.

41. Air Vice Marshal Sir William Sefton Brancker KCB, AFC, (1877–1930), was trained for the Army and during the First World War held important administrative posts in the Royal Flying Corps and later the Royal Air Force. In 1922 he was made Director of Civil Aviation and was an ardent supporter of the development of British civilian air services connecting London to British colonies and dominions overseas. He was killed when the airship R 101 crashed near Beauvais France on 5 October 1930 during its maiden voyage to India.

42. The LZ 128 was never built. It would have been 761 feet long and lifted by 5,307,000 cubic feet of hydrogen. But the crash of the R 101 in which passengers and crew were killed by the hydrogen fire that followed the crash, rather than by the impact itself convinced the Zeppelin Company to alter its plans and develop a ship capable of being lifted by helium.

43. At first, the Nazi Party's assumption of power in January 1933, had little effect on the fortunes of the Zeppelin Company, but little Government financial support was forthcoming partly due to Air Minister Hermann Göring's dislike of lighter-than-air flight. But Propaganda Minister Joseph Goebbels was aware of the potential symbolic value of LZ 129 as a showcase for German strength and technology, and in 1934 Goebbels offered Hugo Eckener two million marks toward the completion of LZ 129. Determined to overshadow Goebbels, Göring offered an additional nine million marks from the Air Ministry, but the offer came with conditions: In March, 1935, the Air Ministry split the Zeppelin Company into two firms; the original Luftschiffbau Zeppelin, which would be responsible solely for the construction of airships, and the newly created Deutsche Zeppelin-Reederei (DZR), half-owned by the German national airline Lufthansa, which would be responsible for airship operations. The establishment of the DZR also served the interest of the Nazis by effectively removing Hugo Eckener from the leadership of German Zeppelin operations. Ernst Lehmann, who was much more amenable to the National Socialist government than Hugo Eckener, was put in charge of the DZR, and Eckener became mostly a figurehead.

44 This book was written while LZ 130 was under the first stages of construction. LZ 130 was the last of the rigid airships built by the Zeppelin Luftschiffbau the second and final ship of the *Hindenburg* class named in honour of Paul von Hindenburg. The airship, which made just 30 flights over 11 months in

1938–39 before being scrapped in 1940, was the second Zeppelin to carry the name 'Graf Zeppelin' (after the LZ 127) and is often referred to as *Graf Zeppelin II*. On 14 September 1938 the ship was christened and flew the first time. Unlike the christening of the *Hindenburg*, only Zeppelin Company officials and Hermann Göring were present; no other government representatives came to the christening to congratulate Eckener. The speech was given by Dr Eckener. By the time the *Graf Zeppelin II* was completed, it was obvious that the ship would never serve its intended purpose as a passenger liner; the lack of a supply of inert helium was one cause. The Reich Air Ministry permitted the *Graf Zeppelin* to fly for one year until 1 September 1939 'without any transportation of passengers and outside from tropical areas', during which time up to 30 experimental flights were made of short duration. Between 2–4 August *Graf Zeppelin II* made an espionage flight over the UK up to Scotland to investigate radar masts. *Graf Zeppelin II* never crossed the Atlantic. In April 1940, Hermann Göring issued the order to scrap both *Graf Zeppelins* and the unfinished framework of LZ 131, since the metal was needed for other aircraft. By 27 April, work crews had finished cutting up the airships. On 6 May, the enormous airship hangars in Frankfurt were levelled by explosives— three years to the day after the destruction of the *Hindenburg*.

45. After the fire and crash of the *Hindenburg*, First Officer Captain Albert Sammt found Captain Max Pruss trying to re-enter the wreckage to look for survivors. Pruss's face was badly burned, and he required months of hospitalization and reconstructive surgery, but he survived. Captain Ernst Lehmann escaped the crash with burns to his head and arms and severe burns across most of his back. Though his burns did not seem quite as severe as those of Pruss, he died at a nearby hospital the next day.

46. Carl Christiansen, (b. 1884), was Polizeipräsident in Magdeburg, 1934–1937. He had served in the Imperial German Navy during the First World War and in April 1915 he was in command of the *Rubens* which was carrying supplies to Von Lettow-Vorbeck's troops in East Africa—a command which ended in disaster. In June 1940 Carl served as Fregattenkapitän der Reserve zur Verfügung (dRzV) in the staff of his brother in the Netherlands. On 20 April 1941 he was promoted to NSFK-Brigadeführer. From September 1942 until the end of Second World War Carl was Generalinspekteur beim Reichskommissar für die Seeschiffart (Gauleiter Karl Kaufmann). His brother Friedrich was Korpsführer of the NSFK, and was later tried for war crimes.

47. Completed in May 1936, *Ostmark* was a catapult vessel of Deutsche Lüfthansa. Seaplanes were handled by a 15 tonne crane. *Ostmark* was sunk by British submarine *Tuna* 24 September 1940 south-west of St Nazaire after she had received an order to proceed to Germany for commissioning by the Kreigsmarine.

48. *Westfalen* was much older than *Ostmark*. She was an ex-cargo vessel of Nord-Deutsche Lloyd, completed in 1906. She was converted to a catapult vessel

for Deutsche Lüfthansa in 1933. Seaplanes were handled by a 15 tonne crane. *Westfalen* was sunk by a mine, 7 September 1944 in Skagerrak.

49. Edward [Eddie] Vernon Rickenbacker, (1890–1973), was an American fighter ace in the First World War and Medal of Honor recipient. With 26 aerial victories, he was America's most successful fighter ace in the war. He was also a racing car driver and automotive designer, a government consultant in military matters and a pioneer in air transportation—particularly as the long-time head of Eastern Air Lines.

50. Ernst 'Putzi' Hanfstaengl, (1887–1976), had an American mother and was brought up and educated in the USA where, in 1920, he married Helene Elise Adelheid Niemeyer. He returned to Germany in 1922 and soon became one of Hitler's most intimate followers. For much of the 1920s, Hanfstaengl introduced Hitler to Munich's high society and helped polish his image. He also helped to finance the publication of *Mein Kampf,* and the Party's official newspaper, the *Völkischer Beobachter*. Hanfstaengl wrote both Brownshirt and Hitler Youth marches, based on his memories of Harvard football songs; he later claimed that he devised the chant 'Sieg Heil'. Several disputes arose between Hanfstaengl and Goebbels which led to him being removed from Hitler's staff in 1933. He and Helene divorced in 1936. Hanfstaengl fell completely out of Hitler's favour after he was denounced by Unity Mitford, a close friend of both the Hanfstaengls and Hitler. He moved to England where he was imprisoned as an enemy alien after the outbreak of the Second World War. In 1942 he was turned over to the US and worked for President Roosevelt's 'S-Project', revealing information on approximately 400 Nazi leaders.

51. Ernst Udet, (1896–1941), was the second-highest scoring German flying ace of the First World War. Udet rose to become a squadron commander under Richthofen, and later, under Hermann Göring. After the war Udet spent the 1920s and early 1930s as a stunt pilot, international barnstormer, light aircraft manufacturer, and playboy. In 1933, he joined the Nazi Party and became involved in the early development of the Luftwaffe. By 1939, Udet had risen to the post of Director-General of Equipment for the Luftwaffe. However, the stress of the position and his distaste for administrative duties led to an increasing dependence on alcohol. When the Second World War commenced, the Luftwaffe's needs for equipment outstripped Germany's production capacity. Hermann Göring, first lied to Hitler about these material shortcomings when the Germans lost the Battle of Britain, then deflected the Führer's wrath onto Udet. Udet committed suicide on 17 November 1941 by a bullet to the head.